LEAVING CERTIFICATE MATHS
ORDINARY LEVEL

GW00417566

Power of
Maths

PAPER
1

Tony Kelly and
Kieran Mills

PUBLISHED BY:
Educate.ie
Walsh Educational Books Ltd
Castleisland, Co. Kerry, Ireland
www.educate.ie

EDITORS:
Finola McLaughlin, Fiona McPolin and
Antoinette Walker

DESIGN:
Kieran O'Donoghue

COVER DESIGN:
Kieran O'Donoghue

LAYOUT:
Compuscript

PROOFREADER:
Ciara McNee

PRINTED AND BOUND BY:
Walsh Colour Print, Castleisland,
Co. Kerry, Ireland

Copyright © Tony Kelly and Kieran Mills 2016

Without limiting the rights under copyright, this book is sold subject to the condition that it shall not, by way of trade or otherwise, be lent, resold, hired out, reproduced, stored in or introduced into a retrieval system, or transmitted, in any form or by any means (electronic, mechanical, photocopying, recording or otherwise), or otherwise circulated, without the publisher's prior consent, in any form other than that in which it is published and without a similar condition, including this condition, being imposed on the subsequent publisher.

PHOTOGRAPHS AND ILLUSTRATIONS:
Dreamstime.com; Gil C/Shutterstock.com; iStockphoto.com; muzsy/Shutterstock.com; Photographerlondon/Dreamstime.com; Radu Razvan/Shutterstock.com; Shutterstock.com; Thinkstock.com; urbanbuzz/Shutterstock.com; Wikicommons (public domain)

The authors and publisher have made every effort to trace all copyright holders. If any have been overlooked we would be happy to make the necessary arrangements at the first opportunity.

ISBN: 978-1-910052-94-5

ACKNOWLEDGEMENTS

The authors would like to thank Pat Saville for her invaluable assistance in writing this book. We would also like to thank Ian Wilkinson and Owen Wardell for providing additional mathematical expertise.

Contents

SECTION 8

Introduction

Power of Maths is the first new Leaving Certificate Ordinary Level series since the full implementation and examination of the new Maths syllabus. The new syllabus encourages teachers and students to engage deeply with mathematical content. *Power of Maths* promotes this engagement by developing students' mathematical knowledge and problem-solving skills.

The *Power of Maths Ordinary Level* package includes two textbooks (with free ebooks), two Activity Books, step-by-step instructional videos and fully worked-out solutions. *Power of Maths* introduces content in a staged and graded manner and ensures that the principles of Maths are firmly established before students are guided through more complex material. Students who use the *Power of Maths* series will be fully prepared for the demands of the most recent Leaving Certificate exam papers.

Content covered in *Power of Maths Paper 1* and *Power of Maths Paper 2*:

Power of Maths Paper 1 Ordinary Level has been divided into 8 major sections: Number, Algebraic Expressions, Algebraic Equations, Sequences and Series, Financial Maths, Complex Numbers, Functions, and Differentiation. This reflects the content that can be examined in the Ordinary Level Leaving Certificate Paper 1 examination.

Geometry, Mensuration, Trigonometry, Co-ordinate Geometry, Probability, and Statistics are covered in *Power of Maths Paper 2 Ordinary Level*. This reflects the content that can be examined in the Ordinary Level Leaving Certificate Paper 2 examination.

The first three sections of *Power of Maths Paper 1* and *Power of Maths Paper 2* provide the foundations for the rest of the course. We recommend completing Sections 1, 2 and 3 of *Power of Maths Paper 1* first, followed by Sections 1, 2 and 3 of *Power of Maths Paper 2*. Sections can then be completed sequentially, alternating between *Power of Maths Paper 1* and *Power of Maths Paper 2,* as you please.

Key features of *Power of Maths Paper 1*:

Learning outcomes

- Each chapter begins with a set of learning outcomes to guide students through the content.

Tips and key terms

- Tip and key term boxes appear throughout to aid understanding.

Examples

- *Power of Maths* is packed with examples. **Worked Examples** explain the reasoning behind a given approach to solving a problem. These examples underpin the philosophy behind the new approach to learning Maths.

- **Numbered Examples** apply the principles learnt to all types of situations. They utilise the more traditional approach to teaching Maths.

- **Short Examples** appear throughout the text and are indicated by a green arrow. These examples give students short and snappy explanations, helping them to undertake the exercises that follow.

Exercises

- Exercises appear at **regular intervals** in the text so that students can carry out questions with a minimum amount of teaching.

- **Questions in the exercises are graded**. Earlier questions provide plenty of practice and rigour to allow students to become totally familiar with the techniques required for carrying out a particular mathematical procedure. Gradually students are asked to use these techniques and **apply them to real-life situations**.

Activity boxes

- Activity boxes in the margin direct students to optional extra activities in the Activity Book.

Digital icons

- Digital icons link to step-by-step instructional videos and other digital resources on **www.educateplus.ie**.

Revision questions

- Revision questions at the end of each section provide plenty of practice of the type of questions examined in the Leaving Certificate examination.

Revision summaries

- Revision summaries at the end of each section reinforce and embed learning.

Activity Book

Power of Maths Paper 1 Ordinary Level comes with an Activity Book. The optional activities are signposted in the margin of this textbook and are designed to allow students to discover mathematical concepts on their own and to acquire a deep understanding of the material. This enhances the enjoyment of the subject, allowing students to learn complex material as effortlessly as possible.

Digital resources

Digital icons in the Algebraic Expressions, Algebraic Equations, and Differentiation sections in this textbook link to step-by-step instructional videos. Students can access the videos by clicking on the icon in the ebook or by visiting **www.educateplus.ie**.

These step-by-step instructional videos are designed to make the learning of difficult concepts as easy as possible. They also provide further exercises to complement the material in the textbook and Activity Book.

Students and teachers also receive a **free ebook** with the textbook. It can be downloaded using the redeem code on the inside front cover of this textbook.

Additional teachers' resources

Fully worked-out solutions for all of the exercises are available for teachers on **www.educateplus.ie**.

Finally, enjoy the experience of learning a beautiful subject.

Tony Kelly and Kieran Mills

Number

'Mathematics is the queen of sciences and number theory is the queen of mathematics' – Carl Friedrich Gauss. This section introduces the different types of numbers that we use today. Arithmetic is a set of rules for manipulating these numbers.

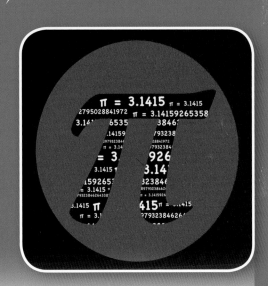

CHAPTER 1

Number Systems

Learning Outcomes

- To carry out natural number operations.

- To know the symbols used in set operations and to be able to carry out such operations.

- To understand that the set of natural numbers is made up of composite and prime numbers.

- To understand that the set of integers includes natural numbers but also zero and whole negative numbers.

- To understand that the set of rationals are fractions which are the ratio of integers. Rationals can be written as either terminating or recurring decimals.

- To understand the concept of an irrational number and that the set of real numbers is the union of rational and irrational numbers.

- To understand that there is a set of complex numbers (imaginary numbers). All the other number sets are subsets of this set. (The set of complex numbers is so important that a whole section is devoted to it in Section 6.)

- To understand what is meant by the absolute value or modulus of a number.

Our present system of numbers was developed by dealing with progressively more difficult problems as they arose throughout the history of humankind.

1.1 Natural numbers

Natural number operations

ACTIVITY 1

ACTION
Understanding natural number operations

OBJECTIVE
To work with the various natural number operations

The language of mathematics is important. Later on, you will have to turn problems in words into mathematical statements. This is called real-life modelling. This book aims to increase your vocabulary of mathematical terms.

The natural numbers are the counting numbers: 1, 2, 3, 4, 5, 6, …

The three dots at the end mean the counting numbers go on forever, that is, they never stop. We say there is an **infinite** number of counting numbers. Therefore, no matter what counting number is in your head, you can always pick a bigger one.

There are several natural number operations that you need to be able to carry out.

Operation 1: Addition

Adding natural numbers: $2 + 3 = 5$

In words: The **sum** of 2 and 3 is equal to 5.

Operation 2: Subtraction

Taking natural numbers away: $10 - 6 = 4$

In words: The **difference** of 10 and 6 is equal to 4.

Operation 3: Multiplication

Multiplying natural numbers: $3 \times 2 = 6$

In words: The **product** of 3 and 2 is equal to 6.

3 **times** 2 is equal to 6.

$3 \times 2 = 2 + 2 + 2 = 6$

3 times 2 is telling you to add 2 and 2 and 2.

3 times 2 can also be written as 3(2).

Operation 4: Division

Dividing natural numbers: $18 \div 3 = \dfrac{18}{3} = 6$

In words: The **quotient** of 18 and 3 is equal to 6.

The **ratio** of 18 and 3 ($18 : 3$) is equal to 6.

$18 : 3 = \dfrac{18}{3} = \dfrac{6}{1} = 6 : 1$

3 is called a **divisor** of 18 because it divides in exactly to give a quotient of 6.

Operation 5: Powers

The power of a number tells you how many times the number (known as the base) gets multiplied by itself: $2^3 = 2 \times 2 \times 2 = 8$

In words: 2 to the power of 3 is equal to 8.

2 is called the **base**. 3 is the **power**. It is also called the **index** or **exponent**.

> **TIP**
>
> Do you understand which operation you need to carry out in the following situations?
>
> $3(2) = 2 + 2 + 2 = 6$ [The big 3 in front of the bracket tells you to add 2 and 2 and 2.]
>
> $(2)^3 = 2 \times 2 \times 2 = 8$ [The little 3 on the top right-hand corner of the bracket tells you to multiply 2 by 2 by 2.]

Order of operations

When several operations come together in the same problem, follow this procedure.

First: Do the calculation inside the **brackets**.

Next: Do the **powers**.

Next: Do the **multiplication** or **division**.

Next: Do the **addition** or **subtraction**.

WORKED EXAMPLE Natural number operations

Calculate $\dfrac{6 + 2 \times (2 + 1)^3}{4}$.

$\dfrac{6 + 2 \times (2 + 1)^3}{4}$ [Brackets first]

$= \dfrac{6 + 2 \times (3)^3}{4}$ [Powers next]

$= \dfrac{6 + 2 \times 27}{4}$ [Simplify the top line of the fraction – it is like a bracket. Multiplication next]

$= \dfrac{6 + 54}{4}$ [Addition next]

$= \dfrac{60}{4}$ [Divide]

$= 15$

Input the numbers into your calculator exactly as shown to check your answer.

Sets of natural numbers

The natural numbers are the counting numbers. The set of **whole positive numbers** is called the set of natural numbers. This set is denoted by $\mathbb{N}$.

$\mathbb{N}$ is the set of natural numbers.

$\mathbb{N} = \{1, 2, 3, 4, 5,...\}$

TIP

↑ Zero (0) is not a natural number.

Revisiting sets

▸ Consider the set of natural numbers less than 10. Call this set A.

$A = \{1, 2, 3, 4, 5, 6, 7, 8, 9\}$

KEY TERM

↑ Each individual member of a set is called an **element** of the set.

▸ 3 is an element of A.

$3 \in A$

ACTIVITY 2

ACTION
Revising sets

OBJECTIVE
To revise the set of natural numbers

▸ $B = \{5, 6, 7, 8, 9, 10, 11\}$

The number of elements in set B is called its **cardinal number** and is represented by #(B).

#(B) = 7: Set B has 7 elements. B has a **finite** number of elements.

KEY TERM

The **universal set** U is the set of all elements under consideration.

Set operation symbols (operators)

union	∪
intersection	∩
less	\
is an element of	∈
is not an element of	∉
is a subset of	⊂
is not a subset of	⊄
complement	′

WORKED EXAMPLE Set operations

U = set of the first 10 natural numbers
 = $\{1, 2, 3, 4, 5, 6, 7, 8, 9, 10\}$

A = set of even natural numbers less than 10
 = $\{2, 4, 6, 8\}$

B = set of natural numbers between 5 and 9 inclusive
 = $\{5, 6, 7, 8, 9\}$

This information can be represented on a Venn diagram.

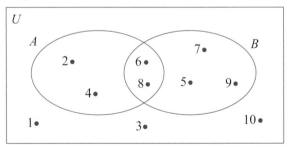

Union: $A \cup B = \{2, 4, 6, 8\} \cup \{5, 6, 7, 8, 9\}$
 = $\{2, 4, 5, 6, 7, 8, 9\}$

A union B is the set formed by joining the elements in set A and in set B into a single set $A \cup B$. Remember to not repeat common elements. $A \cup B$ is represented by the shaded part of the Venn diagram, as shown.

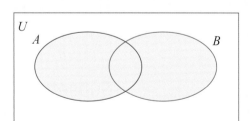

Intersection: $A \cap B = \{2, 4, 6, 8\} \cap \{5, 6, 7, 8, 9\}$
$$= \{6, 8\}$$

A intersection *B* is the set of elements that set *A* and set *B* have in common. You can find the answer from where the sets *A* and *B* overlap in a Venn diagram. $A \cap B$ is represented by the shaded part of the Venn diagram, as shown.

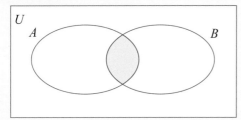

Less: $A \backslash B = \{2, 4, 6, 8\} \backslash \{5, 6, 7, 8, 9\} = \{2, 4\}$

A less *B* means the set of elements that are in *A* but not in *B*. $A \backslash B$ is represented by the shaded part of the Venn diagram, as shown.

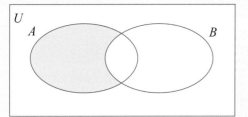

$B \backslash A = \{5, 6, 7, 8, 9\} \backslash \{2, 4, 6, 8\} = \{5, 7, 9\}$

B less *A* means the set of elements that are in *B* but not in *A*. $B \backslash A$ is represented by the shaded part of the Venn diagram, as shown.

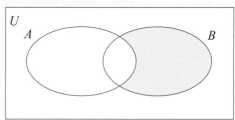

Complement: $A' = \{1, 3, 5, 7, 9, 10\}$

The complement of *A* is the set of all the elements that are outside *A*. A' is represented by the shaded part of the Venn diagram, as shown.

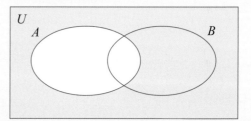

Null set

A **null** set is an empty set and is represented by {} or Ø. It is a set with no elements in it.

▸ $A = \{1, 2, 3\}$
  $B = \{4, 5\}$
  $A \cap B = \{\}$

Subsets

If **every** element of a set *B* is also a member of set *A*, then *B* is a **subset** (⊂) of *A*.

▸ $A = \{1, 2, 3, 4, 5, 6\}$
  $B = \{1, 2, 3\}$

  $B \subset A$ because **every** element in *B* is also in *A*.

  This situation can be represented by drawing the Venn diagram, as shown, with set *B* drawn inside set *A*.

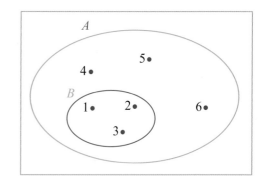

Number line

The natural numbers can be displayed on a number line, as shown.

The numbers increase in size as you go from left to right on the number line.

▸ 6 is greater than 2 (6 > 2)

▸ 3 is less than 5 (3 < 5)

Prime numbers and composite numbers

The set of natural numbers can be divided into the following subsets:

| Prime Numbers | *and* | Composite Numbers | *and* | 1 |

Every natural number is a prime number, a composite number or 1.

KEY TERM

A **prime number** is a natural number greater than 1, which can be divided only by itself and 1.

All other natural numbers are composite numbers or 1.

17 is a prime number because its only divisors are 1 and 17.

18 is not a prime number as its divisors are 1, 2, 3, 6, 9 and 18. So 18 is a composite number.

KEY TERM

The **factors** of a natural number are its whole positive number divisors.

1, 2, 3, 6, 9 and 18 are factors of 18.

WORKED EXAMPLE

Factors tell you whether a number is a prime or a composite number

Consider the number 14.

$\frac{14}{1} = 14 \Rightarrow 1$ is a factor of 14

$\frac{14}{2} = 7 \Rightarrow 2$ is a factor of 14

$\frac{14}{7} = 2 \Rightarrow 7$ is a factor of 14

$\frac{14}{14} = 1 \Rightarrow 14$ is a factor of 14

The factors of 14 are: 1, 2, 7, 14.
So 14 is a composite number.

Consider the number 19.

$\frac{19}{1} = 19 \Rightarrow 1$ is a factor of 19

$\frac{19}{19} = 1 \Rightarrow 19$ is a factor of 19

These are the only factors of 19.
So 19 is a prime number.

Prime numbers are extremely important as they are the building blocks from which **all natural numbers** greater than 1 can be built. Every composite number can be expressed as a product of prime numbers. The first 10 prime numbers are: 2, 3, 5, 7, 11, 13, 17, 19, 23, 29

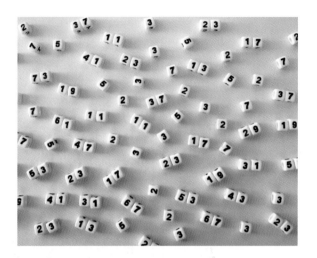

ACTIVITY 3

ACTION
Identifying composite and prime numbers

OBJECTIVE
To investigate whether numbers are composite or prime and to find prime factors

EXAMPLE 1

Find the prime factors of 100.

Solution

Starting with the smallest prime number, divide in prime numbers that are divisors (no remainder). Move in order through the list until you end up with 1. 100 is the product of all these divisors.

$$
\begin{array}{r|r}
2 & 100 \\
2 & 50 \\
5 & 25 \\
5 & 5 \\
& 1
\end{array}
$$

$\therefore 100 = 2 \times 2 \times 5 \times 5 = 2^2 \times 5^2$

Every composite number can be written as a product of its primes.

WORKED EXAMPLE

Is 1457 a prime number?

Divide the prime numbers in order, starting at 1457, until one of them divides in exactly. If no prime number divides in exactly, then the number being tested is itself a prime number.

Prime factor	$N = 1457$
2	$1457 = 2 \times 728 + 1$
3	$1457 = 3 \times 485 + 2$
5	$1457 = 5 \times 291 + 2$
7	$1457 = 7 \times 208 + 1$
11	$1457 = 11 \times 132 + 5$
13	$1457 = 13 \times 112 + 1$
17	$1457 = 17 \times 85 + 12$
19	$1457 = 19 \times 76 + 13$
23	$1457 = 23 \times 63 + 8$
29	$1457 = 29 \times 50 + 7$
31	$1457 = 31 \times 47$
	Stop

$\therefore 1457 = 31 \times 47$

1457 is a composite number.

How can you tell if a number is a prime or a composite number? There are a few tests you can apply to a number to see whether or not it is prime.

Techniques for testing for primes

Test 1

With the exception of the number 2, all numbers with a last digit 0, 2, 4, 6 or 8 are composite. Why?

169 471 468 214 is a composite number.

> **TIP**
> ↑ 2 is the only even prime number.

Test 2

With the exception of the number 5, all numbers with a last digit 0 or 5 are composite numbers. Why?

52 745 is a composite number because $52\,745 = 5 \times 10\,549$.

62 150 is a composite number because $62\,150 = 5 \times 12\,430$.

Test 3

With the exception of the number 3, all numbers whose digits add to a multiple of 3 are divisible by 3 and so are composite.

$12\,356\,781 = 3 \times 4\,118\,927$ because the digits of 12 356 781 add up to 33.

EXAMPLE 2

Are the following numbers prime?

(a) 45 621 438   **(b)** 53 821 470   **(c)** 147 321

Solution

(a) 45 621 43<u>8</u> is not prime because it is even.   [**Test 1**]

(b) 53 821 47<u>0</u> is not prime because it is divisible by 5 and 10.   [**Test 2**]

(c) 147 321 is not prime as $1 + 4 + 7 + 3 + 2 + 1 = 18$, which is a multiple of 3.   [**Test 3**]

147 321 divisible by 3

$147\,321 = 3 \times 49\,107$

EXAMPLE 3

U = set of the first 20 natural numbers

P = set of prime numbers less than 20

C = set of composite numbers less than and including 20

(a) List the elements of all three sets.

(b) Represent these sets on a Venn diagram.

(c) Is $1 \in (P \cup C)$?

(d) List the elements of $P \cap C$. What name is given to $P \cap C$?

(e) E = set of even numbers less than and including 20. List the elements of E. Is $E \subset C$?

Solution

(a) $U = \{1, 2, 3, 4, 5, 6, 7, 8, 9, 10, 11, 12, 13, 14, 15, 16, 17, 18, 19, 20\}$

$P = \{2, 3, 5, 7, 11, 13, 17, 19\}$

$C = \{4, 6, 8, 9, 10, 12, 14, 15, 16, 18, 20\}$

(b)

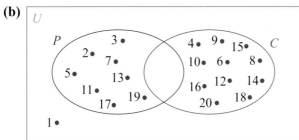

(c) $(P \cup C) = \{2, 3, 4, 5, 6, 7, 8, 9, 10, 11, 12, 13, 14, 15, 16, 17, 18, 19, 20\}$

$1 \notin (P \cup C)$

(d) $P \cap C = \{\}$

This is called the null set.

(e) $E = \{2, 4, 6, 8, 10, 12, 14, 16, 18, 20\}$

$E \not\subset C$, as not all elements in E are also in C: $2 \notin C$

EXERCISE 1

1. (a) What is the sum of 2, 3 and 5?

(b) What is the difference of 20 and 6?

(c) List the first 15 natural numbers.

(d) What is the product of 6 and 8?

(e) What is 4 times 8?

(f) Find the quotient of 10 and 2? What is 2 called in this situation?

(g) Write 2 to the power of 4 mathematically. Calculate it.

(h) Find the product of 2, 3 and 5. Also find the product of 3, 5 and 2. What do you notice?

(i) Write out 5×2 in longhand and then calculate it.

(j) Write out 2^5 in longhand and then calculate it.

2. Calculate the following operations. Do them first without a calculator and then check your answers on your calculator:

(a) $25 + 6 - 2 + 1 - 3$

(b) $(4 + 3) - (2 - 1)$

(c) $(2 + 1)^3 - 1$

(d) $2(6 - 2) + 7 \times 3 - 5$

(e) $3(20 - 19)^5 + 5 \times 3$

(f) $\dfrac{1 + 5 \times 3}{8}$

(g) $\dfrac{2^2 + 4 \times 2 - 3}{3}$

(h) $\dfrac{4 + 2(5) + 7}{2^2 - 1}$

(i) $\dfrac{2^4 - (1 + 1)^2 + 2^3}{2^2}$

(j) $\dfrac{21 + 4 \times 2 + 3^2}{20 - 1}$

3. List the elements for each set described below and draw a Venn diagram to represent the situation:

(a) U = set of the first 12 natural numbers

A = set of odd numbers between 3 and 9 inclusive

B = set of natural numbers between 1 and 5 inclusive

List the elements of the following sets:

(i) $A \cup B$ **(v)** A'

(ii) $A \cap B$ **(vi)** B'

(iii) $A \backslash B$ **(vii)** $(A \cup B)'$

(iv) $B \backslash A$ **(viii)** $(A \backslash B)'$

(b) U = set of the natural numbers between 5 and 20 inclusive

C = set of even numbers between 6 and 14 inclusive

D = set of natural numbers between 5 and 20 divisible by 5 inclusive

List the elements of the following sets:

(i) $C \cup D$ **(v)** C'

(ii) $C \cap D$ **(vi)** D'

(iii) $C \backslash D$ **(vii)** $(C \cup D)'$

(iv) $D \backslash C$ **(viii)** $(D \backslash C)'$

4. (a) Using the Venn diagram below:

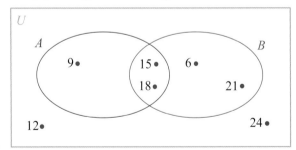

(i) List the elements of the universal set U and sets A and B.

(ii) Is $12 \in A$?

(iii) State the universal set U in words.

(iv) List the elements of $A \cup B$.

(v) List the elements of $A \cap B$.

(vi) List the elements of $A \backslash B$.

(vii) List the elements of A'.

(b)

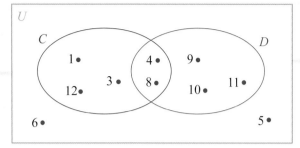

(i) List the elements of the universal set U and sets C and D.

(ii) Evaluate $\#(C)$ and $\#(D)$.

(iii) List the elements of $C \cup D$.

(iv) List the elements of $C \cap D$.

(v) List the elements of $C \backslash D$.

(vi) List the elements of $(C \cup D)'$.

(vii) Is $3 \in D \backslash C$?

5. Say whether the numbers are prime, composite or neither. Find the prime factors of the composite numbers:

(a) 18   **(d)** 28   **(g)** 62

(b) 45   **(e)** 90   **(h)** 79

(c) 11   **(f)** 85   **(i)** 51

6. Which of the following natural numbers are prime?

27, 38, 47, 91, 80, 1, 123, 465, 530.

7. Is 413 625 914 856 a prime number? Why?

8. Is 32 794 221 a prime number? Why? Check it on your calculator.

9. (a) Evaluate 2^3, 2^4, 2^5 and 2^6. Is 2^{2013} a prime number? Why?

(b) Evaluate 5^2, 5^3, 5^4 and 5^5. Is 5^{27} a prime number? Why?

10. There are 36 students in a class. The numbers of boys and girls are prime numbers. If there are two more boys than girls in the class, how many of each are there?

11. 'Every number between 1 and 100 can be written as a sum of two primes.' Give a simple example to show that this is not true.

1.2 Integers

Why do we need more numbers?

As you know, $3 - 3 = 0$ (zero). Mathematicians had debated for centuries whether or not zero (0) was actually a number. What about $3 - 5$? Such an operation would bring you to the left of 0 on the number line. It was therefore obvious that a whole new group of numbers had to be invented to deal with this new situation.

▸ Using the number line: $3 - 5 = -2$

The set consisting of all positive and negative whole numbers is known as the set of integers. This set is denoted by the symbol $\mathbb{Z}$.

$\mathbb{Z} = \{..., -3, -2, -1, 0, 1, 2, 3, ...\}$

> **KEY TERM**
> **Integers** are whole numbers (positive and negative) and zero.

The natural counting numbers are part of this set of integers. Numbers increase in size as you go from left to right on the number line.

▸ 2 is greater than -3 $(2 > -3)$

▸ 0 is less than 4 $(0 < 4)$

Integer operations

Operation 1: Combining (addition and subtraction)

Same sign:

▸ $+3 + 5 = +8$ [Adding two positive numbers]

▸ $-3 - 5 = -8$ [Adding two negative numbers]

Different signs:

▸ $+3 - 5 = -2$ [Take the numbers away. The sign of the answer is the sign of the bigger number.]

▸ $-7 + 12 = +5$

▸ $+4 - (+2) = +4 - 2 = 2$ [A negative sign outside the bracket changes the sign inside the bracket.]

▸ $-4 - (-2) = -4 + 2 = -2$

Operation 2: Multiplication

▸ $(+3)(+5) = +15$ [Multiplying two positive integers gives a positive integer.]

▸ $(-3)(-4) = +12$ [Multiplying two negative integers gives a positive integer.]

▶ $(+3)(-5) = -15$ [Multiplying a positive integer by a negative integer gives a negative integer.]

▶ $(-3)(+4) = -12$ [Multiplying a negative integer by a positive integer gives a negative integer.]

> **Rule:** Integers with **like** signs (both positive or both negative) multiply to give a positive integer.
>
> Integers with **unlike** signs (one positive and one negative) multiply to give a negative integer.

Operation 3: Division

▶ $(+12) \div (+6) = +2$

▶ $\dfrac{-12}{-3} = +4$

▶ $\dfrac{-12}{+3} = -4$

▶ $\dfrac{+15}{-5} = -3$

The rule for the division of integers is the same as the rule for the multiplication of integers.

> **Rule:** Integers with **like** signs (both positive or both negative) divide to give a positive integer.
>
> Integers with **unlike** signs (one positive and one negative) divide to give a negative integer.

ACTIVITY 4

ACTION
Understanding integer operations

OBJECTIVE
To investigate properties of integers

Operation 4: Powers

▶ $(-2)^2 = (-2)(-2) = +4$

▶ $(-2)^3 = (-2)(-2)(-2) = -8$

> **Rule:** A negative integer to a power that is **even** gives a positive integer.
> A negative integer to a power that is **odd** gives a negative integer.

EXAMPLE 4

Simplify the following:

(a) $-7 + 6$

(b) $-7 - 8$

(c) $-7 - (-6)$

(d) $(-7) \times (-6)$

(e) $\dfrac{-8}{-4}$

(f) $(-1)^3$

(g) $(-7)^2$

Solution

(a) $-7 + 6 = -1$

(b) $-7 - 8 = -15$

(c) $-7 - (-6) = -7 + 6 = -1$

(d) $(-7) \times (-6) = +42$

(e) $\dfrac{-8}{-4} = +2$

(f) $(-1)^3 = -1 \times -1 \times -1 = -1$

(g) $(-7)^2 = -7 \times -7 = 49$

EXAMPLE 5

A woman has a direct debit account with a digital TV provider. The company withdraws €55 per month from her account. If she has €450 to start in the account, how much will be left after three withdrawals?

Solution

Balance left after three withdrawals:

$= €(450 - 55 - 55 - 55)$

$= €(450 - 3 \times 55)$

$= €(450 - 165)$

$= €285$

EXAMPLE 6

A golf course has a par of 72. If a golfer takes 70 strokes to complete the course, he is 2 under par (−2). If he takes 75 strokes, he is 3 over par (+3). A score of 72 is even par (0). In a golfing tournament, the golfer has the following scores in his four rounds: 74, 69, 70 and 73. What is his total score? What is his par score?

Solution

	Round 1	Round 2	Round 3	Round 4	Total
Score	74	69	70	73	286
Par score	+2	−3	−2	+1	−2

Score = 74 + 69 + 70 + 73 = 286

Par score = +2 − 3 − 2 + 1 = −2 (2 under par)

EXAMPLE 7

Place the following numbers in the Venn diagram below: 1, −2, 4, 5, −5, 0, 20, −10

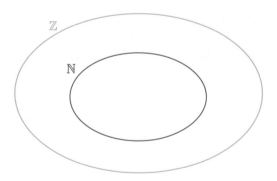

Is $\mathbb{N} \subset \mathbb{Z}$? Explain.

Solution

Put the number 1 into the natural number section. Because the set $\mathbb{N}$ is drawn inside the set $\mathbb{Z}$, the number 1 is also inside $\mathbb{Z}$. So 1 is a natural number that is also an integer.

Put the number −2 outside the set $\mathbb{N}$ but inside $\mathbb{Z}$, as −2 is an integer but not a natural number.

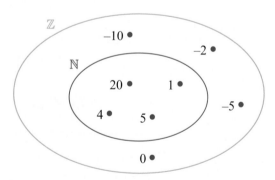

The set of natural numbers $\mathbb{N}$ is a subset of the set of integers $\mathbb{Z}$ because every natural number is also an integer.

$\therefore \mathbb{N} \subset \mathbb{Z}$ [The set of natural numbers is a subset of the set of integers.]

EXAMPLE 8

Write out the following sets:

(a) $\mathbb{Z} \setminus \mathbb{N}$

(b) $\mathbb{Z} \cap \mathbb{N}$

Is $\mathbb{Z} \cup \mathbb{N} = \mathbb{Z}$?

Solution

$\mathbb{Z} = \{\ldots, -3, -2, -1, 0, 1, 2, 3, \ldots\}$

$\mathbb{N} = \{1, 2, 3, 4, \ldots\}$

(a) $\mathbb{Z} \setminus \mathbb{N} = \{\ldots, -3, -2, -1, 0, 1, 2, 3, \ldots\} \setminus \{1, 2, 3, 4, \ldots\}$

$= \{\ldots, -3, -2, -1, 0\}$ [All the negative whole numbers and 0]

(b) $\mathbb{Z} \cap \mathbb{N} = \{\ldots, -3, -2, -1, 0, 1, 2, 3, \ldots\} \cap \{1, 2, 3, 4, \ldots\}$

$= \{1, 2, 3, 4, \ldots\} = \mathbb{N}$

$\mathbb{Z} \cup \mathbb{N} = \{\ldots, -3, -2, -1, 0, 1, 2, 3, \ldots\} \cup \{1, 2, 3, 4, \ldots\}$

$= \{\ldots, -3, -2, -1, 0, 1, 2, 3, 4, \ldots\} = \mathbb{Z}$

Consecutive integers

Consecutive integers are whole numbers in which the difference between one integer and the previous one is 1, when written in ascending order of magnitude.

5, 6, 7, 8 are four consecutive integers because $6 - 5 = 7 - 6 = 8 - 7 = 1$.

$-74, -73, -72$ are three consecutive integers because $-73 - (-74) = -72 - (-73) = 1$.

If a is an integer: a, $a + 1$, $a + 2$ and $a - 1$, a, $a + 1$ are consecutive integers.

▸ Write down three consecutive integers if -23 is one of them. There are three possibilities:

$-23, -22, -21$ *or* $-24, -23, -22$ *or* $-25, -24, -23$

EXERCISE 2

1. A = the set of integers between -3 and 4 inclusive.

   (a) Write out the elements of set A.

   (b) Plot this set on a number line.

   (c) Insert the appropriate symbol $(<, >)$ in the space provided:

        (i) $0 \,\square\, 4$ **(iv)** $2 \,\square\, -3$

        (ii) $-1 \,\square\, -3$ **(v)** $-4 \,\square\, -3$

        (iii) $0 \,\square\, -2$

2. Simplify the following operations and check each answer on your calculator:

   (a) $3 - 4 + 5 - 6$

   (b) $2(3 - 6) - 3(5 - 6)$

   (c) $5(-3) + 6(-1) - 2(-2)$

   (d) $\dfrac{6}{-3} + \dfrac{-2}{2}$

   (e) $\dfrac{-2 - 10}{3}$

   (f) $\dfrac{6(2 - 5) + 3(4 - 2)}{2 - 6}$

   (g) $(-3)^3$

   (h) $\dfrac{(-2)^2 - (2)^4}{4}$

   (i) $\dfrac{3(2 - 4)^2 + 8}{5}$

   (j) $(-3)^2 + (-2)^3$

3. Place the following numbers in the Venn diagram: $5, -6, 2, 0, 1, -3, -10$

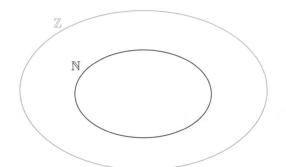

4. A gannet dives from 20 metres above sea level. If the bird descends 2 metres below sea level, what integer represents:

   (a) its initial position,

   (b) its final position,

   relative to sea level, if positive integers are heights above sea level.

5. A submarine at 1200 metres below sea level dives at 50 metres per minute for 10 minutes. What integer represents:

   (a) its initial position,

   (b) its final position,

   relative to sea level, if positive integers are heights above sea level.

6. The highest point in North America is the summit of Mount McKinley at 6168 metres above sea level. The lowest point in North America is the bottom of Death Valley at 86 metres below sea level. Positive integers represent heights above sea level.

   (a) What integer represents:

      (i) the height of the summit of Mount McKinley relative to sea level,

      (ii) the depth of the bottom of Death Valley relative to sea level?

   (b) What is the distance from the bottom of Death Valley to the top of Mount McKinley?

7. The melting point of mercury is −39 °C. The freezing point of ethanol is −114 °C. How much hotter is the melting point of mercury than the freezing point of ethanol?

8. The Roman Empire started in 27 BC and ended in AD 476. How long did the Roman Empire last?

9. The mean temperature in a city falls by 1 °C from 4 °C on the first day of the month for the next 9 days and then rises by 2 °C for the next 2 days. What is the mean temperature on the 12th day?

10. An investment is in the red by €10 000 on 31 December 2012. The investment increases in value by €3000 every month on the first of the month, starting on 1 January 2013. What is its value on 31 December 2013?

11. A very high temperature of 54 °C was once recorded in the Middle East. A very low temperature of −71 °C was once recorded in Siberia. What was the difference in temperature from highest to lowest?

12. The highest temperature reading on a thermometer is 212 °F and the lowest temperature reading is 32 °F. What is the temperature range of this thermometer?

13. The starting balance in Sarah's current account was €285. If she made two withdrawals of €52 and €28 on Monday and Tuesday, respectively, and a deposit of €88 on Wednesday, how much was in her account on Thursday morning?

14. The average daytime temperature on a certain planet is −18 °C and the average night-time temperature is −55 °C. How much hotter is the planet during the day than at night?

15. The population of three cities in one country in 2010 is shown together with the change in population in 2014.

City	Population in 2010	Change in population in 2014
Marley	1 500 725	+54 330
Wagawaca	754 263	−21 456
Brum	55 253	−2780

   (a) Find the total population of all three cities in 2010.

   (b) Find the net (overall) change in the population of the three cities combined in 2014.

   (c) Use the two previous answers to find the total population of the three cities in 2014.

16. A group of 100 integers alternates between −2 and 4, as shown: −2, 4, −2, 4, … Find the sum of this group of numbers.

17. Write down three consecutive integers in ascending order, starting at -27.

18. Three consecutive integers add to -24. What are they, if one of the integers is -8?

19. Evaluate:

(a) $(-1)^3$

(b) $(-1)^{105}$

(c) $(-1)^{2014}$

(d) $(-1)^n$, $n \in \mathbb{N}$, n even

(e) $(-1)^n + (-1)^{n+1}$, $n \in \mathbb{N}$

(f) $(-1)^{2n+1}$, $n \in \mathbb{N}$

1.3 Rational numbers

Why do we need even more numbers?

The fraction $\frac{6}{3} = 2$ is easily calculated and poses no problems. However, what about $\frac{5}{2}$? As you know, $\frac{5}{2} = 2\frac{1}{2}$.

This can be plotted on the number line, as follows:

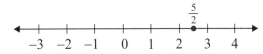

$\frac{5}{2}$ is a number halfway between 2 and 3. It is not a whole number. So it is not an integer.

The set of integers must therefore be extended to include both positive and negative fractions which are not whole numbers. This new set of numbers is called the set of rational numbers and is denoted by $\mathbb{Q}$.

> **KEY TERM**
>
> A **rational number (fraction)** is a number of the form $\frac{a}{b}$, where a and b are both integers.

In other words, a rational number is a ratio of two integers.

> **KEY TERMS**
>
> The top number in the fraction is called the **numerator**.
>
> The bottom number in the fraction is called the **denominator**.

Some examples of rational numbers are: $-\frac{48}{53}, \frac{79}{23}, -\frac{5}{1}, \frac{-5}{-2}, \frac{0}{1}$

All integers themselves are rational numbers, as every integer can be written as a ratio of the integer and 1:

$6 = \frac{6}{1}, -42 = -\frac{42}{1}, -7 = -\frac{7}{1}$

There are infinitely many rational numbers between any two integers:

$1, ..., \frac{1}{4}, ..., \frac{1}{2}, ..., \frac{3}{4}, ..., 2$

ACTIVITY 5

ACTION
Working with rationals

OBJECTIVE
To perform rational number operations and to write numbers in decimal form as rationals

EXAMPLE **9**

Place the following numbers in the Venn diagram, as shown: $4, \frac{6}{2}, -3, -\frac{8}{4}, \frac{7}{3}, -\frac{9}{5}$

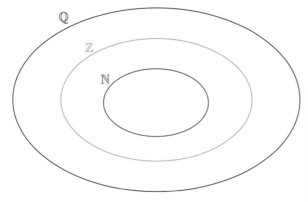

Is $\mathbb{N} \subset \mathbb{Z} \subset \mathbb{Q}$? Explain.

Solution

Put the number 4 into the natural numbers section. Also put $\frac{6}{2}$ into this section, as this number works out to be 3.

Because the set $\mathbb{N}$ is drawn inside the set $\mathbb{Q}$, the number 4 is also inside $\mathbb{Q}$. So 4 is a natural number that is also a rational number, as it could also be written as $\frac{4}{1}$ or $\frac{8}{2}$, and so on.

Put the numbers -3 and $-\frac{8}{4}$ outside the set $\mathbb{N}$ but inside $\mathbb{Z}$, as they are integers but not natural numbers.

Put the numbers $\frac{7}{3}$ and $-\frac{9}{5}$ outside the set $\mathbb{Z}$ but inside $\mathbb{Q}$, as they are rational numbers but not integers.

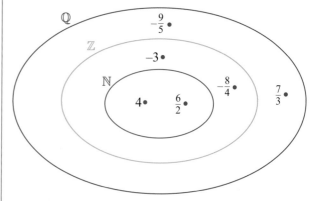

The set of natural numbers $\mathbb{N}$ is a subset of the set of integers $\mathbb{Z}$ because every natural number is also an integer.

The set of integers $\mathbb{Z}$ is a subset of the set of rational numbers $\mathbb{Q}$ because every integer is also a rational number.

$\therefore \mathbb{N} \subset \mathbb{Z} \subset \mathbb{Q}$

The set of natural numbers is a subset of the set of integers, which is a subset of the set of rational number.

Equivalence of fractions

If a number is multiplied by 1, its value remains the same. The number 1 can be written in many equivalent ways:

$$1 = \frac{1}{1} = \frac{2}{2} = \frac{3}{3} = \frac{4}{4} = \frac{-3}{-3} = \frac{p}{p}$$

Multiplying the numerator and denominator of a rational number by the same number produces equivalent fractions, as they all have the same value.

$$\frac{2}{3} \times \frac{2}{2} = \frac{4}{6}$$

$$\frac{2}{3} \times \frac{3}{3} = \frac{6}{9}$$

$$\frac{2}{3} \times \frac{4}{4} = \frac{8}{12}$$

$$\therefore \frac{4}{6} = \frac{6}{9} = \frac{8}{12}$$

Plot the following rational numbers on the number line: $\frac{1}{2}, \frac{7}{10}, \frac{1}{5}$

Solution

These fractions will be easier to compare if you make all of the fractions have the same denominator. The lowest common denominator (LCD) of all these fractions is 10.

$$\frac{1}{2} = \frac{5}{10}, \frac{7}{10} = \frac{7}{10}, \frac{1}{5} = \frac{2}{10}$$

You can now order the fractions from the smallest to the biggest:

$$\frac{2}{10} < \frac{5}{10} < \frac{7}{10} \ or \ \frac{1}{5} < \frac{1}{2} < \frac{7}{10}$$

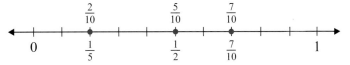

Cancelling fractions

If a fraction (or any number) is divided by 1, its value does not change.

$$\frac{3}{9} = \frac{3}{9} \div \frac{3}{3} = \frac{3 \div 3}{9 \div 3} = \frac{1}{3}$$

This is called cancelling and can be used to reduce fractions to their simplest form.

▸ $\frac{27}{18}$ is simplified by dividing the numerator and denominator by the same number 9.

$$\frac{27}{18} = \frac{{}^3\cancel{27}}{{}^2\cancel{18}} = \frac{3}{2}$$

Your calculator simplifies fractions automatically.

Rational number operations

Operation 1: Addition and subtraction

Rule: You can add and subtract fractions with the same denominators (bottom numbers) by combining their numerators (top numbers).

▸ $\frac{1}{5} + \frac{2}{5} + \frac{3}{5} = \frac{1 + 2 + 3}{5} = \frac{6}{5} = 1\frac{1}{5}$

▸ $\frac{4}{7} - \frac{2}{7} - \left(-\frac{3}{7}\right) = \frac{4}{7} - \frac{2}{7} + \frac{3}{7} = \frac{4 - 2 + 3}{7} = \frac{5}{7}$

If the denominators are different, turn the fractions into equivalent fractions with the same denominator.

▸ $\frac{1}{5} + \frac{3}{10} = \frac{2}{10} + \frac{3}{10} = \frac{2 + 3}{10} = \frac{5}{10} = \frac{1}{2}$

You can also add and subtract fractions by finding the lowest common denominator (LCD) of all fractions, as follows:

▸ $\frac{2}{3} + \frac{4}{5} = \frac{5 \times 2 + 3 \times 4}{15} = \frac{10 + 12}{15} = \frac{22}{15} = 1\frac{7}{15}$

Operation 2: Multiplication

Rule: Multiply the top numbers (numerators) and the bottom numbers (denominators).

▸ $\frac{2}{3} \times \frac{4}{5} = \frac{2 \times 4}{3 \times 5} = \frac{8}{15}$

You can cancel as you proceed.

▸ $\dfrac{1}{4} \times \dfrac{8}{9} \times \dfrac{3}{7} = \dfrac{1}{{}^1\cancel{4}} \times \dfrac{{}^2\cancel{8}}{{}^3\cancel{9}} \times \dfrac{{}^1\cancel{3}}{7} = \dfrac{1 \times 2 \times 1}{1 \times 3 \times 7} = \dfrac{2}{21}$

Operation 3: Division

A fraction divided by a fraction is unofficially called a **double-decker fraction**.

▸ $\dfrac{3}{7} \div \dfrac{2}{5} = \dfrac{\tfrac{3}{7}}{\tfrac{2}{5}}$ is a double-decker fraction.

Rule: To simplify a double-decker fraction, multiply the top fraction and the bottom fraction by the lowest common denominator (LCD) of the denominators of both fractions.

▸ $\dfrac{\tfrac{7}{6}}{\tfrac{3}{2}} = \dfrac{\tfrac{7}{6} \times \tfrac{6}{1}}{\tfrac{3}{2} \times \tfrac{6}{1}} = \dfrac{7}{9}$

Alternatively, multiply the top fraction by the bottom fraction inverted (flipped).

▸ $\dfrac{\tfrac{7}{6}}{\tfrac{3}{2}} = \dfrac{7}{6} \times \dfrac{2}{3} = \dfrac{14}{18} = \dfrac{7}{9}$

Operation 4: Powers

▸ $\left(\dfrac{3}{2}\right)^3 = \dfrac{3}{2} \times \dfrac{3}{2} \times \dfrac{3}{2} = \dfrac{27}{8}$

▸ $\left(2\tfrac{1}{2}\right)^2 = \left(\dfrac{5}{2}\right)^2 = \dfrac{5}{2} \times \dfrac{5}{2} = \dfrac{25}{4} = 6\tfrac{1}{4}$

Rationals and decimals

Every rational number can be expressed as a decimal.

WORKED EXAMPLE

Terminating and recurring decimals

Write $\dfrac{3}{8}$ as a decimal.

$\dfrac{3}{8} = \dfrac{3 \cdot 000}{8}$

$\begin{array}{r} 0 \cdot 375 \\ 8\,\overline{)3 \cdot 000} \quad \text{[By long division]} \\ \underline{24} \\ 60 \\ \underline{56} \\ 40 \\ \underline{40} \\ 0 \end{array}$

$\therefore \dfrac{3}{8} = 0 \cdot 375$

0·375 is called a terminating decimal because it stops. This calculation can be done using your calculator.

However, try writing $\dfrac{11}{9}$ as a decimal.

$\dfrac{11}{9} = \dfrac{11 \cdot 000}{9} = 1 \cdot 222\ldots$

The digit 2 recurs. Decimals such as 1·222... are called non-terminating (never-ending), recurring decimals.

$1 \cdot 22222\ldots = 1 \cdot \dot{2}$ for short. The dot over the 2 indicates it is to be repeated forever (*ad infinitum*).

▸ $1 \cdot 3\dot{7} = 1 \cdot 37777777\ldots$

▸ $0 \cdot \dot{5}\dot{2} = 0 \cdot 525252\ldots$

Every rational number can be expressed either as a terminating decimal or a non-terminating, recurring decimal.

$\dfrac{4}{5} = 0 \cdot 8$ [Terminating decimal]

$\dfrac{2}{3} = 0 \cdot \dot{6}$ [Recurring decimal]

Converting rationals to decimals and vice versa

1. **Changing a rational number into a decimal:** This can be done by division or by using your calculator.

$$\frac{27}{32} = 0\!\cdot\!84375$$

$$4\frac{5}{6} = \frac{29}{6} = 4\!\cdot\!8\dot{3}$$

2. **Changing a terminating decimal into a rational:** This can be done in two ways, as shown below.

EXAMPLE 11

Change $3\!\cdot\!563$ into a rational.

Solution

$$3\!\cdot\!563 = 3 \times 1 + 5 \times \frac{1}{10} + 6 \times \frac{1}{100} + 3 \times \frac{1}{1000}$$

$$= 3 + \frac{5}{10} + \frac{6}{100} + \frac{3}{1000}$$

$$= \frac{3000 + 500 + 60 + 3}{1000}$$

$$= \frac{3563}{1000}$$

or

Multiply above and below by 1000 because there are 3 digits to the right of the decimal point.

$$3\!\cdot\!563 = \frac{3\!\cdot\!563}{1} \times \frac{1000}{1000} = \frac{3563}{1000}$$

Your calculator does this conversion for you.

EXERCISE 3

1. Copy the Venn diagram below:

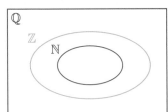

$\mathbb{Q}$ = set of rational numbers

$\mathbb{Z}$ = set of integers

$\mathbb{N}$ = set of natural numbers

(a) Fill the following numbers into the appropriate region of the Venn diagram:

$$-3, 0, \frac{1}{2}, \frac{70}{5}, 27, -\frac{3}{2}, 1$$

(b) (i) Is $\mathbb{Q} \cap \mathbb{Z} = \mathbb{Z}$? Why?

(ii) Is $\mathbb{Q} \cap \mathbb{N} = \mathbb{N}$? Why?

(c) Shade in $\mathbb{Q} \backslash \mathbb{Z}$. How would you describe this set in words?

2.

How many rational numbers are greater than 0 and less than 1?

If x is one of these rational numbers, describe x using mathematical symbols.

3. Plot the following rational numbers on a number line: $\frac{1}{3}, \frac{5}{6}, \frac{1}{6}, \frac{2}{9}$

4. Simplify the following and check each answer on your calculator:

(a) $\frac{1}{5} + \frac{3}{5}$

(b) $\frac{4}{7} - \frac{1}{7}$

(c) $\frac{2}{9} - \frac{5}{9}$

(d) $\frac{2}{3} + \frac{3}{5} - \frac{1}{4}$

(e) $\frac{2}{3} \times \frac{4}{5}$

(f) $\left(\frac{2}{5}\right)^2$

(g) $\left(3\frac{1}{2}\right)^2$

(h) $\frac{2}{3} \times \frac{6}{7}$

(i) $\left(\frac{2}{3}\right)^3 \times \frac{9}{8}$

(j) $\frac{2}{5}\left(-\frac{4}{5}\right) + \frac{3}{5}$

5. Simplify the following:

(a) $\dfrac{\frac{1}{2}}{\frac{1}{3}}$

(d) $\dfrac{-\frac{2}{3}}{3}$

(g) $\dfrac{-3}{\frac{3}{2}}$

(b) $\dfrac{1}{\frac{1}{2}}$

(e) $\dfrac{\frac{7}{6}}{\frac{3}{5}}$

(h) $\dfrac{-2}{\frac{7}{2}}$

(c) $\dfrac{\frac{1}{2}}{2}$

(f) $\dfrac{-\frac{2}{5}}{-\frac{4}{15}}$

(i) $\dfrac{\frac{1}{2}}{\frac{1}{4}}$

6. Change the rationals into terminating decimals:

(a) $\frac{3}{5}$

(f) $-3\frac{2}{5}$

(b) $\frac{3}{4}$

(g) $\frac{6}{25}$

(c) $\frac{121}{100}$

(h) $-\frac{41}{8}$

(d) $\frac{39}{50}$

(i) $\frac{36}{5}$

(e) $-\frac{23}{80}$

(j) $\frac{6}{75}$

7. Write the following terminating decimals as rationals and reduce them to the simplest form using your calculator:

(a) 0·625   **(c)** −2·14

(b) −0·713   **(d)** 5·64

8. Michael won €57 000 in the National Lottery. He gave two-thirds to charity and divided the remainder equally among his four children. How much money did each child receive?

9. On each visit to the gym, Miriam spends an hour and a half there. She spends two-fifths of her time on the treadmill, one-third in the swimming pool and the remainder on the weights. Find how many minutes Miriam spends on each activity and the fraction of time she spends on weights.

10. Mr O'Brien buys a pizza and divides it into two equal portions. He takes one of these portions for himself, gives one-third of the other half to his three-year-old son and the remainder to his seven-year-old daughter. What fraction of the whole pizza does each child get?

11. A university engineering course admits 840 first-year students. Three-eighths of these students opt for mechanical engineering and one-sixth opt for chemical engineering. The remainder choose electrical engineering. Find how many opt for each type of engineering. What fraction opts for electrical engineering?

12. From 2000 to 2014 the population of a city increased by two-fifths. If the population was 205 625 in 2000, what was the population in 2014?

13. A quick way to convert speed from kilometres per hour (km/h) to miles per hour (mph) is to multiply the speed in km/h by five-eighths. If a speed limit is 120 km/h, what is this limit in mph?

14. A tank contained $25\frac{2}{3}$ litres of water. If half a litre leaks out every hour, how much water is left after $35\frac{1}{2}$ hours?

15. A pipe has an external radius of $5\frac{1}{4}$ cm and an internal radius of $2\frac{3}{8}$ cm. What is the thickness of the pipe?

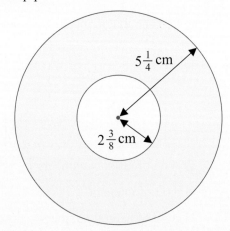

16. A triathlon athlete swims $1\frac{1}{2}$ km, cycles $5\frac{3}{4}$ km and runs $6\frac{3}{8}$ km in training. What is the total distance she covers?

17. In a sale, a television is advertised at four-fifths of its original price. If a customer has a coupon giving him one-quarter off the advertised price, what fraction of the original price does he pay?

18. Of the first 42 presidents of the USA, one-third were elected exactly twice. Of those elected twice, one-seventh were former vice-presidents. How many presidents elected twice were former vice-presidents?

19. How many portions of salt of mass $2\frac{1}{4}$ g can be measured out from a packet of salt of mass $40\frac{1}{2}$ g?

1.4 Real numbers

Irrational numbers

What number squared (multiplied by itself) is equal to 4? Obviously, $(2)^2 = 2 \times 2 = 4$.

The number which when multiplied by itself gives 4 is denoted by $\sqrt{4}$ and is called the square root of 4.

$\therefore \sqrt{4} = 2$

$\sqrt{9} = \sqrt{3^2} = 3$

$\sqrt{16} = \sqrt{4^2} = 4$

What about numbers that are not perfect squares? $\sqrt{2}$ is the number that when multiplied by itself gives 2.

This number is hard to think of but it does exist. It represents a real measurement. Remember Pythagoras:

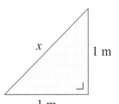

$$x^2 = 1^2 + 1^2$$
$$x^2 = 2$$
$$x = \sqrt{2}\text{ m}$$

The distance $\sqrt{2}$ m does exist.

The calculator gives $\sqrt{2} = 1\cdot41421356237$. It stops at 11 decimal places because no more digits can fit onto the screen of the calculator.

The number goes on forever (non-terminating) with no repeated pattern (non-recurring). This is unlike a rational number and it cannot be written as a rational. It is called an irrational number.

KEY TERM

An **irrational number** is a number that cannot be written as a terminating decimal nor as a non-terminating, recurring decimal.

Pythagoras 🎧

Mathematical murder: A student of Pythagoras called Hippasus recognised these numbers. Pythagoras could not accept the idea that there were numbers which were not rational, so he allegedly killed Hippasus!

The square roots of all rational numbers $\frac{a}{b}$ are irrational, unless a and b are perfect squares. There is an infinite number of irrationals.

$\sqrt{\dfrac{81}{16}} = \dfrac{9}{4}$ is rational but the following are irrational:

$\sqrt{\dfrac{1}{2}} = \dfrac{1}{\sqrt{2}},\ \sqrt{\dfrac{3}{16}} = \dfrac{\sqrt{3}}{4},\ -\sqrt{3} = -1\cdot732050808...,$

$\pi = 3\cdot14159265358979323846264...$

The set of real numbers $\mathbb{R}$ is the union of the set of rational numbers and the irrational numbers. This set can be represented on the number line as follows:

ACTIVITY 6

ACTION
Working with number systems

OBJECTIVE
To understand to which set a particular number belongs

EXAMPLE 12

Show that $\sqrt{2}$ lies between $1\cdot41$ and $1\cdot42$ using your calculator.

Solution

$1\cdot41^2 = 1\cdot9881$

$1\cdot42^2 = 2\cdot0164$

$(\sqrt{2})^2 = 2$

$\therefore 1\cdot41 < \sqrt{2} < 1\cdot42$

EXAMPLE 13

Use your calculator to evaluate $\sqrt[3]{4}$. Is it rational? Why?

Solution

$\sqrt[3]{4}$ means three identical numbers which, when multiplied together, give 4.

$\sqrt[3]{4} = 1\cdot587401052\ldots$ is a non-terminating, non-recurring decimal. Therefore, it is irrational.

EXAMPLE 14

Place the following numbers in the Venn diagram, as shown:

$-4,\ \sqrt{2},\ \sqrt{3},\ \sqrt{4},\ -\dfrac{10}{5},\ -\sqrt{36},\ -\dfrac{11}{3},\ \pi,\ \sqrt{\dfrac{16}{9}},\ -\sqrt{\dfrac{25}{4}}$

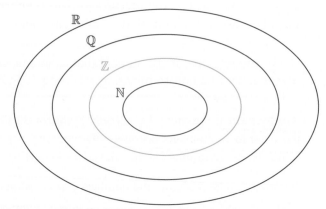

Is $\mathbb{N} \subset \mathbb{Z} \subset \mathbb{Q} \subset \mathbb{R}$? Explain.

Solution

$\mathbb{N} : \sqrt{4} = 2$

$\mathbb{Z} : -4, -\dfrac{10}{5} = -2, -\sqrt{36} = -6$

$\mathbb{Q} : -\dfrac{11}{3}, -\sqrt{\dfrac{25}{4}} = -\dfrac{5}{2}, \sqrt{\dfrac{16}{9}} = \dfrac{4}{3}$

$\mathbb{R} : \sqrt{2}, \sqrt{3}, \pi$

$\therefore \mathbb{N} \subset \mathbb{Z} \subset \mathbb{Q} \subset \mathbb{R}$

The set of natural numbers
is a subset of the set of integers,
which is a subset of the set
of rational numbers, which
is a subset of real numbers.

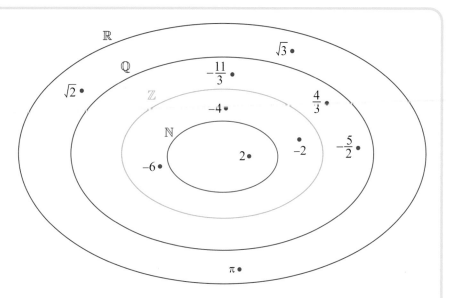

EXERCISE 4

1. Say which real numbers below are rational and which are irrational.

(a) $\sqrt{7}$

(b) $\sqrt{8}$

(c) $\sqrt{9}$

(d) $-\sqrt{16}$

(e) $\sqrt{32}$

(f) 3π

(g) $2\sqrt{2}$

(h) $\sqrt{\dfrac{2}{3}}$

(i) $\sqrt{\dfrac{10}{9}}$

(j) $1 \cdot \dot{3}$

(k) $2 \cdot 497612\ldots$

(l) $-2 \cdot \dot{4} \dot{7}$

(m) $-2 \cdot 474731256\ldots$

(n) $-4 \cdot 721431$

(o) $1 \cdot 2$

(p) $2 \cdot 71314259\ldots$

2. Show that $\sqrt{3}$ is between $1 \cdot 73$ and $1 \cdot 74$.

3. Copy the Venn diagram below. Place the following numbers in their correct positions in the Venn diagram.

$5, \sqrt{5}, \dfrac{15}{13}, 5 \cdot 3, -\dfrac{2}{7}, 0 \cdot \dot{3}, 0 \cdot \dot{2}\dot{9}, \sqrt{4}, \pi, -3, 0, 1$

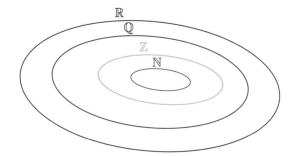

4. The Ancient Greeks discovered that when you divide the circumference of a circle by its diameter, you always get the same real number, which is called π. If the circumference of the circle s with centre O is $37 \cdot 69911184$ cm, estimate π, correct to four decimal places.

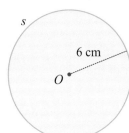

5. π is a real number and is approximately equal to $3{\cdot}14159265358979323846\ldots$ The digits continue with no pattern.

   (a) A boat sails around a circular course of diameter 200 m. How far does it sail in one circuit if the perimeter is given by $2\pi r$, where r is the radius? The length of the radius is half the diameter. Give your answer correct to the nearest metre.

   (b) Using your calculator, estimate π correct to two decimal places, with the following approximation:

   $$\pi \approx 3 + \frac{4}{2 \times 3 \times 4} - \frac{4}{4 \times 5 \times 6} + \frac{4}{6 \times 7 \times 8} - \frac{4}{8 \times 9 \times 10} + \frac{4}{10 \times 11 \times 12}$$

6. The Parthenon in Athens is an example of a golden rectangle, where the length of the longer side divided by the length of the shorter side is $\dfrac{1 + \sqrt{5}}{2}$. Estimate this value correct to one decimal place.

7 The Greek mathematician Heron devised a formula for the area A of a triangle given by: $A = \sqrt{s(s - a)(s - b)(s - c)}$,

   where a, b and c are the lengths of the sides of the triangle and s is equal to half the perimeter. The perimeter is the sum of the three sides of the triangle. Use Heron's formula to estimate the area of the triangle PQR, correct to the nearest centimetre squared.

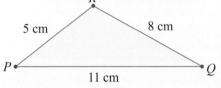

1.5 Complex numbers

Finally, let's introduce the weirdest and most fascinating number of all by considering the answer to $\sqrt{-1}$.

In other words, can you think of two **identical numbers** that when multiplied together give -1. It seems impossible! Don't be put off by this minor inconvenience.

Imagine, like the mathematician Euler did, that $\sqrt{-1}$ does exist and call it i.

Therefore, $i = \sqrt{-1}$. i is called an **imaginary number**.

KEY TERM

An **imaginary number** is a number of the form ib, where $i = \sqrt{-1}$.

▶ $\sqrt{-9} = \sqrt{9 \times (-1)}$
   $= \sqrt{9}\,\sqrt{-1}$
   $= 3 \times i$
   $= 3i$, which can be written as $0 + 3i$

KEY TERM

A **complex number** z is a number of the form $z = a + bi$, where $a, b \in \mathbb{R}$ and $i = \sqrt{-1}$

▶ The number $1 + \sqrt{-9} = 1 + 3i$ with two distinct parts, the 1 and the $3i$, is an example of a **complex number**.

Examples of complex numbers

▶ $3 = 3 + 0i$ ▶ $3 - 5i$ ▶ $-\dfrac{1}{\sqrt{2}} + 3i$

▶ $-\dfrac{2}{3} = -\dfrac{2}{3} + 0i$ ▶ $\sqrt{2} = \sqrt{2} + 0i$

The set $\mathbb{C}$ of complex numbers is the set of numbers that can be written in the form shown in these examples. All real numbers can be written as complex numbers.

The set of natural numbers is a subset of the set of integers, which is a subset of the set of rationals, which is a subset of the set of real numbers, which is a subset of the set of complex numbers.

This is represented mathematically as $\mathbb{N} \subset \mathbb{Z} \subset \mathbb{Q} \subset \mathbb{R} \subset \mathbb{C}$.

The various number systems can be represented by the Venn diagram below:

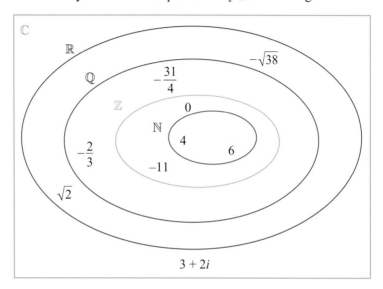

Complex numbers are so important that Section 6 of this book is devoted to them.

1.6 Absolute value

ACTIVITY 7

ACTION
Working with absolute values

OBJECTIVE
To position various numbers on the number line

The absolute value or modulus $|x|$ of a real number x is simply its distance to the origin.

▸ $|-3| = 3$ [The distance of -3 to 0.]

▸ $|3| = 3$ [The distance of 3 to 0.]

▸ $\left|-\frac{1}{2}\right| = \frac{1}{2}$ [The distance of $-\frac{1}{2}$ to 0.]

▸ $\left|\sqrt{2}\right| = \sqrt{2}$

▸ $|-7\cdot35| = 7\cdot35$

The modulus is never negative as it is a distance.

▸ $|7 - 3| = |4| = 4$

▸ $|3 - 7| = |-4| = 4$

This means $|a - b| = |b - a|$

EXERCISE 5

1. Evaluate:

    (a) $|-72|$

    (b) $\left|-\frac{69}{4}\right|$

    (c) $|1\cdot72|$

    (d) $\left|\dfrac{1}{\sqrt{2}}\right|$

    (e) $\left|-\dfrac{3\sqrt{2}}{4}\right|$

    (f) $|0|$

    (g) $|-\pi|$

    (h) $\left|\dfrac{5}{6}\right|$

2. Evaluate:

    (a) $|3 - 5|$

    (b) $|5 - 3|$

    (c) $\left|\sqrt{2} - 1\right|$

    (d) $|\pi - 3|$

    (e) $|3 - \pi|$

    (f) $\left|\sqrt{2} - \sqrt{3}\right|$

    (g) $|a - b|$ if $a > b$

    (h) $|a - b|$ if $b > a$

Arithmetic

Learning Outcomes

- To be able to do all kinds of calculations involving percentages.

- To be able to manipulate numbers written in scientific notation and to use these numbers to make estimates based on order of magnitude.

- To appreciate the importance of tolerance levels and errors.

- To be able to round off numbers and hence estimate and approximate the values of expressions involving such numbers.

- To be familiar with the concept of quantities changing with time, including speed and acceleration.

- To understand how quantities can be directly and inversely proportional to each other.

2.1 Percentages

ACTIVITY 8

ACTION
Working with fractions, decimals and percentages

OBJECTIVE
When presented with various shapes, to write down the shaded area as a fraction, decimal and percentage

Percentages play an important part in our daily lives. You often hear statements like 'The footballer gave 110%' or 'House prices are up by 7%'. A percentage just means part of 100.

$$\blacktriangleright \quad \frac{1}{2} = \frac{4}{8} = \frac{50}{100} = 50 \text{ parts of } 100 = 50 \text{ per cent} = 50\%$$

$$\blacktriangleright \quad 0{\cdot}37 = \frac{37}{100} = 37 \text{ parts of } 100 = 37\%$$

A percentage is simply a fraction in which the denominator is 100. Per cent is represented by %.

$$57\% = \frac{57}{100} = 0{\cdot}57$$

$$100\% = \frac{100}{100} = 1$$

Techniques for working with percentages

1. To convert a number written as a rational number or a decimal into a percentage, multiply the number by 100.

   ▸ $\frac{3}{4} = \left(\frac{3}{4} \times 100\right)\% = 75\%$

   ▸ $0{\cdot}62 = (0{\cdot}62 \times 100)\% = 62\%$

   ▸ $3{\cdot}25 = (3{\cdot}25 \times 100)\% = 325\%$

2. To convert a number written as a percentage into a rational number or a decimal, divide the number by 100.

   ▸ $67\% = \frac{67}{100} = 0{\cdot}67$ [Move the decimal point two places to the left.]

   ▸ $27{\cdot}5\% = 0{\cdot}275$

3. To express one quantity as a percentage of another, write the first quantity as a fraction of the second and then multiply by 100%.   [See Example 1.]

4. To find a percentage of a quantity, multiply the quantity by the decimal equivalent of the percentage.

   ▸ 25% of €230 $= \frac{25}{100} \times €230 = 0{\cdot}25 \times €230 = €57{\cdot}50$

5. To increase a quantity by $r\%$, multiply it by $\left(1 + \frac{r}{100}\right)$.

   ▸ Increase 800 by 20%: $800 + 800 \times 0{\cdot}2 = 800(1 + 0{\cdot}2) = 800 \times 1{\cdot}2 = 960$

6. To decrease a quantity by $r\%$, multiply it by $\left(1 - \frac{r}{100}\right)$.   [See Example 2.]

7. To find a quantity which has been increased by $r\%$ to a given value, divide this given value by $\left(1 + \frac{r}{100}\right)$ to get the original value.   [See Example 3.]

8. To find a quantity that has been decreased by $r\%$ to a given value, divide this given value by $\left(1 - \frac{r}{100}\right)$ to get the original value.   [See Example 4.]

EXAMPLE 1

32 litres (l) of oil leaked from a tank containing 160 l. What percentage of the oil leaked?

Solution

32 l out of 160 l: $\frac{32}{160} = \frac{1}{5} = \frac{1}{5} \times 100\% = 20\%$

EXAMPLE 2

A piece of skirting board of length 1·2 m has to be reduced by 15% to fit. What is the required length?

Solution

$15\% = 0{\cdot}15$

New length $l = 1{\cdot}2 - 1{\cdot}2 \times 0{\cdot}15$

$\qquad = 1{\cdot}2(1 - 0{\cdot}15)$

$\qquad = 1{\cdot}2(0{\cdot}85)$

$\qquad = 1{\cdot}02$ m

EXAMPLE 3

The number of students that sat the Physics exam in 2013 was 8400. This was an increase of 5% on the number that sat the Physics exam in 2012. How many students sat the Physics exam in 2012?

Solution

$$1 + \frac{r}{100} = 1 + \frac{5}{100} = 1 \cdot 05$$

N is the number of students that sat the Physics exam in 2012:

$$1 \cdot 05 N = 8400$$

$$N = \frac{8400}{1 \cdot 05} = 8000$$

or

The percentage that sat the Physics exam in 2012 is 100%. Therefore, the percentage that sat the Physics exam in 2013 is 105%, which is 8400 students.

$$105\% = 8400$$

$$1\% = \frac{8400}{105}$$

$$100\% = \frac{8400}{105} \times 100 = 8000 \text{ students}$$

EXAMPLE 4

The price of a house in 2013 was 43% less than its price in 2008. If the price in 2013 was €342 000, what was the price in 2008?

Solution

$$1 - \frac{r}{100} = 1 - \frac{43}{100} = 0 \cdot 57$$

p was the price in 2008:

$$0 \cdot 57 p = 342\,000$$

$$p = \frac{342\,000}{0 \cdot 57} = €600\,000$$

or

If 100% was the price in 2008:

Price in 2013 = 57% = 342 000

$$1\% = \frac{342\,000}{57}$$

$$100\% = \frac{342\,000}{57} \times 100 = €600\,000$$

EXERCISE 6

1. Write the following as percentages:

   (a) 0·5

   (b) 0·25

   (c) 0·6

   (d) 0·48

   (e) 1·6

   (f) 7·65

   (g) 0·23

   (h) 2

   (i) 0·7

   (j) 0·18

2. Write the following as decimals **and** fractions in their lowest form:

   (a) 20% (d) 18% (g) 4%

   (b) 32% (e) $66\frac{2}{3}\%$ (h) 2·3%

   (c) 67% (f) 82% (i) 24·75%

3. In each of the following, what is the percentage?

   (a) 5 of 20

   (b) 15 of 45

   (c) 10·2 of 27·2

   (d) 520 of 400

   (e) $\frac{1}{3}$ of $\frac{1}{6}$

   (f) $\frac{1}{5}$ of 0·8

   (g) 0·8 of $\frac{1}{5}$

   (h) $\frac{2}{3}$ of $\frac{5}{6}$

   (i) 0·2 of 0·3

   (j) 12·5 of 120

4. (a) Joe's team played 20 games in a season. They won 18 of them. What percentage of the games did Joe's team win?

   (b) The political party Fianna Fáil received 9562 votes out of 26 500 in a constituency. What was its percentage share of the vote, correct to the nearest whole number?

   (c) There are 45 crew members on a ship. Eighteen of them are officers. What percentage of the crew are officers?

   (d) A metal bar has a mass of 23 g. If 21·5 g is pure silver, what percentage of the metal bar is pure silver, correct to one decimal place?

   (e) There are 32 students in a class. Eight of the students are female. What percentage of the students are male?

5. (a) Mary got 80% of the questions in a Maths test right. How many questions did she get right if there were 40 questions in all?

   (b) There are 166 Dáil deputies in Dáil Éireann. 28·3% of them are from Dublin. How many Dublin deputies are there in Dáil Éireann?

   (c) A meal for five in a restaurant costs €152. If the waiter was given a tip of 15% of the cost of the meal, how much did he get?

   (d) If 16% of 62 000 students took the Higher Level Maths exam in 2013, how many students took this exam?

   (e) A woman put €10 000 into a saving account for one year. The rate of interest for one year was 3·2%. How much interest did she get at the end of the year?

6. (a) A sitting-room suite cost €2453 plus 15% delivery charge. What was the total cost?

   (b) A laptop is reduced by 22% in a sale. If the presale price is €530, what was the sale price?

   (c) In 1800, the land area of the USA was 867 980 square miles. In 1803, after the Louisiana Purchase, the land area increased by 95%. What was the land area of the USA after the purchase?

   (d) Cheap Air increased its number of daily flights to Spain by 20% on 1 June. If the number of daily flights to Spain on 31 May was 15, what was the number on 1 June?

   (e) A pharmaceutical company reduces the price of a packet of statins by 28% from €40 per packet. What is the new price of a packet of statins?

7. (a) A clothes shop reduced the price of a brand of jeans by 15%. If the reduced price is €35·70, what was the original price?

   (b) The number of deaths on Irish roads in 2011 was 186. This was a 12·26% decrease on the number of deaths in 2010. How many people died on Irish roads in 2010?

   (c) Between 1990 and 2000, the population of the USA increased by 13%. If the population in 2000 was 281 million, what was the population in 1990, correct to two decimal places?

   (d) The price of a television was €688·80, including tax at 23%. What was the price before VAT was applied?

   (e) The political party Fine Gael won 76 seats in the 2011 general election. This was an increase of 49% over their 2007 election result. How many seats did Fine Gael win in the 2007 election?

2.2 Scientific notation

Some numbers are very big. For example, the radius of the Earth is 6 400 000 m. Other numbers are very, very small. For example, the charge on the electron is 0·0000000000000000016 Coulombs (C).

There is a much better way to write such numbers. It is known as **scientific notation**.

Powers of 10

1. Positive powers of 10

- $1000 = 10 \times 10 \times 10 = 10^3$

- $6 \times 10^4 = 6 \times 10 \times 10 \times 10 \times 10 = 60\,000$

2. Power zero

- $100 = 10 \times 10 = 10^2$

$$1 = \frac{100}{100} = \frac{10^2}{10^2} = 10^{2-2} = 10^0$$

$$\therefore\ 10^0 = 1$$

In words: 10 to the power of zero is equal to 1.

- $3 \times 10^0 = 3 \times 1 = 3$

3. Negative powers of 10

- $\dfrac{1}{100} = \dfrac{1}{10^2}$

$\dfrac{1}{10^2}$ can be written as 1×10^{-2}.

Similarly, $\dfrac{5}{10^3} = 5 \times \dfrac{1}{10^3} = 5 \times 10^{-3}$

Dividing a number by 10^3 is the same as multiplying it by 10^{-3}.

- $\dfrac{1}{10^4} = 1 \times 10^{-4}$

- $\dfrac{6}{10^7} = 6 \times 10^{-7}$

- $0 \cdot 2 = \dfrac{2}{10^1} = 2 \times 10^{-1}$

- $0 \cdot 003 = \dfrac{3}{1000} = 3 \times 10^{-3}$

Negative powers of 10 obey the normal rules of powers.

- $10^{-3} \times 10^{-2} = 10^{-5}$ [Add the powers.]

- $2 \times 10^{-4} \times 3 \times 10^5 = 6 \times 10^1$

- $\dfrac{6 \times 10^{-1}}{3 \times 10^{-3}} = 2 \times 10^2$ [Subtract the powers: $-1 - (-3) = 2$]

4. Multiplying and dividing by powers of 10

Every time you multiply a number by 10, the decimal point moves one place to the **right**.

▸ $4 \cdot 87 \times 10^1 = 48 \cdot 7$

▸ $31 \cdot 425 \times 10^2 = 31 \cdot 425 \times 10^1 \times 10^1$

$$= 314 \cdot 25 \times 10^1$$

$$= 3142 \cdot 5$$

If you move a decimal point two places to the **right**, you have multiplied the number by $100 = 10^2$.

Every time you divide a number by 10, the decimal point moves one place to the **left**.

▸ $\dfrac{3 \cdot 42}{10^1} = 0 \cdot 342$

▸ $\dfrac{467 \cdot 32}{10^2} = \dfrac{467 \cdot 32}{10^1 \times 10^1} = \dfrac{46 \cdot 732}{10^1} = 4 \cdot 6732$

If you move a decimal point two places to the **left**, you have divided the number by 10^2 (or multiplied the number by 10^{-2}).

Writing numbers in scientific notation

To write a number in scientific notation, it must be written in the form $a \times 10^n$, where $1 \le a < 10$ (a number greater than or equal to 1 and less than 10) and n is an integer.

▸ $3 \cdot 24 \times 10^4$ is a number in scientific notation with $a = 3 \cdot 24$ and $n = 4$.

▸ $4 \cdot 325 \times 10^{-7}$ is a number in scientific notation with $a = 4 \cdot 325$ and $n = -7$.

but

▸ $63 \cdot 24 \times 10^3$ is not a number in scientific notation as $63 \cdot 24$ is not between 1 and 10.

▸ 783 is not a number in scientific notation as $783 = 783 \times 10^0$ and 783 is not between 1 and 10.

To write a number in scientific notation, you must move the decimal point in the number so that there is exactly one non-zero digit to the left of the decimal point (in order that a is between 1 and 10) and adjust n accordingly.

WORKED EXAMPLE Writing numbers in scientific notation

1. $247 \cdot 3 = 2 \cdot 473 \times 10^{+2}$ [Two steps left $\Rightarrow$ multiply by 10^{+2}]

By moving the decimal point two places to the left, you have divided the number by 10^2 and so you have changed its value. To keep the same value of the number, you must balance this action by multiplying the number by 10^{+2}.

Similarly:

▸ $37 \cdot 8 = 3 \cdot 78 \times 10^1$ [One step left ⇒ multiply by 10^{+1}]

▸ $27\,415 = 27\,415 \cdot 0 = 2 \cdot 7415 \times 10^{+4}$ [Four steps left ⇒ multiply by 10^{+4}]

2. $0 \cdot 03 = 3 \cdot 0 \times 10^{-2}$ [Two steps right ⇒ multiply by 10^{-2}]

By moving the decimal point two places to the right, you have multiplied the number by 10^2 and so you have changed its value. To keep the same value of the number, you must balance this action by multiplying the number by 10^{-2}, i.e. divide by $10^2 = 100$.

Similarly:

▸ $0 \cdot 00087 = 8 \cdot 7 \times 10^{-4}$ [Four steps right ⇒ multiply by 10^{-4}]

▸ $0 \cdot 0000000324 = 3 \cdot 24 \times 10^{-8}$ [Eight steps right ⇒ multiply by 10^{-8}]

In general:

If you move a decimal point n places to the **left**, you must multiply the new number by 10^{+n}.

If you move a decimal point n places to the **right**, you must multiply the new number by 10^{-n}.

EXAMPLE 5

Write the following numbers in scientific notation:

(a) 3425

(b) $6\,400\,000$ m

(c) $0 \cdot 0000516$

(d) $-457 \cdot 2$

(e) $0 \cdot 00000000000000000016$ C

Solution

(a) $3425 = 3425 \cdot 0 = 3 \cdot 425 \times 10^3$

(b) $6\,400\,000$ m $= 6 \cdot 4 \times 10^6$ m

(c) $0 \cdot 0000516 = 5 \cdot 16 \times 10^{-5}$

(d) $-457 \cdot 2 = -4 \cdot 572 \times 10^2$

(e) $0 \cdot 00000000000000000016$ C $= 1 \cdot 6 \times 10^{-19}$ C

ACTIVITY 9

ACTION
Using scientific notation

OBJECTIVE
To carry out a number of calculations in your head on numbers in scientific notation

Carrying out scientific notation calculations

If numbers are given in scientific notation and the number in front of the power of 10 is a whole number, you can add, subtract, multiply and divide quickly in your head. Otherwise, use your calculator.

1. Multiplying and dividing numbers in scientific notation:

   ▸ $4 \times 10^3 \times 2 \times 10^4 = 8 \times 10^7$ [Add the powers.]

   ▸ $4 \times 10^{-5} \times 3 \times 10^7 = 12 \times 10^2 = 1200 = 1 \cdot 2 \times 10^3$

   ▸ $\dfrac{9 \times 10^{27}}{(3 \times 10^8)^2} = \dfrac{9 \times 10^{27}}{9 \times 10^{16}} = 1 \times 10^{11}$ [Subtract the powers.]

2. Adding and subtracting numbers in scientific notation:

   ▶ $\underline{5} \times 10^4 + \underline{2} \times 10^4 = 7 \times 10^4$ [(5 apples) + (2 apples) = 7 apples]

   Technique: You can only add (subtract) numbers in scientific notation with the same power of 10.

   ▶ $3 \times 10^4 + 2 \times 10^3 = 3 \times 10^4 + 0 \cdot 2 \times 10^4 = 3 \cdot 2 \times 10^4$

   Technique: Always change the number with the smaller power of 10 to a number with the bigger power of 10 before adding or subtracting.

ACTIVITY 10

ACTION
Finding orders
of magnitude

OBJECTIVE
*To write down the
orders of magnitude
of given numbers*

Order of magnitude estimation

In carrying out rough calculations, estimates or comparisons, numbers are often rounded off to the nearest power of 10. A number rounded to the nearest power of 10 is called its **order of magnitude**.

Finding the order of magnitude estimate of a number

1. Write the number in scientific notation, i.e. in the form $a \times 10^n$, where $1 \le a < 10$.

2. If $a < 5$, the order is n. If $a \ge 5$, add 1 to n to get the order of magnitude.

   ▶ The order of magnitude of $1 \cdot 6 \times 10^3$ is 3.   [3 is the power of 10.]

   ▶ The order of magnitude of 9×10^{-3} is −2.   [−2 is the power of 10 plus 1.]

3. Since orders of magnitude are just powers of 10, they can be combined by the rules of powers.

   ▶ The order of magnitude of $2 \times 10^4 \times 6 \times 10^3$ is $4 + 4 = 8$.

   ▶ The order of magnitude of $\dfrac{3 \times 10^{-4}}{2 \times 10^{-5}}$ is $-4 - (-5) = 1$.

EXAMPLE 6

The number of hairs on a human head is between 100 000 and 150 000. What is the order of magnitude of the number of hairs on a human head?

Solution

$100\,000 = 1 \times 10^5$

$150\,000 = 1 \cdot 5 \times 10^5$

1×10^5 to $1 \cdot 5 \times 10^5$: Order of magnitude of 5

EXAMPLE 7

The radius of the Earth is 6 400 000 m and the radius of the Sun is 696 342 000 m. Find an order of magnitude comparison of the radius of the Sun to the radius of the Earth.

Solution

Radius of Sun = 696 342 000 m = $6 \cdot 96342 \times 10^8$
Order of magnitude = 9

Radius of Earth = 6 400 000 m = $6 \cdot 4 \times 10^6$
Order of magnitude = 7

$$\therefore \frac{\text{Radius of Sun}}{\text{Radius of Earth}} = \frac{10^9}{10^7} = 10^2$$

Order of magnitude = $9 - 7 = 2$

$\therefore$ Radius of Sun $\simeq 100 \times$ Radius of Earth

EXERCISE 7

1. Write the following numbers in the form of $a \times 10^{-n}$, where $1 \leq a < 10$ and n is a natural number.

   (a) 0·7

   (b) 0·04

   (c) 0·002

   (d) 0·00004

   (e) 0·000003

   (f) 0·0000000005

   (g) 0·0001

   (h) 0·0000000000008

   (i) 0·000005

   (j) 0·0000009

2. Simplify the following, giving your answer in the form $a \times 10^{n}$, where $1 \leq a < 10$ and $n \in \mathbb{Z}$.

   (a) $10^2 \times 10^3$

   (b) $10^2 \times 10^{-3}$

   (c) $\dfrac{10^3}{10^2}$

   (d) $\dfrac{6 \times 10^3}{2 \times 10^{-2}}$

   (e) $(10^3)^2$

   (f) $(10^{-3})^2$

   (g) $\dfrac{2 \times 10^3 \times 6 \times 10^4}{3 \times 10^2 \times 1 \cdot 25 \times 10^1}$

   (h) $\dfrac{(10^2)^2}{(10^{-3})^2}$

   (i) $\dfrac{10^3 \times 10^{-2}}{10^{-4} \times 10^5}$

   (j) $\dfrac{(10^3)^2 \times 10^{-2}}{10^{-1} \times (10^{-1})^2}$

3. Write the following in scientific notation:

   (a) The number of stars in the Andromeda Galaxy (the closest galaxy to our Milky Way Galaxy): 1 000 000 000 000

   (b) The mass of the Higgs boson (God particle): 0·00000000000000000000000002222 kg

   (c) The speed of light: 300 000 000 m/s

   (d) The population of China: 1 400 000 000

   (e) The mass of the Earth: 6 000 000 000 000 000 000 000 000 kg

   (f) A quintillion: 1 000 000 000 000 000 000

   (g) A ZB (zettabyte) of memory: 1 000 000 000 000 000 000 000

   (h) Planck's constant: 0·000000000000000000000000000000000062 J s

   (i) The temperature at the centre of the Sun: 15 700 000 K

   (j) The diameter of the electron: 0·0000000000000056 m

4. Write the following in the form $a \times 10^n$, $n \in \mathbb{Z}$, $1 \leq a < 10$:

   (a) 0·023

   (b) 1000

   (c) 0·00014

   (d) 2

   (e) 0·0000243

   (f) 12 600 000

   (g) 0·000012

   (h) 14

   (i) 267

   (j) 0·0000000057

5. Write the following numbers, which are written in scientific notion, in standard decimal form:

   (a) $3 \cdot 0 \times 10^{-2}$

   (b) $4 \cdot 12 \times 10^{-4}$

   (c) $3 \cdot 57 \times 10^5$

   (d) 2×10^6

   (e) $5 \cdot 6 \times 10^{-7}$

   (f) 6×10^{-5}

   (g) 1×10^{-4}

   (h) 1×10^5

   (i) $3 \cdot 3 \times 10^0$

   (j) $7 \cdot 8 \times 10^8$

6. Write the following in scientific notation and then write down its order of magnitude:

   (a) 2·3

   (b) 35 642

   (c) 0·00013

   (d) 4 765 314

   (e) 0·0000563

   (f) 7 300 000

7. (a) A quadrillion is 1 000 000 000 000 000. What is its order of magnitude?

   (b) A googol is 10^{100}. What is its order of magnitude?

8. (a) Using $E = mc^2$, find the order of magnitude of E, if $m = 7 \cdot 2 \times 10^{-27}$ kg and $c = 3 \times 10^8$ m s^{-1}.

   (b) Using $f = \dfrac{E}{h}$, find the order of magnitude of f, if $E = 6 \cdot 4 \times 10^{-19}$ J and $h = 6 \cdot 6 \times 10^{-34}$ J s.

   (c) The mass of the Earth is $5 \cdot 98 \times 10^{24}$ kg. The mass of the Great Pyramid of Giza is $5 \cdot 9 \times 10^9$ kg.

   Compare the mass of the Earth to that of the Great Pyramid of Giza using their orders of magnitude as estimates.

9. (a) (i) Which is 4357 nearer to: 1000 or 10000?

    (ii) Estimate the order of magnitude of 4357.

    (iii) What is the order of magnitude of 270 134?

    (b) Mary wants to convert 4357 km into miles. The conversion factor is 1 km = 0·62 miles.

    When she does the calculation, she gets 270 134 miles. She knows this is wrong.

    (i) State, using the order of magnitude of each number, how she knows that she is wrong.

    (ii) Evaluate 4357 × 0·62 on your calculator. How do you think Mary got 270 134 miles?

    (iii) What is 4357 km in miles?

10. The probability of being dealt a royal flush in poker is 649 739 to 1. What is the order of magnitude of this probability?

11. Estimate the number of €20 notes that fill a container with dimensions 2 m × 2 m × 2 m, if the dimensions of a €20 note are 13·3 cm × 7·2 cm × 10^{-2} cm. Use an order of magnitude estimation. (Convert cm to m first.)

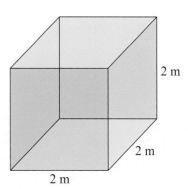

2 m

2 m

2 m

2.3 Errors

No physical measurement is ever exact. The accuracy of a measurement is always determined by the sensitivity and accuracy of the apparatus and the skill of the observer. The accuracy of a measurement is how close the result of the measurement is to the true or accepted value.

Tolerance level (margin of error)

A machine requires steel rods of length $(2\cdot3 \pm 0\cdot1)$ cm. This means that any rod of length in the range $(2\cdot3 - 0\cdot1)$ cm to $(2\cdot3 + 0\cdot1)$ cm is acceptable, i.e. all values from 2·2 cm to 2·4 cm.

The range of values of quantity that is acceptable (allowed/permitted/tolerated) is known as its **tolerance level**.

> **KEY TERM**
>
> The **tolerance level** is the greatest range of variation in the values of a quantity that is acceptable.

▶ Quality Food only accepts bananas from their growers with a tolerance level of (160 ± 8) g for the mass of a banana. This means the maximum acceptable mass is 168 g and the minimum acceptable mass is 152 g.

▶ For safety reasons, an acceptable bolt for a car part must have a diameter between 45·8 mm and 46·2 mm. What is the tolerance level for the diameter of the bolts?

$$\text{The mid-value} = \frac{45\cdot8 + 46\cdot2}{2} = \frac{92\cdot0}{2} = 46$$

Tolerance level = $(46 \pm 0\cdot2)$ mm

Since no measurement is exact, a measurement is quoted with a tolerance level that gives the range within which the true value lies. The temperature of a boiling liquid measured as $(78\cdot6 \pm 0\cdot2)$ °C means that the true value lies between 78·4 °C and 78·8 °C.

ACTIVITY 11

ACTION
Understanding errors

OBJECTIVE
To understand how errors accumulate when results are added and subtracted

Experimental results and the accumulation of errors

When the results of a measurement are added or subtracted, their errors always **accumulate** (add).

▸ A metre stick is used to measure the length of a wooden plank. The plank is longer than 1 m so two measurements must be made.

  The first measured length is $(96\cdot0 \pm 0\cdot1)$ cm and the remaining length is $(13\cdot0 \pm 0\cdot1)$ cm. The total length of the plank is $(109 \pm 0\cdot2)$ cm.

Even when you subtract two measurements, their errors add.

EXAMPLE 8

A weighing scales can measure the mass of objects to an accuracy of $\pm 0\cdot002$ g. The mass of a beaker is measured as 42·056 g. The mass of the beaker with a copper sulfate solution is measured as 42·863 g. What is the possible range of values of the mass of the copper sulfate solution?

Solution

Mass of beaker = $(42\cdot056 \pm 0\cdot002)$ g

Mass of beaker plus copper sulfate solution = $(42\cdot863 \pm 0\cdot002)$ g

Mass of copper sulfate solution = $(0\cdot807 \pm 0\cdot004)$ g

The true value of the mass of copper sulfate solution lies in the range = 0·803 g to 0·811 g

Absolute and percentage error

WORKED EXAMPLE
Understanding absolute and percentage errors

A 750 g box of cornflakes in a consignment of food is weighed by Customs. It is found to have a mass of 820 g.

The accepted mass of the box of cornflakes = 750 g

The measured mass = 820 g

The absolute error = $\left|820 \text{ g} - 750 \text{ g}\right| = 70$ g

The percentage error = $\dfrac{70 \text{ g}}{750 \text{ g}} \times 100\% = 9\frac{1}{3}\%$

Do you think that Customs will suspect that the box of cornflakes is concealing something?

Absolute error in a quantity = $\left|\text{Measured value of quantity} - \text{Accepted value of quantity}\right|$

Percentage error in a quantity = $\dfrac{\text{Absolute error in quantity}}{\text{Accepted value of quantity}} \times 100\%$

EXAMPLE 9

A piece of metal piping used in a washing machine has an accepted length of 21·00 cm. A percentage error of 7% is permitted. If a machinist starts with a pipe of length 30 cm, what is:

(a) the maximum length,

(b) the minimum length

that he can cut off to produce a pipe which can be used?

Solution

Maximum permitted length = 21 × 1·07

$$= 22·47 \text{ cm}$$

Minimum permitted length = 21 × 0·93

$$= 19·53 \text{ cm}$$

(a) Maximum length of cut-off = 30 − 19·53 = 10·47 cm

(b) Minimum length of cut-off = 30 − 22·47 = 7·53 cm

EXERCISE 8

1. **(a)** The recommended retail price (RRP) of a certain model of calculator is €(13 ± 5%). What is the maximum price the retailer should charge?

    (b) The tolerance level of the volume of a bottle of washing-up liquid is (550 ± 10) ml. What is:

    (i) the maximum volume,

    (ii) the minimum volume,
    of liquid a bottle could contain?

    (c) The resistance of a resistor in a washing machine must have a value between 3·5 Ω and 3·9 Ω. What tolerance level is written on the resistor?

    (d) The maximum value of the diameter of a battery that can fit into a slot in a phone is 4·2 mm. The minimum diameter that can fit is 3·8 mm. What is its tolerance level?

    (e) The maximum value of the area of the square cover for a book is 16 cm^2 and the minimum value is 12·96 cm^2. Find the tolerance level of the side of the square in the picture. (Hint: Find the length of each side first.)

    (f) In the square shown, the tolerance level of the side of the square is (2·4 ± 0·3) cm. What is the tolerance level of the area? (Hint: Find the maximum and minimum lengths of the side of the square.)

    x

    x

2. **(a)** A scientist gave the density of mercury as (13 600 ± 4%) kg/m^3. Quote her result with an absolute error.

    (b) A 400 g tin of beans is weighed at the airport. It is found to have a mass of 480 g. Find:

    (i) the absolute error,

    (ii) the percentage error.

    (c) A man was weighed accurately in a gym. His mass was recorded as 80 kg. When he weighed himself at home, the scales recorded 74 kg. What is the percentage error in the home scales' reading? When his wife weighed herself at home, the scales read 62 kg. What was her true mass, correct to the nearest kilogram?

2.4 Approximation and estimation

Technique for rounding off decimals

▸ Write 16·1238732 correct to three decimal places.

Go to the **fourth** digit after the decimal point. If this digit is greater than or equal to 5, increase the digit in the third place after the decimal point by 1:

16·123**8**732 is 16·124 correct to three places of decimal.

▸ Round 7·62 off to the nearest integer (whole number).

As the first digit after the decimal point is greater than 5, round up the whole number in front of the decimal point by 1.

7·**6**2 is rounded up to 8.

EXAMPLE 10

Evaluate the following using your calculator:

(a) $\sqrt[3]{5\cdot63}$, correct to two decimal places.

(b) $\dfrac{1}{4\cdot6} + \tan 65°$, correct to three decimal places.

(c) $\dfrac{\sqrt{8\cdot4} \times 642\cdot7}{5\cdot63^2}$, correct to the nearest whole number.

Solution

(a) $\sqrt[3]{5\cdot63} = 1\cdot78$

(b) $\dfrac{1}{4\cdot6} + \tan 65° = 2\cdot362$

(c) $\dfrac{\sqrt{8\cdot4} \times 642\cdot7}{5\cdot63^2} = 59$

EXAMPLE 11

If $M = 6 \times 10^{24}$, $R = 6\cdot4 \times 10^6$ and $G = 6\cdot7 \times 10^{-11}$, find g correct to one decimal place, given $g = \dfrac{GM}{R^2}$.

Solution

Put brackets around each letter.

$$g = \frac{(G)(M)}{(R)^2}$$

$$g = \frac{(6\cdot7 \times 10^{-11}) \times (6 \times 10^{24})}{(6\cdot4 \times 10^6)^2} = 9\cdot8$$

Significant figures

Whenever a measurement is given, it is assumed the measurement is accurate to the last written digit. A length of 57·8 m indicates that this measurement can be made accurate to one-tenth of a metre.

The digits in a number that indicate the accuracy of the number are called its significant figures.

Rounding to significant figures: To round off a number to a given number of significant figures, change the number into scientific notation ($a \times 10^n$) first. The number of digits in a corresponds to the specified number of significant figures.

Technique for writing numbers to a certain number of significant figures

Write the following to three significant figures:

▸ $1472 = 1 \cdot 472 \times 10^3$ [Three significant figures means three digits in a.]

$\therefore 1472 = 1 \cdot 47 \times 10^3 = 1470$ to three significant figures

▸ $56\,321 = 5 \cdot 6321 \times 10^4$ [Three significant figures means three digits in a.]

$\therefore 56\,321 = 5 \cdot 63 \times 10^4 = 56\,300$

▸ $0 \cdot 03256 = 3 \cdot 256 \times 10^{-2}$

$\therefore 0 \cdot 03256 = 3 \cdot 26 \times 10^{-2} = 0 \cdot 0326$

Estimation

A quick estimate of a quantity can be made by rounding up or rounding down the numbers that make up the quantity. This allows you to do the calculation in your head.

EXAMPLE 12

Estimate the value of $\dfrac{3 \cdot 8 \times 10^4 \times 6 \cdot 2 \times 10^4}{2 \cdot 95 \times 10^{-3} \times 2 \cdot 1 \times 10^9}$ as a whole number.

Solution

$$\text{Estimate} = \frac{4 \times 10^4 \times 6 \times 10^4}{3 \times 10^{-3} \times 2 \times 10^9} = \frac{24 \times 10^8}{6 \times 10^6}$$
$$= 4 \times 10^2$$
$$= 400$$

EXAMPLE 13

Estimate the volume of a sphere of radius $21 \cdot 5$ cm in cm^3, if the volume is given by $V = \frac{4}{3}\pi r^3$ and $\pi = 3 \cdot 14$. Give your answer as a whole number.

Solution

$$V \approx \frac{4}{3}(\pi)(r)^3 \approx \frac{4}{3}(3)(20)^3 = 4 \times 8000 = 32\,000 \text{ cm}^3$$

EXAMPLE 14

A student buys 5 pens at 58c each, a newspaper at €2·00, a writing pad for €2·89 and a can of coke for 90c. Make a quick estimate to see if he has enough money in a €10 note to buy all the items.

Solution

$$\text{Estimate} = €(5 \times 0 \cdot 6 + 2 + 3 + 1) = €9$$

EXERCISE 9

1. Evaluate the following using your calculator:

   (a) π^2 correct to two decimal places

   (b) $(\tan 18°)^2$, correct to one decimal place

   (c) $\frac{1}{3} + \sqrt{2 \cdot 5}$, correct to one decimal place

   (d) $\sqrt[3]{38 \cdot 3} + 2^{0 \cdot 5}$, correct to three decimal places

   (e) $\dfrac{\sqrt{7 \cdot 3} \times 62 \cdot 56}{8 \cdot 62^3}$, correct to four decimal places

2. **(a)** If $A = \pi r^2$, find A correct to one decimal place, given $r = 3 \cdot 7$ cm.

   (b) If $u = \dfrac{vf}{v - f}$, find u correct to two decimal places, given $f = 23 \cdot 4$ and $v = 43 \cdot 8$.

   (c) If $f = \dfrac{1}{2l}\sqrt{\dfrac{T}{\mu}}$, find f correct to two decimal places, given $l = 0 \cdot 503$, $T = 9 \cdot 8$ and $\mu = 0 \cdot 00032$.

   (d) If $x = y^3$, find y correct to three decimal places, given $x = 27 \cdot 32$.

   (e) If $A = \pi r^2 + 2\pi rh$, find A correct to one decimal place, given $r = 5 \cdot 2$ and $h = 11 \cdot 47$.

3. Round off the following:
   (a) 479 357 correct to four significant figures

   (b) $1 \cdot 3274$ correct to three significant figures

   (c) $57 \cdot 321$ correct to four significant figures

   (d) $6 \cdot 023$ correct to two significant figures

   (e) $0 \cdot 0005734$ correct to three significant figures

   (f) $5 \cdot 1795 \times 10^{-12}$ correct to two significant figures

   (g) $6 \cdot 00057 \times 10^4$ correct to three significant figures

   (h) $0 \cdot 056325$ correct to three significant figures

   (i) 7800 correct to three significant figures

   (j) 82 500 correct to two significant figures

4. Estimate the following, giving a whole number answer in each case:

   (a) $\dfrac{609\,000}{14\,500}$

   (b) $31 \cdot 28 \times 14 \cdot 7$

   (c) 21% of $5 \cdot 32$

   (d) $504 \cdot 2 \times (6 \cdot 89 + 42 \cdot 9)$

   (e) $\dfrac{\sqrt{79 \cdot 3} \times \sqrt[3]{1051}}{(3 \cdot 1)^2}$

   (f) $\dfrac{6 \cdot 1 \times 10^3 \times 4 \cdot 7 \times 10^5}{2 \cdot 9 \times 10^4 \times 2 \cdot 1 \times 10^2}$

   (g) $(2 \cdot 9 \times 10^8)^2 \times (5 \cdot 9 \times 10^{-12})$

   (h) $\dfrac{\sqrt{3 \cdot 9 \times 10^4}}{2 \cdot 1 \times 10^2}$

   (i) 81% of 500

   (j) $\dfrac{\sqrt{0 \cdot 62} \times 5 \cdot 1}{(1 \cdot 9)^2}$

5. If $T = 2\pi \sqrt{\dfrac{k}{g}}$, estimate the value of T, if $\pi = 3 \cdot 14$, $g = 9 \cdot 8$ and $k = 38 \cdot 6$, correct to the nearest whole number.

6. The approximation 60×50 was used for the calculation 61×49. Find the percentage error in the approximation correct to two decimal places.

2.5 Average rate of change (with respect to time)

WORKED EXAMPLE Explaining average rate of change

LeBron James played in a basketball match and scored 6 points after 18 minutes, 20 points after 30 minutes, 28 points after 42 minutes, and 39 points after 48 minutes. This information is set out in the table and represented graphically, as shown.

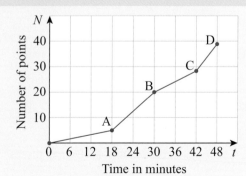

Time in minutes (*t*)	0	18	30	42	48
Number of points (*N*)	0	6	20	28	39

His average scoring rate in the first 18 minutes

$= \dfrac{6-0}{18} = \dfrac{1}{3}$ points per minute.

His average scoring rate in the last 6 minutes

$= \dfrac{39-28}{48-42} = \dfrac{11}{6}$ points per minute.

His average scoring rate for the whole match

$= \dfrac{39-0}{48-0} = \dfrac{39}{48}$ points per minute.

KEY TERM

If Q_1 is the value of a quantity Q at time t_1 and Q_2 is the value of the quantity Q at time t_2, the **average rate of change**

of Q with respect to $t = \dfrac{Q_2 - Q_1}{t_2 - t_1}$.

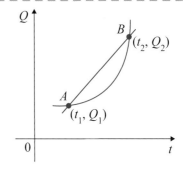

Average rate of change between times t_1 and $t_2 = \dfrac{Q_2 - Q_1}{t_2 - t_1}$ = slope of the line AB.

EXAMPLE 15

If $Q = t^2 + 2t - 1$, find the average rate of change of Q from $t = 2$ to $t = 5$.

Solution

$Q = t^2 + 2t - 1$

$t_1 = 2: Q_1 = 2^2 + 4 - 1 = 7$

$t_2 = 5: Q_2 = 5^2 + 10 - 1 = 34$

Average rate of change between $t = 1$ and $t = 5$

of $Q = \dfrac{34-7}{5-2} = \dfrac{27}{3} = 9$

Speed and acceleration

Speed: When the quantity Q is distance s, the average rate of change is speed v.

$$\text{Speed: } v = \frac{s_2 - s_1}{t_2 - t_1} = \frac{\text{Change in distance}}{\text{Change in time}}$$

Acceleration: When the quantity Q is speed v, the average rate of change is acceleration a.

$$\text{Acceleration: } a = \frac{v_2 - v_1}{t_2 - t_1} = \frac{\text{Change in speed}}{\text{Change in time}}$$

EXAMPLE 16

The first 10 minutes of a warm-up cycle by a racing cyclist is shown on a distance–time graph.

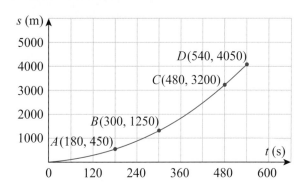

Find the average speed:

(a) between the third minute and eight minute,

(b) between the fifth minute and ninth minute.

Solution

(a) Between the third minute and eight minute:

$$\text{Slope of line } AC: v = \frac{3200 - 450}{480 - 180} = \frac{2750}{300}$$
$$= 9 \cdot 17 \text{ m/s}$$

(b) Between the fifth minute and ninth minute:

$$\text{Slope of line } BD: v = \frac{4050 - 1250}{540 - 300} = \frac{2800}{240}$$
$$= 11 \cdot 67 \text{ m/s}$$

EXERCISE 10

1. A scuba diver is 8 m below the surface of the water 10 seconds after entering the water, and 32 m below the surface after 45 seconds. What is her average rate of descent, correct to two decimal places?

2. If $T = 32 \times 2^{-t}$, find the average rate of change of temperature T (°C) from $t = 2$ to $t = 4$, where t is the time in hours.

3. The table below shows the split times of athlete Usain Bolt in his 2009 world record run in Berlin.

Distance s (m)	0	20	40	60	80	100
Time t (s)	0	2·89	4·64	6·31	7·92	9·58

Find his average speeds, giving your answer correct to two decimal places:

(a) over the first 20 m,

(b) over the last 20 m,

(c) over the whole race.

4. An oil tank is being emptied. The volume V in litres of oil remaining in the tank after time t, in hours, is given by $V = 80(30 - t)^2$, $0 \le t \le 30$. Find the average rate of change of volume:

(a) during the first 10 hours,

(b) during the last 10 hours,

(c) over the whole 30 hours.

5. The population P of a city in millions is given by $P = (0 \cdot 00006)t^2 + (0 \cdot 01)t + 1$, where t is the number of years after the year 2000. Find the average rate of change of the population from 2005 to 2010.

2.6 Direct proportion

ACTIVITY 12

Proportion

ACTION
Understanding direct proportion

OBJECTIVE
To draw a graph from a table of results and answer questions that involve direct proportionality

KEY TERM

A **proportion** is an equation that states that two ratios are equal.

▸ $4:8 = 1:2$
  or $\dfrac{4}{8} = \dfrac{1}{2}$

▸ $a:b = 3:2$
  or $\dfrac{a}{b} = \dfrac{3}{2}$

WORKED EXAMPLE Explaining direct proportion

The table shows the cost y in € of a number x of Yorkie bars:

x	1	2	3	4	5
y	0·9	1·80	2·70	3·6	4·5

The table shows that if the value of x is doubled, the value of y is doubled, and if the value of x is tripled, the value of y is tripled, and so on. This is the meaning of direct proportion.

A variable y is directly proportional to a variable x (and vice versa), if when x is multiplied by any number, then y is multiplied by the same number.

The symbol for 'directly proportional' is $\propto$.

$y \propto x$ means that y is directly proportional to x.

From the above table, for every pair of values (x, y), $\dfrac{y}{x} = 0.9 =$ constant. This is a consequence of the directly proportional relationship between x and y.

$\dfrac{y}{x} = 0.9 \Rightarrow y = 0.9x$

0·9 is called the **constant of proportionality**.

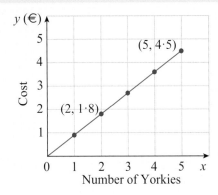

In general, $y \propto x \Leftrightarrow \dfrac{y}{x} = k \Leftrightarrow y = kx$, where k is a constant.

If you plot y (cost) against x (number of Yorkie bars), you get a straight line through the origin. The slope of the straight line is k, the constant of proportionality.

$\text{Slope} = \dfrac{4.5 - 1.8}{5 - 2} = 0.9 = k$

For every directly proportional relationship $y = kx$, the graph of y against x is always a straight line through the origin of slope k.

EXAMPLE 17

If w is directly proportional to t,

(a) write down an equation relating w to t,

(b) find the constant of proportionality if $t = 20$, when $w = 60$,

(c) find t, when $w = 57$.

Solution

(a) $w = kt$

(b) $t = 20$, $w = 60$:
$$60 = 20k$$
$$k = 3 \quad \text{[Constant of proportionality]}$$
$$w = 3t$$

(c) $w = 57$: $57 = 3t$
$$t = 19$$

EXAMPLE 18

The graph below shows the speed of a snowball t seconds after falling from rest from the top of a building. The graph is a straight line.

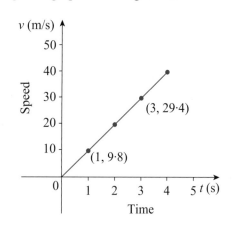

(a) Use the graph to find the constant of proportionality k between the variables. Hence, write an equation linking v to t.

(b) Use the equation to find the speed of the snowball after 2·5 s.

Solution

(a) This is a straight line through the origin.
$$\therefore v \propto t$$
$$v = kt$$
$$\text{Slope} = \frac{29 \cdot 4 - 9 \cdot 8}{3 - 1} = 9 \cdot 8 = k$$
$$v = 9 \cdot 8t$$

(b) $t = 2 \cdot 5$ s: $v = 9 \cdot 8 \times 2 \cdot 5 = 24 \cdot 5$
$$\text{Speed} = 24 \cdot 5 \text{ m/s}$$

WORKED EXAMPLE

WORKED EXAMPLE Looking at another type of direct proportion

Consider the following table of results linking x and y.

x	1	2	3	4	5
y	3	12	27	48	75

Clearly $\dfrac{y}{x}$ is **not** the same for all (x, y) in this table.

However, if the x values are squared, the situation changes.

x^2	1	4	9	16	25
y	3	12	27	48	75

$\dfrac{y}{x^2} = 3$ (a constant) $\Rightarrow y = 3(x^2)$

We say that y is directly proportion to x^2: $y \propto x^2$

A graph of y against (x^2) gives a straight line through the origin.

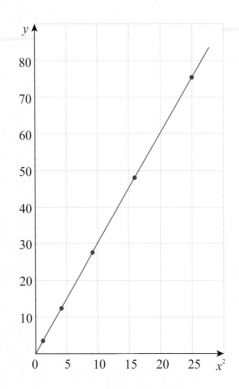

EXERCISE 11

1. A car travels 216 km on 15 litres (l) of petrol. How many kilometres will the car travel using 25 l of petrol, assuming a directly proportional relationship between distance travelled and petrol consumption?

2. y is directly proportional to x and $y = 50$ when $x = 20$. Find an equation relating y to x.

   (a) Find y when $x = 25$.

   (b) Find x when $y = 30$.

3. The force F on a mass is directly proportional to its acceleration a. If $a = 100$ when $F = 400$, write down a formula relating F to a. Find a when $F = 560$.

4. The current I in a resistor is directly proportional to the voltage V across the resistor. If $I = 2$ when $V = 6$, write down a formula relating I to V. If $V = 10$, find I.

5. The graph of y against x is a straight line through the origin.

   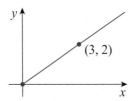

   (a) Write down a formula relating y to x.

   (b) What is the constant of proportionality?

   (c) If $x = 900$, find y.

   (d) If (a, b) and (c, d) are on the straight line, show that $\dfrac{a}{b} = \dfrac{c}{d}$.

6. Hooke's law states that the tension force F (N) in a spring is directly proportional to its extension x (m).

    (a) Write down this statement using mathematical symbols.

    (b) If k is the constant of proportionality, write down the law using F, k and x.

    (c) Find k if $F = 4$ N when $x = 0.005$ m.

    (d) Find F when $x = 3.7$ cm.

    (e) Draw a graph to illustrate the relationship between F and x.

7. If $y \propto x$, find the constant of proportionality given $y = 35$ when $x = 7$. Find x when $y = 72$.

8. If in each case $y \propto x$, find u, v and w.

    (a)

x	2	4	6
y	6	12	w

    (b)

x	1	3	w	8
y	u	9	15	24

    (c)

x	9	12	u	17
y	w	60	75	v

9.

x	2	3	4	5
y	15	22·5	30	37·5

    (a) Is $y \propto x$? Why?

    (b) What is the constant of proportionality?

    (c) Write down an equation relating y to x.

    (d) Draw a graph of y against x.

    (e) What is its slope?

10. In each of the following, state whether or not the relationship between y and x is directly proportional. State a reason for your answer.

    (a) $y = 2x$ **(d)** $y = \dfrac{x}{2}$

    (b) $3x - y = 0$ **(e)** $y = x^2$

    (c) $y = x + 1$

2.7 Inverse proportion

ACTIVITY 13

ACTION
Understanding inverse proportion

OBJECTIVE
To draw a graph from a table of results and to answer questions that involve inverse proportionality

▸ A man driving a 1990 Fiesta completed a journey in 2 hours at 40 km/h. A woman driving a 2014 Ferrari completed the same journey in 1 hour at 80 km/h.

▸ A single pump can fill a swimming pool in 24 hours. If three pumps of the same power as the single pump are used, it takes only 8 hours to fill the pool.

These are examples of **inverse proportion**.

The value of one variable y decreases at the same rate as the value of the other variable x increases. In other words: If x is halved, y is doubled, or if x is quadrupled, y is quartered, and so on.

WORKED EXAMPLE — Explaining inverse proportion

A table of results linking variables x and y is shown.

x	2	3	4	5	6
y	6	4	3	2·4	2

As x increases from 2 to 4 (doubles), y decreases from 6 to 3 (halves).

For every pair (x, y) of variables, $xy = 12 = $ constant.

$$y = \frac{12}{x} \Rightarrow y \propto \frac{1}{x}$$

This is expressed as 'y is directly proportional to one over x (the inverse of x)'

or

'y is inversely proportional to x'.

In general, if $y = \dfrac{k}{x}$, then y is inversely proportional to x and vice versa. k is called the constant of proportionality. A graph of y against $\dfrac{1}{x}$ is a straight line through the origin of slope k.

$$y \propto \frac{1}{x} \Leftrightarrow y = \frac{k}{x} \Leftrightarrow xy = k$$

The product xy is constant.

(graph: y against $\left(\frac{1}{x}\right)$, Slope = k)

EXAMPLE 19

If p is inversely proportional to s, find an expression relating p to s.

If $p = 6$ when $s = 15$:

(a) find the constant of proportionality,

(b) find s when $p = 20$,

(c) find p when $s = 12$.

Solution

$$p \propto \frac{1}{s} \Rightarrow p = \frac{k}{s}$$

(a) $p = 6, s = 15$: $\quad 6 = \dfrac{k}{15}$

$$k = 90$$

$$p = \frac{90}{s}$$

(b) $p = 20$: $\quad s = \dfrac{90}{20} = 4·5$

(c) $s = 12$: $\quad p = \dfrac{90}{12} = 7·5$

EXAMPLE 20

Five computers process a certain amount of information in 12 hours. How long will it take 18 computers to process the same information?

Solution

Clearly, as the number of computers N increases, the processing time t decreases.

$$\therefore\ t \propto \frac{1}{N} \Rightarrow t = \frac{k}{N}$$

$$N = 5, t = 12: \quad 12 = \frac{k}{5}$$

$$k = 60$$

$$t = \frac{60}{N}$$

$$N = 18: \quad t = \frac{60}{18} = \frac{10}{3} = 3\tfrac{1}{3} \text{ hours}$$

$$= 3 \text{ hours } 20 \text{ minutes}$$

EXERCISE 12

1. If $y \propto \dfrac{1}{x}$ and $y = 20$, when $x = 5$, find the constant of proportionality.

   (a) Find x when $y = 25$.

   (b) Find y when $x = 40$.

2. The time t to be served in a restaurant is inversely proportional to the number N of waiters working.

   (a) Write down a formula relating t to N.

   (b) If it takes 30 minutes to be served by 10 waiters, find the constant of proportionality.

   (c) How long does it take to be served by 12 waiters?

3. A bus journey takes 40 minutes at an average speed of 60 km/h.

   (a) Is the relation between the time of a journey t (minutes) and speed v (km/h) a directly or an inversely proportional relation?

   (b) Write down a formula relating t to v.

   (c) How fast must the bus go to cover the same journey in 30 minutes?

4. Boyle's law states that the pressure P in a gas is inversely proportional to the volume V of the gas, at constant temperature.

   (a) Explain what this means by stating what happens to the pressure as the volume increases.

   (b) Write down a formula relating P to V.

   (c) If when the volume is V_1, the pressure is P_1 and when the volume is V_2, the pressure is P_2, show that $P_1 V_1 = P_2 V_2$.

   $$\boxed{\begin{array}{c} P_1 \\ V_1 \end{array}} \longrightarrow \boxed{\begin{array}{c} P_2 \\ V_2 \end{array}}$$

   (d) If $V = 0{\cdot}01$ m^3 when $P = 5$ N m^{-2}, find V when $P = 3{\cdot}2$ N m^{-2}, correct to four decimal places.

5. If x men can complete a job in t days, write down a relationship between x and t. Find the constant of proportionality if 30 men can complete the job in 20 days. How many men are needed to complete the job in 24 days?

6. If it takes 5 pumps to empty a swimming pool in 8 hours, how many pumps will it take to empty the pool in $2\frac{1}{2}$ hours?

7. There is enough food in a refugee camp to feed 300 people for 14 days. If 200 more refugees arrive at that instant, how long will the food last?

8. The frequency of vibration of a violin string varies inversely with the length l of the string.

   A violin string of length $0{\cdot}254$ m vibrates at 512 Hz. Find the frequency of a $0{\cdot}2$ m string.

9. The graph of v (km/h) of a ball against $\dfrac{1}{m}$ (kg^{-1}) is a straight line through the origin, where v is the speed of a ball of mass m (kg).

   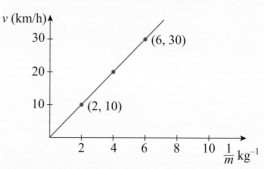

   (a) Find the slope of the graph.

   (b) Write down an equation relating v to m. Find v when $m = 0{\cdot}2$ kg.

10. The acceleration due to gravity g (m/s^2) is inversely proportional to the square of the distance r (m) from the centre of the Earth.

    (a) Write down an equation connecting g and r.

    (b) If $g = 9{\cdot}8$ m/s^2 when $r = 6{\cdot}4 \times 10^6$ m, find g when $r = 3{\cdot}2 \times 10^7$ m.

REVISION QUESTIONS

1. $\mathbb{R}^+$ is the set of positive real numbers.

   (a) Show $\mathbb{R}^+$ on the number line.

   (b) Copy the Venn diagram below. Place the following numbers in the Venn diagram:

     $10, 0, -3, \frac{1}{2}, -\frac{2}{3}, \sqrt{2}, 1$

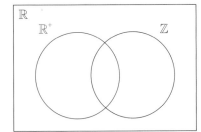

   (c) What set is $\mathbb{R}^+ \cap \mathbb{Z}$?

   (d) Describe in words the set
$A = \{x \mid x < 0, x \in \mathbb{R}\}$

2. **(a)** What is a prime number?

   (b) (i) Find the prime factors of 2457, given that 13 is a factor.

     (ii) Show that:

$$\frac{\text{Product of the first three prime numbers}}{\text{Sum of the first three prime numbers}}$$
$$= \text{The second prime number}$$

   (c) If the sum of the digits of a number is divisible by 3, this means the number is also divisible by 3. Show that 1671 is not a prime number.

3. **(a)** Write out all prime numbers less than 50.

   (b) $\mathbb{Z}$ is the set of integers, $\mathbb{N}$ is the set of natural numbers and P is the set of prime numbers. Copy the diagram as shown and place the following numbers in their correct places in the diagram: $0, 2, 1, -3, 7, 11, -11, 18, 103$

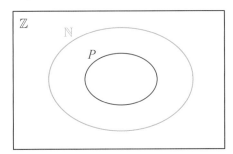

   (c) x, y and z are three prime numbers such that z is six bigger than y and y is six bigger than x. Find the numbers if one of them is 157.

4. **(a)** Write the following in order of increasing size in the form $a \times 10^n$, $1 \le a < 10$:

     $215{\cdot}7 \times 10^7, 22{\cdot}5 \times 10^3, 0{\cdot}032 \times 10^5, 2{\cdot}5 \times 10^4$

   (b) (i) By rounding each number to the nearest whole number, estimate the value of:

$$Q = \frac{132{\cdot}3 - 1{\cdot}74 \times \sqrt{0{\cdot}64}}{35{\cdot}3 - (5{\cdot}2)^2},$$
as a whole number.

     (ii) Evaluate Q, correct to three significant figures, using your calculator.

   (c)

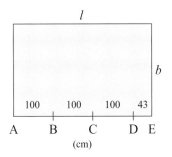

   A man measures the length l of a rectangular room with a metre stick. He needs to use the metre stick four times, as shown. The error in each measurement is $\pm 0{\cdot}1$ cm.

   (i) What is the maximum value of l?

   (ii) What is the minimum value of l?

   Before he measures the width, his friend points out that a tape measure might be useful. Using the tape measure, he measures the width b to a value $(254 \pm 0{\cdot}1)$ cm. Find the maximum and minimum areas of the room in m^2, correct to three decimal places.

5. **(a)** Write $0{\cdot}0000016$ in the form $a \times 10^n$, $1 < a \le 10$.

   (b) The force F in Newtons (N) between two charges $q_1 = 0{\cdot}0000016$ C and $q_2 = 0{\cdot}0000016$ C is given

   by $F = \dfrac{9 \times 10^9 \times q_1 \times q_2}{r^2}$.

   If $r = 1{\cdot}6 \times 10^{-1}$ m, evaluate F without using your calculator. Show your work clearly.

   (c) (i) Estimate $Q = \dfrac{5{\cdot}9 \times \sqrt{16{\cdot}2}}{3{\cdot}2}$ by rounding each number to the nearest whole number.

(ii) Using your calculator, find the exact value of Q correct to one decimal place.

(iii) Find the percentage error in the estimate correct to one decimal place.

6. (a) Light travels at $2 \cdot 9 \times 10^5$ km/s. How many kilometres will light travel in 10 minutes? Give your answer in the form $a \times 10^n$, $1 \le a < 10$.

(b) (i) By rounding each number to the nearest whole number, estimate the value of:

$$Q = \left(\frac{5 \cdot 8 + \sqrt[3]{27 \cdot 1}}{3 \cdot 12} \right)^2, \text{ as a whole number.}$$

(ii) Use your calculator to evaluate Q, correct to two decimal places.

(c) Koola produces cans of cola with a tolerance level of (330 ± 5) ml. If a girl drinks three cans of Koola on a particular day, what is:

(i) the maximum possible volume of Koola she consumes,

(ii) the minimum possible volume of Koola she consumes?

If there are $0 \cdot 11$ g of sugar in 1 ml of Koola, what is the maximum amount of sugar in grams the girl gets from Koola on that day?

7. (a) If $a = 3 \times 10^{-2}$ and $b = 8 \times 10^{-3}$, find $a + 4b$ in the form $a \times 10^n$, $1 \le a < 10$, without using your calculator. Show your work clearly.

(b) The tolerance level of the area A of a square plastic cover for a mobile phone is $(1 \cdot 97 \pm 0 \cdot 28)$ cm^2.

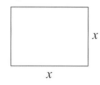

(i) What is the tolerance level of each side?

(ii) If adjacent sides have the minimum and maximum allowed lengths, respectively, what would be the area of the rectangle?

(c) A lunch bill for Joe and Mary is shown.

Joe		Mary	
Soup	€3·95	Salad	€4·10
Salad	€4·10	Beef	€12·95
Salmon	€9·85	Ice cream	€3·10
Apple pie	€5·10		

(i) Make a quick estimate of the bill giving your answer as a whole number.

(ii) Calculate the exact value on your calculator.

(iii) Find the percentage error in the quick estimate, correct to two decimal places.

8. (a) (i) Arrange the following numbers in ascending order:

$2200, 2 \cdot 4 \times 10^3, 2 \cdot 4, 10^3, 2 \cdot 4 \times 10^{-3}$

(ii) Evaluate $7 \times 10^{11} + 9 \times 10^{11} + 8 \times 10^{10}$, giving your answer in the form $a \times 10^n$, $1 \le a < 10$.

(b) The specific gravity of diesel oil has a tolerance level $(0 \cdot 89 \pm 0 \cdot 07)$. Crude oil has a specific gravity of $0 \cdot 79$. What is the least percentage change that the specific gravity of the crude oil must undergo to become diesel oil, correct to one decimal place?

(c) On a certain map, 25 km is represented by 2 cm. If two cities on the map are:

(i) 7 cm apart,

(ii) 12·5 cm apart,

find the actual distance between them.

(d) The current I in amps in an electrical circuit varies inversely as the resistance R of the circuit.

(i) Write down a formula connecting I and R.

(ii) If the current I is 8 amps when the resistance R is 24 ohms, find the current when the resistance is 30 ohms.

9. (a) Plot a graph of y against x using the table of results shown.

x	5	10	15
y	2	4	6

(i) Explain why y is directly proportional to x.

(ii) Find the constant of proportionality.

(iii) Write down a formula connecting y and x.

(iv) Find x when $y = 32 \cdot 5$.

(b) The distance s in metres of a body from a fixed point after t seconds is given by $s = 3t^2$.

Find the average rate of change between $t = 2$ and $t = 6$.

(c) A car with an average speed of r km/h takes t hours to complete a journey.

(i) If r is inversely proportional to t, write down a formula connecting r and t.

(ii) If the car takes 3 hours to complete a journey at an average speed of 75 km/h, how long would it take to complete the journey at an average speed of 85 km/h, correct to two decimal places?

10. (a) In a normal deck of cards, what percentage of the cards are:

(i)   face cards, correct to two decimal places,

(ii) diamonds,

(iii) diamonds or queens, correct to two decimal places?

(b) Express $\frac{7}{371}$ as a decimal, correct to three significant figures.

(c) (i) If $y = x^2$, find the average rate of change of y from $x = -4$ and $x = -1$.

(ii) At a speed of 75 mph, the fuel efficiency of a Subaru is 30 miles/gallon. If the driver slows down to a speed of 60 mph, the fuel efficiency is 35 miles/gallon. What is the average rate of change of the fuel efficiency as the speed drops from 75 mph to 60 mph?

(d) To balance a see-saw, the distance in metres a person is from the pivot P is inversely proportional to his mass in kg. Eamon, whose mass is 60 kg, is sitting 2 m from the pivot. Emma's mass is 48 kg. How far from the pivot must Emma sit so that the see-saw is balanced?

SUMMARY

Number Systems

1. Natural numbers:

   $\mathbb{N} = \{1, 2, 3, \dots\}$

   A prime number is a natural number greater than 1, which can only be divided by itself and 1.

2. Integers:

   $\mathbb{Z} = \{\dots, -3, -2, -1, 0, 1, 2, 3, \dots\}$

   Consecutive integers can be written as:

   $a, a + 1, a + 2, \dots$

   or

   $a - 1, a, a + 1, \dots$

3. Rational numbers:

   $\mathbb{Q} = \left\{\dots, -15, \dots, -\frac{2}{3}, \dots, 0, \dots, \frac{1}{2}, \dots, 5, \dots\right\}$

   Every rational number can be expressed as a terminating decimal or a non-terminating, recurring decimal.

4. Real numbers:

   $\mathbb{R} = \left\{\dots, -\pi, \dots, -\sqrt{3}, \dots, -\frac{2}{3}, \dots, 0, \dots, \sqrt{2}, \dots\right\}$

5. Complex numbers:

   Complex numbers are denoted by $\mathbb{C}$.

   $i = \sqrt{-1}$

   $z = a + bi, \ a, b \in \mathbb{R}, \ i = \sqrt{-1}$

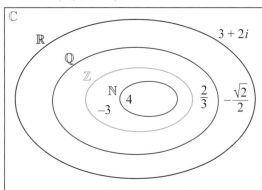

   $\mathbb{N} \subset \mathbb{Z} \subset \mathbb{Q} \subset \mathbb{R} \subset \mathbb{C}$

6. Absolute value (modulus) of a number:

   |Number| = positive value of the number

Arithmetic

1. Percentages:

   (a) A percentage is a fraction expressed as part of 100: $r\% = \dfrac{r}{100}$

   (b) To increase a quantity by $r\%$, multiply it by $\left(1 + \dfrac{r}{100}\right)$

   (c) To decrease a quantity by $r\%$, multiply it by $\left(1 - \dfrac{r}{100}\right)$

2. Scientific notation: $a \times 10^n, \ n \in \mathbb{Z}$ and $1 \le a < 10$

3. The order of magnitude of $a \times 10^n$, $1 \le a < 10$ is n if $a < 5$, and is $n + 1$ if $a \ge 5$.

4. The tolerance level of a measurement is the greatest range of variation in the measurement that is allowable.

5. (a) Absolute error in a quantity
   = |Measured value of the quantity − Accepted value of the quantity|

   (b) Percentage error in a quantity
   $= \dfrac{\text{Absolute error in the quantity}}{\text{Accepted value of the quantity}} \times 100\%$

6. Significant figures: Write the number in the form $a \times 10^n$, $1 \le a < 10$ and give the required number of digits in a.

7. (a) Average rate of change of Q with respect to
   $t = \dfrac{Q_2 - Q_1}{t_2 - t_1}$
   = slope of line AB

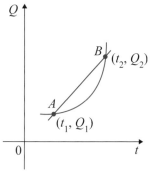

   (b) Speed $v = \dfrac{s_2 - s_1}{t_2 - t_1} = \dfrac{\text{Change in distance}}{\text{Change in time}}$

   Acceleration $a = \dfrac{v_2 - v_1}{t_2 - t_1} = \dfrac{\text{Change in speed}}{\text{Change in time}}$

8. Direct and inverse proportion:

   Direct: $y \propto x \Rightarrow y = kx, \ k \in \mathbb{R}$

   Inverse: $y \propto \dfrac{1}{x} \Rightarrow y = \dfrac{k}{x}, \ k \in \mathbb{R}$

Algebraic Expressions

Algebra is
the gateway
to problem-solving.
It is the language
of mathematics.

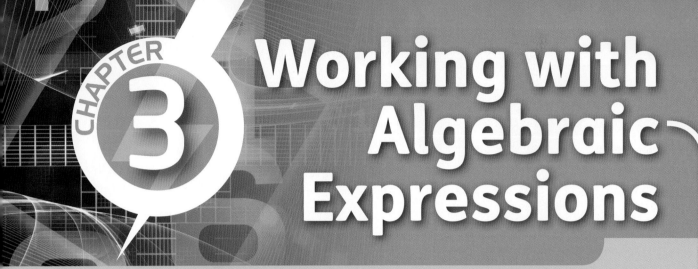

CHAPTER 3

Working with Algebraic Expressions

Learning Outcomes

- To understand the basics of adding and multiplying algebraic expressions.
- To find the value of an algebraic expression by substituting the values of its variables.
- To use various techniques of factorisation to turn algebraic expressions into their factors.
- To apply your knowledge to modelling problems.

3.1 Algebraic basics

ACTIVITY 1

ACTION
Writing out the terms and coefficients in algebraic expressions

OBJECTIVE
To recognise the terms and coefficients in algebraic expressions

Key terms

It is important that you understand the language of algebra.

> **KEY TERM**
> A **variable** is a symbol (letter) that can take on a range of values. The symbols used are generally letters such as x and y, but there is nothing wrong with boxes ($\square$), circles ($\bigcirc$) or brackets ( ).

> **KEY TERM**
> A **term** is a number (constant) multiplied by one or more variables, or just a number on its own.

Examples of terms: $5x$, $-6xy$, $3x^2y$, $-5(2x + 3)$, 7

> **KEY TERM**
> An **expression** is made up of of a number of terms separated by + or – signs.

▶ The expression $3x^2 + 2y - x(y - 1)$ has three terms.

▶ The expression $-2y^2 + 3xy^2 - \frac{1}{2}x + 4$ has four terms.

> **KEY TERM**
> The **coefficient** of a variable or group of variables is the number (constant) multiplying them.

▶ In the expression $4x - 3y + 5x^2y - 2$, the coefficient of x is $+4$, the coefficient of y is -3, the coefficient of x^2y is $+5$ and the constant (numerical) coefficient is -2.

ACTIVITY 2

ACTION
Understanding the meanings of algebraic expressions

OBJECTIVE
To write an algebraic expression in its simplest form

Algebraic expressions explained

- $3 \times 2 = 2 + 2 + 2 = 3(2) = (3)(2)$
- $3 \times x = x + x + x = 3x$
- $-2 \times x = -x - x = -2x$
- $3 \times 2y = 2y + 2y + 2y = 6y = (3 \times 2)y$
- $y^2 = y \times y = (y)(y)$
- $3y^2 = 3 \times y \times y$
- $3x + 2x = x + x + x + x + x = 5x$
- $xy = x \times y$
- $3x^2 + 2xy^2 = 3 \times x \times x + 2 \times x \times y \times y$

ACTIVITY 3

ACTION
Multiplying algebraic terms

OBJECTIVE
To understand the processes involved in multiplying algebraic terms including commutativity and associativity

Multiplication of algebraic terms

1. Commutative property for multiplication:
   - $3 \times 2 = 2 \times 3$
   - $x \times y = y \times x$

   The commutative property means that you can switch the order of multiplication.

2. Associative property for multiplication:
   - $3 \times 2 \times 5 = 3 \times (2 \times 5) = (3 \times 2) \times 5 = 30$
   - $-5 \times 4 \times 2 \times 3 = (-5 \times 4) \times (2 \times 3) = (-20)(6) = -120$
   - $3xy = (3x)y = 3(xy)$

   The associative property means that when you multiply three or more objects, you can group any two together to multiply.
   - $2 \times x \times x = 2 \times (x \times x) = 2x^2$
   - $3 \times x \times 2 \times y = (3 \times 2) \times (x \times y) = 6 \times (xy) = 6xy$

3. Distributive property for multiplication:
   - $2(3 + 5) = 2 \times 3 + 2 \times 5 = 16$
   - $-3x(x - 2y) = -3x^2 + 6xy$

   The distributive property means that you multiply **all terms** in a bracket by an object (number or variable) outside the bracket.

EXAMPLE 1

Multiply out the following:

(a) $3(2x - y + 1)$
(b) $(4x + y - 5)x$
(c) $-4(5x - 11)x$

Solution

(a) $3(2x - y + 1) = 3 \times 2x - 3 \times y + 3 \times 1$
$= 6x - 3y + 3$
(b) $(4x + y - 5)x = x(4x + y - 5)$
$= 4x^2 + xy - 5x$
(c) $-4(5x - 11)x = -4x(5x - 11)$
$= -20x^2 + 44x$

ACTIVITY 4

ACTION
Combining terms using magic squares

OBJECTIVE
To use magic squares to combine terms in algebraic expressions

Combining like terms

You can combine only like terms in an expression. Like terms have exactly the same variable (letters) composition.

▸ $3x + 5x = 8x$

▸ $5y - 8y = -3y$

▸ $5x^2y + 2yx^2 = 7x^2y$ [Both terms have the same variable composition.]

You cannot make an expression such as $2x + 3y$ any simpler, as you cannot combine unlike terms.

EXAMPLE 2

Simplify the following:

(a) $4 + 3x + 2y - 5y + 7x - 2$ **(b)** $4x - 3y + 5z$ **(c)** $4x^2y + 5xy - 6yx^2 + 1 - 2xy$

Solution

(a) $4 + 3x + 2y - 5y + 7x - 2$

     $= 3x + 7x + 2y - 5y - 2 + 4$ [Gather up like terms – you can do this in your head.]

     $= 10x - 3y + 2$

(b) $4x - 3y + 5z = 4x - 3y + 5z$ [There are no like terms – leave the expression as it is.]

(c) $4x^2y + 5xy - 6yx^2 + 1 - 2xy$

     $= 4x^2y - 6yx^2 + 5xy - 2xy + 1$ [Gather up like terms.]

     $= 4x^2y - 6x^2y + 5x - 2xy + 1$ [$6yx^2 = 6x^2y$]

     $= -2x^2y + 3xy + 1$

ACTIVITY 5

ACTION
Expanding brackets and combining like terms (1)

OBJECTIVE
To multiply out brackets term by term and then combine terms

Multiplying out (expanding) brackets and combining like terms

▸ $-4x + 3y - 2 - 3(2y - 5x + 9)$

     $= -4x + 3y - 2 - 6y + 15x - 27$ [Make sure you combine terms **after** the

     $= 11x - 3y - 29$ brackets have been removed.]

▸ $3x(4x - 1) + 2y(4x - 1)$ [Always get rid of the brackets first.]

     $= 12x^2 - 3x + 8xy - 2y$

▸ $3x^2 - x(x + 1) + 2x$

     $= 3x^2 - x^2 - x + 2x$

     $= 2x^2 + x$

▸ $2x(x + 2) - x(2x - 3)$

     $= 2x^2 + 4x - 2x^2 + 3x$

     $= 7x$

WORKED EXAMPLE

Expanding brackets of the type $(x + a)(y + b)$

Multiply out $(x + a)(y + b)$.   [Each bracket has two terms.]

$$(x + a)(y + b) = x(y + b) + a(y + b)$$
$$= xy + xb + ay + ab$$

The same result is obtained by multiplying out term by term. Every term in the first bracket is multiplied by every term in the second bracket.

$$(x + a)(y + b) = xy + xb + ay + ab$$

Observe the following:

To obtain the first term in the answer, multiply the first terms of the two brackets: $x \times y = xy$.

$$(\boldsymbol{x} + a)(\boldsymbol{y} + b) = \boldsymbol{xy} + xb + ay + ab \quad [\text{First} \times \text{First} = \text{First}]$$

To obtain the last term of the answer, multiply the last terms of the two brackets: $a \times b = ab$.

$$(x + \boldsymbol{a})(y + \boldsymbol{b}) = xy + xb + ay + \boldsymbol{ab} \quad [\text{Last} \times \text{Last} = \text{Last}]$$

To obtain the middle terms, multiply the first term of one bracket by the last term of the second bracket. Do this for both brackets: $x \times b = xb$ and $y \times a = ya$. Call these middle terms the mixtures. Now you have all of the terms in the answer.

$$(x + a)(y + b) = xy + \boldsymbol{xb} + \boldsymbol{ay} + ab$$

When you multiply out two brackets with two terms in each bracket, the answers can have four terms, three terms or two terms.

1. Four terms

$$(2x - 1)(4y - 3) = 8xy - 6x - 4y + 3 \quad \text{(four terms)}$$

or

2. Three terms

$$(4x - y)(x + 2y) = 4x^2 + 8xy - xy - 2y^2 \quad [xy = yx]$$
$$= 4x^2 + 7xy - 2y^2 \quad \text{(three terms)}$$

There are three terms in this answer because the mixtures combine into a single term. An expression with three terms is also called a **trinomial**.

or

3. Two terms

$$(2x - 3y)(2x + 3y) = 4x^2 + 6xy - 6xy - 9y^2$$
$$= 4x^2 - 9y^2 \quad \text{(two terms)}$$

There are two terms in this answer because the mixtures cancel. The two terms in this answer are also called the **difference of two squares**.

ACTIVITY 6

ACTION
Expanding brackets and combining like terms (2)

OBJECTIVE
To multiply out more complicated brackets term by term and then combine terms

More multiplication of brackets

1. Difference of two squares

A difference of two squares expression is obtained by the multiplication of two brackets of the type:

> (Difference of two terms) × (Sum of the same two terms)

▶ $(3x - 5y)(3x + 5y) = 9x^2 - 15xy + 15xy - 25y^2 = 9x^2 - 25y^2 = (3x)^2 - (5y)^2$

TIP
▲ (First − Second)(First + Second) = (First)^2 − (Second)^2

▶ $(5x - 2y)(5x + 2y) = (5x)^2 - (2y)^2 = 25x^2 - 4y^2$

2. Perfect squares

A perfect square consists of two identical brackets.

▶ $(3x - 2y)^2 = (3x - 2y)(3x - 2y) = 9x^2 - 6xy - 6yx + 4y^2 = 9x^2 - 12xy + 4y^2$

TIP
▲ (First term + Second term)^2
= (First term)^2 + 2(First term)(Second term) + (Second term)^2

▸ $(2x + 3y)(2x + 3y) = (2x)^2 + 2(2x)(3y) + (3y)^2 = 4x^2 + 12xy + 9y^2$

▸ $(2x - 1)(2x - 1) = (2x)^2 + 2(2x)(-1) + (-1)^2 = 4x^2 - 4x + 1$

ACTIVITY 7

ACTION
Finding the value of an algebraic expression

OBJECTIVE
To find the value of an expression when given the values of the variables

Finding the value of an algebraic expression

To find the value of an algebraic expression, simply fill in the given value(s) of the variable(s).

Method

1. Put a bracket around each variable.
2. Fill in the value of each variable.
3. Simplify each term – always calculate the brackets first.
4. Combine the terms.

EXAMPLE 3

Evaluate $4x^2y - 2xy^2 + 5xy - 7$, if $x = 2$ and $y = -3$.

Solution

$4x^2y - 2xy^2 + 5xy - 7$ [This is a two-variable expression. Put brackets around the variables first.]

$= 4(x)^2(y) - 2(x)(y)^2 + 5(x)(y) - 7$

Substituting in $x = 2$ and $y = -3$ gives:

$4(2)^2(-3) - 2(2)(-3)^2 + 5(2)(-3) - 7$

$= -48 - 36 - 30 - 7$

$= -121$

EXERCISE 1

1. Simplify the following:

   (a) $2 \times x \times x$
   (b) $3 \times x \times y \times y$
   (c) $x(xy)$
   (d) $-2 \times y \times x$
   (e) $3 \times 2y \times 3x$
   (f) $2y \times 3y$
   (g) $-5x \times -3y$
   (h) $(-2x)(-4xy)$
   (i) $5(3x)$
   (j) $x(7y)$

2. Multiply out the following:

   (a) $+2(5x + 3)$
   (b) $-2(5x - 3)$
   (c) $x(2x + 7)$
   (d) $(2x - 7)x$
   (e) $3(5x - 8)x$
   (f) $-2(2x + 1)y$
   (g) $2x(y + 1)y$
   (h) $-3y(x - 1)x$
   (i) $xy(x - y + 1)$
   (j) $2x(y + 2x - 3)y$
   (k) $(x + 2)(y + 3)$
   (l) $(x + 5)(y + 7)$
   (m) $(x - 2)(y + 3)$
   (n) $(-x + 5)(y + 8)$

3. Simplify the following:

   (a) $2x + 3x$
   (b) $5x - 7x$
   (c) $-3y - 2y$
   (d) $-8y + 11y$
   (e) $5x + 3y - 2x + 5y$
   (f) $-11x - 4y + 7y - 8x$
   (g) $2x^2 - 3y^2 + 7y - 2x + 5x^2 + 2y^2 - 4y + 11x$
   (h) $-3xy^2 + 2x^2y - 5xy^2 + 7x^2y - 2$
   (i) $2yz - 3z + 4z - 8y$
   (j) $6y^2 - 2yx + 7xy - 8x^2 - 4y^2 + 11x^2$

4. Multiply out the following, giving your answer in order of descending powers of x:

   (a) $-2(x + 4)$
   (b) $7(x - 7)$

(c) $3x(2x - 8)$

(d) $2x(x^2 - x + 7)$

(e) $4(x - 1) - 5(2x + 11)$

(f) $7x(x + 1) - 3x(x + 2)$

(g) $2x(x - 1) - 3(2x^2 - 5x + 9)$

(h) $x(6x - 2) - (7x^2 - x - 11)$

(i) $x^2(3x + 1) - 2x(3x^2 - x + 5)$

(j) $-2x(x^2 - 1) + 3x^2(3x - 1)$

5. Multiply out and simplify the following:

(a) $(x + 2)(x + 5)$

(b) $(3x + 7)(2x + 3)$

(c) $(y + 5)(y + 8)$

(d) $(3x - 5)(2x - 1)$

(e) $x(x - 3)(2x + 4)$

(f) $(2x^2 + x + 1)(x + 1)$

(g) $(x^2 - x + 5)(x - 3)$

(h) $(x - 1)(3x^2 + 5x - 7)$

(i) $(-2x^2 + 5x - 6)(1 - x)$

(j) $(2x - 1)(x + 2)(x - 1)$

6. Multiply out the following. The answers are a difference of two squares expression, which simplifies the process.

(a) $(x + 2)(x - 2)$ (f) $(4x - 3)(4x + 3)$

(b) $(2x - 1)(2x + 1)$ (g) $(x^2 - 5)(x^2 + 5)$

(c) $(4x - 1)(4x + 1)$ (h) $(y - 3)(y + 3)$

(d) $(x^2 + 1)(x^2 - 1)$ (i) $(3 + x)(3 - x)$

(e) $(3x - 2)(3x + 2)$ (j) $(x + 2y)(x - 2y)$

7. Multiply out the following perfect squares:

(a) $(x + 1)^2$ (g) $(5x - 4)^2$

(b) $(x + 2)^2$ (h) $(x^2 - 11)^2$

(c) $(2x + 1)^2$ (i) $(4x - 5)^2$

(d) $(3x + 2)^2$ (j) $(2x + 3y)^2$

(e) $(x - 4)^2$ (k) $(ax - b)^2$

(f) $(2x - 3)^2$ (l) $(a + 1)^2 - (a - 1)^2$

8. Multiply out and simplify the following:

(a) $(x - 2)(x + 1)(x + 2)$

(b) $(2x - 1)(x + 3)(2x + 1)$

(c) $(2x + 3)(3x - 1)(2x - 3)$

(d) $(x + 1)^3$ [Hint: $(x + 1)^2(x + 1)$]

(e) $(2x - 1)^3$ [Hint: $(2x - 1)^2(2x - 1)$]

(f) $(x - 2)(2x + 1)(x - 3)$

9. (a) If $p = x + 5y - 3$ and $q = 2x - 3y + 7$, find the following, in terms of x and y:

(i) $p + q$ (iii) $2p + 5q$

(ii) $p - q$ (iv) $q - 2p$

(b) If $p = x + 3$ and $q = -2x + 5$, find the following, in terms of x:

(i) $p + q$ (iv) $(p + q)^2$

(ii) $p - q$ (v) $(p - q)^2$

(iii) pq (vi) $p^2 + q^2$

(c) If $p = 5x^2 - 2x + 1$ and $q = -3x^2 + x - 8$, find the following, in terms of x:

(i) $p + q$ (iii) $q - 2p$

(ii) $p - q$ (iv) $3p + 5q$

10. Find the values of the following expressions:

(a) $x + 2y$ if $x = 4$ and $y = 7$

(b) $3x + 11y$ if $x = -2$ and $y = 3·5$

(c) $4x - 3y + 8$ if $x = -1$ and $y = -6$

(d) $5x^2$ if $x = -3$

(e) $-5x^2$ if $x = -3$

(f) $(5x)^2$ if $x = 3$

(g) $x^2 - 3y^2$ if $x = 3$ and $y = -2$

(h) $2x^2 + 5x - 7$ if $x = 5$

(i) $-5x^2 + 7x - 3$ if $x = -2$

(j) $(2x + 3y)^2$ if $x = -3$ and $y = 4$

(k) $2x^2 y - 3xy^2 - 7$ if $x = 3$ and $y = -2$

(l) $3x^2 y^2 - 5x + 7(x - y)^2$ if $x = -2$ and $y = 0·5$

3.2 Factorisation (working backwards)

ACTIVITY 8

ACTION
Factorising algebraic expressions (1)

OBJECTIVE
To revise factorising, concentrating on grouping

KEY TERM

Factorisation means splitting up an algebraic expression into factors that multiply together to give the expression.

Factor technique 1

Highest common factor (HCF)

▶ $5x + 10y + 15$ [5 is the HCF of $5x + 10y + 15$ as it is the largest object that divides into all three terms.]

$= 5 \times x + 5 \times 2y + 5 \times 3$

$= 5(x + 2y + 3)$

EXAMPLE 4

Find the highest common factor of the following and factorise:

(a) $4x^2 - 8x$

(b) $5x^2y^2 - 10xy$

(c) $7x(x - 2y) - 3y(x - 2y)$

Solution

(a) $4x^2 - 8x = 4x(x - 2)$

(b) $5x^2y^2 - 10xy = 5xy(xy - 2)$

(c) $7x(x - 2y) - 3y(x - 2y) = (x - 2y)(7x - 3y)$

 ## Factor technique 2

Grouping

To factorise an expression with four terms with no highest common factor, group the terms into pairs that each have a highest common factor.

WORKED EXAMPLE How grouping works

The terms in the expression $6xy + 3xz + 2y + z$ have no highest common factor (HCF) but the first pair of terms has a HCF and the second pair of terms has a HCF.

$6xy + 3xz + 2y + z$

$= (6xy + 3xz) + (2y + z)$

$= 3x(2y + z) + 1(2y + z)$ [Do not forget to take out the 1.]

Four terms have been combined into two terms. These two terms have a HCF of $(2y + z)$.

$3x(2y + z) + 1(2y + z)$

$= (2y + z)(3x + 1)$

▶ $2x^2 - 5xy + 4kx - 10ky$

$= (2x^2 - 5xy) + (4kx - 10ky)$

$= x(2x - 5y) + 2k(2x - 5y)$

$= (2x - 5y)(x + 2k)$

▶ $ax - bx - ay + by$

$= (ax - bx) + (-ay + by)$

$= x(a - b) - y(a - b)$

$= (a - b)(x - y)$

ACTIVITY 9

ACTION
Factorising algebraic expressions (2)

OBJECTIVE
To revise factorising concentrating on trinomials

Factor technique 3
Trinomials

KEY TERM
A **trinomial** is an expression with three terms such as $6x^2 + 19xy + 10y^2$.

When you multiply $(3x + 2y)$ by $(2x + 5y)$ you get:

$(3x + 2y)(2x + 5y) = 6x^2 + 15xy + 4xy + 10y^2 = 6x^2 + 19xy + 10y^2$

It is tricky to work backwards from $6x^2 + 19xy + 10y^2$ to get its factors of $(3x + 2y)$ and $(2x + 5y)$ because when you multiply these brackets, the middle terms are combined into the single term $19xy$ in the final expression.

WORKED EXAMPLE Technique for factorising trinomials 1

Factorise $x^2 + 12x + 11$.

Step 1: Write down two terms that multiply together to give x^2. [$x \times x = x^2$ or First × First = First]

Step 2: Write down two terms that multiply together to give 11. [$1 \times 11 = 11$ or Last × Last = Last]

Step 3: The cross products are $1x$ and $11x$. Putting the appropriate signs on the cross products, can you combine them to get the middle term of $+12x$? Obviously, $+1x + 11x = +12x$ works.

Step 4: Read straight across on each side to get the factors of $(x + 1)$ and $(x + 11)$.

$\therefore x^2 + 12x + 11 = (x + 1)(x + 11)$.

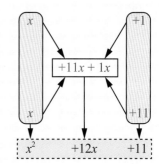

WORKED EXAMPLE Technique for factorising trinomials 2

Factorise $2x^2 + x - 3$.

Step 1: Write down two terms that multiply together to give $2x^2$. [$2x \times x = 2x^2$ or First × First = First]

Step 2: Write down two terms that multiply together to give 3. [$3 \times 1 = 3$ or Last × Last = Last]

Step 3: The cross products are $3x$ and $2x$. Putting the appropriate signs on the cross products, can you combine them to get the middle term of $+1x$? Obviously, $+3x - 2x = x$ works.

Step 4: Read straight across on each side to get the factors of $(2x + 3)$ and $(x - 1)$.

$\therefore 2x^2 + x - 3 = (2x + 3)(x - 1)$.

The order of the factors of 3 is important. If you had put them in the wrong place, it would not have been possible to get the cross products to combine to give the middle term. It is a process of **trial and error**.

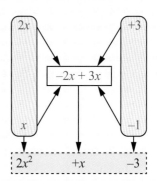

WORKED EXAMPLE Technique for factorising trinomials 3

Factorise $4x^2 - 4x - 15$.

Step 1: Write down two terms that multiply together to give $4x^2$.
$[4x \times x = 4x^2$ or $2x \times 2x = 4x^2]$

Step 2: Write down two terms that multiply together to give 15. $[1 \times 15 = 15$ or $3 \times 5 = 15]$

It will take some trial and error to get the right combination of the cross products. The combination that works is shown:

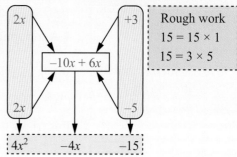

Step 3: The cross products are $6x$ and $10x$. Putting the appropriate signs on the cross products, can you combine them to get the middle term of $-4x$? Obviously, $+6x - 10x = -4x$ works.

Step 4: Read straight across on each side to get the factors of $(2x + 3)$ and $(2x - 5)$.

$\therefore 4x^2 - 4x - 15 = (2x + 3)(2x - 5)$.

WORKED EXAMPLE Technique for factorising trinomials 4

Factorise $3x^2 + 7xy + 2y^2$.

Step 1: Write down two terms that multiply together to give $3x^2$. $[3x \times x = 3x^2]$

Step 2: Write down two terms that multiply together to give $2y^2$. $[2y \times y = 2y^2]$

Step 3: The cross products are $6xy$ and xy. Putting the appropriate signs on the cross products, can you combine them to get the middle term of $+7xy$? Obviously, $+6xy + xy = +7xy$ works.

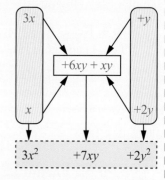

Step 4: Read straight across on each side to get the factors of $(3x + y)$ and $(x + 2y)$.

$\therefore 3x^2 + 7xy + 2y^2 = (3x + y)(x + 2y)$.

EXAMPLE 5

Factorise the following trinomials:

(a) $x^2 - x - 20$
(b) $14y^2 + 13xy - 2x^2$
(c) $30x^2 - 17x + 2$
(d) $49x^2 - 28xy + 4y^2$

Solution

You can speed up the factorisation by doing the combination of the cross products in your head.

(a) $x^2 - 1x - 20 = (x - 5)(x + 4)$ [Sum of cross products $= -1x$]

(b) $14y^2 + 3xy - 2x^2$

$= (7y - 2x)(2y + 1x)$ [Sum of cross products $= +3xy$]

(c) $30x^2 - 17x + 2$

$= (5x - 2)(6x - 1)$ [Sum of cross products $= -17x$]

(d) $49x^2 - 28xy + 4y^2 = (7x - 2y)(7x - 2y)$

$= (7x - 2y)^2$

[A perfect square is a trinomial that has two identical factors.]

Factor technique 4
Difference of two squares

$(x - y)(x + y)$

$= x(x + y) - y(x + y)$

$= x^2 + xy - xy - y^2$

$= x^2 - y^2$

$$\boxed{x^2 - y^2 = (x - y)(x + y)}$$

TIP

▲ **Differences of two squares:**

$(\text{First})^2 - (\text{Second})^2 = (\text{First} - \text{Second})(\text{First} + \text{Second})$

EXAMPLE 6

Factorise the following:

(a) $a^2 - 25b^2$

(b) $400x^2 - 49y^2$

(c) $(x + y)^2 - z^2$

Solution

(a) $a^2 - 25b^2 = (a)^2 - (5b)^2 = (a - 5b)(a + 5b)$

(b) $400x^2 - 49y^2 = (20x)^2 - (7y)^2$

$\qquad\qquad\qquad = (20x - 7y)(20x + 7y)$

(c) $(x + y)^2 - (z)^2 = [(x + y) - z][(x + y) + z]$

$\qquad\qquad\qquad = (x + y - z)(x + y + z)$

 ## Steps for factorisation

1. If you can, always take out a highest common factor (HCF) first. There is not always a HCF.

2. Look at what is left inside the bracket and apply one of the following methods to this:

   (a) grouping **(c)** difference of two squares

   (b) trinomial **(d)** there are no factors

EXAMPLE 7

Factorise the following fully:

(a) $1 - 3x - 4x^2$

(b) $7x^2 - 28y^2$

(c) $2a^2 + 6ac - 4ab - 12bc$

(d) $154x^2 - 50x + 4$

Solution

(a) $1 - 3x - 4x^2$ [−1 is the HCF]

$\quad = -1(4x^2 + 3x - 1)$

$\quad = -1(4x - 1)(x + 1)$

(b) $7x^2 - 28y^2$ [7 is the HCF]

$\quad = 7(x^2 - 4y^2)$

$\quad = 7(x - 2y)(x + 2y)$

(c) $2a^2 + 6ac - 4ab - 12bc$

$\quad = 2(a^2 + 3ac - 2ab - 6bc)$

$\quad = 2[a(a + 3c) - 2b(a + 3c)]$

$\quad = 2(a + 3c)(a - 2b)$

(d) $154x^2 - 50x + 4$

$\quad = 2(77x^2 - 25x + 2)$

$\quad = 2(7x - 1)(11x - 2)$

EXERCISE 2

1. Factorise the following by taking out the HCF:

   (a) $3x + 6y$

   (b) $x^2 + 3x$

   (c) $ab - ac$

   (d) $4x^2 - 16xy$

   (e) $3x^2 + 9x - 18$

   (f) $3x - 9y$

   (g) $8a^2 - 16a^2b^2$

   (h) $7x^2y^2 - 14x^2y$

   (i) $3(x - 2y) - 5x(x - 2y)$

   (j) $m(a + b) - 3n(a + b)$

2. Factorise the following by grouping:

   (a) $ax^2 + 2ax + x + 2$

   (b) $ax + by + ay + bx$

   (c) $ax - bx + ay - by$

   (d) $ab + 7a - 3b - 21$

   (e) $3np + 6nq - ap - 2aq$

   (f) $2x^2 + 2x - 3xy - 3y$

   (g) $2x - 6 - bx + 3b$

   (h) $x^2z - 2x^2 - 2y^2 + y^2z$

   (i) $3x - 8y - 2 + 12xy$

   (j) $21 - 3ax^2 - 14b + 2abx^2$

3. Factorise the following trinomials:

   (a) $x^2 + 12x + 35$ (k) $2x^2 + 5x + 2$

   (b) $x^2 + 12x + 27$ (l) $6x^2 + 23x + 20$

   (c) $x^2 + 11x + 18$ (m) $12x^2 + 53x + 56$

   (d) $x^2 + 20x + 36$ (n) $16x^2 + 46x + 15$

   (e) $x^2 + 21x + 54$ (o) $6x^2 + 5x - 6$

   (f) $x^2 - 15x + 50$ (p) $12x^2 - x - 6$

   (g) $x^2 - x - 110$ (q) $6x^2 - 7x - 24$

   (h) $x^2 + x - 110$ (r) $5x^2 + 33x - 14$

   (i) $x^2 - 21x + 110$ (s) $12x^2 - 4x - 33$

   (j) $x^2 - 18x + 45$ (t) $42x^2 - 5x - 2$

4. Factorise the following trinomials:

   (a) $x^2 + 5xy + 6y^2$ (g) $7x^2 - 22xy + 3y^2$

   (b) $x^2 + 9xy + 14y^2$ (h) $2a^2 + ab - 3b^2$

   (c) $x^2 - 5xy + 6y^2$ (i) $30x^2 - 17x + 2$

   (d) $x^2 + 5xy - 14y^2$ (j) $b^2x^2 + 2bxc + c^2$

   (e) $10x^2 + 13x - 3$ (k) $4p^2 - 4p + 1$

   (f) $2x^2 - x - 15$ (l) $18x^2 + 25x - 3$

5. Factorise the following differences of two squares:

   (a) $4x^2 - 1$ (e) $4m^2 - 81n^2$

   (b) $25x^2 - y^2$ (f) $(x + y)^2 - z^2$

   (c) $9x^2 - 16$ (g) $(x + 1)^2 - 9z^2$

   (d) $x^2 - a^2b^2$ (h) $(\text{Yoke})^2 - (\text{Thing})^2$

6. Factorise and hence evaluate the following without using your calculator:

   (a) $51^2 - 49^2$ (e) $50{\cdot}3^2 - 49{\cdot}7^2$

   (b) $53^2 - 47^2$ (f) $504^2 - 496^2$

   (c) $101^2 - 99^2$ (g) $32^2 - 28^2$

   (d) $21^2 - 19^2$ (h) $10{\cdot}7^2 - 9{\cdot}3^2$

7. Factorise the following fully:

   (a) $2x^2 - 8$

   (b) $18a^2 - 8b^2$

   (c) $36x^2 + 15xy - 9y^2$

   (d) $x^2y + 2x^2 - y - 2$

   (e) $28 - 7x^2$

   (f) $4x^2 - 24xy + 36y^2$

   (g) $-2x^2 + 4xy - 2y^2$

   (h) $(a + 1)^2 - 9$

   (i) $16(x - 1)^2 - 4$

   (j) $2a^2 - 578$

3.3 Algebraic modelling

KEY TERM

Algebraic modelling means translating a problem, stated in words, into an algebraic expression.

WORKED EXAMPLE Words to expressions

Given the words in the left column, write down a corresponding expression in the right column for a number which is:

Words	Expression
7 greater than 5	
12 less than 20	
5 times 4	
6 squared	
5 times the difference of 14 and 11	
The sum of 11 and 4 times 3 squared	

The corresponding number expressions are:

Words	Expression
7 greater than 5	$5 + 7$
12 less than 20	$20 - 12$
5 times 4	5×4
6 squared	6^2
5 times the difference of 14 and 11	$5 \times (14 - 11)$
The sum of 11 and 4 times 3 squared	$11 + 4 \times 3^2$

Given the words in the left column, write down a corresponding expression in the right column for a number which is:

Words	Expression
7 greater than x	
1·5 less than y	
x times y	
x squared multiplied by 3	
2 times x increased by 3 times y	
Twice the difference of x and y	

The corresponding number expressions are:

Words	Expression
7 greater than x	$x + 7$
1·5 less than y	$y - 1·5$
x times y	$x \times y = (x)(y) = xy$
x squared multiplied by 3	$3 \times x^2 = 3x^2$
2 times x increased by 3 times y	$2 \times x + 3 \times y = 2x + 3y$
Twice the difference of x and y	$2 \times (x - y) = 2(x - y)$

WORKED EXAMPLE Modelling a problem 1

1. **(a)** A rugby out-half scores two tries, one conversion and three penalties in a match. How many points does he score in total? (1 try = 5 points, 1 conversion = 2 points, 1 penalty = 3 points)

   Number of points = $2 \times 5 + 1 \times 2 + 3 \times 3 = 10 + 2 + 9 = 21$

(b) A rugby out-half scores x tries, y conversions and three penalties in a match. Write down an expression for the total number of points he scores.

	Tries	Conversions	Penalties
Number of scores	x	y	3
Points per score	5	2	3
Number of points	$5x$	$2y$	9

$\therefore$ Total number of points $= 5x + 2y + 9$

2. When a girl is x years old, her father's age is seven times her age and her brother's age is twice her age.

Write down expressions for:

(a) her father's age,

(b) her brother's age,

(c) their total age in terms of x.

Girl's age	Father's age	Brother's age
x	$7x$	$2x$

(a) Father's age $= 7x$

(b) Brother's age $= 2x$

(c) Total age $= x + 7x + 2x = 10x$

ACTIVITY 10

ACTION
Learning how to turn words into mathematics

OBJECTIVE
To warm up with some solid basics before getting down to the business of algebraic modelling

Guidelines for modelling

1. Identify the quantity to be modelled (cost, price, area, length, etc.) and give it a symbol.

2. Draw a diagram if appropriate (unless given).

3. Identify the number of variables (one or more) and, if appropriate, put them on the diagram.

4. Write the quantity to be modelled in terms of this/these variable(s).

EXAMPLE 8

The breadth of a rectangular field is 20 m longer than its length x m.

Write down, in terms of x, an expression for:

(a) the breadth b,

(b) the perimeter P,

(c) the area A of the field.

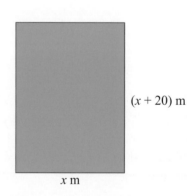

$(x + 20)$ m

x m

Solution

(a) 1. The quantity is the breadth b.

   2. The diagram is given.

   3. The number of variables is one: x

   4. The breadth b is 20 m longer than the length.

   $b = x + 20$

(b) $P = x + (x + 20) + x + (x + 20)$

   $= x + x + 20 + x + x + 20$

   $= 4x + 40$

(c) $A = x(x + 20)$

   $= x^2 + 20x$

EXAMPLE 9

A running track has two straights and two semicircular ends, as shown.

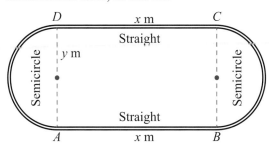

(a) If x m is the length of each straight and y m the radius of each semicircular end, find an expression for the perimeter P, in terms of x and y.

(b) If $x = 100$ m and $y = 31 \cdot 85$ m, find the perimeter to the nearest metre. Use $\pi = 3 \cdot 14$.

(c) If a runner has an average speed of 30 km/h, how long does it take the runner to complete one full circuit of the track?

Solution

(a) 1. The quantity is the perimeter P.

  2. The diagram is given.

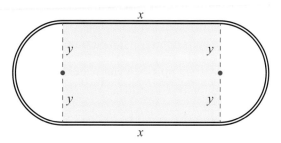

  3. There are two variables: x and y.

  4. $P = 2x + 2\pi y$ [$2\pi y$ is the circumference of a circle of radius y.]

(b) $P = 2(x) + 2\pi(y)$

  Filling in $x = 100$ and $y = 31 \cdot 85$ gives:

  $P = 2(100) + 2\pi(31 \cdot 85)$

  $\quad = 400$ m

(c) Speed = 30 km/h   [Be careful with the units.]

  $= \dfrac{30 \times 1000 \text{ m}}{3600 \text{ s}}$

  $= \dfrac{25}{3}$ m/s

  Time $= \dfrac{\text{Distance}}{\text{Speed}}$

  $= \dfrac{400}{\frac{25}{3}} = 48$ s

EXERCISE 3

1. An entrepreneur bought x phones at €30 each and sold y of them at €98 each. By copying and completing the table, find the entrepreneur's net profit in terms of x and y.

	Sold	Bought
Number of phones		
Price/unit		
Total		

2. An L-shaped flowerbed is shown with $|DC| = x$ m and $|CB| = y$ m. If $[AB]$ is 1 m longer than $[CD]$ and $[ED]$ is 2 m longer than $[CB]$, find expressions for:

  (a) perimeter P,

  (b) area of the flowerbed, in terms of x and y.

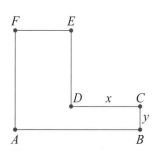

3. A number x, when multiplied by the square of another number y, is greater than the number obtained when the square of the number x is multiplied by the number y.

    Find an expression D for the difference, in terms of x and y, between the bigger number and the smaller number.

4. A petty cash box contains $10x$ one cent coins, $10x$ two cent coins, $5x$ five cent coins, $20x$ ten cent coins, $15x$ twenty cent coins, $7x$ fifty cent coins, $5x$ one euro coins and $3x$ two euro coins. It also contains $2y$ five euro notes, $3y$ ten euro notes and one 20 euro note.

    Copy and complete the table below and find an expression, in terms of x and y, for the total amount A of cash in the box in cents.

Cash type	1c	2c	5c	10c	20c	50c	1€	2€	5€	10€	20€
Number											
Value in cents											

5. (a) For the rectangle shown, find an expression, in terms of x and y:

    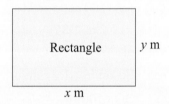

    (i) for the perimeter P of the rectangle,

    (ii) for the area A of the rectangle.

    (b) If $x = 20$ and $y = 30$, what is the length of the perimeter? What is the area of the rectangle?

6. A farmer constructs a fence around a field in the shape of a trapezium $ABCD$ with $[AD]$ parallel to $[BC]$ and $[AB]$ perpendicular to $[BC]$.

    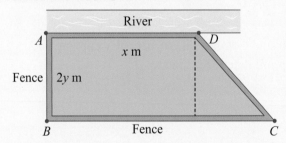

    (a) If $|BC|$ is 4 m longer than $|AD|$ and $|DC|$ is 2 m longer than $|AB|$, find an expression for the length L of fencing, in terms of x and y.

    (b) Find an expression for the area A enclosed by the fence, in terms of x and y.

7. (a) If x is a whole number, find an expression, in terms of x, for:

    (i) the next whole number,

    (ii) the sum of these two consecutive whole numbers.

    (b) Find the values of the sum of two consecutive whole numbers, if x is the first number by copying and completing the table:

	Sum
$x = 1$	$1 + 2 = 3$
$x = 2$	
$x = 3$	
$x = 4$	
$x = 5$	
$x = 6$	
$x = 7$	

    What conclusion can you make?

8. r is the radius of a circle, with centre O, inscribed in a square $ABCD$.

    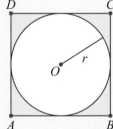

    Find an expression in terms of r for:

    (a) the circumference of the circle,

    (b) the perimeter of the square,

    (c) the area of the circle,

    (d) the area of the square,

    (e) the area of the shaded region.

9. (a) A man can swim at 2 m/s and walk at 1·5 m/s. If he takes x seconds to swim from A to B and y seconds to walk from B to D, find an expression for the length of the journey $ABCD$, in terms of x and y.

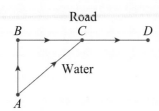

(b) A woman can swim at 1·8 m/s and walk at 1·3 m/s. If she takes $(x + 30)$ seconds to swim from A to C and $(y - 10)$ seconds to walk from C to D, find an expression for the length of the journey ACD, in terms of x and y.

10. $ABCD$ is a rectangular frame with a picture inside, as shown.

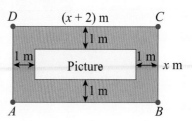

Find an expression, in terms of x, for the area of:

(a) rectangle $ABCD$,

(b) the picture,

(c) the border.

CHAPTER 4

Types of Algebraic Expressions

Learning Outcomes

- To recognise linear and quadratic expressions and to understand how they combine.
- To be able to carry out operations on rational expressions of the form $\dfrac{ax + b}{cx + d}$.
- To be able to apply the rules for carrying out operations on exponentials (powers).
- To understand how to manipulate surd expressions.

4.1 Linear and quadratic expressions

ACTIVITY 11

ACTION
Writing linear expressions in the form $ax + b$

OBJECTIVE
To learn how to recognise linear expressions

KEY TERM

Linear expressions are expressions such as x^1, $2x^1$, $-3x$, $4x + 7$ and $-5x + 9$.

An expression is linear if the highest power of the variable in the expression is 1.

Linear expressions can all be put in the form $ax^1 + b$, where a and b are real constants. a is called the coefficient of x and b is called the constant term.

TIP

Get used to writing linear expressions in the form $ax + b$.

EXAMPLE 1

Write the following expressions in the form $ax + b$ and read off a and b:

(a) $3x - 2$

(b) $-4 + 7x$

(c) $-5x$

Solution

(a) $3x - 2$ is already in this form.

$a = 3$, $b = -2$

(b) $-4 + 7x = 7x - 4$

$a = 7$, $b = -4$

(c) $-5x = -5x + 0$

$a = -5$, $b = 0$

> **KEY TERM**
>
> **Quadratic expressions** are expressions such as x^2, $-2x^2$, $4x^2 - 5$ and $-3x^2 + 5x - 6$.

An expression is quadratic if the highest power of the variable in the expression is 2.

They can all be put in the form $ax^2 + bx + c$, where a, b, c are real constants. a is called the coefficient of x^2. b is called the coefficient of x. c is called the constant term.

> **TIP**
>
> Get used to writing quadratic expressions in the form $ax^2 + bx + c$.

EXAMPLE 2

Write the following quadratic expressions in the form $ax^2 + bx + c$ and read off a, b and c:

(a) $-2x^2$

(b) $2x^2 - 9$

(c) $5 - 2x^2$

(d) $3x^2 - 5 + 2x$

Solution

(a) $-2x^2 = -2x^2 + 0x + 0$

$a = -2$, $b = 0$, $c = 0$

(b) $2x^2 - 9 = 2x^2 + 0x - 9$

$a = 2$, $b = 0$, $c = -9$

(c) $5 - 2x^2 = -2x^2 + 0x + 5$

$a = -2$, $b = 0$, $c = 5$

(d) $3x^2 - 5 + 2x = 3x^2 + 2x - 5$

$a = 3$, $b = 2$, $c = -5$

ACTIVITY 12

ACTION
Writing quadratic expressions in the form $ax^2 + bx + c$

OBJECTIVE
To understand how to recognise quadratic expressions

Your understanding of algebra will be greatly improved if you can recognise patterns and predict results based on the type of expressions involved in any operation.

If you multiply a **linear** expression by a **linear** expression, you get a quadratic expression.

$$(2x - 3)(4x + 1) = 8x^2 + 2x - 12x - 3 = 8x^2 - 10x - 3$$

A quadratic expression is obtained when you multiply two linear expressions.

> Linear × Linear = Quadratic

There is another important observation that we can make. It was discussed in Chapter 3.

Looking at the example above:

Multiplying the first term by the first term in each bracket gives you the highest power in the product as the first term.

$$(2x - 3)(4x + 1) = 8x^2 - 10x - 3 \quad [\text{First} \times \text{First} = \text{First}]$$

Multiplying the last term by the last term in each bracket gives you the constant term in the product as the last term.

$$(2x - 3)(4x + 1) = 8x^2 - 10x - 3 \quad [\text{Last} \times \text{Last} = \text{Last}]$$

The middle term is obtained by adding the products of the first terms by the last terms.

These observations only hold if each linear expression is written in the form $ax + b$.

ACTIVITY 13

ACTION
Dividing quadratic expressions by linear expressions

OBJECTIVE
To divide a quadratic expression by a linear expression to give a linear expression

Division of a quadratic expression by a linear expression

If a linear expression divides into a quadratic expression, it is a factor of the quadratic expression.

You can divide a quadratic expression by a linear expression by factorising the quadratic expression into two linear expressions and cancelling:

▸ $\dfrac{x^2 - 11x + 30}{x - 6} = \dfrac{(x - 6)(x - 5)}{(x - 6)} = x - 5$

▸ $\dfrac{4x^2 - 9}{2x + 3} = \dfrac{(2x - 3)(2x + 3)}{(2x + 3)} = 2x - 3$

▸ $\dfrac{8x^2 - 2x - 21}{4x - 7} = \dfrac{(4x - 7)(2x + 3)}{(4x - 7)} = 2x + 3$

EXERCISE 4

1. Simplify, giving your answer in the form $ax + b$:

   (a) $5x + 7 + 3x + 2$

   (b) $7x - 1 - 2x - 5$

   (c) $3(2x + 1) + 5(3x + 5)$

   (d) $5(x - 3) - 2(4x - 1)$

   (e) $-3(3 - 2x) + 7(x - 2)$

   (f) $2(5x + 1) - 3(7 - 6x) - 5$

   (g) $3 - 5(x - 2) + 5x - 1$

   (h) $x + 3x - 2(x - 4) - 5$

2. Multiply out the brackets, giving your answer in the form $ax^2 + bx + c$:

   (a) $x(x + 2)$ **(f)** $(3x + 2)(5x + 7)$

   (b) $3x(x + 1)$ **(g)** $(x - 1)(x + 4)$

   (c) $-2x(x - 2)$ **(h)** $(2x + 1)(4x - 3)$

   (d) $(x + 1)(x + 2)$ **(i)** $(5x - 6)(3 - 5x)$

   (e) $(2x + 1)(x + 5)$ **(j)** $(6x - 7)(6x + 7)$

3. Simplify the following:

   (a) $\dfrac{x^2 + 10x + 24}{x + 6}$ **(e)** $\dfrac{2x^2 + 5x - 3}{x + 3}$ **(i)** $\dfrac{4x^2 - 1}{2x + 1}$

   (b) $\dfrac{x^2 - 10x + 16}{x - 8}$ **(f)** $\dfrac{15x^2 - 13x + 2}{3x - 2}$ **(j)** $\dfrac{x^2 - 1}{x + 1}$

   (c) $\dfrac{x^2 - 4x - 21}{x - 7}$ **(g)** $\dfrac{6x^2 - 6x - 12}{3(x - 2)}$ **(k)** $\dfrac{x^2 + 5x + 6}{x + 3}$

   (d) $\dfrac{x^2 - 9}{x + 3}$ **(h)** $\dfrac{-15 + 8x - x^2}{x - 5}$ **(l)** $\dfrac{x^2 - 5x}{5 - x}$

4.2 Rational expressions of the form $\dfrac{ax+b}{cx+d}$

ACTIVITY 14

ACTION
Working with rational expressions

OBJECTIVE
To analyse rational expressions involving the ratio of two linear expressions

ACTIVITY 15

ACTION
Adding algebraic fractions by finding the lowest common denominator

OBJECTIVE
To find a lowest common denominator and simplify algebraic expressions

KEY TERM

A **rational expression** of the form $\dfrac{ax+b}{cx+d}$, where $a, b, c, d \in \mathbb{R}$, is a ratio of two linear expressions.

Operations on rational expressions

1. Addition and subtraction

As with numerical fractions, algebraic fractions are added and subtracted by finding their lowest common denominator (LCD).

EXAMPLE 3

Simplify $\dfrac{x}{2} + \dfrac{2x-1}{3}$.

Solution

$\dfrac{x}{2} + \dfrac{2x-1}{3} = \dfrac{x}{2} + \dfrac{(2x-1)}{3}$ [If there are two terms in any part of the ratio, put brackets around them before finding the LCD.]

$= \dfrac{3x + 2(2x-1)}{6}$

$= \dfrac{3x + 4x - 2}{6}$

$= \dfrac{7x - 2}{6}$

EXAMPLE 4

Simplify $\dfrac{2(3x-8)}{11} - \dfrac{2x-8}{4}$.

Solution

$\dfrac{2(3x-8)}{11} - \dfrac{2x-8}{4} = \dfrac{2(3x-8)}{11} - \dfrac{(2x-8)}{4}$

$= \dfrac{4 \times 2(3x-8) - 11(2x-8)}{44}$

$= \dfrac{24x - 64 - 22x + 88}{44}$

$= \dfrac{2x + 24}{44}$ [You should reduce the fraction to its lowest form by factorising and cancelling, if possible.]

$= \dfrac{2(x+12)}{44} = \dfrac{x+12}{22}$

EXAMPLE 5

Simplify $\dfrac{3}{x-1} + \dfrac{4}{2x+1}$.

Solution

$\dfrac{3}{x-1} + \dfrac{4}{2x+1} = \dfrac{3}{(x-1)} + \dfrac{4}{(2x+1)}$

$= \dfrac{3(2x+1) + 4(x-1)}{(x-1)(2x+1)}$ [Do not multiply out the brackets on the bottom until the top has been fully simplified as you may be able to cancel brackets on the top with those on the bottom.]

$= \dfrac{6x + 3 + 4x - 4}{(x-1)(2x+1)}$

$= \dfrac{10x - 1}{(x-1)(2x+1)}$

EXAMPLE 6

Simplify $\dfrac{3x-2}{x-1} - \dfrac{2x+8}{x+1}$.

Solution

$$\frac{3x-2}{x-1} - \frac{2x+8}{x+1} = \frac{(3x-2)}{(x-1)} - \frac{(2x+8)}{(x+1)}$$

$$= \frac{(x+1)(3x-2) - (x-1)(2x+8)}{(x-1)(x+1)}$$

$$= \frac{(3x^2+x-2) - (2x^2+6x-8)}{(x-1)(x+1)}$$

$$= \frac{3x^2+x-2-2x^2-6x+8}{(x-1)(x+1)}$$

$$= \frac{x^2-5x+6}{(x-1)(x+1)} \quad \text{[Always try to factorise the top.]}$$

$$= \frac{(x-3)(x-2)}{(x-1)(x+1)}$$

2. Multiplication

As with numerical fractions, multiply the tops together and multiply the bottoms together and/or cancel.

▸ $\dfrac{x}{2} \times \dfrac{5}{3} = \dfrac{5x}{6}$

▸ $\dfrac{x-1}{3} \times \dfrac{6}{x+2} = \dfrac{6(x-1)}{3(x+2)} = \dfrac{2(x-1)}{x+2}$

ACTIVITY 16

ACTION
Multiplying algebraic fractions

OBJECTIVE
To reduce algebraic fractions by factorising and cancelling

EXAMPLE 7

Simplify $\dfrac{2x-4}{x-1} \times \dfrac{3x-2}{8-4x}$.

Solution

$$\frac{2x-4}{x-1} \times \frac{3x-2}{8-4x} = \frac{2(x-2)(3x-2)}{(x-1)(-4)(x-2)} \quad \text{[Always try to cancel first by factorising the top and/or the bottom.]}$$

$$= \frac{3x-2}{-2(x-1)}$$

$$= \frac{2-3x}{2(x-1)}$$

Be careful when cancelling

You can only cancel a factor on the top with a factor on the bottom.

So $\dfrac{15}{3} = \dfrac{5 \times \cancel{3}}{\cancel{3}} = 5$ is OK, but $\dfrac{15}{3} = \dfrac{12+\cancel{3}}{\cancel{3}} = 12$ is clearly wrong.

However, $\dfrac{15}{3} = \dfrac{12+3}{3} = \dfrac{\cancel{3}(4+1)}{\cancel{3}} = 5$ is fine.

▸ $\dfrac{5x+25}{5} = \dfrac{\cancel{5}(x+5)}{\cancel{5}} = x+5$

▸ $\dfrac{3}{3x+9} = \dfrac{\cancel{3}}{\cancel{3}(x+3)} = \dfrac{1}{x+3}$

▸ $\dfrac{8x-16}{4x-8} = \dfrac{8(x-2)}{4(x-2)} = 2$

EXERCISE 5

1. Simplify the following:

(a) $\dfrac{x}{2} + \dfrac{1}{3}$

(b) $\dfrac{x}{3} - \dfrac{1}{5}$

(c) $\dfrac{x}{2} + \dfrac{x}{7}$

(d) $\dfrac{5x}{4} - \dfrac{2x}{3}$

(e) $x - \dfrac{x}{3}$

(f) $\dfrac{x}{4} - \dfrac{2x}{3} + 1$

(g) $\dfrac{2x}{3} - \dfrac{x+1}{2}$

(h) $\dfrac{x+1}{3} + \dfrac{x+4}{5}$

(i) $\dfrac{2x+1}{3} + \dfrac{5x+1}{12}$

(j) $\dfrac{x-1}{4} - \dfrac{2x+1}{6}$

(k) $\dfrac{3(x+2)}{4} - \dfrac{3x+1}{2}$

(l) $\dfrac{1}{x} + \dfrac{1}{x+1}$

(m) $\dfrac{3}{x+2} + \dfrac{2}{x+3}$

(n) $\dfrac{3}{2(x+1)} + \dfrac{2}{3(x+2)}$

(o) $\dfrac{5}{x+2} - \dfrac{2}{x-3}$

(p) $\dfrac{5}{2x-3} - \dfrac{1}{x}$

(q) $\dfrac{3}{5(x-1)} - \dfrac{1}{(2x+3)}$

(r) $\dfrac{x}{x+1} + \dfrac{x}{x-1}$

(s) $\dfrac{x+2}{x-2} - \dfrac{x-2}{x+2}$

(t) $\dfrac{3x-1}{3x+1} - \dfrac{3x+1}{3x-1}$

2. Simplify the following:

(a) $\dfrac{x}{5} \times \dfrac{17}{2}$

(b) $-\dfrac{2}{3} \times \dfrac{x}{2}$

(c) $\dfrac{x}{3} \times \dfrac{2}{3x}$

(d) $\dfrac{3}{2x} \times \dfrac{x}{6}$

(e) $-\dfrac{5}{7x} \times \dfrac{14x}{35}$

(f) $\dfrac{x}{5} \times \dfrac{x}{3}$

(g) $\dfrac{2x}{7} \times \dfrac{5x}{3}$

(h) $-\dfrac{3x}{5} \times -\dfrac{7x}{27}$

(i) $\dfrac{4x}{11} \times \dfrac{121x}{16}$

(j) $\dfrac{x+1}{5} \times \dfrac{x}{3}$

(k) $\dfrac{x+1}{3} \times \dfrac{x-1}{7}$

(l) $\dfrac{2x+1}{7} \times \dfrac{14}{x-1}$

(m) $\dfrac{3x+2}{12} \times \dfrac{24}{12x+8}$

(n) $\dfrac{-5x+7}{6-4x} \times \dfrac{9-6x}{21-15x}$

(o) $\dfrac{8x+4}{7} \times \dfrac{21x}{16x+8}$

(p) $\dfrac{x+1}{x-2} \times \dfrac{5x-10}{3x+3}$

(q) $\dfrac{2x+2}{2} \times \dfrac{6x-10}{5-3x} \times \dfrac{1}{x+1}$

(r) $\dfrac{7x-14}{(x+2)} \times \dfrac{3}{(x-2)}$

(s) $\dfrac{x-1}{5x+7} \times \dfrac{-25x-35}{3-3x}$

(t) $\dfrac{1-x}{5} \times \dfrac{5x+10}{x-1}$

4.3 Exponential expressions (powers)

KEY TERM

An exponential expression is an expression of the form a^p, $p \in \mathbb{R}$.

ACTIVITY 17

ACTION
Evaluting powers

OBJECTIVE
To simplify powers by multiplying brackets

You already know that $2^3 = 2 \times 2 \times 2$ and $y^4 = y \times y \times y \times y$, but what do $2^{\frac{1}{3}}$, $3^{\frac{2}{5}}$, $3^{-\frac{1}{2}}$ mean? These are all **exponential** expressions.

a is called the base of the expression.

p is called the power or the index or the exponent of the expression.

▸ $(3)^2 = 3 \times 3 = 9$

▸ $(-2)^3 = (-2) \times (-2) \times (-2) = -8$

▸ $\left(\dfrac{y}{2}\right)^4 = \dfrac{y}{2} \times \dfrac{y}{2} \times \dfrac{y}{2} \times \dfrac{y}{2} = \dfrac{y^4}{16}$

▸ $\left(-\dfrac{3}{2}\right)^3 = \left(-\dfrac{3}{2}\right) \times \left(-\dfrac{3}{2}\right) \times \left(-\dfrac{3}{2}\right) = -\dfrac{27}{8}$

▸ $\left(2\dfrac{1}{2}\right)^2 = \left(\dfrac{5}{2}\right)^2 = \left(\dfrac{5}{2}\right) \times \left(\dfrac{5}{2}\right) = \dfrac{25}{4}$

Rules of exponential expressions

1. The multiplication rule

ACTIVITY 18

ACTION
Understanding the multiplication rule for exponential expressions

OBJECTIVE
To understand that when numbers to the same base are multiplied, you add their powers

WORKED EXAMPLE

The multiplication rule for powers

$y^2 \times y^3 = y \times y \times y \times y \times y = y^5$

When you multiply two exponential expressions with the **same base**, you add the powers.

In general, $\boxed{a^p \times a^q = a^{p+q}}$

▸ $10^5 \times 10^3 = 10^8$
▸ $2^4 \times 2^7 = 2^{11}$
▸ $3^{\frac{1}{2}} \times 3^{\frac{1}{4}} = 3^{\frac{3}{4}}$
▸ $(a+2b)^7 \times (a+2b)^4 = (a+2b)^{11}$
▸ $x^{-7} \times x^{-5} = x^{-12}$

2. The division rule

ACTIVITY 19

ACTION
Understanding the division rule for exponentials

OBJECTIVE
To understand that when numbers to the same base are divided, you subtract their powers

WORKED EXAMPLE

The division rule for powers

$\dfrac{y^5}{y^3} = \dfrac{y \times y \times y \times y \times y}{y \times y \times y} = y^2$

When you divide exponential expressions with the **same base**, you subtract the power on the bottom from the power on the top.

In general: $\boxed{\dfrac{a^p}{a^q} = a^{p-q}}$

▸ $\dfrac{10^{23}}{10^{19}} = 10^4$
▸ $\dfrac{2^{3x}}{2^x} = 2^{2x}$

▸ $\dfrac{3^{\frac{3}{4}}}{3^{\frac{1}{2}}} = 3^{\frac{1}{4}}$
▸ $\dfrac{(a^2-2b)^8}{(a^2-2b)^5} = (a^2-2b)^3$
▸ $\dfrac{x^5}{x^{-3}} = x^{5-(-3)} = x^8$
▸ $\dfrac{7^{-2}}{7^{-3}} = 7^{-2-(-3)} = 7^1$

3. The one rule

WORKED EXAMPLE

The one rule for powers

$\dfrac{y^4}{y^4} = \dfrac{y \times y \times y \times y}{y \times y \times y \times y} = 1 = y^{4-4} = y^0$

$(\text{Anything})^0 = 1$

In general: $\boxed{a^0 = 1}$

▸ $2^0 = 1$
▸ $\left(\dfrac{1}{2}\right)^0 = 1$
▸ $(-3)^0 = 1$
▸ $(x^2)^0 = 1$

4. The power of a power rule

ACTIVITY 20

ACTION
Understanding the power of a power rule

OBJECTIVE
To understand that when numbers to a power are raised to a power, you multiply their powers

WORKED EXAMPLE Powers of powers

$(y^2)^3 = y^2 \times y^2 \times y^2 = y^6$

When you put an exponential expression to a power, you multiply the two powers.

In general: $(a^p)^q = a^{pq}$

- $(10^3)^5 = 10^{15}$
- $(2^4)^3 = 2^{12}$
- $(3^{\frac{1}{2}})^2 = 3^1$
- $(x^{-3})^{-2} = x^6$
- $(2^{2x})^{-3} = 2^{-6x}$

5. Powers of products and quotients

ACTIVITY 21

ACTION
Understanding powers of products and quotients

OBJECTIVE
To manipulate more complicated expressions raised to a power

WORKED EXAMPLE Powers of products and quotients

$(2y)^4 = 2y \times 2y \times 2y \times 2y = 2 \times 2 \times 2 \times 2 \times y \times y \times y \times y = 2^4 y^4$

$\left(\frac{y}{2}\right)^3 = \frac{y}{2} \times \frac{y}{2} \times \frac{y}{2} = \frac{y \times y \times y}{2 \times 2 \times 2} = \frac{y^3}{2^3}$

For products and quotients raised to a power, put each factor to the power.

In general: $(ab)^p = a^p b^p$ and $\left(\frac{a}{b}\right)^p = \frac{a^p}{b^p}$

- $\left(\frac{a^2}{b}\right)^3 = \frac{a^6}{b^3}$
- $\left(-\frac{2}{3}\right)^4 = \frac{(-2)^4}{(3)^4} = \frac{16}{81}$
- $\left(\frac{xy}{2z}\right)^4 = \frac{x^4 y^4}{2^4 z^4} = \frac{x^4 y^4}{16 z^4}$
- $\left(\frac{3x^{-2}}{4y^2}\right)^2 = \frac{3^2 \times x^{-4}}{4^2 y^4} = \frac{9x^{-4}}{16 y^4}$

WARNING

Be careful never to apply this rule to a sum of terms raised to a power.

$(a + b)^p \neq a^p + b^p$, except for $p = 1$.

$(a + b)^2 \neq a^2 + b^2$ because $(a + b)^2 = a^2 + 2ab + b^2$.

6. Working with negative powers

ACTIVITY 22

ACTION
Working with negative powers

OBJECTIVE
To understand how to work with negative powers and the procedure for turning them into positive powers

WORKED EXAMPLE Negative powers

Consider y^{-2}:

$$y^{-2} = \frac{y^{-2}}{1} = \frac{y^{-2}}{1} \times \frac{y^2}{y^2} = \frac{y^{-2} \times y^2}{1 \times y^2} = \frac{y^0}{y^2} = \frac{1}{y^2}$$

$$\therefore y^{-2} = \frac{1}{y^2}$$

▸ $3^{-2} = \frac{1}{3^2} = \frac{1}{9}$

Consider $\frac{1}{y^{-3}}$:

$$\frac{1}{y^{-3}} = \frac{1}{y^{-3}} \times \frac{y^3}{y^3} = \frac{1^3 \times y^3}{y^{-3} \times y^3} = \frac{y^3}{y^0} = \frac{y^3}{1} = y^3$$

▸ $\frac{1}{2^{-3}} = 2^3 = 8$

Therefore, if you have an exponential expression with a negative power, you can move the base with the negative power up or down to end up with the same base with the sign of the power changed.

ACTIVITY 23

ACTION
Working with fractional powers

OBJECTIVE
To follow the procedure for working with fractional powers step by step

In general: $\boxed{a^{-p} = \frac{1}{a^p}}$ and $\boxed{\frac{1}{a^{-p}} = a^p}$ ▸ $(-2)^{-3} = \frac{1}{(-2)^3} = \frac{1}{-8} = -\frac{1}{8}$

▸ $5^{-4} = \frac{1}{5^4} = \frac{1}{625}$

▸ $\frac{2^{-3}}{3^{-2}} = \frac{3^2}{2^3} = \frac{9}{8}$

▸ $\frac{4^{-1}}{5^2} = \frac{1}{5^2 \times 4^1} = \frac{1}{100}$

▸ $\frac{3x^{-2}}{zy^{-3}} = \frac{3y^3}{zx^2}$

▸ $(ab)^{-2} = a^{-2}b^{-2} = \frac{1}{a^2 b^2}$

Flipping trick: $\left(\frac{a}{b}\right)^{-p} = \frac{a^{-p}}{b^{-p}} = \frac{b^p}{a^p} = \left(\frac{b}{a}\right)^p$

▸ $\left(\frac{5}{4}\right)^{-2} = \left(\frac{4}{5}\right)^2 = \frac{4^2}{5^2} = \frac{16}{25}$

▸ $\left(-\frac{3}{2}\right)^{-3} = \left(-\frac{2}{3}\right)^3 = \frac{(-2)^3}{(3)^3} = -\frac{8}{27}$

▸ $\left(\frac{3x}{2y^2}\right)^{-3} = \left(\frac{2y^2}{3x}\right)^3 = \frac{2^3 y^6}{3^3 x^3} = \frac{8y^6}{27x^3}$

7. Non-whole number powers

What do $8^{\frac{2}{3}}$, $16^{\frac{1}{2}}$, $25^{-\frac{3}{2}}$ mean?

WORKED EXAMPLE Explaining fractional powers

Both of these statements are true: $2 \times 2 \times 2 = 8$
and $8^{\frac{1}{3}} \times 8^{\frac{1}{3}} \times 8^{\frac{1}{3}} = 8^1 = 8$.   [Add the powers.]

So, if you want to think of three identical numbers

that multiply to give 8, the answer is $8^{\frac{1}{3}}$ or 2.

Each of these numbers is known as the cube root of 8 or $\sqrt[3]{8}$ in symbols.

$\therefore \sqrt[3]{8} = 8^{\frac{1}{3}} = 2$

A fractional power is a root.

In general: $\boxed{a^{\frac{1}{q}} = \sqrt[q]{a}}$

▸ $16^{\frac{1}{4}} = \sqrt[4]{16} = 2$ [$\sqrt[4]{16}$ means the positive 4th root.]

▸ $(-27)^{\frac{1}{3}} = \sqrt[3]{-27} = -3$

What about other fractions?

$8^{\frac{2}{3}} = \left(8^{\frac{1}{3}}\right)^2 = 2^2 = 4$ or $8^{\frac{2}{3}} = (8^2)^{\frac{1}{3}} = (64)^{\frac{1}{3}} = \sqrt[3]{64} = 4.$

In general: $\boxed{a^{\frac{p}{q}} = \sqrt[q]{a^p} = (a^p)^{\frac{1}{q}} = \left(a^{\frac{1}{q}}\right)^p}$

The best way to evaluate $a^{\frac{p}{q}}$ is to evaluate the root before the power (do the q before the p).

▸ $16^{\frac{3}{4}} = \left(16^{\frac{1}{4}}\right)^3 = (2)^3 = 8$

▸ $64^{\frac{3}{2}} = \left(64^{\frac{1}{2}}\right)^3 = (8)^3 = 512$

▸ $27^{\frac{2}{3}} = \left(27^{\frac{1}{3}}\right)^2 = (3)^2 = 9$

EXAMPLE 8

(a) $\dfrac{8^{-\frac{2}{3}}}{4^{-\frac{1}{2}}}.$ (b) Simplify $\dfrac{(-5)^2 \times 25^{\frac{1}{2}}}{5^{-3} \times (25)^3}.$

(b) $\dfrac{(-5)^2 \times 25^{\frac{1}{2}}}{5^{-3} \times (25)^3} = \dfrac{25 \times 5^3 \times 25^{\frac{1}{2}}}{(25)^3}$ [Move 5^{-3} up.]

$\qquad = \dfrac{25 \times 125 \times 5}{25 \times 25 \times 25} = 1$

Solution

(a) $\dfrac{8^{-\frac{2}{3}}}{4^{-\frac{1}{2}}} = \dfrac{4^{\frac{1}{2}}}{8^{\frac{2}{3}}}$ [Get rid of negative powers first.]

$\qquad = \dfrac{2}{\left(8^{\frac{1}{3}}\right)^2} = \dfrac{2}{4} = \dfrac{1}{2}$

EXAMPLE 9

(a) Write $\dfrac{(3^2)^{-3} \times \sqrt{3} \times (3)^4}{(27)^{\frac{1}{3}} \times 9^{-\frac{3}{2}}}$ in the form 3^p, where $p > 0$.

(b) Write $\dfrac{a^5 \times a^{-3}}{(a^2)^{-4} \times (\sqrt{a})^3}$ in the form a^p, where $p > 0$.

Solution

(a) $\dfrac{(3^2)^{-3} \times \sqrt{3} \times (3)^4}{(27)^{\frac{1}{3}} \times 9^{-\frac{3}{2}}} = \dfrac{3^{-6} \times 3^{\frac{1}{2}} \times 3^4}{(3^3)^{\frac{1}{3}} \times (3^2)^{-\frac{3}{2}}}$

$\qquad = \dfrac{3^{-\frac{3}{2}}}{3^1 \times 3^{-3}}$

$\qquad = \dfrac{3^{-\frac{3}{2}}}{3^{-2}}$

$\qquad = 3^{-\frac{3}{2}+2}$

$\qquad = 3^{\frac{1}{2}}$

(b) $\dfrac{a^5 \times a^{-3}}{(a^2)^{-4} \times (\sqrt{a})^3} = \dfrac{a^5 \times a^{-3}}{a^{-8} \times \left(a^{\frac{1}{2}}\right)^3}$

$\qquad = \dfrac{a^5 \times a^8}{a^3 \times a^{\frac{3}{2}}}$

$\qquad = \dfrac{a^{13}}{a^{\frac{9}{2}}}$

$\qquad = a^{\frac{17}{2}}$

EXERCISE 6

1. Evaluate the following without using a calculator:

   (a) 2^2

   (b) 3^2

   (c) 4^2

   (d) 3^3

   (e) 2^5

   (f) 5^4

   (g) 10^8

   (h) 1^{2013}

   (i) $(-1)^4$

   (j) $(-1)^{21}$

   (k) $(-2)^4$

   (l) $(-3)^5$

   (m) $\left(\dfrac{1}{2}\right)^2$

   (n) $\left(\dfrac{2}{3}\right)^2$

   (o) $\left(\dfrac{4}{3}\right)^3$

   (p) $\left(-\dfrac{1}{2}\right)^3$

   (q) $\left(-\dfrac{4}{5}\right)^2$

   (r) $\left(3\dfrac{1}{2}\right)^2$

   (s) $\left(2\dfrac{3}{4}\right)^2$

   (t) $\left(-2\dfrac{1}{2}\right)^3$

2. Evaluate the following without using a calculator:

   (a) 2^{-1}

   (b) 3^{-2}

   (c) 4^{-3}

   (d) 5^{-2}

   (e) 2^{-4}

   (f) $(3 \cdot 6)^{-1}$

   (g) $\left(\dfrac{3}{4}\right)^{-1}$

   (h) $2^{-1} \times 3$

   (i) 2×3^{-1}

   (j) $\dfrac{2}{3^{-1}}$

   (k) $\dfrac{3^{-1}}{2}$

   (l) $\dfrac{1}{3^{-1} \times 2^{-1}}$

   (m) $(-8)^{-2}$

   (n) $(-3)^{-3}$

   (o) $\left(\dfrac{3}{2}\right)^{-3}$

3. Evaluate the following exactly:

   (a) $9^{\frac{3}{2}}$

   (b) $25^{\frac{1}{2}}$

   (c) $25^{\frac{3}{2}}$

   (d) $8^{\frac{4}{3}}$

   (e) $36^{-\frac{1}{2}}$

   (f) $64^{-\frac{1}{3}}$

   (g) $6 \times 36^{-\frac{1}{2}}$

   (h) $2 \times 16^{\frac{1}{2}}$

   (i) $6 \times 100^{-\frac{3}{2}}$

   (j) $4 \times 49^{\frac{1}{2}}$

   (k) $3 \times 4^{-\frac{1}{2}}$

   (l) $\left(\dfrac{1}{9}\right)^{\frac{1}{2}}$

   (m) $(100\,000\,000)^{\frac{3}{4}}$

   (n) $(-8)^{\frac{5}{3}}$

   (o) $100^{-\frac{1}{2}}$

   (p) $\left(\dfrac{4}{9}\right)^{-\frac{1}{2}}$

   (q) $\left(\dfrac{8}{27}\right)^{\frac{1}{3}}$

   (r) $\left(-\dfrac{8}{27}\right)^{\frac{1}{3}}$

   (s) $\left(-\dfrac{8}{27}\right)^{-\frac{1}{3}}$

   (t) 8^0

   (u) $\left(\dfrac{1}{27}\right)^{-\frac{1}{3}}$

   (v) $\left(-\dfrac{1}{27}\right)^{-\frac{1}{3}}$

   (w) $\left(2\dfrac{1}{4}\right)^{-\frac{1}{2}}$

   (x) $\left(\dfrac{25}{16}\right)^{-\frac{1}{2}}\left(\dfrac{3}{2}\right)^2$

4. (a) Write $8\sqrt{2}$ in the form 2^p, $p > 0$.

   (b) Write $\dfrac{27\sqrt{3}}{3}$ in the form 3^p, $p > 0$.

   (c) Write $\dfrac{4\sqrt{2}}{32}$ in the form $\dfrac{1}{2^p}$, $p > 0$.

   (d) Write $\dfrac{49\sqrt{7}}{\sqrt[3]{7}}$ in form 7^p, $p > 0$.

   (e) Write $\dfrac{125^{\frac{2}{3}} \times 5^2}{25 \times \sqrt{5}}$ in the form 5^p, $p > 0$.

5. Write the following in the form a^p or $\dfrac{1}{a^p}$, where $p \in \mathbb{R}$, $p > 0$:

   (a) $a^7 \times a^2$

   (b) $(a^7)^3$

   (c) $a^7 \times a^{-3}$

   (d) $\dfrac{a^7}{a^3}$

   (e) $\sqrt[3]{a}$

   (f) $a\sqrt{a}$

   (g) $\dfrac{a^{14}}{a^2}$

   (h) $\dfrac{a}{a^3}$

   (i) $\dfrac{a^2}{\sqrt{a}}$

   (j) $\dfrac{a^2}{a^{-3}}$

   (k) $\sqrt[3]{a^2}$

   (l) $\dfrac{\sqrt{a} \times (a^2)^3}{a^{-2} \times (a^3)^{-1}}$

   (m) $\dfrac{(a^{-2})^{\frac{1}{2}} \times (a^3)^{-\frac{1}{2}}}{\sqrt{a}}$

   (n) $\dfrac{\sqrt{a^3} \times (a^{-2})^{\frac{3}{2}}}{(a^{-2})^2 \times a^{-1}}$

6. Simplify the following, giving all answers with positive powers:

(a) $\dfrac{x^2 \times (xy)^2}{y}$

(b) $\dfrac{5x^3 \times 6x^4}{15x^2}$

(c) $\dfrac{28x^4}{7x^3}$

(d) $\dfrac{36x^3}{72x^5}$

(e) $\dfrac{42x^5}{7x^2 \times 3x^3}$

(f) $\dfrac{70x^3(xy)^4}{5xy \times 7xy^2}$

(g) $\dfrac{2^x \times 2^{3x}}{2^{2x}}$

(h) $\dfrac{x^4 \times 2^{5x}}{2^x \times x^3}$

(i) $\dfrac{(3xy)^2 \times 2xy}{9(x^2y)^3}$

(j) $\left(\dfrac{x^2y}{3z^3}\right)^4$

(k) $\dfrac{7y^2 \times 25y^2}{5xy^3 \times 14xy}$

(l) $\dfrac{(a+3b)^2(a+3b)^6}{(a+3b)^3}$

(m) $\dfrac{xyab^2}{abx^2y^2}$

(n) $\dfrac{a^{-2}}{2y^2}$

(o) $\dfrac{2a^2}{y^{-2}}$

(p) $\dfrac{25y^{-3}}{5y^{-2}}$

4.4 Surds

ACTIVITY 24

ACTION
Recognising surds

OBJECTIVE
To identify whether numbers are surds or rational numbers

KEY TERM

A **surd expression** is an expression involving square roots.

$\sqrt{2}$, $3\sqrt{2}$, $2 + \sqrt{2}$, $\sqrt{x}$, $\sqrt{3} + \sqrt{x}$, $\sqrt{x} + 3\sqrt{y}$ are all surd expressions.

TIP

Remember: $\sqrt{a} = a^{\frac{1}{2}}$

The rules of exponents apply to surds.

Simplifying surds

To simplify surds, you need two important results:

1. $\sqrt{ab} = (ab)^{\frac{1}{2}} = a^{\frac{1}{2}} b^{\frac{1}{2}} = \sqrt{a} \times \sqrt{b}$

2. $\sqrt{\dfrac{a}{b}} = \left(\dfrac{a}{b}\right)^{\frac{1}{2}} = \dfrac{a^{\frac{1}{2}}}{b^{\frac{1}{2}}} = \dfrac{\sqrt{a}}{\sqrt{b}}$

▸ $\sqrt{8} = \sqrt{4 \times 2} = \sqrt{4} \times \sqrt{2} = 2\sqrt{2}$

▸ $\sqrt{45} = \sqrt{9 \times 5} = \sqrt{9} \times \sqrt{5} = 3\sqrt{5}$

▸ $\sqrt{\dfrac{45}{16}} = \dfrac{\sqrt{45}}{\sqrt{16}} = \dfrac{3\sqrt{5}}{4}$

▸ $\sqrt{2\tfrac{1}{4}} = \sqrt{\dfrac{9}{4}} = \dfrac{\sqrt{9}}{\sqrt{4}} = \dfrac{3}{2}$

WARNING

Never put $\sqrt{a^2 + b^2} = a + b$.

ACTIVITY 25

ACTION
Simplifying surds

OBJECTIVE
To break surds down into their simplest form

Adding and subtracting surds

As usual, you can only add and subtract like terms.

You cannot simplify $\sqrt{2} + \sqrt{3}$ into a single surd,

but $2\sqrt{2} + 5\sqrt{2} + 7\sqrt{2} = 14\sqrt{2}$.   [Just as $2a + 5a + 7a = 14a$.]

▶ $3 + \sqrt{5} + 6 - 2\sqrt{5} + 5\sqrt{5} = 9 + 4\sqrt{5}$

▶ $2\sqrt{5} + \sqrt{45} - 3\sqrt{20}$

$$= 2\sqrt{5} + \sqrt{9 \times 5} - 3\sqrt{4 \times 5}$$

$$= 2\sqrt{5} + 3\sqrt{5} - 3 \times 2\sqrt{5}$$

$$= 2\sqrt{5} + 3\sqrt{5} - 6\sqrt{5}$$

$$= -\sqrt{5}$$

ACTIVITY 26

ACTION
Adding surds

OBJECTIVE
To combine surds into their simplest form

Multiplication of surds

To multiply out brackets with surds, multiply each term in one bracket by each term in the other bracket and combine like terms.

Remember: $\sqrt{a} \times \sqrt{b} = a^{\frac{1}{2}} \times b^{\frac{1}{2}} = (ab)^{\frac{1}{2}} = \sqrt{ab}$

▶ $2(\sqrt{3} + 4\sqrt{2}) = 2\sqrt{3} + 8\sqrt{2}$

▶ $(3 + \sqrt{2})(4 - 5\sqrt{2}) = 12 - 15\sqrt{2} + 4\sqrt{2} - 5\sqrt{4}$ $[\sqrt{2} \times \sqrt{2} = \sqrt{4}]$

$$= 12 - 11\sqrt{2} - 10$$

$$= 2 - 11\sqrt{2}$$

▶ $(\sqrt{3} + \sqrt{2})^2 = (\sqrt{3})^2 + 2(\sqrt{3})(\sqrt{2}) + (\sqrt{2})^2$

$$= 3 + 2\sqrt{6} + 2$$

$$= 5 + 2\sqrt{6}$$ [Perfect square]

▶ $(3\sqrt{2} - 5)(3\sqrt{2} + 5) = (3\sqrt{2})^2 - (5)^2 = 9 \times 2 - 25$

$$= 18 - 25 = -7$$ [Difference of two squares]

ACTIVITY 27

ACTION
Multiplying surds

OBJECTIVE
To multiply surds and to break them down to their simplest form

ACTIVITY 28

ACTION
Rationalising the denominators of surds

OBJECTIVE
To rationalise by multiplying above and below by a surd

Division (rationalising the denominator)

When you divide surds, the answer should never have a surd in the denominator. This process of getting rid of surds on the bottom is called rationalising the denominator.

$$\frac{3}{\sqrt{2}} = \frac{3}{\sqrt{2}} \times \frac{\sqrt{2}}{\sqrt{2}} = \frac{3\sqrt{2}}{2}$$

To rationalise a surd of the form $\frac{a}{\sqrt{b}}$, multiply above and below by $\sqrt{b}$.

▶ $\dfrac{\sqrt{5}}{\sqrt{7}} = \dfrac{\sqrt{5}}{\sqrt{7}} \times \dfrac{\sqrt{7}}{\sqrt{7}} = \dfrac{\sqrt{35}}{7}$

$$\blacktriangleright \quad \frac{4 + \sqrt{3}}{\sqrt{2}} = \frac{(4 + \sqrt{3})}{\sqrt{2}} \times \frac{\sqrt{2}}{\sqrt{2}} = \frac{4\sqrt{2} + \sqrt{6}}{2}$$

$$\blacktriangleright \quad \frac{1}{\sqrt{2}} = \frac{1}{\sqrt{2}} \times \frac{\sqrt{2}}{\sqrt{2}} = \frac{\sqrt{2}}{2}$$

$$\blacktriangleright \quad \frac{\sqrt{2} + 1}{\sqrt{3}} = \frac{(\sqrt{2} + 1)}{\sqrt{3}} \times \frac{\sqrt{3}}{\sqrt{3}} = \frac{\sqrt{6} + \sqrt{3}}{3}$$

EXERCISE 7

1. Write the following in their simplest form:

   (a) $\sqrt{12}$

   (b) $\sqrt{27}$

   (c) $\sqrt{50}$

   (d) $\sqrt{45}$

   (e) $\sqrt{1210}$

   (f) $\sqrt{75}$

   (g) $\sqrt{32}$

   (h) $\sqrt{98}$

   (i) $\sqrt{72}$

   (j) $\sqrt{512}$

   (k) $\sqrt{\dfrac{8}{9}}$

   (l) $\sqrt{\dfrac{18}{25}}$

   (m) $\sqrt{\dfrac{108}{36}}$

   (n) $\sqrt{\dfrac{147}{100}}$

   (o) $\sqrt{\dfrac{75}{36}}$

2. Simplify the following:

   (a) $\sqrt{11} - 2\sqrt{11} + 4\sqrt{11}$

   (b) $5 + 7\sqrt{3} - 9 + 8\sqrt{3}$

   (c) $x + \sqrt{y} - 3\sqrt{y} + 2x - 5\sqrt{y}$

   (d) $\sqrt{28} + \sqrt{63} - \sqrt{175}$

   (e) $\sqrt{125} - 2\sqrt{180} + \sqrt{245}$

   (f) $\sqrt{8} + \sqrt{12} + \sqrt{18} + \sqrt{27}$

   (g) $\sqrt{75} - 3\sqrt{48} + \sqrt{147}$

3. Multiply out and simplify the following:

   (a) $(\sqrt{2})^3$

   (b) $\sqrt{2} \times \sqrt{3}$

   (c) $2\sqrt{6} \times 5\sqrt{18}$

   (d) $\sqrt{6}(3\sqrt{2} + 2\sqrt{3} + \sqrt{6})$

   (e) $(\sqrt{3} + 1)^2$

   (f) $(\sqrt{3} - 1)(\sqrt{3} + 1)$

   (g) $\sqrt{ab}(a\sqrt{b} + b\sqrt{a})$

   (h) $(\sqrt{7} + \sqrt{13})^2$

   (i) $(\sqrt{7} + \sqrt{13})(\sqrt{7} - \sqrt{13})$

4. Rationalise the denominator in the following:

   (a) $\dfrac{1}{\sqrt{5}}$

   (b) $-\dfrac{1}{\sqrt{2}}$

   (c) $\dfrac{2}{\sqrt{3}}$

   (d) $\dfrac{4}{5\sqrt{2}}$

   (e) $\dfrac{-3}{2\sqrt{3}}$

   (f) $\dfrac{\sqrt{6}}{2\sqrt{7}}$

   (g) $\dfrac{x}{\sqrt{y}}$

   (h) $\dfrac{\sqrt{x}}{\sqrt{y}}$

5. If $x = \sqrt{3} + \sqrt{2}$ and $y = \sqrt{3} - \sqrt{2}$, find $x^2 + xy + y^2$.

6. In a random sample of 1000 Irishmen, 560 were married.

   The confidence interval for a population proportion at the 95% significance level is given by $\left(p - \dfrac{1}{\sqrt{n}}\right)\% - \left(p + \dfrac{1}{\sqrt{n}}\right)\%$, where p is the percentage of married men in the sample and n is the size of the sample.

   Find, correct to two decimal places:

   (a) p,

   (b) $\dfrac{1}{\sqrt{n}}$,

   (c) $p - \dfrac{1}{\sqrt{n}}$,

   (d) $p + \dfrac{1}{\sqrt{n}}$.

REVISION QUESTIONS

1. Joe is x years of age. His sister is two years older than him and his brother is three years older than his sister. If his parents' ages are both three times Joe's age, write down an expression for the sum of the ages of all the members of the family.

2. The altitude $|BD|$ of a triangle is one-third longer than its base.

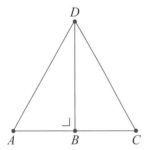

   If the length of the base is $(6x + 3)$ cm, find:

   (a) the length of the altitude,

   (b) the area in terms of x. Write your answer in the form $a(bx + c)^2$.

3. If x is a number, write down an expression for two-thirds of this number. If the resulting number is divided by $\frac{4}{9}$, write down an expression for the final number.

4. The area of the rectangle shown is $6x^2 + 25x + 24$.

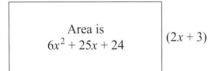

   Area is
   $6x^2 + 25x + 24$ $(2x + 3)$

   If the breadth is $2x + 3$:

   (a) write down an expression for the length,

   (b) find the length in terms of x by factorising $6x^2 + 25x + 24$,

   (c) find an expression for the perimeter, in terms of x.

5. The power of a lens is 1 divided by its focal length in metres (m).

   (a)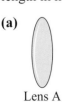
   Lens A

   The focal length of lens A is x m.

   Write down an expression for its power, in terms of x.

   (b)
   Lens B

   Lens B has a focal length $-(x + 2)$ m.

   Write down an expression for the power of lens B, in terms of x.

   (c)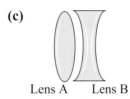
   Lens A   Lens B

   When lenses A and B are combined, the power of the combination is obtained by adding their powers together.

   Find an expression for the power of the combination as a single fraction, in terms of x.

   (d) If $x = \frac{1}{2}$, find the power of this combination as a fraction.

   If the focal length of the combination is 1 divided by the power, find this focal length as a fraction.

6. **(a)** A boy rows downstream for 2 km at a speed of $(x - 2)$ km/h from a point A to a point B. Write down an expression for the time of the journey in terms of x.

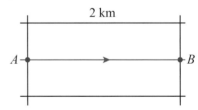

   2 km

   A B

   (b) A man rows the same journey at a speed of $(x + 2)$ km/h. Write down an expression for the time he takes.

   (c) Which person takes the shorter time? Why?

   (d) Write down an expression for the difference in the times. Give your answer as a single fraction in the form $\dfrac{a}{x^2 - b^2}$.

   (e) If $x = 12$, find this difference to the nearest second.

7. The effective area E of a chimney is given by the expression $E = A - \dfrac{\sqrt[3]{A^2}}{4}$, where A is the actual area in m^2.

(a) Write $\sqrt[3]{A^2}$ in two other ways.

(b) If $A = 8$, find $\sqrt[3]{A^2}$ exactly. Show your work.

(c) If $A = 1\cdot728$, find the effective area.

8. The fraction of a sample of a radioactive isotope left after a number of half-lifes is shown below.

(a) Copy and complete the table:

Number of half-lifes	Fraction left	Power of 2	% Left
1	$\frac{1}{2}$	$2^\square$	50
2	$\frac{1}{4}$	$2^\square$	
3	$\frac{1}{8}$	$2^\square$	
4	$\frac{1}{16}$	$2^\square$	
5	$\frac{1}{32}$	$2^\square$	

(b) If the initial mass of a radioactive isotope is 96 g, what mass is left after four half-lifes?

(c) What conclusion can you make about the fraction left after n half-lifes?

9. The volume of a cylinder is given by the expression $\pi r^2 h$.

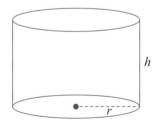

(a) Write down the volume of the cylinder A, in terms of π.

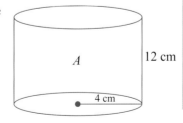

(b) Write down the volume of the cylinder B, in terms of π and x.

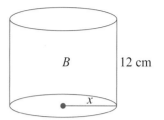

(c) If B is placed inside A, write down the volume of the space between the two cylinders, in terms of π and two linear factors.

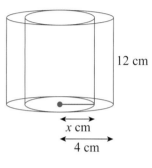

(d) A plastic cylinder has an external radius 4 cm and thickness 1 cm. Find the volume of the plastic in terms of π.

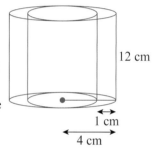

10. (a) The number of bacteria in a sample A after t minutes is given by 3200×2^t.

Find the number of bacteria initially in the sample.

(b) The number of bacteria in a sample B after t minutes is given by the expression 100×2^{2t}.

Find the number of bacteria initially in this sample.

(c) Find the ratio of the number of bacteria in sample B to that in sample A after t minutes in the form $\dfrac{2^t}{k}$. What is this ratio after:

(i) 2 minutes,

(ii) 5 minutes,

(iii) 10 minutes?

(d) Make a conclusion.

SUMMARY

1. Combining terms:

   Multiply out brackets term by term and combine like terms.

   Difference of two squares: $(a-b)(a+b) = (a)^2 - (b)^2$

   Perfect square: $(a+b)^2 = (a)^2 + 2(a)(b) + (b)^2$

2. Evaluating algebraic expressions:

   Put brackets around the variables and then substitute the given values.

3. Factorisation:

   Steps

   (a) Take out the HCF.

   (b) Factorise what is left by one of the following methods:

      (i) grouping

      (ii) trinomial

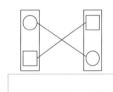

      (iii) difference of two squares

   $$(a)^2 - (b)^2 = [(a) - (b)][(a) + (b)]$$

4. Modelling

5. Linear and quadratic expression:

   Linear: $ax + b$

   Quadratic: $ax^2 + bx + c$

   (a) Multiplication: Linear × Linear = Quadratic

   (b) Division: $\dfrac{\text{Quadratic}}{\text{Linear}} = \dfrac{(\text{Linear})(\text{Linear})}{(\text{Linear})}$

6. Rational expressions:

   (a) Addition and subtraction: lowest common denominator

   (b) Multiplication: multiply the tops and multiply the bottoms (cancel)

7. Exponential expressions:

   (a) $a^p a^q = a^{p+q}$

   (b) $\dfrac{a^p}{a^q} = a^{p-q}$

   (c) $a^0 = 1$

   (d) $(a^p)^q = a^{pq}$

   (e) $a^{-p} = \dfrac{1}{a^p}$

   (f) $a^{\frac{1}{q}} = \sqrt[q]{a}$

   (g) $a^{\frac{p}{q}} = \sqrt[q]{a^p} = (\sqrt[q]{a})^p$

   (h) $(ab)^p = a^p b^p$

   (i) $\left(\dfrac{a}{b}\right)^p = \dfrac{a^p}{b^p}$

8. Surds:

   (a) Addition: add like terms

   $$2\sqrt{a} + 3\sqrt{a} = 5\sqrt{a}$$

   (b) Multiplication

   $$\sqrt{a} \times \sqrt{b} = \sqrt{ab}$$

   (c) Division

   $$\dfrac{\sqrt{a}}{\sqrt{b}} = \sqrt{\dfrac{a}{b}}$$

Algebraic Equations

Modelling a problem mathematically means expressing words in the form of equations that are true statements involving the unknown quantities. The golden rule of equations: Do unto one side of the equation as you do unto the other side.

Linear and Quadratic Equations

Learning Outcomes

- To solve linear equations.
- To solve quadratic equations by factorisation and using the quadratic formula.
- To model and solve word problems leading to linear and quadratic equations.

Introducing equations

An equation is a mathematical statement with two sides. An equation consists of a left-hand side (LHS) and a right-hand side (RHS) with an equality sign (=) between the sides.

Equation: LHS = RHS

Solving an equation means finding the values of the unknown quantity (variable) which make the statement true.

Example:
$$\underbrace{3x + 2}_{\text{LHS}} = \underbrace{5}_{\text{RHS}}$$

The value of 1 for x (the unknown value) makes this statement true. The value 1 for x that makes the statement true is known as a solution or root of the equation. The process of finding the solutions of an equation is known as solving the equation.

🎧 An equation behaves like a balance. Whatever you do to one side, you must do to the other side to maintain equilibrium.

When you solve an equation, you should substitute the values obtained back into the original equation to check whether or not they make the statement true. Only those values that satisfy the original equation are acceptable solutions (roots).

> **The basic technique for solving all equations:** Whatever operation you do to one side of an equation, you must do exactly the same operation to the other side of the equation.

5.1 Linear equations ⚡

ACTIVITY 1

ACTION
Interpreting linear equations

OBJECTIVE
To write linear equations in the form $y = ax + b$ and hence find the x and y intercepts

A linear equation is an equation that can be written in the form $ax^1 + b = 0$, where $a \neq 0$, b are fixed numbers.

a is called the coefficient of x.

b is called the constant term.

An equation is linear if the highest power of the variable in the equation is 1.

Method of solution

$$ax + b = 0$$
$$ax = -b$$
$$x = -\frac{b}{a}$$

There is one, and only one, solution (root) of a linear equation. Every linear equation has one root only.

▸ $3x + 2 = 0$
$$3x = -2$$
$$x = -\frac{2}{3}$$

WORKED EXAMPLE — Graphical solution of a linear equation

(a) $y = f(x) = ax + b$ is the equation of a straight line.

(b) $y = 0$ is the equation of the x-axis.

The solution of $ax + b = 0$ is the value of x at which the straight line crosses the x-axis. Its value is $x = -\frac{b}{a}$.

▸ Find where $y = 4x - 8$ crosses the x-axis:
$$4x - 8 = 0$$
$$4x = 8$$
$$x = \frac{8}{4} = 2$$

$y = 4x - 8$ crosses the x-axis at $(2, 0)$.

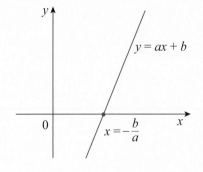

In general, finding the points at which a curve $y = f(x)$ crosses the x-axis means exactly the same thing as solving the equation $f(x) = 0$ or finding the roots of the equation $f(x) = 0$.

Steps for solving linear equations

1. Clear all fractions by multiplying all terms on each side by the common denominator of all terms.

2. Multiply out all brackets.

3. Tidy up each side by combining like terms.

4. Get the variables (usually x) on one side and the numbers on the other side.

5. Solve for the variable (usually x).

EXAMPLE 1

Solve the following for x:

(a) $2x - 7 = 11$

(b) $5x - 1 = 2x + 2$

(c) $7(5x + 2) + 4(8 - 7x) = 60$

(d) $\dfrac{x-8}{7} - \dfrac{x-3}{3} = \dfrac{5}{21}$

Solution

(a) $2x - 7 = 11$

$2x = 11 + 7$

$2x = 18$

$x = 9$ [This is the only solution of this equation.]

(b) $5x - 1 = 2x + 2$

$5x - 2x = 2 + 1$

$3x = 3$

$x = 1$

(c) $7(5x + 2) + 4(8 - 7x) = 60$

$35x + 14 + 32 - 28x = 60$

$7x + 46 = 60$

$7x = 60 - 46$

$7x = 14$

$x = 2$

(d) $\dfrac{x-8}{7} - \dfrac{x-3}{3} = \dfrac{5}{21}$

$\dfrac{(x-8)}{7} - \dfrac{(x-3)}{3} = \dfrac{(5)}{21}$ [Put brackets around terms on top before multiplying by 21.]

$\dfrac{21(x-8)}{7} - \dfrac{21(x-3)}{3} = \dfrac{21(5)}{21}$

$3(x - 8) - 7(x - 3) = (5)$

$3x - 24 - 7x + 21 = 5$

$-4x - 3 = 5$

$-4x = 5 + 3$

$-4x = 8$

$x = \dfrac{8}{-4}$

$x = -2$

Checking a solution

To show that a value is a solution of an equation, substitute it back into the original equation.

EXAMPLE 2

Show that 27 is a solution of $\dfrac{x+3}{2} - \dfrac{x-3}{4} = 9$.

Solution

LHS	RHS
$\dfrac{(x+3)}{2} - \dfrac{(x-3)}{4}$	9
$x = 27:\ \left(\dfrac{27+3}{2}\right) - \left(\dfrac{27-3}{4}\right)$	
$= 15 - 6$	
$= 9$	

LHS = RHS

$x = 27$ is a solution.

EXAMPLE 3

Investigate if $g = \frac{1}{2}$ is a solution of $\dfrac{2g-2}{4} - \dfrac{g}{4} = 1$.

Solution

LHS	RHS
$\dfrac{(2g-2)}{4} - \dfrac{(g)}{4}$	1
$g = \frac{1}{2}:\ \dfrac{(2(\frac{1}{2})-2)}{4} - \dfrac{(\frac{1}{2})}{4}$	
$= -\dfrac{1}{4} - \dfrac{1}{8}$	
$= -\dfrac{3}{8}$	

LHS ≠ RHS. It is not a solution.

ACTIVITY 2

ACTION
Learning techniques for modelling linear problems

OBJECTIVE
To learn some basic techniques to aid the modelling of linear problems

EXAMPLE 4

Find $k \in \mathbb{R}$, if $x = 1$ is a solution of $2(kx - 2) - 5(2x - 1) = -3$.

Solution

Substituting $x = 1$ into $2(kx - 2) - 5(2x - 1) - 3$ gives:

$$2(k - 2) - 5(1) = -3$$
$$2k - 4 - 5 = -3$$
$$2k = 6$$
$$k = 3$$

Mathematical modelling (word problems)

WORKED EXAMPLE Modelling a linear problem

A pipe 55 cm in length is cut into three pieces: a long piece, a short piece and an intermediate-length piece. The short piece is 20 cm shorter than the long piece. The long piece is twice as long as the intermediate piece. What are the lengths of all three pieces?

This is an example of a mathematical problem that is stated in words (a word problem). Mathematical modelling is the technique of translating these words into a mathematical equation and hence solving it.

1. Read the problem carefully and draw a diagram, if appropriate.

2. Assign a variable to one of the quantities to be found and hence assign variables to the other quantities.

   Let x = length of the intermediate piece

Long	Intermediate	Short
$2x$	x	$(2x - 20)$

3. Translate the word problem into an equation:

   $2x + x + (2x - 20) = 55$ [All of the pieces add up to the total length.]

4. Solve the equation:

   $$2x + x + 2x - 20 = 55$$
   $$5x - 20 = 55$$
   $$5x = 75$$
   $$x = 15$$

5. List all answers:

Long	Intermediate	Short
30 cm	15 cm	10 cm

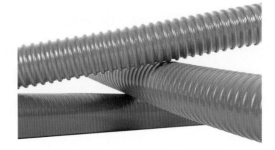

EXAMPLE 5

Four consecutive integers add to –38.
What are they?

Solution

1. Consecutive integers mean adding 1 to one of them gives the next one.

2. Let x = smallest integer.

   The four consecutive integers are:
   (x), $(x + 1)$, $(x + 2)$, $(x + 3)$.

3. $x + (x + 1) + (x + 2) + (x + 3) = -38$
   [They add to –38.]

4. $x + x + 1 + x + 2 + x + 3 = -38$
   $$4x + 6 = -38$$
   $$4x = -44$$
   $$x = -11$$

5. The integers are –11, –10, –9, –8.

EXAMPLE 6

Part of €3000 was invested at 6% per annum (p.a.) and the remainder was invested at 5% per annum. If the total interest earned at the end of the first year was €167, find the amount invested at each rate.

Solution

1. $6\% = 0·06 = \dfrac{6}{100}$

   $5\% = 0·05 = \dfrac{5}{100}$

2. Let x = amount invested at 6%
   $(3000 - x)$ = amount invested at 5%

3. $(x \times 0·06) + (3000 - x) \times 0·05 = 167$

4. $0·06x + 150 - 0·05x = 167$
   $$0·01x = 17$$
   $$x = \frac{17}{0·01}$$
   $$x = €1700$$

5. €1700 at 6% p.a.
   €1300 at 5% p.a.

EXAMPLE 7

Eimear wants to get an A1 mark as an average for four Maths tests. To do this, her average mark must be 90 or more. In her first three tests, she scored 86, 91 and 94, respectively. What is the lowest mark she can get on the final test to get an A1 average?

Solution

1. Her total marks over four tests must be at least 360.

2. Let x = mark in the final test

3. $x + 86 + 91 + 94 = 360$

4. $x + 271 = 360$
   $$x = 89$$

5. The lowest mark is 89.

EXERCISE 1

Solve the following equations:

1. (a) $x + 3 = 12$
    (b) $3 - x = 7$
    (c) $3x - 9 = -3$
    (d) $10x - 25 = 5$
    (e) $4x + 1 = 2x + 7$
    (f) $7x - 1 = 2x + 14$
    (g) $x + 4 = 4x + 10$
    (h) $-3x + 5 = -7x + 11$
    (i) $11 - 3x = -2x + 9$
    (j) $4x - 7 = -7x + 4$

2. (a) $3(2x - 1) = -15$
    (b) $-2(y + 7) = 0$
    (c) $6(1 - 3z) = -12$
    (d) $5(x - 3) - 2(7x - 4) = 43$
    (e) $5(3 - 2p) - 4(1 - 2p) = 12$
    (f) $5 - 4(x - 3) = x - 2(x - 1)$

(g) $0{\cdot}2(4 + 2f) - 0{\cdot}1(f + 2) = 2$

(h) $2\left(x - \frac{3}{2}\right) - 6x = 3(x - 12) - 23$

(i) $4 - 2\left(3x - \frac{7}{2}\right) = 3\left(2x - \frac{2}{3}\right) - 2\left(\frac{1}{2} - x\right)$

(j) $3x - 2(x + 1) = -4(x - 2) - (1 - x)$

3. **(a)** $\dfrac{x}{2} = 1$ **(f)** $\dfrac{x}{2} + 3 = 5$

   (b) $\dfrac{1}{6x} = -\dfrac{2}{3}$ **(g)** $x - 6 = \dfrac{3x}{4} - 2$

   (c) $\frac{1}{2}(x + 2) = 8$ **(h)** $\dfrac{x}{2} + 3 = \dfrac{x}{4} + 5$

   (d) $\dfrac{x + 3}{2} = 5$ **(i)** $\dfrac{x}{2} + \dfrac{x}{3} = \dfrac{5}{2}$

   (e) $\frac{1}{3}(x - 4) = 1$ **(j)** $\dfrac{3x}{4} - \dfrac{1}{2} = \dfrac{5x}{8}$

4. **(a)** $\dfrac{x - 8}{7} + \dfrac{x - 3}{3} = \dfrac{5}{21}$

   (b) $\dfrac{x + 2}{4} + \dfrac{x - 3}{2} = \dfrac{1}{2}$

   (c) $\dfrac{2x + 7}{3} - 5 = \dfrac{x - 3}{2}$

   (d) $\dfrac{x + 3}{2} + \dfrac{2(2 - x)}{3} = \dfrac{3x + 1}{4} - 2$

   (e) $\frac{3}{2}(x - 1) - \frac{1}{4}(x - 19) = \frac{2}{3}(x + 2)$

   (f) $\dfrac{2(x - 2)}{5} - 2(x - 2) = \dfrac{4(1 - 2x)}{3}$

5. **(a)** Show that $x = 2$ is not a solution of
$\dfrac{x + 4}{2} + x = 0$.

   (b) Show that $x = 5$ is a solution of the
equation $\dfrac{x}{2} + \dfrac{2x - 1}{6} = 4$.

   (c) Find k, if $x = 1$ is a solution of
$\dfrac{kx + 3}{4} - \dfrac{kx + 2}{3} = \dfrac{1}{2}$.

   (d) Investigate if $x = 1 - \sqrt{2}$ is a solution of
$x(1 + \sqrt{2}) = -1$.

6. Solve the following:

   (a) A piece of rope, 92 cm long, is cut into
two pieces so that the longest piece is
three times the length of the shorter piece.
How long are the two pieces?

(b) The ratio of the length to breadth of a
rectangle is 5:3. If the perimeter is 44 m,
find the length, breadth and area of the
rectangle.

(c) A ribbon, 60 cm long, is cut into three
pieces such that each piece is 5 cm longer
than the next piece. Find the length of
each piece.

(d) The sum of two numbers is 20. If the
difference between the bigger number
and half the smaller number is 8, find the
numbers.

(e) The sum of three consecutive numbers
is 48. Find the numbers.

(f) If Sandra is two years older than Anna and
the sum of half of Sandra's age and one-third
of Anna's age is 11, what is the age of each
girl?

(g) Polly and her **twin** brother will have a
total age of 38 in four years' time. What
are their present ages?

(h) Of 25 plants purchased, some cost €1·50
each and some cost €1 each. If the total
cost was €33, how many of each was
purchased?

(i) An electricity supply company has a fixed
charge of €42 for every two months and
9·5c per unit of electricity used. If the
Wilson family got a bill of €76·20 for
the last two months, how many units of
electricity did they use?

(j) The average of five consecutive natural
numbers is 9. What are they?

(k) A car covers part of a 100 km journey at 60
km/h and the remainder at 80 km/h. If the
total time for the journey was 1 hr 20 min,
find the distance travelled at 80 km/h.

(l) Josh deposits €10 per week in a bank
after an initial deposit of €500. His
brother Noah deposits €6 per week after
an initial deposit of €980. If they made
their initial deposits at the same time,
after how many weeks will they have the
same amount of money in their accounts?

(m) The difference between half a number and one-third of the same number is 69. What is the number?

(n) A man is twice as old as his son now. If he was three times as old as his son 10 years ago, how old is each now?

5.2 Quadratic equations

A quadratic equation is an equation that can be written in the form $ax^2 + bx + c = 0$, where a, b, c are fixed real numbers and $a \neq 0$.

a is called the coefficient of x^2 and must not be zero. (Why?)

b is called the coefficient of x.

c is called the constant term.

If the highest power of the variable in an equation is 2, the equation is a quadratic equation.

Methods of solution

There are two methods of solving quadratic equations:

1. Factorisation
2. The quadratic formula

1. Factorisation

Factorisation is the fastest way of solving quadratic equations. However, it does not always work. It depends on a fundamental idea in mathematics called the zero factor property, which states that if $pq = 0$, then $p = 0$ or $q = 0$, or both are equal to zero.

WORKED EXAMPLE Solving a quadratic by factorisation

Solve $6x^2 - x - 2 = 0$. This is a sum of three terms. Convert it into a product of two linear factors:

$(3x - 2)(2x + 1) = 0$
$\quad\ p \qquad\quad q$

By the zero factor property:

$3x - 2 = 0 \quad or \quad 2x + 1 = 0$

$\qquad 3x = 2 \qquad\qquad 2x = -1$

$\qquad\ x = \frac{2}{3} \qquad\qquad\ x = -\frac{1}{2}$

1. These are the solutions or roots of the equation $6x^2 - x - 2 = 0$. They are the **only** numbers in the universe for which $6x^2 - x - 2 = 0$.

2. They are the x co-ordinates of the points at which the curve $y = 6x^2 - x - 2$ crosses the x-axis.

3. You can check your solution by substituting them back into the LHS of the original expression:

LHS	RHS
$6(x)^2 \ (x) \ 2$	
$x = \frac{2}{3}$: $6\left(\frac{2}{3}\right)^2 - \left(\frac{2}{3}\right) - 2 = 0$	0
$x = -\frac{1}{2}$: $6\left(-\frac{1}{2}\right)^2 - \left(-\frac{1}{2}\right) - 2 = 0$	0

Summary of the process (Equation, Factors, Roots):

Equation: $6x^2 - x - 2 = 0$

Factors: $(3x - 2)(2x + 1) = 0$

Roots: $\frac{2}{3}, -\frac{1}{2}$

EXAMPLE 8

Solve the following:

(a) $x^2 - 5x = 0$ (b) $6x^2 + 27x - 15 = 0$

Solution

(a) $x^2 - 5x = 0$ [Always take out a HCF first, if there is one.]

$x(x - 5) = 0$

$x = 0$ | $x - 5 = 0$

$x = 5$

$x = 0, 5$

(b) $6x^2 + 27x - 15 = 0$

$3(2x^2 + 9x - 5) = 0$

$2x^2 + 9x - 5 = 0$

$(2x - 1)(x + 5) = 0$

$2x - 1 = 0$ | $x + 5 = 0$

$x = \frac{1}{2}$ | $x = -5$

$x = \frac{1}{2}, -5$

EXAMPLE 9

A variable current I in amps in an electric circuit after t seconds is given by $I = t^2 - 12t + 25$.

Find the times at which the current is 5 amps.

Solution

$I = t^2 - 12t + 25$

$I = 5$: $t^2 - 12t + 25 = 5$

Equation: $t^2 - 12t + 20 = 0$

Factors: $(t - 2)(t - 10) = 0$

Roots: $t - 2 = 0$ | $t - 10 = 0$
$t = 2$ | $t = 10$

Therefore, the current is 5 amps after 2 seconds and 10 seconds.

EXAMPLE 10

If $g = -3$ is a solution of the quadratic equation $kg^2 - 2kg - 60 = 0$, find $k \in \mathbb{R}$.

Solution

$kg^2 - 2kg - 60 = 0$

Since $g = -3$ is a solution of the equation, when you substitute in this value, it makes the equation true.

$k(g)^2 - 2k(g) - 60 = 0$

$g = -3$: $k(-3)^2 - 2k(-3) - 60 = 0$
$9k + 6k - 60 = 0$
$15k = 60$
$k = 4$

ACTIVITY 3

ACTION
Using the quadratic formula

OBJECTIVE
To practise using the quadratic formula by solving a number of equations

2. The quadratic formula (magic formula)

It is impossible to solve $x^2 - 2x - 2 = 0$ by factorisation as it does not factorise obviously. The quadratic formula can be used to solve all quadratic equations whether they can be factorised or not.

It states: The solutions (roots) of the quadratic equation $ax^2 + bx + c = 0$,

where a, b, c are constants and $a \neq 0$, are given by:

$$x = \frac{-b \pm \sqrt{b^2 - 4ac}}{2a}$$

EXAMPLE 11

Solve $x^2 - 2x - 2 = 0$.

Solution

$1x^2 - 2x - 2 = 0$

$a = 1, b = -2, c = -2$

$$x = \frac{-(-2) \pm \sqrt{(-2)^2 - 4(1)(-2)}}{2(1)}$$

$$x = \frac{2 \pm \sqrt{4 + 8}}{2}$$

$$x = \frac{2 \pm \sqrt{12}}{2}$$

$x = 1 + \sqrt{3}, 1 - \sqrt{3}$ [Using a calculator.]

The two roots of the equation $x^2 - 2x - 2 = 0$ are $1 + \sqrt{3}, 1 - \sqrt{3}$.

These are both irrational numbers.

EXAMPLE 12

The height h in metres of a ball thrown up into the air at a certain speed after t seconds is given by $h = 14t - 4 \cdot 9t^2$. Find the times at which the height of the ball is 5 m, correct to one decimal place.

Solution

$h = 14t - 4 \cdot 9t^2$

$h = 5$: $14t - 4 \cdot 9t^2 = 5$

$4 \cdot 9t^2 - 14t + 5 = 0$

$a = 4 \cdot 9, b = -14, c = 5$

$$t = \frac{-(-14) \pm \sqrt{(-14)^2 - 4(4 \cdot 9)(5)}}{2(4 \cdot 9)}$$

$$t = \frac{14 \pm \sqrt{98}}{9 \cdot 8}$$

$t = 0 \cdot 4$ s and $t = 2 \cdot 4$ s.

What do these two answers mean?

Properties of the quadratic formula

$$x = \frac{-b \pm \sqrt{b^2 - 4ac}}{2a}$$

The quantity $(b^2 - 4ac)$ under the square root is known as the **discriminant** because it discriminates between different types of roots.

1. If $(b^2 - 4ac) > 0$, you always get two **different**, real roots.
2. If $(b^2 - 4ac) = 0$, you always get two **equal**, real roots.
3. If $(b^2 - 4ac) < 0$, you get **no** real roots.

WORKED EXAMPLE

Exploring the roots of quadratics

1. If $(b^2 - 4ac) > 0$, you always get two **different**, real roots.

   Consider the equation: $2x^2 - 7x + 4 = 0$

   $a = 2$, $b = -7$, $c = 4$

   $\therefore (b^2 - 4ac) = (-7)^2 - 4(2)(4) = 49 - 32 = 17 > 0$

   This means when you solve this equation, you should get two **different** roots.

   These are: $x = \dfrac{7 \pm \sqrt{17}}{4} = 0.72, 2.78$

2. If $(b^2 - 4ac) = 0$, you always get two **equal**, real roots.

   Consider the equation: $4x^2 - 12x + 9 = 0$

   $a = 4$, $b = -12$, $c = 9$

   $\therefore (b^2 - 4ac) = (-12)^2 - 4(4)(9) = 144 - 144 = 0$

   This means that when you solve this equation, you should get two **equal** roots.

   They are: $x = \dfrac{12 \pm \sqrt{0}}{2(4)} = 1.5, 1.5$

   In this case, the quadratic is a perfect square because:

   $4x^2 - 12x + 9$

   $= (2x - 3)(2x - 3)$

   $= (2x - 3)^2$

   Its two factors are identical.

3. If $(b^2 - 4ac) < 0$, you get **no** real roots.

   Consider the equation: $x^2 - 2x + 2 = 0$

   $a = 1$, $b = -2$, $c = 2$

   $\therefore (b^2 - 4ac) = (-2)^2 - 4(1)(2) = -4 < 0$

   The quadratic formula gives $x = \dfrac{2 \pm \sqrt{-4}}{2}$.

   The calculator gives an error reading.

   There are no real solutions.

Graphical solutions of quadratic equations

$y = ax^2 + bx + c$ is the equation of the quadratic function. The general shape of the graph of such a function is either:

$a > 0$
CUP

or

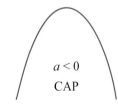

$a < 0$
CAP

This general shape is known as a **parabola**. $y = 0$ is the equation of the x-axis. Therefore, the solutions of $ax^2 + bx + c = 0$ are the values of x at which the parabola crosses the x-axis.

EXAMPLE 13

Find the points at which the curve $y = 3x^2 - 5x + 1$ crosses the x-axis. Give your answers correct to two decimal places. Draw a rough sketch of its graph.

Solution

$y = 3x^2 - 5x + 1$

x-axis: It crosses the x-axis when $y = 0$:

$$3x^2 - 5x + 1 = 0$$

$$a = 3, b = -5, c = 1$$

$$x = \frac{5 \pm \sqrt{(-5)^2 - 4(3)(1)}}{2(3)}$$

$$x = \frac{5 \pm \sqrt{13}}{6} = 0{\cdot}23, \ 1{\cdot}43$$

The curve crosses the x-axis at:
$(0{\cdot}23, 0)$, $(1{\cdot}43, 0)$

Rough sketch: $a > 0 \Rightarrow \cup$ is the shape.

y-axis: It crosses the y-axis when $x = 0$:
$x = 0 \Rightarrow y = 0 - 0 + 1 = 1$

$(0, 1)$ is the y-intercept.

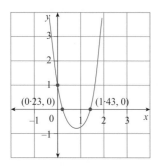

EXAMPLE 14

The curve shown has an equation $y = x^2 + x - 12$. Find the co-ordinates of the points U, V and W.

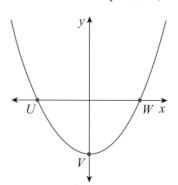

Solution

$y = x^2 + x - 12$

x-axis

$y = 0$: $x^2 + x - 12 = 0$

$(x - 3)(x + 4) = 0$

$x = -4, \ 3$

$U(-4, 0), \ W(3, 0)$

y-axis

$x = 0$: $y = 0^2 + 0 - 12 = -12$

$V(0, -12)$

EXAMPLE 15

A tunnel in the shape of a parabola is described by the equation $y = -x^2 + 11x - 21{\cdot}25$, where x is in metres. Find $|SL|$, the maximum width of the tunnel.

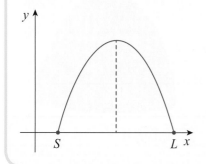

Solution

S and L are the points where the curve crosses the x-axis.

$$-x^2 + 11x - 21{\cdot}25 = 0$$

$$a = -1, b = 11, c = -21{\cdot}25$$

$$x = \frac{-11 \pm \sqrt{(11)^2 - 4(-1)(-21{\cdot}25)}}{2(-1)} = 2{\cdot}5, \ 8{\cdot}5$$

$S(2{\cdot}5, 0), \ L(8{\cdot}5, 0)$

$|SL| = 8{\cdot}5 - 2{\cdot}5 = 6$ m

Finding the quadratic equation from its roots (working backwards)

WORKED EXAMPLE | Finding a quadratic from its roots

Given the equation $12x^2 + x - 6 = 0$, the roots can be found as follows:

Equation: $12x^2 + x - 6 = 0$

Factors: $(3x - 2)(4x + 3) = 0$

Roots: $x = \frac{2}{3}$, $x = -\frac{3}{4}$

The equation can be found from the roots by reversing the process.

Given the roots $x = -\frac{3}{5}$, $x = \frac{4}{3}$ of a quadratic equation, the equation can be found as follows:

Roots: $x = -\frac{3}{5}$ | $x = \frac{4}{3}$

$5x = -3$ | $3x = 4$

$5x + 3 = 0$ | $3x - 4 = 0$

Factors: $(5x + 3)(3x - 4) = 0$

Equation: $15x^2 - 11x - 12 = 0$

In general: If $\dfrac{q}{p}$ and $\dfrac{r}{s}$ are the roots of a quadratic equation, the equation is $(px - q)(sx - r) = 0$.

EXAMPLE 16

Find the quadratic equation with roots:

(a) $-2, -3$ **(b)** $\frac{1}{2}, \frac{1}{3}$

Solution

(a) Roots: $x = -2$, $x = -3$

Factors: $(x + 2)(x + 3) = 0$

Equation: $x^2 + 5x + 6 = 0$

(b) Roots: $x = \frac{1}{2}$, $x = \frac{1}{3}$

Factors: $(2x - 1)(3x - 1)$

Equation: $6x^2 - 5x + 1 = 0$

Trick: There is a trick for doing this reverse process all in one go and it makes harder questions much simpler.

> A quadratic equation can be written as $x^2 - Sx + P = 0$, where S is the sum of the roots and P is the product of the roots.

Example: Roots: 2, 5

$S = 2 + 5 = 7 =$ sum of the roots

$P = 2 \times 5 = 10 =$ product of the roots

Equation: $x^2 - 7x + 10 = 0$

Steps for solving quadratic equations

1. Factorise all denominators.
2. Multiply all terms by the lowest common denominator (LCD).
3. Multiply out all brackets.
4. Get all terms on one side in the form $ax^2 + bx + c = 0$.
5. Take out the highest common factor (HCF).
6. Solve by factorisation or by using the quadratic formula.
7. Check your solutions.

EXAMPLE 17

Solve $\dfrac{3}{x-2} - \dfrac{1}{x} = \dfrac{5}{4}$.

Solution

$\dfrac{3}{(x-2)} - \dfrac{1}{(x)} = \dfrac{5}{4}$ [Multiply across by LCD: $4x(x-2)$]

$\dfrac{3(4)(x)(x-2)}{(x-2)} - \dfrac{(4)(x)(x-2)}{x} = \dfrac{5(4)(x)(x-2)}{4}$

$3(4)(x) - 4(x-2) = 5x(x-2)$

$12x - 4x + 8 = 5x^2 - 10x$

$8x + 8 = 5x^2 - 10x$

$5x^2 - 18x - 8 = 0$

$(5x + 2)(x - 4) = 0$

$x = -\dfrac{2}{5},\ 4$

Check:

	LHS	RHS
$x = -\dfrac{2}{5}:$	$\dfrac{3}{-\frac{2}{5}-2} - \dfrac{1}{-\frac{2}{5}} = \dfrac{5}{4}$	$\dfrac{5}{4}$
$x = 4:$	$\dfrac{3}{4-2} - \dfrac{1}{4} = \dfrac{5}{4}$	$\dfrac{5}{4}$

Using quadratics to solve other equations

The equations: $3x^2 + 5x - 1 = 0$, $3g^2 + 5g - 1 = 0$ and $3(\text{yoke})^2 + 5(\text{yoke}) - 1 = 0$ all have the same solutions for **their** variable because they have the same coefficients:

$a = 3,\ b = 5,\ c = -1$

$$\begin{matrix} x \\ g \\ \text{yoke} \end{matrix} = \left\{ \dfrac{-5 \pm \sqrt{(5)^2 - 4(3)(-1)}}{6} = \dfrac{-5 \pm \sqrt{37}}{6} \right.$$

EXAMPLE 18

(a) Solve $x^2 + 3x - 54 = 0$.

(b) Hence, solve $\left(t + \dfrac{8}{t}\right)^2 + 3\left(t + \dfrac{8}{t}\right) - 54 = 0$ for $t \neq 0$.

Solution

These two equations have the same coefficients: $a = 1$, $b = 3$, $c = -54$. Hence, they have the same solutions for their variable.

(a) $x^2 + 3x - 54 = 0$

$(x - 6)(x + 9) = 0$

$x = 6, -9$

(b)

$t + \dfrac{8}{t} = 6$	$t + \dfrac{8}{t} = -9$
$t^2 + 8 = 6t$	$t^2 + 8 = -9t$
$t^2 - 6t + 8 = 0$	$t^2 + 9t + 8 = 0$
$(t - 4)(t - 2) = 0$	$(t + 8)(t + 1) = 0$
$t = 4, 2$	$t = -8, -1$

The solutions are: $-8, -1, 2, 4$

ACTIVITY 4

ACTION
Using techniques for modelling quadratic problems

OBJECTIVE
To learn some basic techniques to aid the modelling of quadratic problems and hence solve them

Steps for mathematical modelling (word problems)

The steps used for modelling problems leading to quadratic equations are the same used for modelling problems leading to linear equations.

1. Read the problem carefully and draw a diagram, if appropriate.
2. Assign a variable to one of the quantities to be found and hence assign variables to the other quantities.
3. Translate the word problem into an equation.
4. Solve the equation.
5. List all answers.

EXAMPLE 19

The perimeter of a rectangular garden is 36 m. If its area is 72 m², find the length and breadth of the garden.

Solution

1. Area = Length × Breadth

$A = 72$ b

l

2. Let l = length of the garden

$l + b = 18$

$b = (18 - l)$

3. $A = l \times b$

$A = l(18 - l) = 72$

4. $18l - l^2 = 72$

$l^2 - 18l + 72 = 0$

$(l - 6)(l - 12) = 0$

$\therefore l = 6, 12$

5. $l = 6$ | $l = 12$

     $b = 12$ | $b = 6$

Answer: 12 m and 6 m

EXAMPLE 20

A rectangular metal frame has an area of metal of 76 cm² as a border. If the dimensions of the glass on the inside of the frame are 10 cm × 5 cm, find the uniform width of the frame.

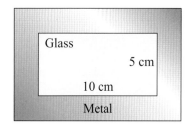

Glass

5 cm

10 cm

Metal

Solution

1. The area A of the metal region = 76 cm^2

2. Let x = width of the frame

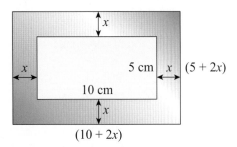

3. Metal area A = area of frame – area of glass

$A = (10 + 2x)(5 + 2x) - 10 \times 5$

$76 = 4x^2 + 30x$

4. $4x^2 + 30x = 76$

$4x^2 + 30x - 76 = 0$

$2x^2 + 15x - 38 = 0$

$(2x + 19)(x - 2) = 0$

$2x + 19 = 0 \qquad\qquad x - 2 = 0$

$x = -\dfrac{19}{2} \qquad\qquad x = 2 \text{ cm}$

[Reject this solution as you cannot have a negative width.]

Answer: The width of the metal frame is 2 cm.

EXAMPLE 21

The profit P in euro per week of a local newspaper is given by $P = -0.0025x^2 + 10x - 6000$, $0 \le x \le 2500$, where x is the number of newspapers sold per week.

Find:

(a) the break-even point (the value of x for which there is no profit),

(b) the number of newspapers that must be sold to give a profit of €2400 per week.

Solution

$P = -0.0025x^2 + 10x - 6000$

(a) Break-even point:

$\mathbf{P = 0:} \quad -0.0025x^2 + 10x - 6000 = 0$

$0.0025x^2 - 10x + 6000 = 0$

$$x = \frac{10 \pm \sqrt{(-10)^2 - 4(0.0025)(6000)}}{2(0.0025)}$$

$\therefore x = 3264.9, \ 735.09$

Reject 3264·9 because it is not in the domain.

Answer: 735 newspapers

(b) $\mathbf{P = €2400:} \quad -0.0025x^2 + 10x - 6000 = 2400$

$-0.0025x^2 + 10x - 8400 = 0$

$0.0025x^2 - 10x + 8400 = 0$

$$\therefore x = \frac{10 \pm \sqrt{(-10)^2 - 4(0.0025)(8400)}}{2(0.0025)} = 2800, \ 1200$$

Answer: 1200 [2800 is not in the domain.]

EXERCISE 2

1. Solve the following quadratic equations:

   (a) $(x + 2)(x - 1) = 0$

   (b) $(x - 3)(2x + 1) = 0$

   (c) $(2x - 7)^2 = 0$

   (d) $x(x - 3) = 0$

   (e) $2x(3x - 7) = 0$

   (f) $x^2 - 2x = 0$

   (g) $5x^2 - 15x = 0$

   (h) $x^2 - \dfrac{x}{9} = 0$

   (i) $3x^2 - 27 = 0$

   (j) $4x^2 - x = 0$

2. Solve the following quadratic equations by factorisation:

   (a) $x^2 - 25 = 0$

   (b) $3x^2 - 12 = 0$

   (c) $x^2 - 2x - 15 = 0$

   (d) $3x^2 + 24x - 99 = 0$

   (e) $2x^2 + 3x + 1 = 0$

   (f) $12x^2 - 23x + 10 = 0$

   (g) $3x^2 + 16x - 12 = 0$

   (h) $21x^2 + 3x - 24 = 0$

   (i) $-4x^2 + 20x - 24 = 0$

3. Simplify the following and solve the resulting quadratics by factorisation:

   (a) $x(x + 24) = 25$

   (b) $(x + 3)(x + 5) = 3 + x$

   (c) $2x - 2(x - 1) = x(x - 1)$

   (d) $5(2x^2 - 3x - 2) = 3(x^2 - 6x - 2)$

   (e) $(2x - 1)^2 - (x + 2)^2 = 0$

4. (a) If -2 is a root of the quadratic equation $kx^2 - 4x - 2 = 0$, find $k \in \mathbb{R}$.

   (b) Show that $1 + \sqrt{2}$ is a solution of the equation $x^2 - 2x - 1 = 0$.

   (c) Investigate if $-\dfrac{3}{2}$ is a solution of the equation $2x^2 + 5x + 3 = 0$.

5. Solve the following by using the quadratic formula, giving your answers as a rational or in surd form and then as decimals, correct to two decimal places:

   (a) $x^2 - 2x - 30 = 0$

   (b) $x^2 = 2x + 9$

   (c) $4x^2 - 19x + 1 = 0$

   (d) $6x^2 + x - 2 = 0$

   (e) $6x^2 - 15x - 18 = 0$

   (f) $3x^2 - 8x - 2 = 0$

   (g) $7x^2 + 8x = 2$

   (h) $(3x - 2)(2x + 4) - 4x^2 + 5 = 0$

   (i) $x^2 - 3 = 0$

   (j) $4x^2 - 32 = 0$

6. The graph of $y = ax^2 + bx + c$ is shown. State how many real roots there are of the equation $ax^2 + bx + c = 0$ and read them off from the graph. Check your answers.

   (a)

   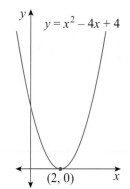

   (b)

   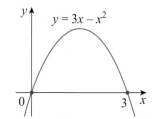

   (c)

   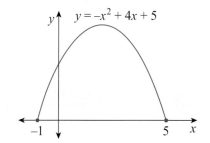

7. If $y = x^2 + px$ is the equation of the curve below, find p.

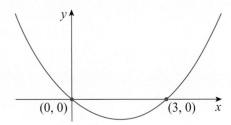

8. Form the quadratic equations with the following roots:

    (a) 1, 2

    (b) 3, 3

    (c) −1, −2

    (d) 5, −6

    (e) $\frac{1}{2}, \frac{3}{2}$

9. Solve the following:

    (a) $x^2 = \dfrac{13x + 5}{6}$

    (b) $\dfrac{3}{x} + \dfrac{5}{x + 2} = 2$

    (c) $\dfrac{6}{x - 1} - \dfrac{1}{x - 1} = 1$

    (d) $\dfrac{x(x - 7)}{x - 5} + \dfrac{8}{x - 5} = \dfrac{x}{3}$

    (e) $\dfrac{1}{x + 1} - \dfrac{1}{3} = \dfrac{1}{x + 2}$, correct to one decimal place

10. Solve the following:

    (a) $x^2 - 7x + 10 = 0$ for x and hence $(y - 2)^2 - 7(y - 2) + 10 = 0$ for y

    (b) $6x^2 - 11x - 10 = 0$ for x and hence $6(t - 1)^2 - 11(t - 1) - 10 = 0$ for t

    (c) $3x^2 - 7x + 4 = 0$ for x and hence $3\left(\dfrac{y}{3} - 1\right)^2 - 7\left(\dfrac{y}{3} - 1\right) + 4 = 0$ for y

    (d) $x^2 - 10x + 21 = 0$ for x and hence $\left(x - \dfrac{18}{x}\right)^2 - 10\left(x - \dfrac{18}{x}\right) + 21 = 0$ for x

    (e) $5x^2 - 23x + 12 = 0$ for x and hence $(y - 2)^2 - 4{\cdot}6(y - 2) = -2{\cdot}4$ for y

11. (a) In a round-robin hockey tournament, each team is paired with every other team once. If there are x teams, the number N of games that are played is given by $N = \dfrac{x^2 - x}{2}$. If 66 games are played, how many teams entered?

    (b) When the sum of 6 and twice a natural number is subtracted from the square of the number, the result is 2. Find this number.

    (c) The profit P in € made by selling x computers is modelled by the equation $P = -5x^2 + 1200x + 6000$. How many computers must be sold to make a profit of €53 500?

    (d) The total resistance R of two resistors in parallel is given by $\dfrac{1}{R} = \dfrac{1}{r} + \dfrac{1}{r + 3}$.

    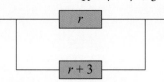

    If $R = 2$ ohms, find r in ohms.

    (e) A golf ball is thrown up on the moon. The equation of the ball's height h (m) above the lunar surface t seconds after launch is given by $h = 12{\cdot}8t - 0{\cdot}8t^2$. Find when it is 22·4 m above the surface.

    (f) A regulation tennis court for a doubles match is laid out so that its length is 1·85 m longer than twice its width. The area of the doubles court is 267 m². Find the length and breadth of a doubles court, correct to two decimal places.

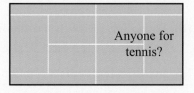

Anyone for tennis?

(g) A house owner wants to build an extension in the shape of a cuboid so that the length l is 3 m longer than the width. Find l in terms of w.

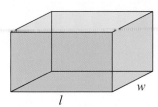

The planning regulations state that the area of the floor space occupied by the extension must not exceed 50% of the floor space of the house to which it is attached. The floor space of the house is 14 m by 12 m. Show that $w^2 + 3w - 84 = 0$, if the largest extension is built. Find l and w, correct to one decimal place.

(h) Rectangle P has length $(x + 10)$ and breadth x.

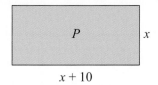

Rectangle Q has length $(x + 4)$ and breadth 4.

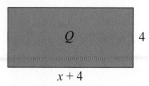

Find x if the rectangles have the same area.

(i) In a right-angled triangle, the length of $[PR]$ is 7 cm longer than $[PQ]$. The length of the hypotenuse is 8 cm longer than $[PQ]$. Find the lengths of all sides.

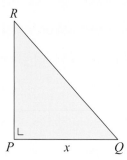

CHAPTER 6

Other Types of Equations

Learning Outcomes

- To solve surd equations (equations with square roots).

- To solve literal equations where a given variable is isolated and written in terms of the other variables.

- To solve exponential or power equations.

6.1 Equations with square roots

A surd equation is an equation with one or more square roots.

ACTIVITY 5

ACTION
Working with surd equations

OBJECTIVE
To learn the techniques needed to solve surd equations

EXAMPLE 1

Solve $\sqrt{3x + 1} = 4$.

Solution

$\sqrt{3x + 1} = 4$ [Square both sides.]

$(\sqrt{3x + 1})^2 = 4^2$

$3x + 1 = 16$ [Solve for x.]

$3x = 15$

$x = 5$

Check your answer:

$x = 5$: $\sqrt{15 + 1} = \sqrt{16} = 4$

$x = 5$ is a solution.

EXAMPLE 2

Solve $4 - \sqrt{5x + 1} = 0$.

Solution

$4 - \sqrt{5x + 1} = 0$ [Isolate the square root on one side of the equation.]

$4 = \sqrt{5x + 1}$ [Square both sides and solve for x.]

$16 = 5x + 1$

$15 = 5x$

$x = 3$

Check your answer:

$x = 3$: $4 - \sqrt{15 + 1} = 4 - \sqrt{16}$

$= 4 - 4 = 0$

$x = 3$ is a solution.

EXAMPLE 3

Solve $\sqrt{2x-1} - \sqrt{x+8} = 0$.

Solution

$\sqrt{2x-1} - \sqrt{x+8} = 0$ [If there are two square roots, get them on opposite sides of the equation.]

$\quad\quad \sqrt{2x-1} = \sqrt{x+8}$ [Square both sides.]

$\quad\quad\quad 2x-1 = x+8$ [Solve for x.]

$\quad\quad\quad\quad\quad x = 9$

Check your answer:

$x = 9$: $\sqrt{17} - \sqrt{17} = 0$

EXERCISE 3

1. Solve the following for x:

  (a) $\sqrt{x} = 4$ (c) $\sqrt{x} = 10^2$ (e) $\sqrt{x} = e$ (g) $\sqrt{x} = \sqrt[3]{4}$ (i) $\dfrac{1}{\sqrt{x}} = \dfrac{3}{2}$

  (b) $\sqrt{x} = \dfrac{1}{2}$ (d) $\sqrt{x} = a^{\frac{1}{2}}$ (f) $\sqrt{x} = \sqrt{2}$ (h) $\sqrt{x} = a-1$ (j) $\sqrt{x} = 1{\cdot}2$

2. Solve the following for x:

  (a) $\sqrt{x-1} = 2$ (e) $3\sqrt{x+1} - 15 = 0$ (i) $x = \sqrt{6x-8}$

  (b) $\sqrt{x+14} = 5$ (f) $2\sqrt{5x+4} = 16$ (j) $\sqrt{3}x = \sqrt{13x+10}$

  (c) $\sqrt{2x+11} = 5$ (g) $3 - 2\sqrt{x+19} = -5$ (k) $2x = \sqrt{4x+3}$

  (d) $\sqrt{3x+1} - 4 = 0$ (h) $7 + 3\sqrt{2x-1} = 22$

6.2 Literal equations

A literal equation is an equation with more than one unknown variable (letter).

▶ $S = ut$ (3 letters)

▶ $F = x + \dfrac{3}{x}$ (2 letters)

▶ $\dfrac{h}{p} = \sqrt{\dfrac{p}{z} + \dfrac{x}{3}}$ (4 letters)

ACTIVITY 6

ACTION
Working with literal equations

OBJECTIVE
To learn the techniques needed to solve literal equations

Steps for solving literal equations

Follow the steps outlined below to solve for a stated letter in terms of the other(s):

1. Get rid of fractions by multiplying both sides by the common denominator of all fractions.

2. Multiply out all brackets.

3. Get rid of square roots by isolating them and squaring.

4. Bring all terms containing the required letter to one side of the equation.

5. Take out the required letter as a factor (if necessary).

6. Solve for the letter.

Note: Sometimes Steps 2 and 3 are easier to do before Step 1.

In the following examples, the letter in red is to be written in terms of the other letters:

▸ $b = u + t$

$b - u = t$

$\therefore t = b - u$

▸ $V = IR$

$\dfrac{V}{I} = R$

$\therefore R = \dfrac{V}{I}$

▸ $x + \dfrac{tz}{y} = z$ [Get rid of the fractions. Multiply across by y.]

$xy + tz = zy$ [Move all terms with y to right.]

$tz = zy - xy$ [Take out a factor of y on right.]

$tz = y(z - x)$ [Solve for y.]

$\dfrac{tz}{z - x} = y$

$\therefore y = \dfrac{tz}{z - x}$

▸ $A - \sqrt{r^2 + h^2} = 0$

$A = \sqrt{r^2 + h^2}$ [Isolate the square root.]

$A^2 = r^2 + h^2$

$A^2 - h^2 = r^2$

$\pm\sqrt{A^2 - h^2} = r$

$\therefore r = \pm\sqrt{A^2 - h^2}$

EXAMPLE 4

The amount of energy in joules released in a nuclear reaction is given by $E = mc^2$, where m is the mass of Uranium-235 in kg and c is the speed of light in m/s. Solve for c and find c if $m = 3 \times 10^{-3}$ kg and $E = 2 \cdot 7 \times 10^{14}$ J.

Solution

$E = mc^2$

$\dfrac{E}{m} = c^2$

$\sqrt{\dfrac{E}{m}} = c$

$\therefore c = \sqrt{\dfrac{E}{m}}$

$m = 3 \times 10^{-3}$ kg

$E = 2 \cdot 7 \times 10^{14}$ J

$c = \sqrt{\dfrac{2 \cdot 7 \times 10^{14}}{3 \times 10^{-3}}}$

$= 3 \times 10^8$ m/s

EXAMPLE 5

The concentration C of a certain drug in the bloodstream in mg/l after t hours is given by $C = \dfrac{4t}{t+2}$. Solve for t and find the time for the concentration to become 2 mg/l.

Solution

$$C = \frac{4t}{(t+2)}$$
$$C(t+2) = 4t$$
$$Ct + 2C = 4t$$
$$2C = 4t - Ct$$
$$2C = t(4 - C)$$
$$t = \frac{2C}{4 - C}$$

$C = 2$: $t = \dfrac{2 \times 2}{4 - 2} = 2$ hours

EXAMPLE 6

The distance of an image v from a mirror is given by $\dfrac{1}{u} + \dfrac{1}{v} = \dfrac{1}{f}$, where u is the distance of the object from the mirror and f is the focal length of the mirror. u, v and f are all measured in centimetres. Express v in term of u and f. If $u = 30$ cm and $f = 20$ cm, find v.

Solution

$$\frac{1}{u} + \frac{1}{v} = \frac{1}{f} \quad \text{[Multiply all terms by } uvf.\text{]}$$
$$vf + uf = uv$$
$$uf = uv - vf$$
$$uf = v(u - f)$$
$$\frac{uf}{u - f} = v$$
$$v = \frac{uf}{u - f}$$

$u = 30$ and $f = 20$: $v = \dfrac{30 \times 20}{30 - 20} = 60$ cm

EXERCISE 4

1. Solve the following for the letter in the bracket:

   (a) $y = x + 4$ $\quad(x)$

   (b) $y = 3x$ $\quad(x)$

   (c) $y = 3x + 4$ $\quad(x)$

   (d) $I = \dfrac{PRT}{100}$ $\quad(T)$

   (e) $\dfrac{w}{p} = \dfrac{2\pi l}{d}$ $\quad(d)$

   (f) $v^2 = u^2 + 2as$ $\quad(a)$

   (g) $S = 2\pi r(r + h)$ $\quad(h)$

   (h) $(m + n)V = na$ $\quad(n)$

   (i) $A = \pi r^2 h$ $\quad(r)$

   (j) $V = \tfrac{1}{3}\pi r^2 h$ $\quad(r)$

   (k) $v = \sqrt{5gh}$ $\quad(h)$

   (l) $T = 2\pi\sqrt{\dfrac{k}{MH}}$ $\quad(M)$

   (m) $D = \sqrt{\dfrac{3h}{2}}$ $\quad(h)$

   (n) $H = \tfrac{1}{2}gT^2$ $\quad(T)$

   (o) $A = \tfrac{1}{2}r^2 x$ $\quad(r)$

   (p) $r = a + bt^2$ $\quad(t)$

   (q) $P = \tfrac{1}{3}(a - b)$ $\quad(a)$

   (r) $Q = \dfrac{3(3v - l)}{5}$ $\quad(v)$

   (s) $L = 9 + \dfrac{6}{y}$ $\quad(y)$

   (t) $d = \dfrac{k - s}{t}$ $\quad(k)$

   (u) $Q = p^2 + 3f$ $\quad(p)$

   (v) $M = R^2 z - 1$ $\quad(R)$

   (w) $A = \sqrt{b^2 - 4ac}$ $\quad(a)$

   (x) $E = \tfrac{1}{2}CV^2$ $\quad(V)$

   (y) $v^2 = u^2 + 2as$ $\quad(u)$

2. If $q = 2\sqrt{s} + p$, express s in terms of q and p. Find s when $q = 7$ and $p = 4\cdot4$.

3. The volume V of a cylinder is given by $V = \pi r^2 h$. Solve this equation for r. If $V = 16\pi \text{ cm}^3$ and $h = 4$ cm, find the radius r.

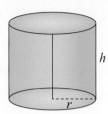

4. The distance D (km) of the horizon from a point h (m) above the Earth's surface is given by $D = \sqrt{\dfrac{Rh}{500}}$, where R is the radius of the Earth in km.

Express R in terms of h and D. A balloonist determines that the horizon is 26·87 km away for a height of 56·7 m. Use these figures to estimate the radius of the Earth, correct to one decimal place.

5. The formula for the recommended dose C (mg) of a drug for a child is related to the recommended adult dose A (mg) by $\dfrac{17C}{A} - 1 = t$, where t is the age of the child in years. Solve for A in terms of C and t. If $C = 28$ mg for a six-year-old child, find the corresponding recommended adult dose. At what age is the adult dose the same as the child dose?

6.3 Exponential equations (power equations)

Exponential equations are equations in which the unknown quantity is a power.

ACTIVITY 7

ACTION
Working with exponential equations

OBJECTIVE
To learn the techniques needed to solve exponential equations

Steps for solving exponential equations

1. Get both sides to the same base raised to a single power using the rules of powers.
2. Equate the powers to solve for the unknown quantity.

▸ $2^x = 8$ [Get the same base on each side.]

$2^x = 2^3$ [Equate the powers.]

$x = 3$

▸ $(5)^{x-3} = 25$

$(5)^{x-3} = (5)^2$

$x - 3 = 2$

$x = 5$

▸ $4^{2x+1} = 8^{x-3}$

$(2^2)^{2x+1} = (2^3)^{x-3}$

$(2)^{4x+2} = (2)^{3x-9}$

$4x + 2 = 3x - 9$

$x = -11$

▸ $16^x = 64$

$(2^4)^x = 2^6$

$2^{4x} = 2^6$

$4x = 6$

$x = \dfrac{3}{2}$

▸ $(\sqrt{32})^{2x+4} = 8^{-x+2}$

$\left(2^{\frac{5}{2}}\right)^{2x+4} = (2^3)^{-x+2}$

$2^{5x+10} = 2^{-3x+6}$

$5x + 10 = -3x + 6$

$8x = -4$

$x = -\dfrac{1}{2}$

EXAMPLE 7

The percentage P of light transmitted by n sheets of plastic is given by $P = 25 \times 2^{2-n}$.

(a) What percentage is transmitted by 0 sheets?

(b) What percentage of light is transmitted by four sheets?

(c) How many sheets transmit $0 \cdot 78125\%$ of light?

Solution

$P = 25 \times 2^{2-n}$

(a) **$n = 0$:** $P = 25 \times 2^2 = 100\%$

(b) **$n = 4$:** $P = 25 \times 2^{-2} = 6 \cdot 25\%$

(c) $0 \cdot 78125 = 25 \times 2^{2-n}$

$2^{2-n} = 0 \cdot 03125 = \dfrac{1}{32} = \dfrac{1}{2^5} = 2^{-5}$

$2 - n = -5$

$n = 7$

Answer: 7 sheets

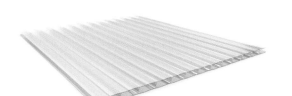

EXERCISE 5

1. Write the following in the form 2^k:

(a) 4

(b) 16

(c) 128

(d) 8^4

(e) $8^{\frac{1}{3}}$

(f) $8^{\frac{4}{3}}$

(g) $\dfrac{1}{8^{\frac{4}{3}}}$

(h) $\dfrac{1}{8^{-\frac{4}{3}}}$

(i) $\dfrac{\sqrt{8}}{32}$

(j) $\dfrac{16\sqrt{2}}{32}$

(k) $\dfrac{4^2 \times 16^{\frac{1}{2}}}{8^{\frac{1}{3}} \times 2}$

(l) $\dfrac{2^{-2}}{4^{-1}}$

2. Write the following in the form 3^p:

(a) 9

(b) $\dfrac{1}{3}$

(c) $\dfrac{1}{9}$

(d) $\dfrac{1}{9^{-2}}$

(e) $9^{-\frac{3}{2}}$

(f) $\dfrac{1}{9^{-\frac{3}{2}}}$

(g) $(3\sqrt{3})^4$

(h) $\left(\dfrac{\sqrt{27}}{3}\right)^3$

(i) $\dfrac{3^{-2}}{9}$

(j) $\dfrac{3^{-2}}{3^{-4}}$

(k) $\dfrac{9}{3^{-2}}$

(l) $\left(\dfrac{3}{\sqrt{3}}\right)^4$

3. Write the following in the form with base 2:

(a) 4^x

(b) $\dfrac{1}{2^x}$

(c) $(\sqrt{2})^x$

(d) 8^x

(e) $\dfrac{16}{2^x}$

(f) 2×8^x

(g) $\dfrac{32^x}{2}$

(h) $(4^x)^2$

(i) $\left(\dfrac{16^x}{\sqrt{2}}\right)^2$

(j) $\dfrac{2^x}{2^{4x}}$

(k) $\dfrac{4^{x+1}}{2^x}$

4. Write the following in the form with base 3:

(a) 9^x

(b) $\dfrac{1}{9^x}$

(c) 9^{-x}

(d) $\dfrac{1}{9^{-x}}$

(e) 9^{x+2}

(f) $\dfrac{3^x}{9^x}$

(g) $\dfrac{9^{x+1}}{3}$

(h) $(3^x)^2 \times 3$

(i) $\left(\dfrac{3^x}{9}\right)^2$

5. Solve the following for x:

(a) $4^x = 16$

(b) $4^x = \dfrac{1}{16}$

(c) $4^x = 8^2$

(d) $\dfrac{1}{4^x} = 16$

(e) $8^x = 16$

(f) $4^x = \dfrac{1}{8}$

(g) $25^x = 125$

(h) $9^x = \dfrac{1}{27}$

(i) $3^{x+1} = 81$

(j) $8^{x+2} = 4^{x-1}$

(k) $2^x = \sqrt{8}$

(l) $9^{x-1} = 3^{x+2}$

(m) $27 \times 9^{x+1} = 3 \times 3^{x-2}$

(n) $\dfrac{3}{9^x} = \dfrac{\sqrt{3}}{27}$

(o) $2^{2x-5} = 4^{3x}$

(p) $9^{\frac{1}{2}x} = 81$

(q) $2^{3x-5} = 8^{3x+1}$

(r) $(25)^{x+1} = (125)^{2x}$

(s) $4^{2x} = \dfrac{64}{2^x}$

6. (a) Express $\dfrac{\sqrt{8}}{32}$ in the form 2^k. Hence, solve $\left(\dfrac{\sqrt{8}}{32}\right)^4 = 2^{2x+1}$.

(b) Express $27 \times \sqrt[3]{81}$ in the form 3^k. Hence, solve $(27 \times \sqrt[3]{81})^{3x} = 3^{x-2}$.

(c) Express $\dfrac{64}{\sqrt{32}}$ in the form 2^k. Hence, solve $\left(\dfrac{64}{\sqrt{32}}\right)^{2x+1} = 8^{x+2}$.

(d) Express $\dfrac{5 \times 25^3}{\sqrt{125}}$ in the form 5^p. Hence, solve $\left(\dfrac{5 \times 25^3}{\sqrt{125}}\right)^2 = 5^{3x-1}$.

7. An insect population P increases according to the law $P = 153 \times 9^{2t-1}$, where P is the number of insects in the colony t months after the population is observed. Find:

(a) the initial population,

(b) when the population is $12\,393$.

8. Another insect population P increases according to the formula $P = 17 \times 3^{3t+1}$, where P is the number of insects in the sample t months after the observation begins. Find:

(a) the initial population,

(b) when the number of insects in the colony is $37\,179$.

9. If the two populations in questions 7 and 8 are observed beginning at the same time, when will they be equal?

10. A man's risky investment grows according to the equation $A = 8000 \times 2^{\frac{1}{5}t-1}$, where A is the amount of investment in euro after t years. Find:

(a) the initial investment,

(b) the value of the investment after 20 years,

(c) when the investment will be worth €256 000.

Systems of Simultaneous Equations

CHAPTER 7

Learning Outcomes

- To solve simultaneous linear equations in two unknowns.
- To solve simultaneous equations involving linear equations and equations of order two in two unknowns.
- To model and solve word problems involving simultaneous equations.

Systems of simultaneous equations

A system of simultaneous equations consists of two or more equations in two or more unknowns.

$$2x + 3y = 7$$

$$3x - 5y = 1$$

This set of two equations has two unknowns, x and y. The solution of this system of simultaneous equations is the values of x and y that make both equations true at the same time (simultaneously). There are two different types to be considered.

7.1 Linear equations in two unknowns

ACTIVITY 8

ACTION
Working with simultaneous equations

OBJECTIVE
To learn the techniques needed to solve linear simultaneous equations

These are simultaneous equations of the form: $ax + by = d$
$$ex + fy = g$$

1. The unknowns are x and y in this case.
2. The coefficients of x and y are a, e and b, f, respectively. The constants are d and g.
3. They are called linear equations because if you plot y against x for each equation, you get a straight line.

The method of solution is called **elimination by addition**.

WORKED EXAMPLE

Solving linear equations in two unknowns

Solve $2x + 3y = 7$ and $3x - 5y = 1$ using elimination by addition.

Step 1: Write the x term under the x term, the y term under the y term, and the constant under the constant. Decide which letter to eliminate by looking at the coefficients of x and y.

$2x + 3y = 7 \dots$ **(1)**

$3x - 5y = 1 \dots$ **(2)**

Step 2: Multiply equation **(1)** by 3 and equation **(2)** by –2. Their x coefficients will then become –6 and +6. Remember that when you multiply an equation by a number, you must multiply all terms in the equation. Add both equivalent equations so that the terms in x are eliminated. Solve for y.

$$6x + 9y = 21 \dots \textbf{(1)} \, (\times 3)$$
$$\underline{-6x + 10y = -2 \dots \textbf{(2)} \, (\times -2)}$$
$$19y = 19$$
$$y = 1$$

Step 3: Find the value of x by substituting $y = 1$ back into any of the previous equations. Putting $y = 1$ into equation **(1)**:

$$2x + 3(1) = 7$$
$$2x = 4$$
$$x = 2$$

Step 4: Present your answer in the form $(x, y) = (2, 1)$. This is the point of intersection of the two lines $2x + 3y = 7$ and $3x - 5y = 1$ when plotted on co-ordinated rectangular axes.

EXAMPLE **1**

A bird's speed v (m/s) against time t (seconds) is plotted by an observer. The graph of v against t is a straight line, as shown. The equation of the straight line is $v = u + at$. Find u and a, if $v = 10$ m/s at $t = 1$ s and $v = 18$ m/s at $t = 5$ s.

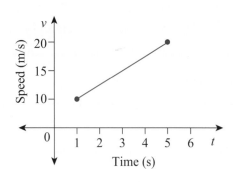

Solution

$v = u + at$

$t = 1, v = 10$: $10 = u + a \ \dots$ **(1)**

$t = 5, v = 18$: $\underline{18 = u + 5a \dots \textbf{(2)}}$

$$-10 = -u - a \dots \textbf{(1)} \times (-1)$$
$$\underline{18 = u + 5a \dots \textbf{(2)}}$$
$$8 = 4a$$
$$\underline{2 = a}$$

Into (1): $10 = u + a$

$$u = 8$$

If your equation(s) has fractions, get rid of these first by multiplying across by the common denominator of all the fractions. If your equation has brackets, multiply them out after getting rid of any fractions.

EXAMPLE 2

Solve: $\dfrac{(x+2)}{3} + \dfrac{(y-3)}{2} = 6$

$\dfrac{(x-2)}{5} - \dfrac{(y+3)}{6} = -1$

Solution

$\dfrac{(x+2)}{3} + \dfrac{(y-3)}{2} = 6 \ (\times 6)$ [Get rid of fractions first.]

$2(x+2) + 3(y-3) = 36$

$2x + 4 + 3y - 9 = 36$

$2x + 3y = 41 \ \dots (1)$

$\dfrac{(x-2)}{5} - \dfrac{(y+3)}{6} = -1 \ (\times 30)$

$6(x-2) - 5(y+3) = -30$

$6x - 12 - 5y - 15 = -30$

$6x - 5y = -3 \ \dots (2)$

Step 1: Eliminate x.

$2x + 3y = 41 \dots (1) \quad (\times -3)$

$6x - 5y = -3 \dots (2)$

Step 2: Solve for y.

$-6x - 9y = -123 \ \dots (1) \quad (\times -3)$

$\underline{6x - 5y = -3 \qquad \dots (2)}$

$-14y = -126$

$y = 9$

Step 3: Solve for x.

$6x - 5y = -3 \dots (2)$

$y = 9: \quad 6x - 5(9) = -3$

$6x = 42$

$x = 7$

Step 4: $(x, y) = (7, 9)$

Word problems using two simultaneous linear equations in two unknowns

The following example illustrates the approach to modelling a problem with two variables using simultaneous equations.

WORKED EXAMPLE Modelling a simultaneous equation problem

Some 800 tickets were sold for a basketball match. An adult ticket cost €13·50 and a child ticket cost €8. A total of €10 140 was collected from selling all tickets. How many adult tickets were sold and how many child tickets were sold?

Solution

1. Always let x and y be the answers to the questions asked and be absolutely clear what they represent. There are two unknowns, x and y, so you need two equations. Let x be the number of adult tickets sold and y the number of child tickets sold.

2. Translate the words in the problem into two linear equations:

   (a) The total number of tickets was 800: $x + y = 800$

   (b) The total amount of money collected was €10 140.

   The money collected from selling x adult tickets at €13·50 per ticket $= 13 \cdot 5x$

   The money collected from selling y child tickets at €8 per ticket $= 8y$

   $13 \cdot 5x + 8y = 10\,140$

3. Now solve the equations using the elimination by addition method:

$$x + y = 800 \quad \dots (1)$$

$$13{\cdot}5x + 8y = 10\,140 \dots (2)$$

$$-8x - 8y = -6400 \dots (1) \quad (\times -8)$$

$$13{\cdot}5x + 8y = 10\,140 \dots (2)$$

$$5{\cdot}5x = 3740$$

$$x = 680$$

Using (1): $\quad x + y = 800$

$x = 680$: $\quad 680 + y = 800$

$$y = 120$$

Answer: 680 adult tickets and 120 child tickets.

Type 1: Numbers

EXAMPLE 3

Five times a number and three times a second number add to 27. Twice the second number and three times the first add to 17. Find these numbers.

Solution

Let x = first number

Let y = second number

$$5x + 3y = 27 \quad \dots (1)$$

$$3x + 2y = 17 \quad \dots (2)$$

$$10x + 6y = 54 \quad \dots (1) \quad (\times 2)$$

$$-9x - 6y = -51 \dots (2) \quad (\times -3)$$

$$x = 3$$

Using (2): $\quad 3x + 2y = 17$

$x = 3$: $3(3) + 2y = 17$

$$2y = 8$$

$$y = 4$$

Answer: The two numbers are 3 and 4.

Type 2: Geometry

EXAMPLE 4

The perimeter of a rectangle is 82 m. The length is 8 m longer than twice the breadth. Find the length, the breadth and the area of the rectangle.

Solution

Let x = length

Let y = breadth

Breadth = y

Length = x

Perimeter = $2x + 2y = 82 \quad \dots (1)$

Length = 2(Breadth) + 8: $x = 2y + 8 \Rightarrow x - 2y = 8 \dots (2)$

$$2x + 2y = 82 \quad \dots (1)$$

$$x - 2y = 8 \quad \dots (2)$$

$$3x = 90$$

$$x = 30 \text{ m}$$

Using (2): $\quad x - 2y = 8$

$x = 30$: $(30) - 2y = 8$

$$22 = 2y$$

$$y = 11 \text{ m}$$

Area = $30 \times 11 = 330 \text{ m}^2$

Type 3: Business and finance

EXAMPLE 5

Enda has more money than Mícheál. If Enda gave Mícheál €55 000, they would have the same amount. However, if Mícheál gave Enda €8000, Enda would have twice as much as Mícheál. How much money does each have?

Solution

Let x = amount of Enda's money

Let y = amount of Mícheál's money

$x - 55\,000 = y + 55\,000$

$\quad x - y = 110\,000 \ldots (\mathbf{1})$

$(x + 8000) = 2(y - 8000)$

$\quad x + 8000 = 2y - 16\,000$

$\quad\quad x - 2y = -24\,000 \ldots (\mathbf{2})$

$$x - y = 110\,000 \ldots (\mathbf{1})$$
$$x - 2y = -24\,000 \ldots (\mathbf{2})$$
$$x - y = 110\,000 \ldots (\mathbf{1})$$
$$-x + 2y = 24\,000 \ldots (\mathbf{2}) \quad (\times -1)$$
$$y = 134\,000$$

Using (1): $x - y = 110\,000$

$y = \mathbf{134\ 000}$: $x = 134\,000 + 110\,000$

$\quad\quad\quad\quad\quad x = 244\,000$

Answer: Enda has €244 000 and Mícheál has €134 000.

Type 4: Mixtures

A solution of one substance in another is simply a mixture of the two. If you are told that a 20% solution of sugar in water is made up, this simply means that 1 litre of a mixture of water and sugar has 0·2 litres of sugar and 0·8 litres of water. So x litres of such a solution would have $0\cdot2x$ litres of sugar and $0\cdot8x$ litres of water.

EXAMPLE 6

Twenty litres of a 15% solution of a disinfectant in water is made up of two solutions. One solution is made up of 22% of the disinfectant in water and the other solution is made up of 8% of the disinfectant in water. How many litres of each solution are there?

Solution

Let x = number of litres of 22% solution

Let y = number of litres of 8% solution

The total is 20 litres.

$x + y = 20 \ldots (\mathbf{1})$

The total amount of disinfectant in the 20 litres:

$0\cdot15 \times 20 = 3$ litres

$0\cdot22x + 0\cdot08y = 3 \ldots (\mathbf{2})$

$$x + y = 20 \quad \ldots (\mathbf{1})$$
$$0\cdot22x + 0\cdot08y = 3 \quad \ldots (\mathbf{2})$$
$$-0\cdot22x - 0\cdot22y = -4\cdot4 \quad \ldots (\mathbf{1}) \quad (\times -0\cdot22)$$
$$0\cdot22x + 0\cdot08y = 3 \quad \ldots (\mathbf{2})$$
$$-0\cdot14y = -1\cdot4$$
$$y = 10 \text{ litres}$$

Using: $x + y = 20 \quad \ldots (\mathbf{1})$

$y = \mathbf{10}$: $x + (10) = 20$

$\quad\quad\quad x = 10$ litres

EXERCISE 6

(A) CONCEPTS AND SKILLS

Solve the following pairs of linear simultaneous equations:

1. $2x + y = 7$
$2x - y = 1$

2. $3x + y = 7$
$2x - y = 3$

3. $2x + y = 8$
$5x - y = 6$

4. $2x - 3y = -5$
$x + y = 5$

5. $x - 5y = 11$
$2x + y = 0$

6. $2x + 3y = 5$
$3x + 4y = 7$

7. $5x + 4y = 22$
$3x + 5y = 21$

8. $5x + 3y = 29$
$4x + 7y = 37$

9. $2x - 5y = 8$
$2x - 3y = -6$

10. $3y - 4x = -10$
$y + 4x = 8$

11. $2x - 5y = 3$
$x - 3y = 1$

12. $3x - 5y = 44$
$5x + 7y = 12$

13. $2x - 3y = 24$
$\dfrac{5x}{3} - \dfrac{y}{2} = 12$

14. $\dfrac{x}{2} + \dfrac{y}{5} = 4$
$\dfrac{x}{4} + \dfrac{y}{2} = 6$

15. $4x + 11 = 3y$
$3(x - 2) - 7y = 0$

16. $7 - 6(x - 3y) = 4$
$3(x + 2y) + 6 = 5x + 10y$

17. $\dfrac{3(x + 2)}{4} - \dfrac{(y + 3)}{2} = 1$
$\dfrac{5(x - y + 2)}{6} = \dfrac{5}{2}$

18. If $y = a + bx$, find a and b, given $y = 7$ when $x = -2$ and $y = 10$ when $x = 4$.

19. The straight-line graph of $y = a + bx$ is shown. Find a and b.

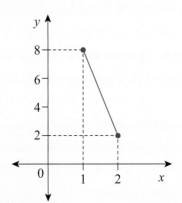

20. The volume of oil in a tank is decreasing linearly with time. Find the equation of the straight line $V = a + bt$ by finding a and b. Find V when $t = 0$.

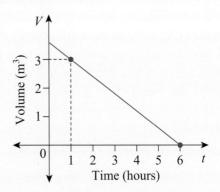

(B) CONTEXTS AND APPLICATIONS

Numbers

1. The sum of two numbers is 135. Their difference is 7. Find them.

2. The difference of two numbers is 3. If three times the larger number less twice the smaller one is 13, find them.

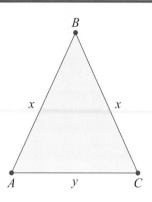

3. Three times a number and twice a second number add to –1. If twice the first number added to three times the second number is –9, find these numbers.

4. The difference between two numbers is 5. If three times the larger number plus five times the smaller number is 111, find them.

5. One half of the sum of two numbers is equal to their difference. What are the numbers if their sum is 96?

6. Two numbers add to 12. If one of these is subtracted from three times the other, the answer is also 12. Find them.

Geometry

7. The perimeter of a rectangular field is 114 m. The length is 7 m greater than the breadth. Find the length, the breadth and the area of the rectangle.

8. The lengths of the rectangle shown are all written in centimetres.

   (a) Find x and y.

   (b) Find the perimeter and area of the rectangle.

   $4x + y - 14$

   $2y + 3$ x

   $2x - 3y$

9. The lengths of the sides of the equilateral triangle shown are given in centimetres.

   (a) Find x and y.

   (b) Find the perimeter and area of the triangle in surd form.

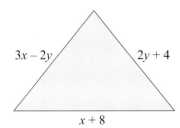

   $3x - 2y$ $2y + 4$

   $x + 8$

10. The shortest side of the isosceles triangle ACB is $[AC]$. If the perimeter is 17 cm and $|AC|$ is 4 cm shorter than $|AB|$, find the length of all sides.

Business and finance

11. Peter invested €20 000. Part of his money was invested at 2% per annum and the rest at 3% per annum. If the interest at the end of a year was €450, find how much was invested at each rate.

12. Mr Nolan bought 100 shares in Bankwin and 50 shares in Academic Enterprise. The total cost of all 150 shares was €790.

    Mrs Harvey bought 40 shares in Bankwin and 110 shares in Academic Enterprise. The total cost of all 150 shares was €874.

    Find the price of a Bankwin share and of an Academic Enterprise share.

Mixtures

13. A woman has €2·25 in her pocket, consisting of 5 cent and 10 cent coins only. If the total number of coins in her pocket is 41, find the number of each coin in her possession.

14. A test consists of 13 questions. There are 5-mark questions and 12-mark questions. If the test is worth 100 marks in total, how many of each type of question are there?

15. A parking lot has 162 spaces in total. It has twice as many spaces for cars as it has for trucks. How many spaces has the lot for cars? How many spaces has it for trucks?

16. How many litres of a 30% alcohol solution and how many litres of a 50% alcohol solution must be mixed to produce 20 litres of a 40% alcohol solution?

17. A goldsmith uses two gold alloys. The first alloy is 90% gold and the second is 80% gold. How many grams of each should she mix together to produce 53·1 g of an alloy that is 87% gold?

7.2 One linear equation and one equation of order two in two unknowns

An equation of order two is an equation that in at least one term the powers of the variables add to exactly 2 and that no powers of the variables add to more than 2.

Examples: $x^2 + y^2 = 4$, $x^2 - y = 7x$, $xy + x^2 = 2y^2$

The technique for solving one linear equation and one equation of order two is **substitution**.

ACTIVITY 9

ACTION
Using simultaneous equations involving a linear and an equation of order two

OBJECTIVE
To learn the techniques needed to solve linear and order two simultaneous equations

WORKED EXAMPLE
Solving linear and order two simultaneous equations

Solve $x - y = -3$ and $x^2 + xy = -1$ simultaneously.

Step 1: Start with the linear equation $x - y = -3$ and solve for x or y. Choose cleverly.

$y = (x + 3) \ldots$ **(1)**

Put a bracket around the terms on the right-hand side.

Step 2: Substitute this expression for y into $x^2 + x(y) = 1 \ldots$ **(2)**
$x^2 + x(x + 3) = -1$

Multiply out the brackets:

$x^2 + x^2 + 3x = -1$

$2x^2 + 3x + 1 = 0$ [This is a quadratic in x.]

Step 3: Solve the quadratic by factorisation or by using the magic formula:

$(2x + 1)(x + 1) = 0$

$x = -\frac{1}{2}, x = -1$

Step 4: Get the corresponding values for y using equation **(1)**.

$x = -\frac{1}{2}$: $y = \left(-\frac{1}{2} + 3\right) = \frac{5}{2}$

$x = -1$: $y = (-1 + 3) = 2$

$\left(-\frac{1}{2}, \frac{5}{2}\right)$ and $(-1, 2)$ are the solutions.

What do these solutions mean?

They are the points of intersection of the straight line with equation $x - y = -3$ and the curve with equation $x^2 + xy = -1$.

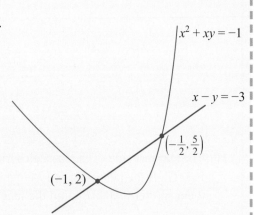

Word problems involving one linear equation and one equation of order two

The strategy is pretty much the same as for two linear equations word problems. Always let x and y be the answers to the questions asked and be absolutely clear what they represent.

EXAMPLE 7

The sum of two numbers is 3 and the sum of their squares is 65. What are the numbers?

Solution

Let x = one number

Let y = the other number

$$x + y = 3 \quad \ldots (1)$$
$$x^2 + y^2 = 65 \ldots (2)$$
$$\overline{}$$
$$x + y = 3 \quad \ldots (1)$$
$$y = (3 - x)$$

Into (2): $x^2 + (3 - x)^2 = 65$
$$x^2 + 9 - 6x + x^2 = 65$$
$$2x^2 - 6x - 56 = 0$$
$$x^2 - 3x - 28 = 0$$
$$(x + 4)(x - 7) = 0$$
$$x = -4, 7$$

$\boldsymbol{x = -4}$: $y = (3 - x) = (3 - (-4)) = 7$

$\boldsymbol{x = 7}$: $y = (3 - x) = (3 - (7)) = -4$

The numbers are –4 and 7.

EXAMPLE 8

A television screen has diagonals of length 100 cm. If the perimeter of the screen is 280 cm, find the length, breadth and area of the screen.

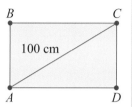

Solution

Let x = length of screen

Let y = breadth of screen

Perimeter: $2x + 2y = 280$
$$x + y = 140 \ldots (1)$$

Diagonals: $x^2 + y^2 = 10\,000 \ldots (2)$
$$\overline{x + y = 140 \ldots (1)}$$
$$y = (140 - x)$$

Into (2): $x^2 + (140 - x)^2 = 10\,000$
$$x^2 + 19\,600 - 280x + x^2 = 10\,000$$
$$2x^2 - 280x - 9600 = 0$$
$$x^2 - 140x - 4800 = 0$$
$$(x - 80)(x - 60) = 0$$
$$x = 80, 60$$

$\boldsymbol{x = 80}$: $y = (140 - x) = (140 - 80) = 60$

$\boldsymbol{x = 60}$: $y = (140 - x) = (140 - 60) = 80$

Solutions: length = 80 cm, breadth = 60 cm *or* length = 60 cm, breadth = 80 cm

Area = $80 \times 60 = 4800$ cm^2

EXERCISE 7

(A) CONCEPTS AND SKILLS

Solve the following for x and y:

1. $x + y = 7$
   $xy = 12$

2. $x - y = 1$
   $xy = 42$

3. $x + y = 3$
   $x^2 + y^2 = 5$

4. $x - y - 1 = 0$
   $x^2 + y^2 = 13$

5. $x^2 + xy + y^2 = 52$
   $x + y = 8$

6. $x + y - 6 = 0$

   $x^2 + 2y^2 - 24 = 0$

What can you conclude about $x + y - 6 = 0$ in terms of its intersection with the curve $x^2 + 2y^2 - 24 = 0$?

7. $3x + y = 10$

   $2x^2 + y^2 = 19$

8. $2x + y + 1 = 0$

   $4x^2 + y^2 = 25$

9. $2x - y = 5$

   $xy = 0$

10. $2x + y = 1$

   $y = x^2 - 4x - 2$

(B) CONTEXTS AND APPLICATIONS

1. The difference of two numbers is 3. The sum of their squares is 185. Find one pair of such numbers.

2. The sum of two numbers is 42. The difference of their squares is 168. Find the pair of such numbers.

3. The product of two positive numbers is 120. Their difference is 7. If x is the larger and y the smaller of the numbers, find x and y.

4. Find two numbers such that their sum is 3 and their product is 1.

5. The area of a rectangular section of a field for playing sports is 3600 m². If the perimeter is 250 m, find the length and breadth of the field.

6. The equation of the circle s is $x^2 + y^2 = 34$. The equation of the line l is $2x - y = -1$. Find the co-ordinates of the points of intersection of the line and the circle.

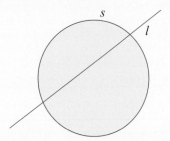

7. The lengths of all sides of the rectangle shown are in centimetres. Find x and y, the length, breadth and area of the rectangle.

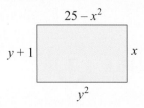

8. A tank with no lid has a total area of 1·88 m². If the sum of the length, the breadth and the height is 1·9 m, find x, y and the volume of the tank.

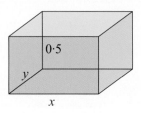

9. Two ferries run by Irish Ferries leave every day from Dublin Port to Holyhead by exactly the same route. The distance of the trip is 148 km. The average speed of the *Jonathan Swift* is 34 km/h greater than the average speed of the slower *Ulysses* ferry. As a result, the *Jonathan Swift* arrives 1 hour 42 minutes ahead of the *Ulysses*. Find the average speed of each ferry.

10. The ellipse has the formula $x^2 + 9y^2 = 9$. Find where the line $x - y = 3$ intersects the ellipse.

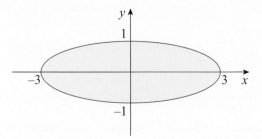

Inequalities

CHAPTER 8

Learning Outcomes

- To understand the rules for dealing with inequalities.
- To solve linear inequalities.
- To plot the solutions to inequalities on a number line.

The previous chapters examined mathematical statements in which one side is equal to (=) the other side. Inequalities involve mathematical statements where one side is not equal to the other side.

▸ $5 > 2$ (5 is greater than 2)

▸ $2 < 4$ (2 is less than 4)

▸ $x \leq -4$ (x is less than or equal to -4)

▸ $y \geq 3$ (y is greater than or equal to 3)

8.1 Techniques for handling inequalities

Inequalities are tricky to handle. If you see an inequality, take your time and think about it. To illustrate the techniques for handling inequalities, consider the following numerical example:

> **WORKED EXAMPLE** Understanding inequalities
>
> Start with $8 > 4$.
>
> Add +5 to both sides: $13 > 9$ [This is a true statement.]
>
> Subtract 5 from both sides: $3 > -1$ [This is a true statement.]
>
> Move all terms to the left: $8 - 4 > 0$ [This is a true statement.]
>
> Move all terms to the right: $0 > 4 - 8$ [This is a true statement.]
>
> Switch sides: $-4 > -8$ [This is a true statement.]
>
> Multiply both sides by +2: $16 > 8$ [This is a true statement.]
>
> Divide both sides by +2: $4 > 2$ [This is a true statement.]

But

Multiply both sides by –2: $-16 > -8$ [This is a false statement.]

Divide both sides by –2: $-4 > -2$ [This is a false statement.]

It seems that you can do the same operations to inequalities as you can do to equations, except multiply or divide by a negative number.

ACTIVITY 10

ACTION
Understanding basic inequality operations

OBJECTIVE
To learn the techniques needed to carry out basic inequality operations

Rules of inequalities

The same operations can be carried out for inequalities as for equalities, except multiplying and dividing by a negative number. To deal with a negative number in front of the variable, simply switch the sides of the variable term and the number, and change their signs so that you end up with a positive number in front of the variable.

▸ $-2x > 8$

$-8 > 2x$

$-4 > x$

$x < -4$

Reading an inequality

$8 > 4$ can be read as '8 is greater than 4' as you read from left to right. It can be rewritten as $4 < 8$, which reads as '4 is less than 8'. So $7 > x$ can be rewritten as $x < 7$.

TIP

The smaller number is always at the tip of the arrow of the inequality sign.

▸ $-6 \leq x \Leftrightarrow x \geq -6$ [–6 stays at the tip of the inequality sign whichever way you write the inequality.]

WARNING

If you multiply the sides of an inequality by a negative number, you must also reverse the direction of the inequality sign.

▸ $-x < 5 \Leftrightarrow x > -5$ [Inequality sign reverses after multiplying by –1 on both sides.]

8.2 Solving linear inequalities

ACTIVITY 11

ACTION
Working with linear inequalities

OBJECTIVE
To learn the techniques needed to solve linear inequalities

Linear inequalities involve linear functions of a variable of the form $ax + b$.

Steps for solving linear inequalities

1. Multiply both sides by a positive common denominator to get rid of any fractions.

2. Multiply out any brackets.

3. Get all the terms in the variable on one side and the numbers on the other side.

4. Simplify each side.

5. If there is a – sign in front of the variable term, switch the sides of the variable term and the number and change their signs.

6. Solve for the variable.

7. Give your answer as a range of values for the variable.

Remember:

$\mathbb{N}$ = Natural numbers = {1, 2, 3, …}

$\mathbb{Z}$ = Integers = {…, −3, −2, −1, 0, 1, 2, 3, …}

$\mathbb{R}$ = Real numbers

▸ $x - 1 \leq 5$
  $\quad x \leq 6$

▸ $3x - 1 > 2x + 5$
  $\quad 3x - 2x > 1 + 5$
  $\quad x > 6$

▸ $-x < 5$
  $\quad -5 < x$
  $\quad x > -5$

EXAMPLE 1

Solve $3(1 - x) \geq -2x - 7, x \in \mathbb{R}$.

Solution

$3(1 - x) \geq -2x - 7$

$3 - 3x \geq -2x - 7$

$-3x + 2x \geq -3 - 7$

$\quad\quad -x \geq -10$ [Switch sides to get $+x$.]

$\quad\quad 10 \geq x$

This can be written as: $x \leq 10, x \in \mathbb{R}$.

EXAMPLE 2

Solve $\dfrac{(x - 3)}{2} \leq \dfrac{(5x - 1)}{3}, x \in \mathbb{R}$.

Solution

$\dfrac{(x - 3)}{2} \leq \dfrac{(5x - 1)}{3}$ [Multiply both sides by 6.]

$\dfrac{6(x - 3)}{2} \leq \dfrac{6(5x - 1)}{3}$

$3(x - 3) \leq 2(5x - 1)$

$\quad 3x - 9 \leq 10x - 2$

$\quad -9 + 2 \leq 10x - 3x$

$\quad\quad -7 \leq 7x$

$\quad\quad -1 \leq x$

This can be written as: $x \geq -1, x \in \mathbb{R}$

Plotting the solution set of an inequality on the number line

EXAMPLE 3

Solve $2x - 1 \leq 5, x \in \mathbb{R}$ and plot the solution set on the number line.

Solution

$2x - 1 \leq 5, x \in \mathbb{R}$

$\quad 2x \leq 6$

$x \leq 3, x \in \mathbb{R}$

The solution set is all values of x less than or equal to 3.

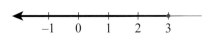

EXAMPLE 4

Solve $\dfrac{4-10x}{5} > 2(4-3x)$, $x \in \mathbb{N}$, and plot the solution set on the number line.

Solution

$\dfrac{4-10x}{5} > 2(4-3x)$, $x \in \mathbb{N}$

$4 - 10x > 10(4 - 3x)$

$4 - 10x > 40 - 30x$

$30x - 10x > 40 - 4$

$20x > 36$

$\therefore x > 1{\cdot}8$, $x \in \mathbb{N}$

The solution set is all natural numbers greater than $1{\cdot}8$.

Solution set = $\{2, 3, 4, ...\}$

EXAMPLE 5

(a) Find A, the solution set of $x + 6 > 2x + 1$, $x \in \mathbb{N}$.

(b) Find B, the solution set of $4(x - 1) \le x + 2$, $x \in \mathbb{N}$.

(c) List the elements $A \cap B$.

Solution

(a) $x + 6 > 2x + 1$, $x \in \mathbb{N}$

$6 - 1 > 2x - x$

$5 > x$

$\therefore x < 5$, $x \in \mathbb{N}$

$A = \{1, 2, 3, 4\}$

(b) $4(x - 1) \le x + 2$, $x \in \mathbb{N}$

$4x - 4 \le x + 2$

$4x - x \le 2 + 4$

$3x \le 6$

$\therefore x \le 2$, $x \in \mathbb{N}$

$B = \{1, 2\}$

(c) $A = \{1, 2, 3, 4\}$

$B = \{1, 2\}$

$A \cap B = \{1, 2, 3, 4\} \cap \{1, 2\} = \{1, 2\}$

EXERCISE 8

1. Solve the following for x.

   (a) $x - 4 > 5$, $x \in \mathbb{R}$

   (b) $x - 5 < 4$, $x \in \mathbb{N}$

   (c) $x + 2 \le 1$, $x \in \mathbb{R}$

   (d) $x - 5 \ge 7$, $x \in \mathbb{R}$

   (e) $2x > 30$, $x \in \mathbb{R}$

   (f) $-x \ge 9$, $x \in \mathbb{R}$

   (g) $-3x \le 12$, $x \in \mathbb{R}$

   (h) $4x \ge -8$, $x \in \mathbb{R}$

   (i) $x > 2x + 1$, $x \in \mathbb{R}$

   (j) $2x > x - 5$, $x \in \mathbb{R}$

   (k) $3(x - 1) > 4 - x$, $x \in \mathbb{R}$

   (l) $-5(x + 1) \le 2 - 3x$, $x \in \mathbb{R}$

   (m) $\dfrac{x}{3} - 2 \le \dfrac{x}{5}$, $x \in \mathbb{Z}$

   (n) $\dfrac{2x - 1}{4} \ge 5x$, $x \in \mathbb{R}$

   (o) $\dfrac{3x - 2}{4} \le \dfrac{1}{2}$, $x \in \mathbb{R}$

   (p) $-\dfrac{4x + 7}{3} > \dfrac{2 - x}{4}$, $x \in \mathbb{R}$

   (q) $-\dfrac{x}{3} > \dfrac{x}{5} - \dfrac{1}{15}$, $x \in \mathbb{R}$

   (r) $-3x + \dfrac{5}{3} > 2$, $x \in \mathbb{R}$

   (s) $\dfrac{2x - 1}{4} - \dfrac{1}{2} \le \dfrac{5x - 1}{2}$, $x \in \mathbb{R}$

   (t) $\dfrac{x + 1}{3} + \dfrac{x - 1}{7} \le \dfrac{1}{3}$, $x \in \mathbb{R}$

2. Plot the solution sets of questions **1(b)**, **(i)**, **(l)** and **(t)** on the number line.

3. **(a)** Find the solution set of $4x - 15 < 1, x \in \mathbb{N}$.

   (b) Find the solution set of $2(3 - x) < x + 15, x \in \mathbb{Z}$.

   (c) Find the solution set of $2x + 1 \geq -8, x \in \mathbb{Z}$.

   (d) Find A, the solution set of $x + 3 > 2x - 9, x \in \mathbb{N}$. Find B, the solution set of $2(x - 3) \geq x + 1, x \in \mathbb{N}$. List the elements $A \cap B$.

   (e) Find A, the solution set of $x - 2 \geq 2x - 6, x \in \mathbb{N}$. Find B, the solution set of $\dfrac{x - 1}{2} < 4, x \in \mathbb{N}$. List the elements B/A.

   (f) Find P, the solution set of $x + 2 < 2x + 7, x \in \mathbb{Z}$. Find Q, the solution set of $\dfrac{x + 7}{4} \geq 1, x \in \mathbb{Z}$. List the elements P/Q.

REVISION QUESTIONS

1. (a) Solve $\frac{1}{x} = x + 1$, giving your answer in the form $\frac{a \pm \sqrt{b}}{c}$, $a, b, c \in \mathbb{N}$.

   (b) Solve:

   (i) $(\sqrt{2})^x = 8$

   (ii) $\sqrt{x} - 1 = 7$

   (iii) $x^2 - 8 = 0$

   (c) Paul took part in a triathlon which involved swimming, running and cycling. He spent twice as long running as swimming, and three times as long cycling as running. His total time was 36 minutes. Write down an equation to represent this situation. Find t, the time he spent swimming.

2. (a) Solve:

   $2x - 3y = 7$
   $5x + 8y = 64$

   (b) Find:

   (i) The solution set A of $2x - 3 \leq 5$, $x \in \mathbb{Z}$.

   (ii) The solution set B of $\frac{1 - 2x}{3} < 3$, $x \in \mathbb{Z}$.

   (iii) List the elements of $A \cap B$.

   (c) The graph shown below has the equation of $y = ax^2 + bx + c$.

   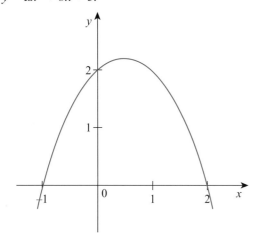

   If the curve crosses the y-axis at $(0, 2)$, find c. If it crosses the x-axis at $(-1, 0)$ and $(2, 0)$, find a and b.

3. Market research for a phone app shows that if it is sold for €1, then 24 000 are sold, but if it is sold for €4, none are sold. This research is modelled by the straight line in the diagram below.

   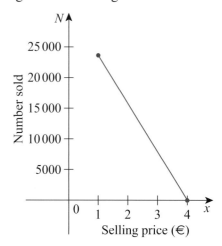

   (a) Find the equation connecting the number N sold and the selling price x. (Hint: $N = ax + b$)

   (b) If the cost of producing the app is €10 000, write down a formula for the profit P made by selling N apps at €x each, in terms of N and x.

   (c) Hence, show that

   $P = -8000x^2 + 32\,000x - 10\,000$.

   (d) Find the profit if the selling price is €3.

   (e) Find the selling price needed to make profit of €22 000.

4. (a) The time t in seconds for a child to slide down a slide is given by $t = \frac{kL}{\sqrt{H}}$, where L is the length in metres of the slide and H is its height in metres.

   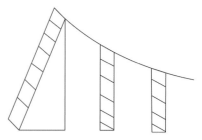

   It takes 8 seconds for a child to slide from the top to the bottom. Find k, if $L = 4$ m and $H = 2 \cdot 56$ m for a given slide. Express H in terms of t and L.

(b) The cost per night for staying in a hotel is €x and the cost of breakfast is €y. Mr Tierney stays for three nights and has breakfast on two mornings. Ms Prism stays for five nights and has breakfast on three mornings. If Mr Tierney's bill is €240 and Ms Prism's bill is €396, find the cost of a room per night and the cost of the breakfast.

(c) Find the points of intersection of the straight line $l: 3x + y - 7 = 0$ and the circle $s: x^2 + y^2 = 5$.

5. (a) Solve $\dfrac{4}{x-1} = 1 + \dfrac{1}{x}$. Write your answer in the form $a \pm \sqrt{b}$, $a, b \in \mathbb{Z}$.

(b) The amount of an investment after n years is given by $A = 2000(1\cdot2)^n$. How long does it take for the investment to amount to €3456?

(c) A patient is prescribed medication daily that must contain 9 units of vitamin A and 6 units of vitamin B. The vitamins are available in tablet and capsule form. Each tablet has 2 units of vitamin A and 1 unit of vitamin B. Each capsule has 1 unit of vitamin A and 2 units of vitamin B. If x is the patient's daily dose of tablets and y her daily dose of capsules, find x and y.

6. (a) Solve $\dfrac{4^{3x}}{\sqrt{8}} = \dfrac{16^x}{\sqrt{32}}$.

(b) Find k, if 2 is a root of the quadratic equation $2x^2 - kx + 9 = 0$.

(c) Form the quadratic equation with roots:

(i) $-1, 5$

(ii) $\dfrac{2}{3}, \dfrac{1}{4}$

(d) A boat, which can travel at x m/s, travels $1\cdot2$ km upstream and $1\cdot2$ km back to its original point in 24 minutes.

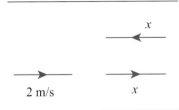

If the speed of the current is 2 m/s, find x and the time to go upstream and downstream.

7. (a) Solve:
$$\frac{3}{2}x - y = -1$$
$$\frac{2}{3}x - \frac{y}{5} = 2$$

(b) The sum S of the first n natural numbers $1, 2, 3, \ldots, n$ is given by $S = \dfrac{n}{2}(n + 1)$.

(i) Find the sum of the first 100 natural numbers.

(ii) Write out the first N natural numbers which add to 66.

(c) The production costs of a jeans manufacturer are fixed costs of €2500 per week and €15 for each pair of jeans made. Market research shows that if the selling price of a pair of jeans is €50 each, the manufacturer will sell 600 per week, but if the price is €60, it will only sell 100 per week.

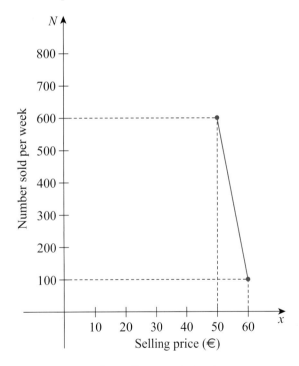

(i) Assuming a linear relation between the number N of jeans sold per week and the selling price x, show that $N = -50x + 3100$.

If the company sells N pairs per week:

(ii) Write down an expression for the weekly cost C in terms of x.

(iii) Write down an expression for the weekly revenue R.

(iv) Write down an expression for the weekly profit P.

(v) Find the selling price x for a profit of €13 100 per week, $50 \leq x \leq 60$.

8. (a) $ABCD$ is a rectangle and AEF is a right-angled triangle. If the area of $FEBCD$ is 324 cm^2, find x.

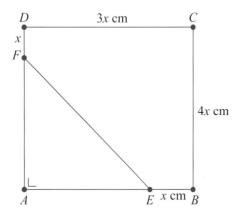

(b) A tiling company produces two samples of a square metre of tiling for a conservatory, sample A and sample B, consisting of white tiles and red tiles. Find the cost x of a white tile and the cost y of a red tile, if the cost of pattern A is €165 and the cost of pattern B is €160.

Sample A: cost = €165 per 1 m^2

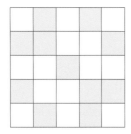

Sample B: cost = €160 per 1 m^2

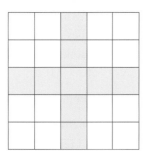

(c) Solve $\dfrac{x-1}{x+2} - \dfrac{x-2}{x+1} = \dfrac{1}{10}$.

9. (a) If $E = I(R + r)$, solve for r.

(b) If $\dfrac{1}{x+f} + \dfrac{1}{y+f} = \dfrac{1}{f}$, show that $xy = f^2$.

(c) The diagram below shows the graph of $y = 3x^2 + 6x - 1$. Find U and V, correct to two decimal places. Find W.

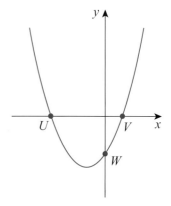

10. (a) In the triangle shown, find x if all angles are in degrees.

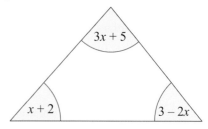

(b) The product of two consecutive even numbers is 624. Find them.

(c) A firework is launched upwards from a platform above the ground. Its height h, in metres, above the ground after t seconds is given by $h = -4{\cdot}9t^2 + 49t + 2$. Find:

(i) its height after 3 seconds,

(ii) the time it is 124·5 m above the ground,

(iii) the times for which it is 104·9 m above the ground.

SUMMARY

1. Linear equations: $ax + b = 0$:

   Solution: $x = -\dfrac{b}{a}$

2. Quadratic equations: $ax^2 + bx + c = 0$

   (a) Solution:

      (i) By factorisation

      (ii) By using the quadratic formula:

   $$x = \frac{-b \pm \sqrt{b^2 - 4ac}}{2a}$$

   (b) Properties of quadratics:

      (i) $b^2 - 4ac > 0$ gives two different, real roots:

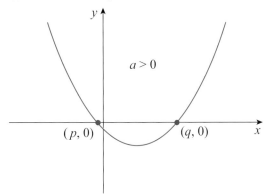

   or

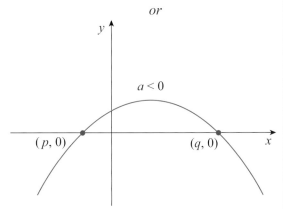

      (ii) $b^2 - 4ac = 0$ gives two equal, real roots:

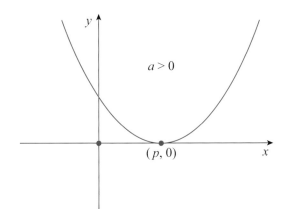

   or

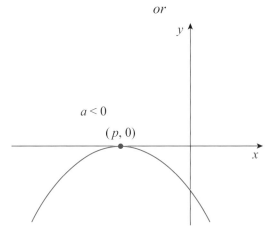

      (iii) $b^2 - 4ac < 0$ gives no real roots:

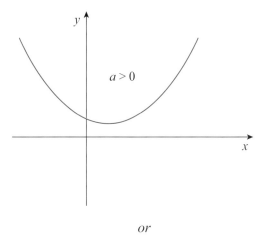

   or

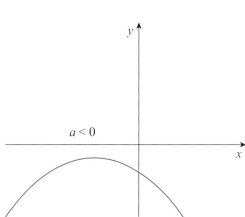

   (c) Forming a quadratic equation from its roots p and q:

   $$(x - p)(x - q) = 0$$

   or

   $x^2 - Sx + P = 0$, where S is the sum of the roots and P is the product of the roots.

3. Equations with square roots:

    Solve by isolating the square root and squaring both sides. Always check the answers.

4. Literal equations: Solve by isolating the specified variable.

5. Exponential equations:

    Solve by getting the same base and equating the powers:

    $$a^p = a^q$$

    $$\Rightarrow p = q$$

6. Simultaneous equations:

    (a) Two linear equations in two unknowns: Solve using elimination by addition.

    (b) One linear and one equation of order two: Solve using substitution by addition.

7. Word problems:

    Write down:

    (a) one equation for one unknown,

    (b) two equations for two unknowns

    Solve the equation(s).

8. Inequalities:

    For linear inequalities $ax + b \geq 0$, move ax to ensure a is positive, then solve by dividing both sides by a.

Sequences and Series

Seeing and understanding patterns is important for many reasons.

- Patterns enable you to make order out of apparent chaos.
- Patterns enable you to make accurate predictions.
- Patterns enable you to see mathematical relationships and hence to take short cuts.

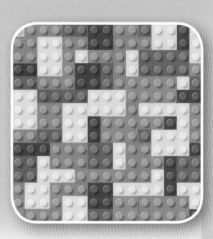

CHAPTER 9

Patterns

Learning Outcome

- To recognise patterns of numbers, shapes and objects and to construct a formula connecting the value of the nth T_n in a pattern with its place number (position) n in the pattern.

ACTIVITY 1

ACTION
Completing the pattern

OBJECTIVE
To recognise patterns and to fill in the missing terms in the sequence

ACTIVITY 2

ACTION
Writing down terms from sequences

OBJECTIVE
To write down specified terms from given sequences

It is very important to be able to recognise patterns in symbols, numbers and shapes and to be able to predict the next symbol, number or shape in a pattern.

It is even better if you can predict **any** symbol, number or shape using a rule (formula) as then you really do understand the underlying connection between them.

One of the most famous patterns in maths is the Fibonacci sequence (pattern). This was discovered in 1202 by Leonardo of Pisa, who was nicknamed Fibonacci (meaning 'the good-natured son').

The sequence is 1, 1, 2, 3, 5, 8, 13, 21, 34, …

It is an **infinite** sequence as it never ends. We have listed the first nine terms of the sequence. Can you predict the tenth term?

Of course, it is 55 as 21 + 34 = 55.

Fibonacci in nature (spirals) 🎧

This sequence occurs in nature in describing the population growth of rabbits and the spiral in a snail's shell.

9.1 What is a sequence?

KEY TERM

A **sequence** is a set of objects (symbols, numbers or shapes) listed in order from left to right with commas between the objects.

▸ Mo, Tu, We, Th, Fr, Sa, Su. [The days of the week]

▸ 0·9, 0·99, 0·999, …

▸ Δ, ○, □, Δ, ○, □, …

An individual object in a sequence is known as a term of the sequence. Each term is assigned a label which specifies its position in the list.

WORKED EXAMPLE | Infinite and finite sequences

Consider the following list of numbers: 1, 3, 5, 7, 9, …

This is the sequence of the odd natural numbers.

It is an **infinite** sequence as it does not end. The … (three dots) means that it goes on forever.

Each object in order is called a term.

1, 3, 5, 7, 9, …

1 is the first term, 3 is the second term, 5 is the third term, 7 is the fourth term …

Now look at the following list of numbers: 57, 48, 39, 30, 21, 12, 3. This is a **finite** sequence as it ends at 3.

The first term is 57. The symbol T_1 (T for term, 1 for first) is used to label this term.

The second term is labelled as T_2 and its value is 48.

T_5 is the value of the object in fifth place in the list reading from left to right. So $T_5 = 21$.

▸ In the sequence −5, −3, 1, 9, 25, …

▸ $T_1 = -5$, $T_2 = -3$, $T_3 = 1$, $T_4 = 9$, $T_5 = 25$, but what is T_{69} for example?

WORKED EXAMPLE | Predicting terms by recognising patterns

Triangular numbers are made by forming triangular patterns with circular discs, as shown.

, , , …

The number of discs in each shape generates the 'triangular numbers'.

Shape number	Number of discs
1	1
2	3
3	6
4	10

The sequence is: 1, 3, 6, 10, …

Can you predict the number of discs in the fifth shape? It is 15, of course.

The question of how to predict the value of terms that are not listed will now be examined by finding the rule of a sequence.

9.2 Rule of a sequence

ACTIVITY 3

ACTION
Generating a rule from a sequence

OBJECTIVE
To recognise patterns in sequences and to write down a rule for the sequence

A sequence usually has a rule. This is a way of finding the value of any specified term in the sequence.

WORKED EXAMPLE | Finding the rule of a sequence

The sequence 3, 8, 13, 18, 23, … starts at 3 and jumps by 5 from term to term.

The statement above is a rule of sorts but it does not really help you to find the 58th term in a simple and quick way. If you had a formula that related the value (T_n) of the nth term to its position (n) in the list, then you could find any specified term.

The rule above gives you a clue for finding a formula for T_n.

$T_1 = 3$

$T_2 = 8 = 3 + (2 - 1)$ jumps of 5

$T_3 = 13 = 3 + (3 - 1)$ jumps of 5

$T_4 = 18 = 3 + (4 - 1)$ jumps of 5

$\therefore T_n = 3 + (n - 1)$ jumps of $5 = 3 + (n - 1)5 = 5n - 2$

Another way to look at this sequence is to try to relate the value of any term T_n to its place number n in the list. In a table, the sequence is as follows:

Number of the term	Value of the term
$n = 1$	$3 = T_1 = 5 \times 1 - 2$
$n = 2$	$8 = T_2 = 5 \times 2 - 2$
$n = 3$	$13 = T_3 = 5 \times 3 - 2$
$n = 4$	$18 = T_4 = 5 \times 4 - 2$
$n = 5$	$23 = T_5 = 5 \times 5 - 2$

$\therefore T_n = 5 \times n - 2 = 5n - 2$

$T_n = 5n - 2$ is the value of the nth term of the sequence and is known as the **general term**.

This is a very powerful formula for a sequence as it enables you to:

1. **Find the value of any term in the list**

   To find the value of a term, simply replace n by the number of the term.

   To find the value of the 37th term in the sequence $T_n = 5n - 2$, replace n with 37.

   $T_{37} = 5 \times 37 - 2 = 183$

   The 37th term is 183.

2. **Find the position of a term in the list, given its value**

   Using the sequence above, find which term has a value of 158. Since 158 is some term in the list it must have a name (label). Call this T_n.

   $T_n = 158 = 5n - 2$

   $\qquad 5n = 160$

   $\qquad n = 32$

   The 32nd term in the list has a value of 158.

   In general, it is very difficult to find a general term T_n for a sequence, given its first few terms.

WORKED EXAMPLE

Finding the general term T_n of a sequence is not always easy

Find T_n for the sequence 5, 13, 35, 97, …, given that $5 = 2^1 + 3^1$.

Number of the term	Value of the term
$n = 1$	$T_1 = 5 = 2^1 + 3^1$
$n = 2$	$T_2 = 13 = 2^2 + 3^2$
$n = 3$	$T_3 = 35 = 2^3 + 3^3$
$n = 4$	$T_4 = 97 = 2^4 + 3^4$

$\therefore T_n = 2^n + 3^n$

This would have been extremely difficult to find without the hint.

However, given T_n for a sequence, it is very easy to find any specified term because you simply replace n, wherever it appears, by the specified value.

EXAMPLE 1

For a sequence $T_n = 3n - 2$:

(a) write out the first five terms,

(b) find the 85th term,

(c) find which term has a value of 49.

Solution

$T_n = 3n - 2$

(a) $n = 1$: $T_1 = 3(1) - 2 = 1$

   $n = 2$: $T_2 = 3(2) - 2 = 4$

   $n = 3$: $T_3 = 3(3) - 2 = 7$

   $n = 4$: $T_4 = 3(4) - 2 = 10$

   $n = 5$: $T_5 = 3(5) - 2 = 13$

   The first five terms in the sequence are: 1, 4, 7, 10, 13, …

(b) $n = 85$: $T_{85} = 3(85) - 2 = 255 - 2 = 253$

   The 85th term is 253.

(c) 49 is some term T_n, but which one?

   $T_n = 3n - 2 = 49$

   $3n = 51$

   $n = 17$

   The 17th term has a value of 49.

EXAMPLE 2

For a sequence $T_n = 3 \times 2^{n-1}$:

(a) find the first four terms,

(b) find the 12th term,

(c) find which term has a value of 192.

Solution

$T_n = 3 \times 2^{n-1}$

(a) $n = 1$: $T_1 = 3 \times 2^{1-1} = 3 \times 2^0 = 3$

   $n = 2$: $T_2 = 3 \times 2^{2-1} = 3 \times 2^1 = 6$

   $n = 3$: $T_3 = 3 \times 2^{3-1} = 3 \times 2^2 = 12$

   $n = 4$: $T_4 = 3 \times 2^{4-1} = 3 \times 2^3 = 24$

   The first four terms are: 3, 6, 12, 24, …

(b) $n = 12$: $T_{12} = 3 \times 2^{12-1} = 3 \times 2^{11} = 6144$

(c) $T_n = 3 \times 2^{n-1} = 192$

   $2^{n-1} = 64$

   $2^{n-1} = 2^6$

   $n - 1 = 6$

   $n = 7$

   The seventh term in the sequence has a value of 192.

EXERCISE 1

1. For the sequence $-8, -3, 2, 7, \ldots$

   (a) find T_1

   (b) find $T_4 - T_3$

   (c) write down a rule, in words, for this sequence

   (d) using your rule, find the values of the following terms: T_7, T_8, T_9, T_{10}

   (e) show that $T_8 - T_7 = T_{10} - T_9$

   (f) complete $T_n = -8 + (\ \ ) \times 5$

   (g) find T_{34}

   (h) state if it is a finite or an infinite sequence

2. For the sequence $11, 14, 17, 20, 23, 26, \ldots$

   (a) complete the statement: Any term minus the previous one = _____

   (b) copy and complete the table:

Number of the term	Value of the term
$n = 1$	$11 = T_1 = 3 \times 1 + 8$
$n = 2$	$14 = T_2 = 3 \times 2 + 8$
$n = 3$	$17 = T_3 =$
$n = 4$	$20 = T_4 =$
$n = 5$	$23 = T_5 =$
$n = 6$	$26 = T_6 =$

   (c) write down a formula for T_n for this sequence,

   (d) using this formula, find:

   (i) T_{37}
   (ii) T_{100}
   (iii) T_{101}

   (e) show that $T_{101} - T_{100} = 3$.

3. For the sequence $1, 8, 27, 64, \ldots$

   (a) copy and complete the table:

Number of the term	Value of the term
$n = 1$	$1 = T_1 = 1^3$
$n = 2$	$8 = T_2 = 2^3$
$n = 3$	
$n = 4$	

   (b) a formula for the general term of this sequence might be: $T_n =$ _____

   (c) using your calculator, find T_{22}

4. For the sequence $6, 18, 54, 162, \ldots$

   (a) complete the statement: Any term divided by the previous one = _____

   (b) copy and complete the table:

Number of the term	Value of the term
$n = 1$	$6 = T_1 = 2 \times 3^1$
$n = 2$	$18 = T_2 = 2 \times 3^2$
$n = 3$	$54 = T_3 =$
$n = 4$	$162 = T_4 =$

   (c) write down a formula for T_n for this sequence,

   (d) using the formula in part (c), find $\dfrac{T_{100}}{T_{99}}$ without using your calculator.

5. The formula for the general term of a sequence is $T_n = 3n - 2$.

   (a) Find:

   (i) T_1 (iii) T_7

   (ii) T_2 (iv) T_{11}

   (b) Which term has a value of 94?

6. For a sequence $T_n = n^2 + 2n$:

   (a) find the first five terms,

   (b) which term has a value of 120?

7. The general term of a sequence is
$T_n = -5n + 2$.

(a) Find:

(i) T_5 (iii) T_{51}

(ii) T_6 (iv) T_{52}

(b) Show that $T_{52} - T_{51} = T_6 - T_5$.

8. The general term for a sequence is $T_n = \dfrac{4}{2^n}$.

(a) Write out the first five terms.

(b) Which term has a value of $\dfrac{1}{128}$?

(c) Show that $\dfrac{T_{15}}{T_{14}} = \dfrac{1}{2}$.

9. A fence is constructed by starting with a five-bar section consisting of two vertical bars and three horizontal bars.

Four-bar sections are then added.

The first few stages in the construction are shown.

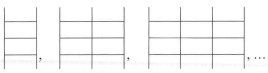

Stage 1   Stage 2   Stage 3

(a) Draw the fourth pattern.

(b) Write a sequence to show the number of bars in each stage.

(c) Copy and complete the table:

Stage number n	Number of bars T_n
1	$5 = 5 + 4 \times 0$
2	
3	
4	

(d) Find a formula for T_n.

(e) How many bars are there in the tenth stage?

(f) Which stage has 61 bars?

10. (a) For the polygons below:

(i) copy and complete the table:

Polygon	Number of sides	Sum of interior angles
Triangle	3	180°
Quadrilateral		
Pentagon	5	540°
Hexagon		

(ii) hence, copy and complete the table:

Number of sides of a polygon N	Sum of interior angles T_n
3	$180° = 180° \times 1 = 180° \times (3 - 2)$
4	
5	$540° = 180° \times 3 = 180° \times (5 - 2)$
6	

(iii) write down a formula for T_n

(b) What is the sum of the interior angles of a decagon (a 10-sided figure)?

(c) How many sides does a polygon have if the sum of the interior angles is 3780°?

11. Copy and complete the tables below:

(a)

Pattern number n	Shape	Number of small squares T_n
1		$T_1 = 5 = 6 \times 1 - 1 = \boxed{}$
2		$T_2 = 11 = 6 \times \boxed{} - \boxed{} = \boxed{}$
3		$T_3 = \boxed{} = 6 \times \boxed{} - \boxed{} = \boxed{}$

Find:

(i) T_4 **(ii)** T_n

(b)

Pattern number n	Shape	Number of circles T_n
1		$T_1 = 4 = 3 \times 1 + 1 = 4$
2		$T_2 = \boxed{} = 3 \times \boxed{} + 1 = \boxed{}$
3		$T_3 = \boxed{} = 3 \times \boxed{} + \boxed{} = \boxed{}$

Find:

(i) T_5 **(ii)** T_{10} **(iii)** T_n

Sequences and Series

CHAPTER 10

Learning Outcomes

- To understand the difference between an arithmetic sequence and a geometric sequence.
- To understand what is meant by a series.
- To solve problems involving arithmetic sequences and series.
- To explore quadratic sequences

10.1 Special types of sequences

ACTIVITY 4

ACTION
Exploring arithmetic sequences

OBJECTIVE
To explore the properties of arithmetic sequences

Arithmetic sequence

Consider the following sequences:

▸ 1, 3, 5, 7, 9, …

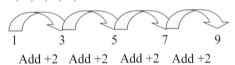

1   3   5   7   9
Add +2   Add +2   Add +2   Add +2

▸ −3, 2, 7, 12, 17, …

−3   2   7   12   17
Add +5   Add +5   Add +5   Add +5

▸ 5, 3, 1, −1, −3, …

5   3   1   −1   −3
Add −2   Add −2   Add −2   Add −2

▸ −4, −7, −10, −13, −16, …

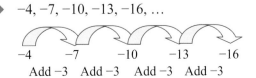

−4   −7   −10   −13   −16
Add −3   Add −3   Add −3   Add −3

All of these sequences have one thing in common: you add the same number to any term to get the next term.

> Arithmetic sequence: Any term − Previous term = Constant

ACTIVITY 5

ACTION
Exploring geometric sequences

OBJECTIVE
To explore the properties of geometric sequences

Geometric sequence

Consider the following sequences:

▸ 1, 2, 4, 8, 16, …

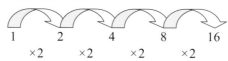

▸ 16, 8, 4, 2, 1, …

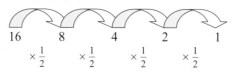

▸ 4, −12, 36, −108, +324, …

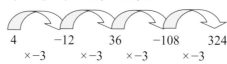

▸ 27, −9, 3, − 1, $\frac{1}{3}$, …

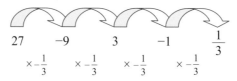

All of these sequences have one thing in common: you multiply each term by the same number to get the next term.

> Geometric sequence: $\dfrac{\text{Any term}}{\text{Previous term}} = \text{Constant}$

Test for an arithmetic sequence

A sequence is an arithmetic sequence if: Any term − Previous term = Constant.

▸ $\frac{5}{2}, 3, \frac{7}{2}, 4, \ldots$ is an arithmetic sequence because:

Any term − Previous term = Constant = $\frac{1}{2}$

$3 - \frac{5}{2} = \frac{7}{2} - 3 = 4 - \frac{7}{2} = \frac{1}{2}$

▸ −11, −2, +7, +16, … is an arithmetic sequence because:
Any term − Previous term = Constant = 9

$-2 - (-11) = 7 - (-2) = 16 - 7 = 9$

▸ $1, \frac{1}{2}, \frac{1}{3}, \frac{1}{4}, \ldots$ is **not** an arithmetic sequence because:

Any term − Previous term ≠ Constant.

$\frac{1}{2} - 1 \neq \frac{1}{3} - \frac{1}{2} \neq \frac{1}{4} - \frac{1}{3}$

Test for a geometric sequence

A sequence is a geometric sequence if: $\dfrac{\text{Any term}}{\text{Previous term}} = \text{Constant}$

▸ 2, −6, 18, … is a geometric sequence because $\dfrac{-6}{2} = \dfrac{18}{-6} = -3$.

EXERCISE 2

State which of the following sequences are arithmetic, geometric or neither, giving a reason for your answer.

1. 3, 11, 19, …
2. 3, 6, 12, …
3. 1, 3, 6, 10, …
4. 5, 10, 20, …
5. $\frac{1}{2}$, 2, 8, …
6. 5, −6, −17, …

7. 3, 9, 27, …
8. $1, -\frac{1}{2}, \frac{1}{4}, …$
9. −8, 16, −32, …
10. −17, −20, −23, …
11. 6, 12, 20, …
12. $x, x+1, x+2, …$

13. $x, x^2, x^3, …$
14. $\frac{1}{3}, \frac{1}{4}, \frac{1}{5}, …$
15. $\frac{2}{3}, \frac{4}{9}, \frac{8}{27}, …$
16. $\frac{a}{b}+11, \frac{a}{b}+12, \frac{a}{b}+13, …$
17. $p-1, p, p+1, …$
18. $\frac{a}{b}, a, ab, …$
19. $3x, 9x^2, 27x^3, …$
20. $\frac{1}{2}, 3, \frac{11}{2}, …$

10.2 Arithmetic sequences

Defining an arithmetic sequence

ACTIVITY 6

ACTION
Understanding an arithmetic sequence

OBJECTIVE
To follow a simple, practical example of an arithmetic sequence

WORKED EXAMPLE ## Arithmetic sequence 1

Jane saves €60 in the first week of opening a savings account and increases it by €10 per week after that. Write out how much Jane saves, week by week, for the first six weeks.

Week 1	Week 2	Week 3	Week 4	Week 5	Week 6
€60	€70	€80	€90	€100	€110

Therefore, Jane's weekly savings in euro form the sequence 60, 70, 80, 90, 100, 110, …

This sequence starts with €60. This is the first term T_1 and it increases at a **constant rate** of €10.

This means that the **difference** between any term and the previous term is a constant equal to 10.

WORKED EXAMPLE

Arithmetic sequence 2

As dry air moves up in the atmosphere, it cools down. In fact, it cools by 3 °C for every 300 m rise. If the ground temperature is 20 °C, write out as a sequence the temperature of the air at heights of 300 m, 600 m, 900 m, 1200 m and 1500 m above the surface of the ground.

Height (m)	300	600	900	1200	1500
Temperature (°C)	17	14	11	8	5

The sequence of temperatures in °C is 17, 14, 11, 8, 5, …

The sequence starts at 17 °C. This is the first term T_1 and it decreases at a constant rate of 3 °C.

This means that the difference between any term and the previous term is a constant equal to -3.

EXAMPLE 1

For the sequence $\frac{3}{2}, \frac{7}{4}, 2, \frac{9}{4}, \frac{5}{2}, \ldots$, find:

(a) T_1

(b) T_2

(c) T_4

(d) T_5

Show that $T_2 - T_1 = T_5 - T_4$.

Solution

$\frac{3}{2}, \frac{7}{4}, 2, \frac{9}{4}, \frac{5}{2}, \ldots$

(a) $T_1 = \frac{3}{2}$ (c) $T_4 = \frac{9}{4}$

(b) $T_2 = \frac{7}{4}$ (d) $T_5 = \frac{5}{2}$

$T_2 - T_1 = \frac{7}{4} - \frac{3}{2} = \frac{1}{4}$

$T_5 - T_4 = \frac{5}{2} - \frac{9}{4} = \frac{1}{4}$

KEY TERM

An **arithmetic sequence** or **progression** is a list of terms in which you start with any object (number, symbol, shape, function) and keep on adding the same constant to each term to get the next term.

ACTIVITY 7

ACTION
Working with arithmetic sequences (1)

OBJECTIVE
To write down the first term and common difference of a number of arithmetic sequences

▶ Start with +2 and keep on adding 5.

+2,   7,   12,   17,   22, …

Add +5   Add +5   Add +5   Add +5

▶ Start with −3 and keep on adding 6.

−3,   3,   9,   15,   21, …

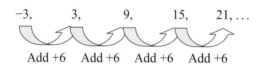

Add +6   Add +6   Add +6   Add +6

▶ Start with 7 and keep on adding −3.

7,   4,   1,   −2,   −5, …

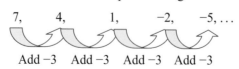

Add −3   Add −3   Add −3   Add −3

ACTIVITY 8

ACTION
Working with arithmetic sequences (2)

OBJECTIVE
To explore various arithmetic sequences and to gain an understanding of how these sequences operate

▸ Start with −3 and keep on adding −7.

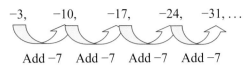

$$-3, \quad -10, \quad -17, \quad -24, \quad -31, \ldots$$

Add −7   Add −7   Add −7   Add −7

It is important to note the following:

1. Every arithmetic sequence has a starting term T_1 (the first term).

2. Any term minus the previous term is the same constant, called d (the common difference).

   Any term − Previous term = d = Constant

3. If you know the first term T_1 and the constant d, you can generate the whole sequence.

EXAMPLE 2

The first term of an arithmetic sequence is 50 and the constant that is to be added on to each term is −4. Write down the first five terms of the sequence.

Solution

$T_1 = 50$

$T_2 = 50 + (-4) = 46$

$T_3 = 46 + (-4) = 42$

$T_4 = 42 + (-4) = 38$

$T_5 = 38 + (-4) = 34$

Arithmetic sequence:
50, 46, 42, 38, 34, …

EXAMPLE 3

In the arithmetic sequence 4, 7, 10, … , what is the first term T_1 and the constant you add on to get the next term?

Solution

Arithmetic sequence 4, 7, 10, …

$T_1 = 4$

Constant $= 7 - 4 = 3 = 10 - 7$.

EXERCISE 3

1. **(a)** For the sequence 3, 11, 19, … find:

   (i) T_1 **(iii)** $T_2 - T_1$

   (ii) T_3 **(iv)** $T_3 - T_2$

   (b) Assuming the same pattern continues, find T_5 and T_6.

2. **(a)** For the sequence 5, 3, 1, … find:

   (i) T_1

   (ii) T_2

   (iii) T_3

   (iv) $T_2 - T_1$

   (v) $T_3 - T_2$

   (b) Assuming the same pattern continues, find T_4, T_5 and T_6.

3. For the sequence 4, 11, 18, 25, …

   (a) Find:

   (i) T_1

   (ii) the difference d between any term and the previous one

(b) Show that:

   (i) $T_2 = T_1 + 1d$

   (ii) $T_3 = T_1 + 2d$

   (iii) $T_4 = T_1 + 3d$

(c) Assuming the same pattern continues, find T_{42}.

4. For the sequence $-3, -7, -11, -15, \ldots$

  (a) Find:

   (i) the first term T_1

   (ii) the difference d between any term and the previous one

  (b) Show that:

   (i) $T_2 = T_1 + 1d$

   (ii) $T_3 = T_1 + 2d$

   (iii) $T_4 = T_1 + 3d$

(c) Assuming the same pattern continues, find T_{21}.

5. For the sequence $\frac{1}{2}, \frac{5}{6}, \frac{7}{6}, \frac{3}{2}, \ldots$

  (a) Find:

   (i) the first term T_1

   (ii) the difference d between any term and the previous one

  (b) Show that:

   (i) $T_2 = T_1 + 1d$

   (ii) $T_3 = T_1 + 2d$

   (iii) $T_4 = T_1 + 3d$

  (c) Assuming the same pattern continues, find T_{17}.

The general arithmetic sequence and the general term T_n

If you start with a first term a and keep on adding a constant d you generate the general arithmetic sequence:

$$a, \quad a+d, \quad a+2d, \quad a+3d, \ldots$$

$$\uparrow \qquad \uparrow \qquad \uparrow \qquad \uparrow$$

$$T_1, \quad T_2, \quad T_3, \quad T_4 \ldots$$

$T_1 = a = $ the first term

$T_2 = a + 1d$

$T_3 = a + 2d$

$T_4 = a + 3d$

$\therefore T_{57} = a + 56d$

The sequence $a, a + d, a + 2d, a + 3d, \ldots$ is known as the general arithmetic sequence with first term $T_1 = a$ and common difference d.

> **TIP**
>
> If you are told the 57th term of an arithmetic sequence is -82, you can write $a + 56d = -82$.

The general term T_n of the arithmetic sequence with first term a and common difference d is:

$$\boxed{T_n = a + (n - 1)d}$$

This general term is also known as the nth term of an arithmetic sequence.

EXAMPLE 4

For the arithmetic sequence 15, 18, 21, ... find:

(a) the first term a,

(b) the common difference d,

(c) the 38th term,

(d) the general term.

Solution

Arithmetic sequence: 15, 18, 21, ...

(a) $a = 15 = $ first term $= T_1$

(b) $d = $ Any term − Previous term $= 18 - 15 = 3$

(c) $T_{38} = a + 37d = 15 + 37 \times 3 = 15 + 111 = 126$

(d) $T_n = a + (n-1)d = 15 + (n-1)3 = 3n + 12$

As already stated, for any arithmetic sequence:

1. $T_1 = a = $ first term.

2. $d = $ common difference $= $ Any term − Previous term.

3. If you know a and d, you can find any other term.

EXAMPLE 5

A cyclist freewheels downhill travelling 1·2 m in the first second and, in each succeeding second, 1·5 m more than in the previous second. Write out as a sequence the distances travelled in the first four seconds. Find the distance travelled in the 12th second.

Solution

1st second	2nd second	3rd second	4th second
1·2 m	2·7 m	4·2 m	5·7 m

Arithmetic sequence: 1·2, 2·7, 4·2, 5·7, ...

$a = 1·2, d = 1·5$

$T_{12} = a + 11d = 1·2 + 11 \times 1·5 = 1·2 + 16·5 = 17·7$ m

Given the general term of an arithmetic sequence, you can find any specified term.

EXAMPLE 6

For an arithmetic sequence with general term $T_n = 5 - 2n$,

(a) find: **(i)** a

        (ii) d

        (iii) T_{34}

(b) show that $T_{n+1} - T_n = d$

(c) write out the first four terms

Solution

$T_n = 5 - 2n$

(a) **(i)** $a = T_1 = 5 - 2 \times 1 = 3$

    (ii) $T_2 = 5 - 2 \times 2 = 1$

         $\therefore d = T_2 - T_1 = 1 - 3 = -2$

    (iii) $T_{34} = 5 - 2 \times 34 = 5 - 68 = -63$

(b) $T_{n+1} = 5 - 2(n+1) = 5 - 2n - 2 = 3 - 2n$

    $T_n \qquad\qquad\qquad\qquad\quad = 5 - 2n$

$$\overline{\qquad\qquad T_{n+1} - T_n = -2 = d}$$

(c) $a = 3, d = -2$.

Arithmetic sequence: 3, 1, −1, −3, ...

If you know the value of the nth term of an arithmetic sequence, you can find what position it is in the sequence (the number of the term).

EXAMPLE 7

Which term is 97 in the arithmetic sequence $-14, -11, -8, -5, \ldots$?

Solution

Arithmetic sequence: $-14, -11, -8, -5, \ldots$

Write down what you know: $a = -14, d = 3$

You do not know which term 97 is, so call it T_n.

$$T_n = a + (n-1)d = -14 + (n-1)3$$
$$= 3n - 17$$

$\therefore 3n - 17 = 97$

$\qquad 3n = 114$

$\qquad n = 38$

97 is the 38th term.

TIP

↑ Remember, in all sequences, $n \in \mathbb{N}$.

EXAMPLE 8

Is 305 a term of the arithmetic sequence $7, 10, 13, \ldots$?

Solution

Arithmetic sequence: $7, 10, 13, \ldots$

If 305 is a term in this arithmetic sequence, you should be able to say which term it is.

Write down what you know: $a = 7, d = 3$

$$T_n = 7 + (n-1)3 = 3n + 4$$

$T_n = 305$

$3n + 4 = 305$

$\qquad 3n = 301$

$\qquad n = 100\frac{1}{3}$

305 is not a term of the arithmetic sequence because n is not a natural number.

EXAMPLE 9

How many terms are in the finite arithmetic sequence $7, 3, -1, -5, -9, \ldots, -129$?

Solution

Arithmetic sequence: $7, 3, -1, -5, -9, \ldots, -129$.

$T_1 = a = 7, d = -4$

$$T_n = a + (n-1)d = 7 + (n-1)(-4) = 11 - 4n$$

Call the last term T_n: $T_n = 11 - 4n = -129$

$\qquad 4n = 140$

$\qquad n = 35$

There are 35 terms in the sequence.

-129 is the 35th term.

EXERCISE 4

1. **(a)** An arithmetic sequence has $a = 4$ and $d = 5$. Find $T_1, T_2, T_3, T_5, T_{11}$ and T_{122}.

   (b) For the arithmetic sequence $4, 2, 0, \ldots$, find T_1, T_2, T_3, T_{55} and T_{105}.

   (c) For an arithmetic sequence $a = 5$ and $d = \frac{1}{2}$, find T_1, T_7, T_9, T_{50} and T_{73}.

   (d) Find the fifth, eighth and 22nd terms of the arithmetic sequence $3, 6, 9, 12, \ldots$.

   (e) A baker receives a delivery of 520 kg of flour. He uses no flour on the day it is delivered (day 1). He uses 20 kg every day after that. How much flour will the baker have left at the end of the 18th day?

(f) Joe walks 2 km on the first day of his fitness programme and increases the distance by 550 m every day after that. How far does Joe walk on the 14th day?

(g) At the start of 1 April, Mary has 192 sweets left over from Easter. She eats six sweets per day starting on 1 April until they are finished. How many sweets will she have at the start of 15 April?

(h) A coin collection is valued at €24 000 in 2002. Its value increases by €3000 annually.

    (i) Write out, as a sequence, the value of the collection from 2002 to 2006 inclusive.

    (ii) Is the sequence arithmetic? Why?

    (iii) Find a and d.

    (iv) How much would the collection be worth in 2041?

2. Find a, d and the general term for the arithmetic sequences:

(a) 2, 4, 6, 8, …

(b) 1, 3, 5, 7, 9, …

(c) 7, 5, 3, …

(d) 3, 3·5, 4, 4·5, …

(e) −1, −4, −7, …

(f) −6, −2, 2, …

(g) $x, x − 1, x − 2, …$

(h) $b, b + c, b + 2c, …$

(i) $\frac{1}{2}, 1, 1\frac{1}{2}, …$

(j) A walker increases the distance she walks by 0·1 km every day starting with 4 km on 1 September. Write out the distances she walks every day from 1 September as a sequence. Find a, d and the distance she walks on 8 September.

3. Calculate the first term a and the common difference d of the following arithmetic sequences and write down the first five terms of each sequence:

(a) $T_n = n + 1$

(b) $T_n = 2n$

(c) $T_n = 2n + 3$

(d) $T_n = 3n − 2$

(e) $T_n = 5n − 7$

(f) $T_n = \dfrac{n + 1}{3}$

4. Find the general term T_n of the following arithmetic sequences and hence, the specific term in the bracket:

(a) 2, 4, 6, 8, … (T_7)

(b) 7, 5, 3, 1, … (T_{17})

(c) −1, 2, 5, 8, … (T_{21})

(d) −3, −5, −7, −9, … (T_{42})

(e) $1, \frac{1}{2}, 0, -\frac{1}{2}, …$ (T_{35})

(f) $\frac{3}{2}, 2, \frac{5}{2}, 3, \frac{7}{2}, …$ (T_{58})

(g) $5, \frac{5}{2}, 0, -\frac{5}{2}, …$ (T_{37})

(h) $a, a + 1, a + 2, a + 3, …$ (T_{12})

(i) $a, a + d, a + 2d, a + 3d, …$ (T_{45})

(j) $\frac{1}{2}, \frac{7}{6}, \frac{11}{6}, \frac{5}{2}, …$ (T_{48})

5. (a) Which term has a value of 27 in the arithmetic sequence 3, 5, 7, …?

(b) Which term has a value of 126 in the arithmetic sequence 4, 6, 8, …?

(c) Which term has a value of 342 in the arithmetic sequence 12, 67, 122, …?

(d) Which term has a value of −112 in the arithmetic sequence 5, −8, −21, …?

(e) At the start of 1 April, John has 110 sweets in a box. He eats five sweets per day starting on 1 April. At the start of what date will he have 35 sweets left?

(f) How many terms are there in the following arithmetic sequences?

    (i) 2, 4, 6, …, 48

    (ii) 5, 7, 9, 11, …, 135

    (iii) −3, 2, 7, …, 92

    (iv) 6, 2, −2, …, −190

10.3 The sum of a sequence (series)

ACTIVITY 9

ACTION
Writing series

OBJECTIVE
To write the corresponding series when presented with a sequence

KEY TERM

A **series** is simply the sum of the individual terms of a sequence.

Given the sequence 1, 2, 6, 24, …, the corresponding series is $1 + 2 + 6 + 24 + …$.

The individual terms in both are exactly the same. The only difference between a sequence and a series is that the **commas are replaced by + signs**.

Arithmetic series: $-5 - 2 + 1 + 4 + 7 + …$

$T_1 = -5$ $\qquad\qquad$ $T_3 = 1$

$T_2 = -2$ $\qquad\qquad$ $T_5 = 7$

The corresponding sequence is $-5, -2, 1, 4, 7, …$.
The general term T_n is exactly the same for both.

EXAMPLE 10

A sequence has a general term given by $T_n = 3n + 5$. Write out the first five terms of the series.

Solution

$T_n = 3n + 5$

$T_1 = 3 \times 1 + 5 = 8$

$T_2 = 3 \times 2 + 5 = 11$

$T_3 = 3 \times 3 + 5 = 14$

$T_4 = 3 \times 4 + 5 = 17$

$T_5 = 3 \times 5 + 5 = 20$

Series: $8 + 11 + 14 + 17 + 20 + …$

So how do you add up the terms in an arithmetic series?

ACTIVITY 10

ACTION
Writing out the sums of sequences

OBJECTIVE
To write out the partial sums of a number of sequences

The partial sums of a series

It is relatively easy to work out the sums of the first few terms (partial sums) of a series, but the sums of large numbers of terms are difficult to compute.

WORKED EXAMPLE — Exploring partial sums

For the series
$1 + 3 + 5 + 7 + 9 + 11 + …$, find:

(a) the sum of the first term,
(b) the sum of the first three terms,
(c) the sum of the first six terms.

Series: $1 + 3 + 5 + 7 + 9 + 11 + …$

(a) The sum of the first term is known as the first partial sum and is denoted by S_1.

$S_1 = 1 = T_1$ is, of course, just the first term.

(b) The sum of the first three terms is known as the 3rd partial sum and is denoted by S_3.

$S_3 = 1 + 3 + 5$
$\quad = T_1 + T_2 + T_3 = 9$

(c) The sum of the first six terms is known as the 6th partial sum and is denoted by S_6.

$S_6 = 1 + 3 + 5 + 7 + 9 + 11$
$\quad = T_1 + T_2 + T_3 + T_4 + T_5 + T_6$
$\quad = 36$

You can imagine how difficult it would be to work out S_{98}, S_{1002}, etc.

ACTIVITY 11

ACTION
Using the summing formula for arithmetic series

OBJECTIVE
To add up the terms of a sequence and to check the answer using the summing formula

The sum S_n of the first n terms of an arithmetic series

The formula for the sum S_n of the first n terms of an arithmetic sequence was worked out by a famous mathematician named Gauss.

For any arithmetic series (sequence), with first term a and common difference d, the sum S_n of the first n terms is given by:

$$S_n = \frac{n}{2}[2a + (n-1)d]$$

It is important to note the following:

1. S_n = the sum of the first n terms of an arithmetic series (sequence)
   $S_1 = T_1 = a$
   $S_2 = T_1 + T_2$
   $S_n = T_1 + T_2 + \ldots + T_n$

2. n = the number of terms to be added

3. $a = T_1$ = first term

4. d = common difference = any term − previous one

5. Once you know a and d for an arithmetic series, you can add up any number of terms.

EXAMPLE 11

For the arithmetic series $6 + 10 + 14 + \ldots$ find:

(a) S_1 (c) S_n

(b) S_{20} (d) S_{72}

Solution

Arithmetic series: $6 + 10 + 14 + \ldots$

$a = 6, d = 4$

(a) $S_1 = T_1 = 6$

(b) $S_{20} = \frac{20}{2}[2 \times 6 + (20-1) \times 4]$

$\qquad = 10[12 + 76]$

$\qquad = 880$

This means that when you add up the first 20 terms of this arithmetic series, you get 880.

(c) $S_n = \frac{n}{2}[2 \times 6 + (n-1) \times 4]$

$\qquad = \frac{n}{2}[12 + 4n - 4]$

$\qquad = \frac{n}{2}(4n + 8) = 2n(n + 2)$

This is the sum of the first n terms of the arithmetic series.

(d) To find S_{72}, use S_n in part (c) and $n = 72$.

$\qquad \therefore S_{72} = 2 \times 72(72 + 2) = 144(74) = 10\,656$

EXAMPLE 12

Mr Casey repays a loan over 24 months. His monthly repayments form an arithmetic sequence. There are 24 repayments in total. He repays €139 in the first month, €135 in the second month, €131 in the third month, and so on.

(a) How much does he pay in the 24th month?

(b) Find his total payments for 24 months.

Solution

Month	1st month	2nd month	3rd month
Repayment	€139	€135	€131

Arithmetic sequence: 139, 135, 131, ...

$a = 139, d = -4$

(a) $T_{24} = a + 23d = 139 + 23(-4) = €47$

(b) $S_{24} = \frac{24}{2}[2 \times 139 + (24-1)(-4)]$

$\qquad = €2232$

EXAMPLE 13

For the arithmetic series $7 + 10 + 13 + 16 + \ldots$, find:

(a) T_1 **(f)** T_{32}

(b) S_1 **(g)** S_{32}

(c) a **(h)** T_n

(d) d **(i)** S_n

(e) S_3 **(j)** S_{74}

Solution

$7 + 10 + 13 + 16 + \ldots$

(a) $T_1 = 7$

(b) $S_1 = T_1 = 7$

(c) $a = T_1 = 7$

(d) $d = 10 - 7 = 3$

(e) $S_3 = T_1 + T_2 + T_3 = 7 + 10 + 13 = 30$

(f) $T_{32} = a + 31d = 7 + 31 \times 3 = 100$

(g) $S_{32} = \frac{32}{2}[2 \times 7 + (32 - 1) \times 3] = 1712$

(h) $T_n = 7 + (n - 1)3 = 3n + 4$

(i) $S_n = \frac{n}{2}[14 + (n - 1)3] = \frac{n}{2}(3n + 11)$

(j) $S_{74} = \frac{74}{2}(3 \times 74 + 11) = 8621$

EXAMPLE 14

Find the sum of the finite series $4 + 9 + 14 + \ldots + 349$.

Solution

Calculate the number of terms in the series.

$a = 4, d = 5, n = ?$

$T_n = a + (n - 1)d = 4 + (n - 1)5 = 5n - 1$

$5n - 1 = 349$

$\quad 5n = 350$

$\therefore n = 70$

Find the sum of 70 terms.

$S_n = \frac{n}{2}[2a + (n - 1)d]$

$S_n = \frac{70}{2}[2(4) + (70 - 1)5]$

$\quad = 35[8 + 69(5)]$

$\quad = 12\,355$

EXAMPLE 15

(a) Find the sum of the first 100 natural numbers $1 + 2 + 3 + \ldots + 100$.

(b) In an arithmetic series the fourth term is 12 and the ninth term is 37.

  (i) Find the common difference.

  (ii) Find the first term.

  (iii) Find the sum of the first 17 terms.

Solution

(a) Arithmetic series: $1 + 2 + 3 + \ldots + 100$

$a = 1, d = 1, n = 100$

$S_{100} = \frac{100}{2}[2 \times 1 + (100 - 1) \times 1] = 5050$

(b) (i) $T_4 = a + 3d = 12 \ldots \textbf{(1)}$

$\quad\quad T_9 = a + 8d = 37 \ldots \textbf{(2)}$

$\quad\quad\quad\quad\quad 5d = 25 \ldots \textbf{(2)} - \textbf{(1)}$

$\quad\quad\quad\quad\quad\quad d = 5$

(ii) Substituting $d = 5$ into equation **(1)**:

$a + 3(5) = 12$

$a + 15 = 12$

$a = -3$

(iii) $S_{17} = \frac{17}{2}[2(-3) + (17 - 1)5]$

$\quad\quad = \frac{17}{2}[-6 + 80]$

$\quad\quad = \frac{17}{2}[74]$

$\quad\quad = 629$

TIP ———

$\uparrow$ Given S_n, you can find a, d and hence, T_n.

EXAMPLE 16

For an arithmetic series $S_n = 2n^2 + n$, find a, d and the 15th term.

$S_2 = 2 \times 2^2 + 2 = 10$

Solution

$S_2 = T_1 + T_2 = 10$

$S_1 = 2 \times 1^2 + 1 = 3$

$\therefore T_2 = 7$

$T_1 = S_1 = 3$

$d = T_2 - T_1 = 7 - 3 = 4$

$a = T_1 = 3$

$T_{15} = a + 14d = 3 + 14 \times 4 = 59$

EXERCISE 5

1. Find the given sums for each of the following arithmetic series:

   (a) $8 + 10 + 12 + \dots S_n$ and S_{22}

   (b) $12 + 16 + 20 + \dots S_n$ and S_{32}

   (c) $-17 + 3 + 23 + \dots S_n$ and S_{30}

   (d) $3 + 2\frac{1}{2} + 2 + \dots S_n$ and S_{40}

   (e) $-8 - 5 - 2 + 1 + \dots S_n$ and S_{54}

   (f) $\frac{1}{4} + \frac{7}{12} + \frac{11}{12} + \dots S_n$ and S_{48}

   (g) $11 + 9 + 7 + \dots S_n$ and S_{37}

   (h) $x, x + 3, x + 6, \dots S_n$ and S_{12}

   (i) $\frac{1}{4} + \frac{1}{2} + \frac{3}{4} + \dots S_n$ and S_{72}

   (j) $-3 + 0 + 3 + \dots S_n$ and S_{25}

2. Find the sum of the following finite series:

   (a) $2 + 4 + 6 + \dots + 100$

   (b) $1 + 3 + 5 + 7 + \dots + 99$

   (c) $1 + 2 + 3 + \dots + 1000$

   (d) $11 + 22 + 33 + \dots + 275$

   (e) $10 + 20 + 30 + \dots + 2000$

3. (a) In an arithmetic series, the 10th term is 47 and the 20th term is 97. Find the common difference and the first term.

   (b) In an arithmetic series, the 15th term is 66 and the 24th term is 102. Write out the first four terms.

   (c) In an arithmetic series, the 5th term is −2 and the 16th term is −35. Find the sum of the first ten terms.

   (d) In an arithmetic series, the 6th term is −10 and the 10th term is 22. Find the sum of the first six terms.

4. (a) Michael saves € 80 in the first week and increases this by € 10 per week every week for the next 14 weeks. How much will Michael have saved after 15 weeks?

   (b) Fiona's starting salary is € 32 000. It increases incrementally every year by € 800. What are her gross earnings if she retires after 40 years? What is Fiona's final salary?

   (c) Mr Phillips buys a new car every two years. The first car he bought in 1990 cost € 22 000. If the price of each new car is € 3500 more than the previous one, how much did Mr Phillips spend on cars between 1990 and 2008 inclusive?

   (d) Gemma got a new mobile phone on 1 September. She sent five texts on the day she got the phone. Every day after that, she sent two more texts per day than the previous day. How many texts did Gemma send on 30 September? How many texts in all did she send during September?

(e) In an arena there are 120 seats in the front row, 115 in the second row, 110 in the third row, and so on. This pattern continues until the last row which has 55 seats. How many rows are there and what is the total number of seats in the arena?

(f) A dressmaker uses 60 buttons on her first day of business. As business gets better, the number of buttons she uses increases by 12 each day after that. If the dressmaker works 22 days in the month, how many buttons will she have used in the month?

5. **(a)** For an arithmetic series $T_n = 5n - 3$, find:

(i) T_1 (iii) a (v) S_n
(ii) T_2 (iv) d (vi) S_{37}

(b) For the arithmetic series $-5 + 1 + 7 + \ldots$, find:

(i) T_1 (iv) d (vii) S_{32}
(ii) a (v) T_{15} (viii) S_n
(iii) S_1 (vi) T_n (ix) S_{100}

(c) For an arithmetic series $S_n = n^2 + 2n$, find:

(i) S_1 (iv) T_1 (vii) T_{34}
(ii) S_2 (v) T_2
(iii) S_{50} (vi) d

10.4 Quadratic sequences

What is a quadratic sequence?

ACTIVITY 12

ACTION
Investigating quadratic sequences

OBJECTIVE
To write down the sequences of first and second differences

Consider the sequence: 1, 4, 9, 16, 25, …

If you form a new sequence from the difference of consecutive terms you get the sequences: 3, 5, 7, 9, …

This new sequence is called the sequence of first differences and is clearly an arithmetic sequence with first term 3 and common difference 2.

KEY TERM
A **quadratic sequence** is a sequence in which the differences of consecutive terms form an arithmetic sequence.

▸ 2, 5, 9, 14, 20, …

Sequence of first differences: 3, 4, 5, 6, …

This is an arithmetic sequence with $a = 3$ and $d = 1$.

WORKED EXAMPLE

Properties of a quadratic sequence

A sequence has a general term given by $T_n = 2n^2 + 3n - 1$.

The first five terms of this sequence are as follows:

$T_n = 2n^2 + 3n - 1$
$T_1 = 2(1)^2 + 3(1) - 1 = 2 + 3 - 1 = 4$
$T_2 = 2(2)^2 + 3(2) - 1 = 8 + 6 - 1 = 13$
$T_3 = 2(3)^2 + 3(3) - 1 = 18 + 9 - 1 = 26$
$T_4 = 2(4)^2 + 3(4) - 1 = 32 + 12 - 1 = 43$
$T_5 = 2(5)^2 + 3(5) - 1 = 50 + 15 - 1 = 64$

Sequence: 4, 13, 26, 43, 64, …

Show that the sequence of first differences is an arithmetic sequence. Also show that the sequence of second differences is a sequence of the same constant.

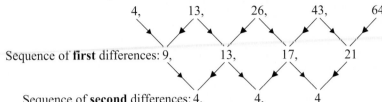

The sequence of first differences: 9, 13, 17, 21, ... is an arithmetic sequence.

The sequence of second differences: 4, 4, 4, ... is a sequence of the same constant.

> **TIP**
>
> ▲ A sequence is quadratic if the sequence of second differences is a sequence of the same constant.

WORKED EXAMPLE Finding the general term of a quadratic sequence

A floor is tiled, as shown, starting with pattern 1 and progressively increasing the area of floor space covered.

   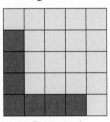

Pattern 1   Pattern 2   Pattern 3   Pattern 4

Pattern number	Number of red tiles	Number of blue tiles	Total number of tiles
1	1	3	4
2	3	6	9
3	5	11	16
4	7	18	25

For the red tiles, the sequence is the arithmetic sequence: 1, 3, 5, 7, ... with $a = 1$ and $d = 2$.

General term: $T_n = a + (n-1)d = 1 + (n-1)2 = 2n - 1$

For the blue tiles, the sequence is the quadratic sequence:

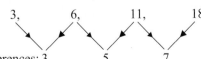

Sequence of **first** differences: 3,   5,   7

$T_1 = 3 = 1^2 + 2$

$T_2 = 6 = 2^2 + 2$

$T_3 = 11 = 3^2 + 2$

$T_4 = 18 = 4^2 + 2$

$T_n = n^2 + 2$

For the total number of tiles, the sequence is the quadratic sequence: 4, 9, 16, 25

$T_1 = 4 = (1 + 1)^2$

$T_2 = 9 = (2 + 1)^2$

$T_3 = 16 = (3 + 1)^2$

$T_4 = 25 = (4 + 1)^2$

$T_n = (n + 1)^2 = n^2 + 2n + 1$

EXERCISE 6

1. For each quadratic sequence given, write out the sequences of first and second differences:

   (a) 1, 3, 6, 10, 15, …

   (b) 6, 11, 18, 27, 38, …

   (c) 1, 3, 7, 13, 21, …

   (d) 2, 10, 24, 44, 70, …

   (e) 3, 0, –5, –12, –21, …

   (f) 0, –6, –16, –30, –48

   (g) 3, –1, –7, –15, –25, …

   (h) $a, a + 2, a + 5, a + 9, a + 14,$ …

   (i) $x, x + 5, x + 13, x + 24, x + 38$…

   (j) $t, 4t + 1, 9t + 2, 16t + 3, 25t + 4,$ …

2. Write out the next two terms in the quadratic sequences:

   (a) 1, 11, 25, …   **(d)** 2, 17, 38, …

   (b) 22, 36, 52, …   **(e)** –3, –17, –25, …

   (c) 7, 35, 71, …

3. Write out the first four terms in each of the quadratic sequences below given its general term:

   (a) $T_n = n^2 + 1$ **(d)** $T_n = -n^2 + 3$

   (b) $T_n = 2n^2$ **(e)** $T_n = 2n^2 - 5n + 3$

   (c) $T_n = n^2 - 3n + 1$

4. For the patterns of dots shown,

   (a) copy and complete the table:

   Pattern 1   Pattern 2   Pattern 3   Pattern 4   Pattern 5

   (b) Write out the first six terms for the number of dots in each successive pattern starting at pattern 1.

   (c) For the sequence in part **(b)**:

   (i) write out the sequence of first differences,

   (ii) write out the sequence of second differences.

   What can you say about the sequence in part **(b)**?

Pattern number n	Number of dots T_n
1	$T_1 = 1 = \dfrac{1^2 + 1}{2}$
2	$T_2 = 3 = \dfrac{2^2 + 2}{2}$
3	$T_3 = \square = \dfrac{\square^2 + \square}{2}$
4	$T_4 = \square = \dfrac{\square^2 + \square}{2}$
5	$T_5 = \square = \dfrac{\square^2 + \square}{2}$
6	$T_6 = \square = \dfrac{\square^2 + \square}{2}$
7	$T_7 = \square = \dfrac{\square^2 + \square}{2}$
n	$T_n = \square = \dfrac{\square^2 + \square}{2}$
20	$T_{20} = \square = \dfrac{\square^2 + \square}{2}$

REVISION QUESTIONS

1. A garden wall is constructed by building right-angled triangular sections on consecutive days.

Day 1 :

Day 2 :

Day 3 :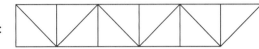

(a) Draw the pattern for the number of sections on day four and day five.

(b) Copy and complete the table below:

Day n	1	2	3	4	5
Number of sections N					

(c) Write down a formula connecting N and n.

(d) How many sections were in the wall on day 10?

(e) On what day were there 68 sections in the wall?

2. The first term of an arithmetic sequence is 5 and the common difference is –2.

(a) Write down the general term T_n.

(b) Use T_n to find T_2, T_3, T_4, T_5.

(c) Plot a graph of T_n against n on graph paper.

(d) Draw the line joining these points and use two of these points to find its slope.

(e) For another arithmetic sequence $T_n = 4 + \dfrac{3n}{2}$.
What is the slope of the line of the graph of T_n against n?

What is:

(i) the first term,

(ii) the common difference of this sequence?

3. (a) Use your calculator to complete the table:

n	1	2	3	4	5	6	7	8
7^n			343		16 807			

(b) Using the table above, write down the sequence of unit digits for all of the numbers in the second row. The first two unit digits are: 7, 9, ….

(c) What is the unit digit in 7^{199}?

(d) Using the table, write down the sequence of tens digits for all numbers in the second row. The first three tens digits are: 0, 4, 4 …. What is the tens digit in 7^{199}?

4. An oil tank contains 1000 litres of oil at the start of day one. The tank develops a leak and oil leaks out of the tank at a rate of 5 litres a day.

(a) Copy and complete the table below:

At the start of	Day 1	Day 2	Day 3	Day 4	Day 5
Volume of oil in the tank					

(b) State why these volumes form an arithmetic sequence.

(c) For this sequence, write down:

(i) the first term

(ii) the common difference

(d) How much oil does the tank contain at the start of the 12th day?

(e) At the end of which day will the tank be half full?

5. A path is made from two different types of paving slabs – black (B) slabs and white (W) slabs – as shown. The diagrams show how the path develops after each hour.

W	B	W
	B	
	B	

After
1 hour

W	W	B	W	W
		B		
		B		
		B		

After
2 hours

W	W	W	B	W	W	W
			B			
			B			
			B			
			B			

After
3 hours

(a) Draw the shape of the path after 4 hours.

(b) Copy and complete the table below:

After	1 hour	2 hours	3 hours	4 hours	5 hours
Number of white tiles					
Number of black tiles					
Total number of tiles					

(c) Write down a formula for the number T_n of white tiles laid after n hours.

(d) Write down a formula for the number T_n of black tiles laid after n hours.

(e) Write down a formula for the total number T_n of tiles laid after n hours.

(f) How long will it take to lay 296 tiles in total?

6. An athlete's training programme consists of increasing the distance she runs by 350 m every day. She runs 2 km on the first day.

(a) Write out the distance in metres the athlete runs on the first 4 days of the programme.

(b) Explain why the sequence of distances forms an arithmetic sequence.

(c) Find the first term and common difference of this arithmetic sequence.

(d) Find the general term T_n of this arithmetic sequence.

(e) What distance does the athlete cover on the 10th day of the programme?

(f) When will she cover a distance of 4·1 km in one day?

(g) Find the total distance she runs in the first 12 days.

(h) How many days will it take the athlete to run a total distance of 21·35 km?

7. An ironmonger makes gates from metal rods bolted together. Each rod is 0·5 m long.

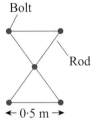

Length = 0·5 m

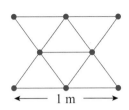

Length = 1 m

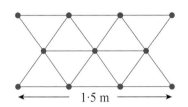

Length 1·5 m

(a) Draw a gate of length 2 m.

(b) Copy and complete the table below:

Length l (m)	0·5	1	1·5	2
Number of rods n				
Number of bolts N				

(c) Write down a formula connecting N and l.

(d) Write down a formula relating n and l.

(e) Find a formula connecting N and n.

(f) How many rods are needed to make a fence of length 22·5 m?

(g) How many bolts are needed to make a fence of length 13 m?

(h) How many bolts are needed to make a fence containing 314 rods?

8. The sum of the first n terms of an arithmetic sequence is given by $S_n = n^2 - 12n$.

(a) Find S_1 and S_2.

(b) Find T_1 and T_2.

(c) Find a and d.

(d) Find T_n.

(e) Find n if $S_n = -11$.

9. (a) For the arithmetic sequence
$-7, -4, -1, 2, \ldots 116$, find:

(i) a

(ii) d

(iii) which term has a value of 116

(iv) the number of terms listed

(v) the sum of the terms in the sequence

(b) Find the sum of all even natural numbers from 10 to 54, inclusive.

10. (a) An experiment shows that as dry air moves upwards in the atmosphere above the Arctic, it cools about 2 °C for every 100 m rise.

(i) Copy and complete the table below:

Height n above the ground in hundreds of metres	1	2	3	4	5
Temperature T_n in °C	20				

(ii) Write down a formula connecting T_n and n.

(iii) Find the temperature at 1·8 km.

(b) A supermarket employee is given the job of stacking cans of beans. The number of cans in each row forms an arithmetic sequence. The top three rows are shown. There are 22 cans in the fourth row from the bottom and 16 cans in the 10th row from the bottom.

    (i) How many cans are there in the first row?

    (ii) How many cans are there in the 13th row?

    (iii) How many rows are there in total?

    (iv) How many cans are there in total?

11. The fifth term of an arithmetic sequence is 23 and the eighth term is 44.

    (a) Find:

        (i) the first term,

        (ii) the common difference.

    (b) Write out the first four terms of the sequence.

    (c) Find the sum of the first 30 terms of the sequence.

12. Peter has matchsticks all of the same length. He arranges them in squares in rows, as shown.

Row 1: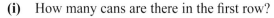

Row 2: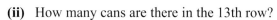

Row 3:

    (a) Write out, as a sequence, the number of matchsticks in each row.

    (b) How many matchsticks are there in the 20 squares in row 20?

    (c) How many matchsticks in total are needed to complete 20 rows?

SUMMARY

1. An arithmetic sequence is a sequence in which: Any term − Previous term = Constant.

2. A geometric sequence is a sequence in which: $\dfrac{\text{Any term}}{\text{Previous term}} = \text{Constant.}$

3. Formulae for arithmetic sequences and series:

    (a) The general term T_n of an arithmetic sequence: $T_n = a + (n-1)d$

    Example: $T_{27} = a + 26d$

    Example: $T_{48} = a + 47d$

    (b) A series is a sum of a sequence.

    (c) The sum S_n of the first n terms of an arithmetic series: $S_n = \frac{n}{2}[2a + (n-1)d]$

    (d) Notation

    $T_1 = S_1 = a = $ first term

    $n = $ the number of terms to be added

    $d = $ common difference = Any term − Previous term

    $T_n = $ value of the term in the nth place

    $S_n = $ sum of the first n terms

4. A sequence is quadratic if the sequence of second differences is a sequence of the same constant.

SECTION 5

Financial Maths

Understanding how money works is an essential part of living and planning for your future. 'I think the whole issue of a debt ceiling makes no sense to me whatsoever. Anybody who is remotely adroit at arithmetic doesn't need a debt ceiling to tell you where you are' – Alan Greenspan, former chairman of the US Federal Reserve.

CHAPTER 11

Financial Maths 1

Learning Outcomes

- To calculate unit rates.
- To convert from one system of units to another.
- To use exchange rates.
- To calculate value added tax (VAT).
- To calculate income tax, PRSI and USC.

11.1 Unit rates

ACTIVITY 1

ACTION
Working with unit rates

OBJECTIVE
To understand the idea of solving problems by finding the unit value first

Have you ever looked at two products side by side on a supermarket shelf and asked yourself which is better value? Crunchy Peanuts are priced at €3·70 for 250 g. Beside them on the shelf are Munchy Peanuts priced at €3·90 for 300 g. To decide which is the better value, you need to find the price of each product per gram.

Crunchy	**Munchy**
250 g costs 370 c	300 g costs 390 c
1 g costs $\dfrac{370}{250}$ c = 1·48 c	1 g costs $\dfrac{390}{300}$ c = 1·3 c
Cost: 1·48 c/g	Cost: 1·3 c/g

This is the unit rate for each product and compares like with like. The Munchy Peanuts are better value for money.

EXAMPLE 1

35 kg of coal is priced at €17·15. How much will 80 kg of coal cost?

Solution

35 kg costs €17·15.

1 kg costs $\dfrac{€17·15}{35}$ = €0·49

80 kg costs €0·49 × 80 = €39·20

ACTIVITY 2

ACTION
Converting to different units

OBJECTIVE
To understand the idea of solving problems by converting to different units

Conversion factors

For everyday measurement of length, area, volume, mass and time, most countries use the **metric system** of units. A few countries, notably the UK and the US, use an older system of units to measure these quantities. This older system is called the **imperial system**. For example, the Square Mile is the financial district in London. Scientists in every part of the world use the metric system.

Quantity	Metric system	Imperial system
Length	Centimetre (cm), metre (m), kilometre (km)	Inch, foot, yard, mile
Area	cm^2, m^2, km^2	Square inch, square foot, square yard, square mile
Volume	cm^3, m^3, litre (l)	Fluid ounce, pint, gallon
Mass	Gram (g), kilogram (kg), tonne	Ounce, pound, stone, ton
Time	Second (s), minute, hour	Second, minute, hour

You can convert between units in the same system and between units in different systems. All you need to know is the **conversion factor**.

1. Metric to metric

TIP
↑ Bracket a unit before you convert it.

▸ If $1 \text{ km} = 10^3 \text{ m}$, what is 5 km^2 in m^2?
$$5 \text{ km}^2 = 5 \times (1 \text{ km})^2 = 5 \times (10^3 \text{ m})^2 = 5 \times 10^6 \text{ m}^2 \quad [(10^3)^2 = 10^6]$$

▸ If $1 \text{ cm} = 10^{-2} \text{ m}$, what is $25 \cdot 6 \text{ cm}^3$ in m^3?
$$25 \cdot 6 \text{ cm}^3 = 25 \cdot 6 \times (1 \text{ cm})^3 = 25 \cdot 6 \times (10^{-2} \text{ m})^3 = 25 \cdot 6 \times 10^{-6} \text{ m}^3$$
$$= 2 \cdot 56 \times 10^{-5} \text{ m}^3 \quad [\text{You can use your calculator at any point in the calculation.}]$$

EXAMPLE 2

Convert 1 litre (l) to m^3 if $1 \text{ cm} = 10^{-2} \text{ m}$ and $1 \text{ litre (l)} = 10^3 \text{ cm}^3$.

Solution
$$1 \text{ l} = 1 \times (1 \text{ l}) = 1 \times (10^3 \text{ cm}^3)$$
$$= 1 \times 10^3 \times (1 \text{ cm})^3$$
$$= 1 \times 10^3 \times (10^{-2} \text{ m})^3$$
$$= 1 \times 10^3 \times 10^{-6} \text{ m}^3 \quad [\text{Add the powers of 10}]$$
$$1 \text{ l} = 1 \times 10^{-3} \text{ m}^3$$

EXAMPLE 3

(a) If $1 \text{ km} = 10^3 \text{ m}$ and $1 \text{ h} = 3600 \text{ s}$, convert 90 km/h to m/s.

(b) Convert 6 m/s to km/h.

Solution

(a) $90 \text{ km/h} = 90 \times \dfrac{(1 \text{ km})}{(1 \text{ h})} = 90 \times \dfrac{(10^3 \text{ m})}{(3600 \text{ s})} = \dfrac{90 \text{ m}}{3 \cdot 6 \text{ s}} = 25 \text{ m/s}$

(b) $6 \text{ m/s} = 6 \times \dfrac{(1 \text{ m})}{(1 \text{ s})} = 6 \times \dfrac{(10^{-3} \text{ km})}{\left(\dfrac{1}{3600} \text{ h}\right)} = 6 \text{ km} \times 3 \cdot 6 \text{ h} = 21 \cdot 6 \text{ km/h}$

TIP
↑ km/h → m/s: Divide by 3·6
m/s → km/h: Multiply by 3·6

2. Metric to imperial and vice versa

▸ If 1 inch = 2·54 cm, what is 12 inches (1 foot) in cm?

1 inch = 2·54 cm

12 inches = 12 × 2·54 cm = 30·48 cm

12 inches = 1 foot

∴ 1 foot = 30·48 cm

EXAMPLE 4

(a) A driver from the Republic of Ireland crosses the border into Northern Ireland. The speed limits in the Republic are in kilometres per hour (km/h). Speed is measured in Northern Ireland in miles per hour (mph). What is 120 km/h in mph if 1 km = 0·62137 miles?

(b) A quick method to convert a speed in km/h to a speed in mph is to multiply the speed in km/h by $\frac{5}{8}$. Find the percentage error this gives when converting 120 km/h to mph, correct to one decimal place.

Solution

(a) $120 \text{ km/h} = 120 \times \dfrac{(1 \text{ km})}{(1 \text{ h})}$

$= 120 \times \dfrac{(0 \cdot 62137 \text{ miles})}{(1 \text{ h})}$

$= 74 \cdot 5644 \text{ mph}$

(b) $120 \text{ km/h} = 74 \cdot 5644 \text{ mph}$

Quick method: $120 \text{ km/h} = 120 \times \dfrac{5}{8} \text{ mph}$

$= 75 \text{ mph}$

Percentage error in quick answer

$= \dfrac{(75 - 74 \cdot 5644)}{74 \cdot 5644} \times 100\%$

$= 0 \cdot 6\%$

EXERCISE 1

1. **(a)** A car travels 251·2 km in 4 hours. Its average speed is how far it travels in 1 hour. What is its average speed?

   (b) A shop has an offer of six cans of cola for the price of five. If the price of one individual can is €1·08, how much do you pay for six cans? How much are you paying per can?

   (c) A shop has a 'special offer' on a large 200 g jar of coffee for €6·50. A smaller 100 g jar costs €3·00. Is this really a 'special offer'?

   (d) A 160-page refill pad costs €2·50. A 200-page 'jumbo' refill pad costs €3·60. Which is better value?

   (e) An 870 ml bottle of washing-up liquid costs €2·99. The 530 ml bottle of the

same liquid costs €2·22 and the 433 ml costs €1·51. Which is the best value?

   (f) 60% of a building site has area 312 m². What is the area of 80% of the site?

   (g) Forty cars occupy 58% of a parking lot. What percentage of the lot is occupied by 25 cars?

   (h) In a cinema 120 patrons means the cinema is half-full. What fraction of the seats in the cinema is filled by 160 patrons?

2. Convert the following, giving your answer in the form $a \times 10^n$, $1 \leq a < 10$.

   (a) 5 cm to m

   (b) 2·7 m to km

   (c) 5·4 km² to m²

(d) 2·6 cm² to m² (g) 5·6 cm³ to m³

(e) 680 cm³ to m³ (h) 5 l to cm³

(f) 5 tonne to kg (i) 5 l to m³

3. Convert the following:

   (a) 72 km/h to m/s

   (b) 108 km/h to m/s

   (c) 100 km/h to m/s

   (d) 45 km/h to m/s

   (e) 10 m/s to km/h

   (f) 15·6 m/s to km/h

   (g) 3 m/s to km/h

   (h) 25 m/s to km/h

   (i) 75 km/h to m/s

   (j) 9 m/s to km/h

4. The capacity of a family saloon petrol tank is 49·2 l. How many gallons is this correct to the nearest gallon? (1 gallon = 3·785 l)

5. The River Nile is 4160 miles long. How long is the Nile in km? (1 mile = 1·61 km)

6. Mount Everest is 29 029 feet high. What is its height in metres, correct to one decimal place? (1 metre = 3·281 feet)

7. The mean density of the Earth is 5·515 g/cm³. Compare this density with the mean density of Jupiter, which is 1326 kg/m³, correct to two decimal places.

8. Javier Sotomayor set a world high jump record at 8·02 feet in 1993 in Salamanca, Spain. What is this height in metres? Javier's height is 1·95 m. How many feet can he jump above his height? Give both answers correct to two decimal places. (1 foot = 0·3048 m)

9. A building site measures 125 m by 420 m, as shown.

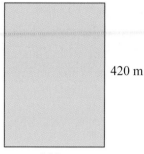

420 m

125 m

What is its area in:

   (a) m²,

   (b) km²,

   (c) hectares
   (1 hectare = 100 m × 100 m = 10⁴ m²),

   (d) acres, to the nearest acre?
   (1 hectare = 2·471 acres)

10. A house is built on a rectangular plot with an area of 3 acres. Its length is 121 yards. What is its breadth? (1 acre = 4840 square yards)

121 yards

11. The speed of light is 3 × 10⁸ m/s. What is this speed in:

   (a) km/h,

   (b) mph, correct to two significant figures? (1 mile = 1·61 km)

Currency exchange

Currency exchange is the same as converting units of measurement except it involves money. If you visit a country outside the eurozone or buy goods on the internet from another country, you normally use the currency of that country. It is easy to convert from one currency to another once you are given the **exchange rate**. This allows you to work out unit rates. The exchange rate is simply the conversion factor between two currencies.

EXAMPLE 5

On a certain day, the exchange rate between the euro and the dollar is €1 = $1·32.

(a) How many dollars will you get for €500?

(b) How many euro will you need to get $594? (Assume there is no commission charged.)

Solution

(a) €1 = $1·32

€500 = $500 × 1·32 = $660

(b) $1·32 = €1

$1 = €\dfrac{1}{1·32}$

$594 = €\dfrac{594}{1·32} = €450$

Most banks and foreign exchange companies charge a commission on transactions. They take a slice of the money you wish to convert *before* they convert it.

EXAMPLE 6

Peter wants to change €600 into roubles as he is travelling to St Petersburg. The bank charges a fixed commission of 1·5% on all foreign exchange transactions. If the exchange rate is €1 = 47·32 roubles, how many roubles does he get?

Solution

A commission of 1·5% means Peter has only 98·5% of €600 to convert to roubles.

98·5% of €600 = 0·985 × 600 = €591

€1 = 47·32 roubles

€591 = 591 × 47·32 = 27 966·12 roubles

Have you ever noticed when you walk into a bank there is a foreign exchange board that looks like the table below?

	Country	Currency	Buys	Sells
1	USA	Dollar	**1·3949**	**1·3266**
2	UK	Pound	0·8394	0·7983
3	UAE	Dirham	5·2061	4·8093
4	Canada	Dollar	1·5702	1·4505
5	South Africa	Rand	15·7342	14·5349

Banks are currency traders. They make a profit on all foreign exchange transactions. The table above gives the conversion rate for €1. On a particular day, the table shows that the bank will buy dollars at a rate of €1 = $**1·3949**, but will sell dollars at a rate of €1 = $**1·3266**.

EXAMPLE 7

(a) A man returning from a trip to the US has $556 left. He goes to the bank on his way home from the airport to convert this money. According to the foreign exchange board, how many euro does he get? (Assume there is no commission.)

(b) When the man arrives home his son says he is off to New York the following day. His father gives him €398·59 and tells him to go to the bank to convert it to dollars. According to the foreign exchange board, how many dollars does he get? (Assume there is no commission.)

Solution

(a) The bank is buying the man's dollars, so he gets the 'buy rate'.

$$€1 = \$1·3949$$

$$\$1 = €\frac{1}{1·3949}$$

$$\$556 = €\frac{556}{1·3949} = €398·59$$

(b) The bank is selling dollars, so the son gets the 'sell rate'.

$$€1 = \$1·3266$$

$$€398·59 = \$528·77$$

The bank makes a nice profit!

EXERCISE 2

1. Change €800 into the stated currency with the given exchange rate:

   (a) Pounds sterling (£): rate €1 = £0·8242

   (b) US dollars ($): rate €1 = $1·364

   (c) Canadian dollars (CAD$): rate €1 = CAD$1·521

   (d) South African rand (R): rate €1 = R15·31

   Give all answers correct to two decimal places.

2. Change the following, giving all answers correct to two decimal places:

   (a) $500 into euro if €1 = $1·364

   (b) £650 into euro if €1 = £0·8242

   (c) 70 000 roubles into euro if €1 = 48·03 roubles

   (d) 553 000 yen (¥) into US dollars ($) if ¥1 = $0·009776

   (e) $200 into pounds (£) if £1 = $1·655

   (f) 95 Malaysian ringgit into Indian rupees if 1 Indian rupee = 0·05326 ringgits

3. Joanne went on a Christmas trip to New York.

   (a) She changed €1200 into US dollars ($) at an exchange rate of €1 = $1·364. How many dollars did she receive if a commission of 1% was charged on the €1200?

   (b) In New York, she bought a coat for $230 and Christmas presents for $482. She spent $220 on other expenses. She changed the dollars she had left at JFK Airport in New York at a rate of €1 = $1·34 and no commission. How many euro did she have when she arrived home?

4. The table below shows the exchange rates between three currencies: euro (€), Thai bahts (THB) and Hong Kong dollars (HKD).

	€	THB	HKD
€	1	44·96	10·60

   (a) Convert 3000 THB to **(i)** €, **(ii)** HKD.

   (b) How many THB can you get for €50?

   (c) How many THB can you get for 600 HKD?

5. A foreign exchange office exchanges €1 for US dollars with the buy rate of $1·3949 and the sell rate of $1·3266.

   (a) If Seán walks into the office with $900 to exchange, how many euro will he get?

   (b) Ten minutes later, Michael walks into the office looking for $900. How many euro will he have to pay for these?

   (c) What profit does the office make on these two transactions?

6. The graph shows the relationship between euro (€) and pounds sterling (£) over a particular period of time.

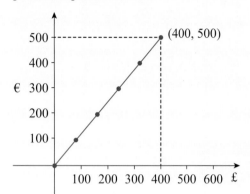

Find:

(a) the slope of the straight line,

(b) the equation of the straight line,

(c) how many euro you get for £200,

(d) how many pounds you get for €300,

(e) the exchange rate from euro to pounds (how many pounds you get for €1).

What does the slope tell you about the relationship between € and £ over this period of time?

11.2 Tax

VAT

Value added tax (VAT) is a government tax on consumer spending. Everyone who pays for goods and services pays VAT. Usually the VAT is built into the price of the goods or services. For example, the price of *The Irish Times* newspaper is €2 (including VAT). This means that you pay €2 for the paper, but the Government gets a cut of the €2.

Rates of VAT

The rates of VAT vary from country to country in the EU and from year to year. In 2015, in Ireland the **standard rate** of VAT was 23%. This rate applies to all goods and services that do not fall into the reduced rate categories of 13·5% and 9%. Some goods and services are VAT exempt. This means they have a zero rating (0%) of VAT.

VAT rates in Ireland in 2015

Standard rate	23%	Cars/televisions/paper/food/consultancy services
Reduced rate	13·5%	Fuel/electricity/building services
Reduced rate	9%	Restaurants/cinemas/newspapers
Zero rate	0%	Bread/milk/educational services

TIP

Always assume the price of goods or services excluding VAT is 100%.

EXAMPLE 8

A laptop is advertised on television as costing €420, excluding VAT. If the VAT rate is 23%, what is the actual cost to the buyer?

Solution

Cost without VAT = 100% = €420

Actual cost = 123% = €420 × 1·23 = €516·60

EXAMPLE 9

A restaurant bill comes to €59·95 including VAT at 9%. If eating in restaurants was VAT exempt, what would the bill have cost?

Solution

Bill with VAT = 109% = €59·95

Bill without VAT = 100% = €$\frac{59\cdot95}{109}$ × 100 = €55

EXAMPLE 10

Mary buys a pair of shoes in Spain at a bargain price of €48 (VAT included). The sales assistant tells her that the price would have been €40 if VAT had not been included.

(a) What is the VAT rate on shoes in Spain?

(b) What would she have paid in Ireland for a pair of shoes that cost €40 excluding VAT of 23%?

Solution

(a) Rate of VAT = $\frac{(48-40)}{40}$ × 100 = 20%

(b) Cost excluding VAT = €40

Cost including VAT = €40 × 1·23 = €49·20

EXAMPLE 11

The Kennys decide to redecorate their kitchen. They sit down to calculate the cost and set out their estimates as follows:

1. Measurements:

   (a) Area of floor to be tiled = 13 m^2

   (b) Area of walls to be tiled = 7·7 m^2

2. Raw material costs:

   (a) Cost of floor tiles = €60 per m^2

   (b) Cost of wall tiles = €42 per m^2

   (c) Cost of paint = €88

   These costs all include VAT.

3. Labour costs:

   The tiler charges €45 per hour excluding VAT at 13·5%.

4. Other:

   The cost of grout and adhesive is €44 excluding VAT at 23%.

What is the Kennys' estimate, assuming the tiler takes 20 hours to complete the job?

Solution

Cost of floor tiles	€60 × 13	= €780
Cost of wall tiles	€42 × 7·7	= €323·4
Cost of paint		= €88
Cost of grout and adhesive	€44 × 1·23	= €54·12
Labour costs	€45 × 20 × 1·135	= €1021·50
Estimated cost		= €2267·02

Taxes on earnings

ACTIVITY 3

ACTION
Calculating tax on earnings

OBJECTIVE
To calculate the tax to be paid on a single person's and a married person's salary

The total amount of money (gross income) you earn in a year is subject to various taxes. What you see at the top of your payslip is not what you get. The Government takes its cut of your earnings.

1. PRSI and USC

PRSI (Pay Related Social Insurance) and USC (Universal Social Charge) are taxes on your gross income. A person on a gross yearly salary of €42 000 would pay PRSI of €1680 and USC of €1603·06 in 2016.

Most employees pay PRSI at a rate of 4%. USC is levied in bands. The first €12 012 is levied at 1%, the next €6656 is levied at 3%, the next €51 376 at 5·5%, and the remainder at 8%.

2. Income tax

Income tax is applied to your gross income at two rates. In 2016, the rates were as follows:

- The **standard rate** of 20% is applied to the first €33 800 of your salary.
- The **higher rate** of 40% is applied to the remainder of your salary.

EXAMPLE 12

A person has a gross yearly salary of €46 000. What is their gross yearly income tax if the first €33 800 is taxed at 20% and the remainder is taxed at 40%?

Solution

Gross income = €46 000

20% of €33 800 = €6760

40% of €12 200 = €4880

Gross income tax = €6760 + €4880 = €11 640

To reduce their income tax every person is given **tax credits.**

3. Tax credits

A tax credit is an amount of money which is used to reduce your gross income tax. The amount depends on personal circumstances. For most single workers, it is €3300 per year. So after all of this, how do you calculate your yearly take-home (net) pay?

Steps to calculate your net yearly income:

1. Calculate your gross income tax and then reduce this by your tax credits to get your net income tax deduction.
2. Calculate your PRSI and USC deductions on your gross income.
3. Subtract your PRSI, USC and net income tax deductions from your gross income to get your net income.

EXAMPLE 13

An IT worker has a gross salary of €52 000 per year.

(a) Calculate his gross income tax per year if the first €33 800 is taxed at 20% and the remainder is taxed at 40%.

(b) Calculate his net income tax per year if his tax credits amount to €3300 per year.

(c) Calculate his total deductions if his PRSI and USC deductions amount to €4233·06.

(d) Calculate his net yearly income.

Solution

Gross yearly income = €52 000

(a) Gross income tax:

€33 800 at 20% = €6760

€18 200 at 40% = €7280

Gross income tax = €6760 + €7280 = €14 040

(b) Net income tax = €14 040 − €3300 = €10 740

(c) Net income tax = €10 740

USC/PRSI = €4233·06

Total deductions = €10 740 + €4233·06

= €14 973·06

(d) Gross yearly income = €52 000

Total deductions = €14 973·06

Net yearly income = €52 000 − €14 973·06

= €37 026·94

EXAMPLE 14

A teacher has a gross yearly income of €47 000. Her yearly tax credits are €3300.

(a) Find her gross yearly income tax if the first €33 800 is taxed at 20% and the remainder at 40%.

(b) Find her net income tax per year.

(c) Find her USC and PRSI deductions, if her net yearly income is €34 502.

Solution

Gross yearly income = €47 000

(a) €33 800 at 20% = €6760

€13 200 at 40% = €5280

Gross income tax = €6760 + €5280 = €12 040

(b) Net income tax = €12 040 − €3300 = €8740

(c) Net income = €34 502

Total deductions = €47 000 − €34 502

= €12 498

PRSI and USC deductions = €12 498 − €8740

= €3758

EXERCISE 3

1. A jacket costs €220 before VAT is applied at 23%. How much does the customer pay for the jacket?

2. A camera costs £289 before VAT is applied at 20%. What price does the buyer pay for the camera?

3. A game console is listed online at US $250 excluding VAT. If Paula in Dublin wants to buy this console, she will have to pay VAT at 23% on the price in euro. How much will she actually pay for the console if the exchange rate applied is $1 = €0·714?

4. An LED TV costs €357 including VAT. What price does the customer pay?

5. A laptop costs €458 including VAT at 21% in Spain. What is the cost of the laptop before VAT?

6. A meal in a restaurant in Cork cost €68 including VAT at 9%. What is the cost of the meal before VAT is applied?

7. A tourist to Ireland buys silver costing €325·47 including VAT at 23%. She is told by the sales assistant that she will get a refund of the amount of VAT paid if she presents her receipt at Dublin Airport. How much of a refund is she due?

8. The price of a car is €33 000 excluding VAT. The table below shows the VAT rates in all 19 eurozone countries:

Country	Standard VAT rate (%)
Austria	20
Belgium	21
Cyprus	19
Estonia	20
Finland	24
France	20
Germany	19
Greece	23
Ireland	23
Italy	22
Latvia	21
Lithuania	21
Luxembourg	17
Malta	18
The Netherlands	21
Portugal	23
Slovakia	20
Slovenia	22
Spain	21

(a) What is the lowest price you could pay for this car?

(b) What is the highest price you could pay for this car?

9. A car dealership in a European country has VAT at 18% included in its car prices. If the price of a Sports Spitfire is €42 000, find the price of the car excluding VAT. In the Budget the VAT rate was increased to 20%. What is the price of the car to the consumer after the Budget?

10. The O'Connors get an extension to their house costing €17 700 before VAT. VAT on labour is 13·5% and VAT on material is 23%. How much will the extension cost if the labour costs were €7600 excluding VAT.

11. A woman has a salary of €30 000 per year. She pays income tax at 20% on all of her salary. What is her gross income tax? If her tax credits are €3300, find her net income tax.

12. AJ pays income tax, USC and PRSI on his income. His gross weekly wages are €500.

    (a) He pays income tax at 20% on all of his wages. He has a weekly tax credit of €63. How much income tax does he pay?

    (b) He pays USC at 1% on the first €231, 3% on the next €128 and 5·5% on the remainder of his gross weekly wages. What are his USC deductions?

    (c) He also pays PRSI at a rate of 4% on his gross weekly wages. How much PRSI does he pay?

    (d) What are his total weekly deductions?

    (e) What is his net weekly wage?

13. Sarah's gross yearly salary is €56 000.

    (a) Her PRSI is 4% of her gross salary. What is her PRSI?

    (b) Her USC is 1% on the first €12 012, 3% on the next €6656 and 5·5% on the remainder. How much USC is deducted?

    (c) Her income tax is 20% on the first €33 800 of her salary and 40% on the remainder. Her yearly tax credits are €3370. Find her net income tax.

    (d) Find her net yearly salary and her net monthly take-home pay.

14. A man pays PRSI at 4% of his gross yearly income. If his PRSI amounts to €1920, find his gross yearly income. If USC is applied to the first €12 012 of his gross yearly income at 1%, the next €6656 at 3% and the remainder at 5·5%, find his total USC deductions.

15. A man pays tax on the first €33 800 of his gross yearly income at 20% and the remainder at 40%. Find his gross yearly income if his tax credits are €3300 and his net income tax is €12 936.

16. A computer programmer pays USC at 1% on the first €12 012 of her gross yearly income, 3% on the next €6656 and 5·5% on the remainder. If her total USC deductions are €3068·48, find:

    (a) her gross yearly income,

    (b) her PRSI contributions at 4% of her gross income,

    (c) her net yearly income if the first €33 800 is taxed at 20% and the remainder at 40%, given her tax credits are €3300 per annum.

Financial Maths 2

Learning Outcomes

- To understand cost price, selling price, profit and loss, and profit margin.
- To distinguish between simple interest and compound interest and to solve problems involving both.
- To understand AER and APR.
- To solve problems on depreciation by the reducing balance method.

12.1 Buying and selling

Profit and loss

1. Profit

WORKED EXAMPLE Understanding profit and loss

A man buys a painting in an auction for €150. He sells it three years later for €450.

The price at which you buy something is known as the **cost price** (CP).

The cost price of the painting: CP = €150

The price at which you sell something is known as the **selling price** (SP).

The selling price of the painting: SP = €450

The man has made a **profit** (P) of €300.

His profit: P = SP – CP = €450 – €150 = €300

He has made this profit on a purchase price of €150.

His **percentage profit**: $(\%P) = \dfrac{300}{150} \times 100\% = 200\%$

$$\text{Percentage profit } (\%P) = \dfrac{\text{Profit}}{\text{Cost price}} \times 100\%$$

Percentage profit is also known as **percentage mark-up**.

The **profit margin** is the percentage of the selling price that is turned into profit.

The profit margin on the painting $= \dfrac{300}{450} \times 100\% = 66\frac{2}{3}\%$

$$\begin{aligned} \text{Profit (P)} &= \text{Selling price (SP)} - \text{Cost price (CP)} \\ \text{Percentage profit} &= \frac{\text{Profit}}{\text{Cost price}} \times 100\% \\ \text{Profit margin} &= \frac{\text{Profit}}{\text{Selling price}} \times 100\% \end{aligned}$$

2. Loss

WORKED EXAMPLE — Calculating percentage loss

NAMA bought a hotel for €540 000 in 2010 and sold it in 2013 for €400 000.

NAMA has made a loss (L): €540 000 − €400 000 = €140 000

The loss L = CP − SP = €140 000

Percentage loss (%L) $= \dfrac{140\,000}{540\,000} \times 100\% = 25.9\%$

This **percentage loss** is also known as **percentage discount**.

$$\begin{aligned} \text{Loss (L)} &= \text{Cost price (CP)} - \text{Selling price (SP)} \\ \text{Percentage loss (\%L)} &= \frac{\text{Loss}}{\text{Cost price}} \times 100\% \end{aligned}$$

EXAMPLE 1

In a sale a shop gives a discount of 40% on the original price of a bicycle. If the sale price is €168, find the original price.

Solution

SP = €168 = 60% of CP

CP $= \dfrac{€168}{0.6} = €280$

EXAMPLE 2

A retail games store buys game consoles from a wholesaler for €180 each. The store marks up the price by 62%. What is the selling price of a console?

Solution

Cost price = €180

SP = 162% of CP = €180 × 1.62 = €291.60

EXAMPLE 3

A furniture store has a New Year's sale in which there is a 20% discount on all items less than €1000 and a discount of 30% on all items that are priced at €1000 or more. Ms Rice buys a table for €700, a bed for €1200 and a sideboard for €1000. How much does she pay for all three items?

Solution

Cost of table = €700 × 0.8 = €560

Cost of bed = €1200 × 0.7 = €840

Cost of sideboard = €1000 × 0.7 = €700

Total spend = €560 + €840 + €700 = €2100

EXERCISE 4

1. Copy and complete the following tables:

   (a)

Cost price	Selling price	Profit	% Profit	Profit margin
€100	€150			
	€300	€120		
€250			25%	
	€72			30%
€72		€88		

   (b)

Cost price	Selling price	Loss	% Loss
€100	€75		
€172		€85	
	€100	€70	

2. (a) What percentage is €137·52 of €687·60?

   (b) A ring is bought for €852 and sold for a profit of 26%. What is the selling price?

3. Bucket Electronics wants to decrease the price of a laptop from €560 to €480. What percentage discount must they advertise, correct to one decimal place?

4. A man goes to Northern Ireland to buy a television set priced at £420. During a sale there is a discount on this price of 15%. How many euro must the man change into pounds sterling to cover the cost of the television in the sale if €1 = £0·80.

5. A retailer bought 150 games for Christmas at €23·50 each. She sold 90 at €45 each and the remainder at a 20% discount.

   (a) What was the value of her total sales?

   (b) What was her percentage profit, correct to one decimal place?

   (c) What was her profit margin, correct to one decimal place?

6. PC Universe bought 100 external hard drives at €78 each and 58 USB cables at €12 each. It made a 55% profit on the sale of each hard drive. All items were sold. If the total amount of sales was €12 925·20, find the percentage profit on the USB cables.

7. The selling price S in euro of a car after t years can be expressed as follows:
   $$S = 30\,000(0·87)^t$$

   (a) What is the current selling price?

   (b) What will the selling price be in 3 years?

12.2 Borrowing and lending

When individuals or financial institutions lend money, they expect that the original amount of money will be repaid in full. In addition, they expect the borrower to pay them a charge for the privilege of using their money.

The original amount of money is called the **principal** P and the charge for the privilege of using the money is called the **interest** I.

▸ Mr O'Brien repaid a loan of €12 000 (principal) with interest of €1585. This means for the privilege of using the €12 000, he has to pay an extra €1585.

▸ Mrs Brown invested €5000 in a building society for a year. At the end of the year she withdrew her investment, which amounted to €5250. Therefore, the building society paid her interest of €250 for using her money.

The **interest** on an investment or a loan can be calculated in two ways: simple interest or compound interest.

Simple interest

ACTIVITY **4**

ACTION
Working with simple interest

OBJECTIVE
To go through the steps to calculate the simple interest on a sum of money

Simple interest is the interest applied to an investment or a loan by calculating the interest on the **original principal only** at the end of each period of interest (usually per year).

For simple interest, only the original principal earns interest.

WORKED EXAMPLE — How simple interest is calculated

€1200 is invested for 3 years at 4% per annum simple interest.

Note: Per annum (p.a.) means per year.

The interest after 1 year = 4% of €1200
= €1200 × 0·04 = €48

The value of the investment after 1 year is €1248.

During the second year, the interest is applied to the original principal of €1200 only, and not on €1248.

The interest for the second year is also €48.

After 2 years, the total interest = 2 × €48 = €96.

After 3 years, the total interest = 3 × €48 = €144.

The interest on €1200 invested for **3 years** at simple interest of 4% p.a. is given by:

$$I = €1200 × 0·04 × 3 = €1200 × \frac{4}{100} × 3 = €144$$

This idea can be generalised into the simple interest

formula: $$I = \frac{P × r × t}{100}$$

where:

I is the simple interest.

P is the principal (the amount borrowed or lent).

r is the percentage rate of interest (per year).

t is the duration or term of the loan or investment (in years).

EXAMPLE **4**

Calculate the simple interest on a loan of €22 000 at a rate of 6·5% p.a. over 2 years and 6 months.

Solution

$P = €22\,000$

$r = 6·5\%$

$t = 2·5$ years

$$I = \frac{P × r × t}{100} = \frac{22\,000 × 6·5 × 2·5}{100} = €3575$$

EXAMPLE **5**

What interest rate per annum will I have to get so that €10 000 will earn €1260 simple interest in 3 years?

Solution

$P = €10\,000$

$I = €1260$

$t = 3$ years

$r = ?$

$$I = \frac{P × r × t}{100}$$

$$r = \frac{100I}{Pt}$$

$$r = \frac{100 × 1260}{10\,000 × 3} = 4·2\%$$

Simple interest repayments

Normally loans are repaid in regular equal amounts over the term of the loan rather than at the end of the term. The principal and the interest must be repaid in full by the end of the term. For simple interest loans, it is easy to work out the amount of each repayment using the formula:

$$\text{Amount of each repayment} = \frac{\text{Total amount to be repaid}}{\text{Number of repayments}}$$

EXAMPLE 6

Calculate the monthly repayments on a car loan of €18 000 at a simple interest rate of 7·2% p.a. over 5 years.

Solution

$P = €18\,000$

$r = 7·2\%$

$t = 5$ years

$I = \dfrac{18\,000 \times 7·2 \times 5}{100} = €6480$

Total repayment $= €18\,000 + €6480 = €24\,480$

Amount of each monthly payment $= \dfrac{€24\,480}{5 \times 12} = €408$

Compound interest

When compound interest is applied to a loan or an investment, the principal at the start of a period of interest is the sum of the principal and interest at the end of the preceding period. Interest of €50 at the end of a year on a principal of €1000 invested at compound interest gives a principal of €1050 at the start of the second year.

For compound interest, both the interest and principal earn interest for the second period and all future periods.

WORKED EXAMPLE How compound interest is calculated

€5000 is invested for 2 years at 2% p.a. compound interest. What is the value of the investment after 2 years?

2% p.a. means the interest is calculated at the end of each year at 2%. The rate of interest p.a. $r = 2$.

Year 1:
$P = €5000 = $ principal at the start of year 1

$I = €5000 \times 0·02 = $ interest at the end of year 1 $= €100$

$F_1 = P + I = €5100 = $ amount at the end of year 1

Year 2:
$P = €5100$

$I = €5100 \times 0·02 = €102$

$F_2 = P + I = €5202$

Amount at end of year 2 $= €5202$

Compound interest formula

The compound interest formula allows you to calculate the value of investments and loans over a given period of time (term) earning compound interest.

ACTIVITY 5

ACTION
Mastering the compound interest formula

OBJECTIVE
To go through the steps to calculate the compound interest on a sum of money

WORKED EXAMPLE

Understanding the compound interest formula

What value will €10 000 have after 3 years if invested at 2% p.a. compound interest?

Information

2% per annum means the interest period is 1 year and the percentage rate for this period is $r = 2$. The term is 3 years.

The initial investment at the start of the term is called the principal P and is €10 000.

Calculation

At the end of year 1, the principal is increased by 2%:

Total amount F_1 of the investment: $F_1 = €10\,000 \times (1 \cdot 02)^1$

At the end of year 2, the amount F_1 is increased by 2% to give a new total F_2:

$F_2 = €10\,000 \times (1 \cdot 02) \times (1 \cdot 02) = €10\,000 \times (1 \cdot 02)^2$

At the end of year 3, the amount F_2 in increased again by 2%, to give the final total of F_3:

$F_3 = €10\,000 \times (1 \cdot 02)^2 \times (1 \cdot 02) = €10\,000 \times (1 \cdot 02)^3$

This pattern can be generalised into the compound interest formula:

$$F = P\left(1 + \frac{r}{100}\right)^t = P(1 + i)^t$$

where:

F is the total (final) amount of the investment or loan to be repaid after t periods.

P is the principal at the start of the term.

r is the percentage compound interest rate per interest period.

t is the number of interest periods in the term.

$i = \dfrac{r}{100}$ is the decimal rate of compound interest.

EXAMPLE 7

A loan of €15 300 is taken out for 4 years at 6% p.a. compound interest. What is the total amount of the repayment and the interest if it is repaid in total at the end of the 4 years?

Solution

$P = €15\,300$

$r = 6\%$

$t = 4$ years

$F = 15\,300\left(1 + \dfrac{6}{100}\right)^4 = 15\,300\,(1 \cdot 06)^4 = €19\,315 \cdot 90$ [Using a calculator.]

$I = €19\,315 \cdot 90 - €15\,300 = €4015 \cdot 90$

Annual equivalent rate (AER) on investments

Interest can be compounded over any period of time: yearly, monthly, daily, etc. This means an investment of €10 000 compounded daily at 5% can give the same return as €10 000 compounded yearly at 5·12%. In other words, a 5% compound interest rate applied daily for 1 year is **equivalent** to a 5·12% compound interest rate applied yearly for 1 year. The annual equivalent rate (AER) is 5·12%, and is the compound interest rate quoted by most financial institutions, even though they may actually apply the interest over a shorter period than 1 year.

EXAMPLE 8

A bank quotes an AER of 2·5% for investments up to €100 000 for a fixed term of 2 years. A retired civil servant invests his retirement lump sum of €85 000 into this account. What is the total value of the investment after 2 years?

Solution

$P = €85\,000, \qquad r = 2·5\%, \qquad t = 2$ years

$F = P\left(1 + \dfrac{r}{100}\right)^t$

$F = 85\,000\left(1 + \dfrac{2·5}{100}\right)^2 = 85\,000(1·025)^2 = €89\,303·13$

Annual percentage rate (APR) on loans

Personal loans are used to finance house purchases, college fees, cars, etc. When you take out a loan, it is for a fixed length of time (the term) and the interest charged by the lender is known as the APR (annual percentage rate) and is compound interest.

The interest can be fixed or variable. A fixed rate does not change over the term. For example, a fixed rate of 3·7% for 5 years will be applied for the full term of the loan.

A variable rate can change over the term depending on domestic and/or global economic conditions.

Loans are normally repaid monthly on the **reducing balance** of the loan because the loan decreases as repayments are made. This makes it difficult to work out monthly repayments.

EXAMPLE 9

A college undergraduate takes out a student loan of €5000 at an APR of 4% to be repaid in full after 3 years. What is the student's single repayment after 3 years?

Solution

$P = €5000$

$r = 4\%$

$t = 3$ years

$F = 5000\,(1·04)^3 = €5624·32$

EXAMPLE 10

Philip has a credit card with a limit of €1500. Interest is charged at 1·75% per month on the amount owed. Philip gets a bill at the end of each month. At the start of June he owes €1200. If he makes no more purchases and no repayments, show that he will exceed his credit limit after 13 months.

Solution

1·75% per month means the interest period is 1 month.

$r = 1·75\%$

$P = €1200$

$t = 13$ (13 periods of interest in 13 months)

$F_{13} = 1200(1·0175)^{13} = €1503 > €1500$

APR repayments on loans can be calculated from an APR table.

The APR table below shows the monthly repayments on each €1000 borrowed at a fixed APR for a fixed term.

Number of payments	4%	4·5%	5%
12	85·15	83·38	85·61
24	43·43	43·65	43·87
36	29·50	29·75	29·97
48	22·60	22·80	23·03
60	18·42	18·64	18·87

EXAMPLE 11

Morgan buys a car for €12 500 by taking out a personal loan from a bank. The bank charges an APR of 5% over a 3 year term. Find:

(a) his monthly repayments using the APR table,

(b) his total repayments,

(c) the interest he has been charged.

Solution

The term is 3 years, which gives 36 monthly repayments at 5% APR.

(a) This is a monthly repayment per €1000 of €29·97.

The monthly repayments on
€12 500 = €29·97 × 12·5 = €374·63

(b) Total repayments = €374·63 × 36 = €13 486·68

(c) Interest = €13 486·68 − €12 500·00 = €986·68

Depreciation

The value of most assets decreases as time passes for many reasons. They become unfashionable, they may suffer wear and tear or they become inefficient. However, some items increase in price over time, like gold or antiques. Their value appreciates. One method for calculating deprecation is called the **reducing balance method**. In this method, the value of an item is decreased by the same fixed percentage every year.

WORKED EXAMPLE Calculating depreciation

A car bought for €26 000 depreciates by 18% every year. What is its value after 3 years?

At the end of the first year, the value = 82% of €26 000 = €26 000 × 0·82 = €21 320

At the end of the second year, the value = 82% of €21 320 = €21 320 × 0·82

$= €26\,000 \times (0{\cdot}82) \times (0{\cdot}82) = €26\,000 \times (0{\cdot}82)^2$

$= €17\,482{\cdot}40$

At the end of the third year, the value = 82% of €17 482·40

$= €17\,482{\cdot}40 \times (0{\cdot}82)$

$= €26\,000 \times (0{\cdot}82)^2 \times 0{\cdot}82$

$= €26\,000 \times (0{\cdot}82)^3$

$= €14\,335{\cdot}57$

This pattern can be generalised into the depreciation formula:

$$F = P\left(1 - \frac{r}{100}\right)^t = P(1 - i)^t$$

F is the final value.

P is the initial value of the item.

r is the percentage rate of depreciation per depreciation period.

t is the number of depreciation periods.

$i = \dfrac{r}{100}$ is the decimal rate of depreciation.

The general formula for calculating depreciation is given in the *Formulae and Tables* book:

$$F = P(1 - i)^t$$

F = final value

P = principal (present value)

t = number of depreciation periods

i = rate of depreciation as a decimal or fraction

EXAMPLE 12

A washing machine is bought for €580. It depreciates at 15% p.a. What is its value after 5 years? By how much has it depreciated in 5 years?

Solution

$P = €580$

$t = 5$ years

$r = 15\%$

$F = P\left(1 - \dfrac{r}{100}\right)^t = 580\left(1 - \dfrac{15}{100}\right)^5$

$= 580(0{\cdot}85)^5$

$= €257{\cdot}35$

It has depreciated by €580 − €257·35
= €322·65.

EXAMPLE 13

Joe bought a scooter for €1500. After 3 years he estimated its value at €768. Calculate the percentage rate of depreciation p.a. using the reducing balance method.

Solution

$F = €768, \qquad P = €1500, \qquad t = 3$

$F = P(1 - i)^t$

$768 = 1500(1 - i)^3$

$\dfrac{768}{1500} = \dfrac{64}{125} = (1 - i)^3$

$1 - i = \left(\dfrac{64}{125}\right)^{\frac{1}{3}} = \dfrac{4}{5}$

$i = 1 - \dfrac{4}{5} = \dfrac{1}{5} = 0{\cdot}2$

$r = 20\%$

∴ 20% is the percentage rate of depreciation per annum.

EXAMPLE 14

A company purchases an asset for €25 000. The asset has a useful lifetime of 4 years before it is scrapped. The scrap value is estimated to be €4000. The asset is estimated to depreciate at 36·75% p.a. The accountant has two methods available to her for calculating depreciation on this asset: the reducing balance method and the straight line method.

Carry out the calculations for each method showing the value of the asset after each year and the amount by which the asset has depreciated. Comment on which method should be used.

Solution

Reducing balance method:

Use the formula $F = P(1 - i)^t$.

$P = €25\,000$

$r = 36·75\%$

$i = 0·3675$

Year 1: $F = 25\,000(1 - 0·3675)^1 = 15\,812·50$

Loss in value $= €25\,000 - €15\,812·50 = €9187·50$

Year 2: $F = 25\,000(1 - 0·3675)^2 = 10\,001·41$

Loss in value $= €25\,000 - €10\,001·41 = €14\,998·59$

Year	Value	Depreciation
0	€25 000	0
1	€15 812·50	€9187·50
2	€10 001·41	€14 998·59
3	€6325·89	€18 674·11
4	€4001·13	€20 998·87

Straight line method:

The formula for this method is in the *Formulae and Tables* book.

$$A = \frac{P - S}{t}$$

A = annual depreciation amount

P = initial value

S = scrap value

t = useful economic life

In this example, $P = €25\,000$, $S = €4000$, $t = 4$

$$A = \frac{P - S}{t} = \frac{25\,000 - 4000}{4} = €5250$$

Year	Value	Depreciation
0	€25 000	0
1	€19 750	€5250
2	€14 500	€10 500
3	€9250	€15 750
4	€4000	€21 000

One major difference between the two methods is that with the reducing balance method the asset lost much more of its value in the first year compared to the straight line method. The reducing balance method gives you a truer value of your asset. Most of the value of a new car is lost the second you drive it out of the salesroom.

Although the reducing balance depreciation formula, $F = P\left(1 - \dfrac{r}{100}\right)^t = P(1 - i)^t$, is normally applied to monetary problems, it can be used for any item that depreciates.

EXAMPLE 15

Michael goes on a diet. His goal is to decrease his body weight in kg by 1% per week. If he achieves this goal, what will his weight be after 6 weeks correct to one decimal place, given his initial weight is 80 kg? What is his percentage change in weight after 6 weeks, correct to one decimal place?

Solution

$P = 80$ kg, $r = 1\%$, $t = 6$ weeks

$F = 80\left(1 - \dfrac{1}{100}\right)^6 = 80(0{\cdot}99)^6 = 75{\cdot}3$ kg

His percentage change in weight:

$= \dfrac{\text{Change in weight}}{\text{Original weight}} \times 100\%$

$= \dfrac{80 - 75{\cdot}3}{80} \times 100\% = 5{\cdot}9\%$

EXERCISE 5

1. **(a)** Calculate the simple interest on a loan of €15 500 at a rate of 5·5% p.a. over 2 years and 6 months.

    (b) Calculate the simple interest on a loan of €675 at a rate of 8·75% p.a. over 3·5 years.

    (c) What interest rate per annum will I have to get so that €12 000 will yield €1500 in 3 years using simple interest? Give your answer correct to one decimal place.

    (d) What interest rate per annum will I have to get so that €875 will yield €1200 in 4 years using simple interest? Give your answer correct to one decimal place.

    (e) Calculate the monthly repayments on a car loan of €12 700 at a simple interest rate of 6·2% p.a. over 5 years.

2. A suite of furniture has a total purchase price of €4200. John buys the suite on the following terms: 10% deposit with the balance plus simple interest paid monthly at 8% p.a. over 4 years.

    (a) Calculate the amount of the deposit.

    (b) What is the balance owing after the initial deposit?

    (c) Calculate the interest payable.

    (d) What is the total amount to be repaid?

    (e) Find the amount of each monthly repayment.

3. Michelle wants to buy a used car that has a cash price of €13 500. The dealer offers terms of 10% deposit and monthly repayments of €372·94 for 3 years.

    (a) Calculate the amount of the deposit.

    (b) Calculate the total amount to be paid in monthly repayments.

    (c) What is the total amount Michelle pays for the car?

    (d) How much more than the cash price of the car does Michelle pay?

    (e) What is the simple interest per annum charged by the dealer? Give your answer correct to two decimal places.

4. Jack wants to purchase a car. He has saved €1500 as a deposit but the cost of the car is €5000. Jack takes out a loan from the bank to cover the balance of the car plus €1150 to cover his insurance costs.

    (a) How much will Jack need to borrow from the bank?

    (b) Jack takes the loan out over 3 years at 7·5% p.a. simple interest. How much interest will Jack pay?

    (c) What are Jack's monthly repayments?

    (d) What is the total cost of the car after paying off the loan, including the insurance costs?

5. Lara borrows €15 000 over 4 years from the bank. The loan is charged at 7·4% p.a. simple interest. The loan is to be repaid in equal monthly instalments. Calculate the amount of each monthly repayment.

6. (a) How much does €10 000 amount to at 3% p.a. compound interest after:

    (i) 1 year, (ii) 2 years, (iii) 3 years?

    (b) How much does €25 000 amount to at 2·5% p.a. compound interest after:

    (i) 1 year, (ii) 2 years, (iii) 3 years?

7. (a) How much does €10 000 amount to in 2 years at an AER of 1·5%?

    (b) How much does €22 000 amount to in 3 years at an AER of 2·4%?

8. (a) What principal must be invested to amount to €21 500 in 2 years at an AER of 2%?

    (b) What principal must be invested to amount to €15 600 in 3 years at an AER of 3·4%?

9. (a) What is the AER if €12 600 amounts to €13 000 in 2 years? Give your answer correct to two decimal places.

    (b) What is the AER if €28 400 amounts to €30 500 in 3 years? Give your answer correct to one decimal place.

10. Bank of Ireland offered a 9-month fixed term account paying 2·5% on maturity. Find the total value of €10 000 after 9 months.

11. An Post offers a savings bond giving a gross annual interest of 4% for 3 years. What is the total value of €15 500 at the end of 3 years?

12. An Post savings bonds give a gross amount of €12 480 on an investment of €12 000 after 3 years. What is the gross percentage interest rate?

13. An Post savings bonds give an AER of 1·32%. What does an investment of €26 500 amount to in 5 years?

14. A savings bond amounts to €36 404·38 on an investment of €35 000 in 3 years. What is the AER, correct to two decimal places?

15. Susan inherits €15 000. She wants to invest it in a high-risk fund to double her inheritance in 2 years. What must the AER of the fund be, correct to one decimal place?

16. A double-your-interest account earns 2% interest in the first year and 4% in the second year. The interest is added to the account at the end of each year. If a person invests €25 000 in this account, how much will they have in this account at the end of 2 years. How much more interest can be earned by investing the money in an account for 2 years at 3% AER?

17. What sum of money invested at an AER of 4·5% will amount to €22 823·32 in 3 years?

18. €P was invested at r % compound interest. The interest for the first year was €125. The interest for the second year was €131·25. Find r and P.

19. A man borrows €10 000 from a bank for 3 years at an APR of 4·5%. He is given two options to repay the loan.
    Option 1: To repay the total principal and interest in 3 years.
    Option 2: To repay the loan monthly, using the following loan repayments table.

    The APR table below shows the monthly repayments on each €1000 borrowed for a loan at a fixed APR for a fixed term.

Number of payments	4%	4·5%	5%
12	85·15	83·38	85·61
24	43·43	43·65	43·87
36	29·50	29·75	29·97
48	22·60	22·80	23·03
60	18·42	18·64	18·87

Find the total cost of repayment:

(a) using option 1,

(b) using option 2 (use the APR repayment table).

Which option is better?

20. A personal loan of €15 000 is taken out for 5 years by a family to extend their kitchen. If the total repayments were €16 983 and the repayments were made monthly, what was the APR?
(Use the APR table in Question 19.)

21. A motorcycle which cost €4700 depreciates at a rate of 18% p.a. Find its value after 4 years to the nearest euro using the reducing balance method.

22. A 4 × 4 vehicle depreciated to €20 410 in 5 years at a rate of 15% p.a. Find its original value using the reducing balance method, correct to the nearest euro.

23. A photocopier bought at €24 000 depreciated to €12 288 in 3 years. Find the rate of depreciation using the reducing balance method.

24. A car rental company paid €32 000 for a car. The company expects to rent it out for 3 years and then sell it.

    (a) If it depreciates at 25% p.a., find its value after 3 years by the reducing balance method.

    (b) If the company sells it at a percentage loss of 10% on its depreciated value, how much does the company get for the car from its sale?

25. The current value of a car is €22 500. It depreciates by 25% p.a. by the reducing balance method. Find the percentage change in value after 2 years.

REVISION QUESTIONS

1. The specials for the week in a local minimart were advertised on a flyer, as shown:

Pack of
120 nappies

€18·00 reduced by 10%

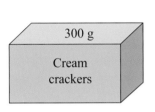

300 g

Cream
crackers

Snipe
cola

€1·70 reduced to €1·30   €2·50 reduced to €1·80

(a) Find:

    (i) the special price of the nappies,

    (ii) the percentage discount on the cream crackers, correct to one decimal place,

    (iii) the percentage discount on the cola.

(b) If a baby needs 6–8 nappies per day:

    (i) what is the maximum number of days a pack of 120 will last,

    (ii) what is the minimum number of days a pack of 120 will last?

2. €10 000 is invested for 3 years at compound interest. The AER for the first year was 3% and the AER for the second year was 2%.

(a) Find the amount of the investment at the end of the second year.

(b) At the beginning of the third year, a further €5000 was invested. The AER for the third year was r%. The total investment at the end of the third year was €15 893·65. Find r.

3. A school play was staged by the second-year students in a secondary school to raise money for a school bus. The ticket pricing was as follows:

Category	Price
Children under 12 years	€5·00
Children between 12 and 18 years	€7·50
Adults	€10·00
Senior citizens	€8·00

On the night of the show, the attendance was 60 adults, 20 senior citizens, 80 children aged between 12 and 18 years, and 40 children under 12 years.

(a) Find the total ticket sales.

(b) During the interval refreshments were sold. If the cost of the refreshments was €78 and the income from them was €228, find the percentage profit from refreshments, to the nearest euro.

(c) The parents association added €34 290 to the net takings of the play and refreshments. If the total amount was invested at an AER of 2·5% for 3 years, what was its total value at the end of this period?

(d) The bus was priced at €42 000 excluding VAT at 23%. What is the price of the bus when VAT is included?

(e) What percentage discount must the motor dealer give to the school in order that its investment will pay for the bus, correct to the nearest euro?

4. The spreadsheet below gives details of the hours worked and the rates of pay for three employees of a supermarket.

	A	B	C	D	E
1	Employee	Weekday hourly rate in €	Weekday hours worked	Weekend hours worked	Gross weekly pay in €
2	Felicity	9	25		297
3	Noah	13·20	24	6	
4	Ciara		40	0	852

The weekend hourly rate is double the weekday hourly rate.

(a) Fill in these cells: (i) D2, (ii) E3, (iii) B4.

(b) What is Ciara's gross weekly salary?

(c) If tax is levied at 20% on the first €650 and 40% on the remainder of Ciara's salary, find her gross tax.

(d) Find her net tax, if Ciara's weekly tax credit is €63.

(e) Find Ciara's PRSI deduction, if PRSI is levied at 4% on her gross salary.

(f) Find Ciara's USC deduction if the first €231 is levied at 1%, the next €128 at 3%, and the remainder at 5·5%.

(g) Find Ciara's net weekly take-home pay, if net pay = gross pay – net tax – PRSI – USC.

5. (a) A company's turnover in 2012 was €325 475. It increased its turnover in 2013 by 3·5%. What was the company's turnover in 2013?

(b) A holiday complex offers three different types of holiday homes, as shown in the table.

Holiday home type	Number of homes	Maximum occupancy	Weekly rent in July per home
A	10	5	€500
B	12	6	€600
C	18	8	€800

If during one week in July, all holiday homes were fully occupied, find:

(i) the maximum number of people staying at the complex during that week,

(ii) the total rental income for that week,

(iii) the percentage profit margin for that week if the total costs C for cleaning, wages, maintenance, administration, mortgages, etc. are given by $C = €(50n + 3000)$, where n is the number of occupants. Give your answer correct to one decimal place.

(iv) During September a discount of 30% is given on each home. Find the rental income for a week in September in which six type A, eight type B and three type C homes were occupied.

6. The metric body mass index (BMI) formula is
$$BMI = \frac{Mass}{(Height)^2},$$ where mass is in kilograms (kg) and height is in metres (m).

(a) On 1 January, Joe's mass was 100 kg and his height was 1·7 m. Find his BMI correct to one decimal place.

(b) Over 3 months, Joe lost 6% of his mass each month. Find his BMI on 1 April, correct to one decimal place.

(c) What was the percentage change in his BMI between 1 January and 1 April, correct to the nearest per cent?

The imperial BMI formula is:
$$BMI = 703 \times \frac{Mass}{(Height)^2},$$ where mass is in pounds and height is in inches.

(d) If 1 kg = 2·20463 pounds and 1 inch = 0·0254 m, find Joe's mass in pounds and height in inches on 1 April, correct to two decimal places.

(e) Show that the imperial BMI gives the same value as the metric BMI for Joe on 1 April.

7. John returns from a weekend in London with £550. At the airport, Hibernian Bank's currency exchange board displays the exchange rate for €1.

Country	Currency	Buys	Sells
USA	Dollar ($)	1·3494	1·3266
UK	Pound (£)	0·8394	0·7983
Canada	Dollar (CAD)	1·5702	1·4505
South Africa	Rand (R)	15·7342	14·5349

(a) What rate will John get to change his £ into €?

(b) How many euro will John get for his £550?

John decides to hang on to his £550. When he gets home, his sister Mary tells him she is going shopping in Belfast the next day. She says she is going to convert €670 to pounds sterling.

(c) What rate will Mary get in the Hibernian Bank?

(d) How many pounds sterling will she get for her €670?

(e) John and Mary decide to do a deal. John gives Mary his £550 for her €670. Explain why both save money from this transaction.

8. (a) Find the compound interest on €6000 invested at 2·3% AER for 4 years.

(b) A loan of €40 000 is to be repaid by a single payment of €45 369, 2 years from now. Find the APR of this loan.

(c) Before going on a holiday to Paris, Joan meets up with two friends, Mia from the US and Kylie from Australia. Mia changes $100 into pounds sterling and her remaining $1000 into euro. Kylie changes AUS$150 into pounds sterling and her remaining AUS$1100 into euro. Joan changes £800 into euro.

Use the exchange rates below to find the total number of euro the three friends bring to Paris, correct to the nearest euro.

£1 = $1·67

£1 = AUS$1·85

£1 = €1·22

9. The value of a car V depreciates according to the straight line graph, as shown (using the straight line method of depreciation). $t = 0$ is 1 January 2010.

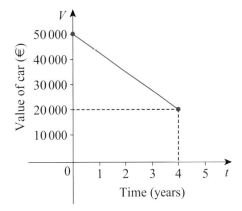

(a) Find the value of the car in:

   (i) January 2010,

   (ii) January 2014 from the graph.

(b) Find the slope of the graph.

(c) Find the equation of the straight line.

(d) Use the equation of the straight line to find when the value of the car will be zero.

(e) Find the rate of depreciation per annum by the reducing balance method that gives the same depreciation from 1 January 2010 to 1 January 2014. Give your answer correct to one decimal place.

10. The length of a kitchen wall is 4·32 m and its height is 1·9 m. It is to be tiled with tiles of dimensions 15 cm × 15 cm.

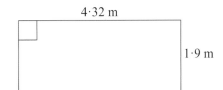

Find:

(a) the area of the wall,

(b) the total number of tiles required,

(c) the percentage wastage, correct to one decimal place.

The tiles come in boxes of 40.

(d) How many boxes are required for the job?

(e) How many spare tiles are left over?

(f) If each box costs €85 excluding VAT at 23%, find the total cost of the tiles.

SUMMARY

1. Unit rates:

   5 objects cost €20.

   1 object costs €4.

   7 objects cost €28.

2. Value added tax (VAT) can be included or not included in a cost price.

3. Income tax and deductions:

   (a) Pay Related Social Insurance (PRSI) is calculated as a percentage of gross income.

   (b) Tax on income:

   (i) Gross tax:

   20% on the first €33 800 of gross income.

   40% on the remainder.

   (ii) Net tax = gross tax – tax credits

   (c) Universal Social Charge (USC): There are different rates for different bands of income.

4. Profit (P) = Selling price (SP) – Cost price (CP):

   $$\text{Percentage profit (\%P)} = \frac{\text{Profit}}{\text{Cost price}} \times 100\%$$

   $$\text{Profit margin} = \frac{\text{Profit}}{\text{Selling price}} \times 100\%$$

5. Loss (L) = Cost price (CP) – Selling price (SP):

   $$\text{Percentage loss (\%L)} = \frac{\text{Loss}}{\text{Cost price}} \times 100\%$$

6. Simple interest:

   $$I = \frac{P \times r \times t}{100}$$

   I = interest

   P = principal

   r = percentage rate per year (p.a.)

   t = time in years

7. Compound interest:

   $$F = P\left(1 + \frac{r}{100}\right)^t = P(1 + i)^t$$

   F = final amount after t periods

   P = principal

   r = percentage rate per interest period

   t = number of interest periods in the term

   $i = \dfrac{r}{100}$ = rate of compound interest expressed as a decimal or fraction

8. Depreciation by the reducing balance method:

   $$F = P\left(1 - \frac{r}{100}\right)^t = P(1 - i)^t$$

   F = value after t periods

   P = principal = initial value

   r = percentage rate per depreciation period

   t = number of depreciation periods

   $i = \dfrac{r}{100}$ = rate of depreciation expressed as a decimal or fraction

SECTION 6

Complex Numbers

Complex numbers may appear strange at first, but with a bit of practice they really are easy. Complex numbers deal with the problem of finding the square root of a negative number.

Imaginary and Complex Numbers

Learning Outcomes

- To understand the idea of imaginary and complex numbers.
- To plot complex numbers on the Argand diagram.

13.1 Why imaginary numbers are needed

ACTIVITY 1

ACTION
Asking: Is it real or imaginary?

OBJECTIVE
To recognise whether numbers are real or imaginary

To solve the equation $x^2 = 4$ or $x \times x = 4$, you have to find two identical numbers which, when multiplied together, give 4.

No problem: $(+2) \times (+2) = 4$ and $(-2) \times (-2) = 4$

$\therefore x = \pm 2$

But now try to solve $x^2 = -1$ or $x \times x = -1$. You have to think of two identical numbers which, when multiplied together, give -1.

$\therefore x = \pm\sqrt{-1}$

↑ Leonhard Euler

Like the great mathematician Euler (pronounced *oiler*), imagine that $\sqrt{-1}$ does exist and give it a name i. From now on *imagine* $i = \sqrt{-1}$.

Hundreds of years ago, Euler imagined $\sqrt{-1}$ did exist and called it i (*iota*). Based on this 'imaginary number', a new system of numbers called complex numbers was developed. These complex numbers have enormous applications in physics, engineering, science and IT.

Imaginary numbers are as normal as every other number. They are a tool to describe the world in the same way that 0 and negative numbers were invented to deal with problems that arose in the development of mathematics.

Square roots of positive and negative integers

$$i = \sqrt{-1} \Rightarrow i^2 = -1$$

▸ $\sqrt{6} = \sqrt{3 \times 2} = \sqrt{3} \times \sqrt{2}$

▸ $-\sqrt{8} = -\sqrt{4 \times 2} = -\sqrt{4} \times \sqrt{2} = -2\sqrt{2}$

▸ $\sqrt{-9} = \sqrt{9 \times -1} = \sqrt{9} \times \sqrt{-1} = 3 \times i = 3i$

▸ $\sqrt{-\dfrac{16}{25}} = \sqrt{\dfrac{16}{25} \times -1} = \sqrt{\dfrac{16}{25}} \times \sqrt{-1} = \dfrac{4}{5} \times i = \dfrac{4}{5}i$

KEY TERM

Numbers of the form bi, with $b \in \mathbb{R}$ and $i = \sqrt{-1}$, are called **imaginary numbers**.

Examples: $\sqrt{3}i$, $-4i$, $-\frac{2}{3}i$, $-7 \cdot 2i$, $3\sqrt{2}\,i$ are all imaginary numbers. If there is no i in a number, the number is a real number.

ACTIVITY 2

ACTION
Exploring powers of i

OBJECTIVE
To write various powers of i in their simplest form

Whole number powers of i

Higher natural number powers of i can be broken down into multiples of i and i^2 using $i^2 = -1$.

$i^3 = i^2 \times i = -1 \times i = -i$

$i^4 = i^2 \times i^2 = -1 \times -1 = +1$

$i^5 = i^2 \times i^2 \times i = -1 \times -1 \times i = i$

$i^6 = i^2 \times i^2 \times i^2 = -1 \times -1 \times -1 = -1$

i	$= i$
i^2	$= -1$
i^3	$= -i$
i^4	$= 1$
i^5	$= i$

Any whole number power of i has one of the four values: $1, i, -1, -i$.

▸ $3i^3 = 3 \times i^2 \times i = 3 \times (-1) \times i = -3i$

▸ $4i^2 + 2i^4 = 4(-1) + 2(i^2)(i^2) = 4(-1) + 2(-1)(-1)$
$$= -4 + 2 = -2$$

TIP

Since $i^4 = 1$, any power of i that is a multiple of 4 is also 1.

▸ $i^{32} = (i^4)^8 = (1)^8 = 1$ [Remember $(a^p)^q = a^{pq}$]

To simplify very high natural number powers of i, just divide the power by 4 and work out i to the power of the remainder.

▸ $i^{27} = (i^4)^6 \times i^3 = (1)^6 \times i^3 = i^3 = -i$

or

TIP

Divide the power by 4 and put i to the power of the remainder.

▸ $i^{27} = i^3 = -i$ [$27 \div 4 = 6$ remainder 3]

▸ $i^{78} = i^2 = -1$ [$78 \div 4 = 19$ remainder 2]

EXERCISE 1

1. Simplify the following and say if the number is real or imaginary:

   (a) $\sqrt{16}$

   (b) $-\sqrt{49}$

   (c) $-\sqrt{18}$

   (d) $\sqrt{-16}$

   (e) $\sqrt{-49}$

   (f) $\sqrt{-81}$

   (g) $-\sqrt{-25}$

   (h) $\sqrt{-3}$

   (i) $\sqrt{-2}$

   (j) $\sqrt{-\frac{1}{7}}$

   (k) $\sqrt{-\frac{3}{16}}$

   (l) $\sqrt{-\frac{9}{16}}$

2. Simplify the following and say if the number is real or imaginary:

   (a) $\sqrt{16} + \sqrt{9}$

   (b) $-\sqrt{16} - \sqrt{25}$

   (c) $\sqrt{-16} + \sqrt{-9}$

   (d) $-\sqrt{-16} - \sqrt{-25}$

   (e) $4\sqrt{2} + 3\sqrt{32}$

   (f) $\sqrt{9} - 2\sqrt{81} + \sqrt{36}$

   (g) $3\sqrt{-16} + 4\sqrt{-25} - 2\sqrt{-49}$

3. Simplify the following:

   (a) i^7

   (b) i^8

   (c) i^9

   (d) i^{10}

   (e) $3i^4$

   (f) $2i^{13}$

   (g) $-3i^{11}$

   (h) $-4i^3$

   (i) $3i^8 + 4i^2$

   (j) $5i^3 - 6i$

   (k) $i^3 \times 3i^2 \times 6i^{12}$

   (l) $3i^5 + 2i^7$

   (m) $i - i^3$

   (n) $(2i)^5$

13.2 The idea of a complex number

ACTIVITY 3

ACTION
Understanding complex numbers

OBJECTIVE
To examine statements about complex numbers and to decide if they are true or false

Real numbers such as 2 and imaginary numbers such as $2i$ exist, but can a number be both real and imaginary at the same time? This question leads to the idea of a **complex number**.

KEY TERM

A **complex number** z is a number that can be written in the form $z = a + bi$, where $a, b \in \mathbb{R}$ and $i = \sqrt{-1}$.

Examples of complex numbers

▶ $z = 3 + 2i = 3 + 2 \times i$ [$a = 3 \in \mathbb{R}$, $b = 2 \in \mathbb{R}$ and $i = \sqrt{-1}$]

▶ $z = -5 - 7i$ [$a = -5 \in \mathbb{R}$, $b = -7 \in \mathbb{R}$ and $i = \sqrt{-1}$]

▶ $z = -\frac{1}{2} + \sqrt{3}\,i$

▶ $z = -7 = -7 + 0i$

▶ $z = -4i = 0 - 4i$

▶ $z = 0 = 0 + 0i$

It is important to note the following:

1. a and b can be any real numbers.

2. a is called the real part (Re) of the complex number.

3. b is called the imaginary part (Im) of the complex number.

4. $a + bi$ is often written as $a + ib$.

ACTIVITY **4**

ACTION
Working with real and imaginary numbers

OBJECTIVE
To pick out the real and the imaginary parts of complex numbers and to put them into sets

Standard form of a complex number

You must get used to putting every complex number in the standard form:

$z = $ (Real part) + (Imaginary part)$i = $ Re + Imi

So, $z = -6 + 2i$ is fine. It is in standard form. But, $w = -2i + 6$ is not in standard form. Rewrite it as $w = 6 - 2i$ before doing anything else.

▸ $z = -3 + 2i$

[Re $= -3$, Im $= +2$]

▸ $z = \frac{2}{3} - \sqrt{5}i$

[Re $= \frac{2}{3}$, Im $= -\sqrt{5}$]

▸ $z = -8 \Rightarrow z = -8 + 0i$

[Re $= -8$, Im $= 0$]

▸ $z = xi + 5 - 7i + 3q, x, q \in \mathbb{R}$

$z = (5 + 3q) + (x - 7)i$

[Re $= 5 + 3q$, Im $= x - 7$]

All real numbers are complex numbers as are all imaginary numbers.

0 is the complex number $0 + 0i$: $0 = 0 + 0i$.

EXERCISE 2

1. Find the real and the imaginary parts of the complex numbers below by writing each one in standard from: $a + bi = $ Re + Imi, where $a, b \in \mathbb{R}, i = \sqrt{-1}$.

(a) $2 + 3i$

(b) $5 - 7i$

(c) $-6 + 5i$

(d) $-7 - 4i$

(e) $-3i$

(f) $\frac{7}{3}$

(g) $\frac{1}{2} + \frac{3}{2}i$

(h) $-8 + \frac{3}{4}i$

(i) $\sqrt{2} - \sqrt{3}i$

(j) $\frac{3}{2}i - \frac{1}{\sqrt{2}}$

(i) $7 - 2i$

(j) $11 - 5i$

(k) $-3 - 6i$

(l) $-7 - 9i$

(m) $-15 - 22i$

(n) -3

(o) $11i - 3$

(p) $-22i + 5$

(q) $\sqrt{2} + 3i$

(r) $3 + 2\sqrt{3}i$

(s) $-\frac{1}{2} - i$

(t) $-\frac{3i}{2} + \sqrt{7}$

(u) $3 - xi + y, x, y \in \mathbb{R}$

(v) $x - 3i + yi, x, y \in \mathbb{R}$

2. Write in the form: $a + bi = $ Re + Imi and read off $a, b \in \mathbb{R}$.

(a) $3 + 4i$

(b) $4 + 7i$

(c) $7 + 11i$

(d) $3 + 7i$

(e) $5 + 13i$

(f) $-3 + 11i$

(g) $-5i$

(h) $-6 + 9i$

3. Write in the form $a + bi$, and read off $a, b \in \mathbb{R}$.

(a) $x - 3i + 2, x \in \mathbb{R}$

(b) $x + 7 - 2i, x \in \mathbb{R}$

(c) $xi + 7 - 2i, x \in \mathbb{R}$

(d) $y - xi + 5i, x \in \mathbb{R}$

13.3 The Argand diagram

ACTIVITY 5

ACTION
Drawing Argand diagrams

OBJECTIVE
To plot complex numbers on Argand diagrams and to explore the properties of these numbers

Complex numbers can be plotted as points on a two-dimensional (2-D), rectangular, co-ordinated diagram known as the Argand diagram.

The real part (Re) is plotted on the real axis (*x*-axis) and the imaginary part (Im) is plotted on the imaginary (*y*-axis).

The complex number $z = 2 + 3i$ with Re = 2 and Im = 3 is plotted as shown:

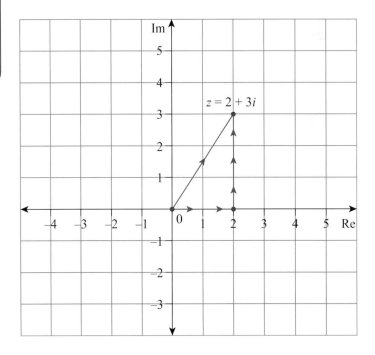

Note: The same scale is used on both axes.

Starting at 0, go +2 units along the real (Re) axis. Then go +3 units up parallel to the imaginary (Im) axis, to reach the point (2, 3).

In general, $z = x + yi$ with Re = x and Im = y is represented by the point (x, y) on the Argand diagram.

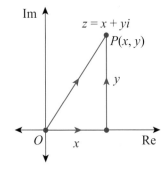

The point $P(x, y)$ represents the complex number $z = x + yi$. The point $O(0, 0)$ represents the complex number $0 = 0 + 0i$.

Every complex number can be represented by a point in 2-D space. Complex numbers are 2-D in the sense they have one foot in the real dimension and one foot in the imaginary dimension. It is this 2-D behaviour that makes them useful. They can be used to store two pieces of information simultaneously. Operations involving complex numbers can be used to process data on two different quantities simultaneously.

WORKED EXAMPLE Plotting complex numbers on
the Argand diagram

Plot the following complex numbers on an Argand diagram.

Complex number		Corresponding point
$z_1 = 0 + 1i$	↔	(0, 1)
$z_2 = 1 + i$	↔	(1, 1)
$z_3 = -4 + 0i$	↔	(-4, 0)
$z_4 = -2 - 5i$	↔	(-2, -5)
$z_5 = 0 - 3i$	↔	(0, -3)
$z_6 = -2 + 4i$	↔	(-2, 4)
$z_7 = 4 - 3i$	↔	(4, -3)
$z_8 = 6 + 0i$	↔	(6, 0)

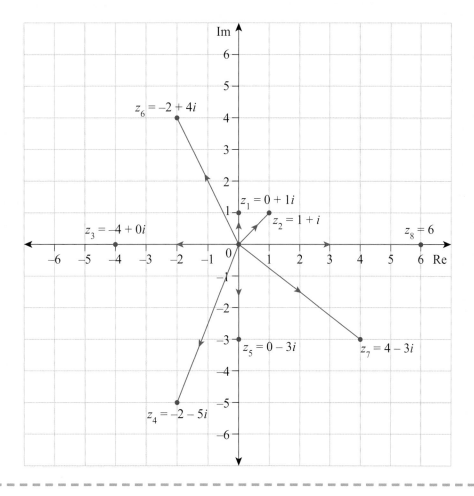

When using the Argand diagram, think of the complex number $z = x + yi$ as represented by the point $P(x, y)$.

When you plot a complex number on the Argand diagram, the distance from the origin $O(0, 0)$ to $P(x, y)$ is written as $|z|$.

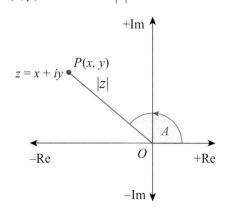

$|z|$ is called the modulus of z.

EXAMPLE 1

For $z = 5 + 12i$, find the corresponding point P on the Argand diagram and plot z on the Argand diagram.

Find:

(a) the slope of $[OP]$, where O is $(0, 0)$,

(b) distance $|OP|$.

Solution

$z = 5 + 12i$

Point P on the Argand diagram is $(5, 12)$

(a) Slope: $O(0, 0)$, $P(5, 12)$

$$m = \frac{y_2 - y_1}{x_2 - x_1}$$

$$\text{Slope} = \frac{12 - 0}{5 - 0} = \frac{12}{5}$$

(b) Distance $|OP| = |z|$:

$$|OP| = \sqrt{(x_2 - x_1)^2 + (y_2 - y_1)^2}$$

$$|z| = \sqrt{(5 - 0)^2 + (12 - 0)^2}$$

$$= 13$$

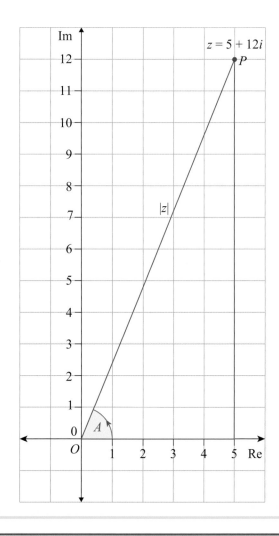

TIP

↑ The formulae used in co-ordinate geometry can be used in complex numbers.

EXERCISE 3

1. Write down the points P on an Argand diagram corresponding to the following complex numbers:

   (a) $2 + 7i$

   (b) $3 + 18i$

   (c) $17 + 52i$

   (d) $11 - 5i$

   (e) $-3 + 7i$

   (f) $-7 - 6i$

   (g) $\frac{1}{2} + \frac{3}{2}i$

   (h) $\sqrt{2} - \frac{7}{2}i$

   (i) $-5i + 6$

   (j) $-11i - 8$

   (k) $x + 1 - 2i, x \in \mathbb{R}$

   (l) $yi + 3i - 2, y \in \mathbb{R}$

2. Write down the complex numbers z corresponding to the given points on an Argand diagram:

   (a) $(1, 0)$

   (b) $(-3, 0)$

   (c) $(0, 5)$

   (d) $(-5, 6)$

   (e) $(-7, -2)$

   (f) $\left(\frac{1}{2}, \sqrt{2}\right)$

   (g) $\left(-\frac{2}{3}, 1\right)$

   (h) $\left(5, -\frac{11}{3}\right)$

   (i) $\left(4, \frac{3}{\sqrt{2}}\right)$

   (j) $\left(\frac{1}{\sqrt{2}}, \frac{1}{\sqrt{2}}\right)$

   (k) $(y - 1, 2), y \in \mathbb{R}$

   (l) $(-3, a - 2), a \in \mathbb{R}$

3. Plot the following complex numbers on the same Argand diagram:

   (a) $z_1 = 5$

   (b) $z_2 = 2 + 3i$

   (c) $z_3 = 4i$

   (d) $z_4 = -3 + 5i$

   (e) $z_5 = -5$

   (f) $z_6 = -4 - 2i$

   (g) $z_7 = -2i$

   (h) $z_8 = 4 + i$

4. Plot $z = 3 + 4i$ on an Argand diagram.

   (a) What point P represents z?

   (b) Find the slope of $[OP]$, where $O(0, 0)$.

   (c) Find the distance $|OP| = |z|$ using the distance formula.

5. The point P on the Argand diagram represents a complex number z. The origin is $O(0, 0)$. Find:

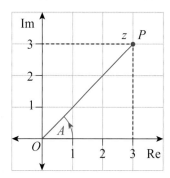

   (a) z in the form $a + bi$, $a, b \in \mathbb{R}$,

   (b) the slope of OP,

   (c) $\tan A$,

   (d) $|OP|$.

CHAPTER 14

Complex Number Operations

Learning Outcomes

- To perform the following operations on complex numbers: addition and subtraction, multiplication by a scalar, modulus, conjugate, multiplication, division.
- To interpret addition and multiplication by i geometrically.
- To solve simple complex number equations.

14.1 Addition and subtraction

To add or subtract complex numbers, combine their real parts and combine their imaginary parts giving your answer in the form $a + bi$.

▶ $3 - 2i + 8 + 4i = 11 + 2i$ [Add the real parts and add the imaginary parts.]

▶ $5 - 7i - 4 - 3i = 1 - 10i$

EXAMPLE 1

If $z = 5 + 7i$ and $w = 3 + 2i$, find:

(a) $z + w$

(b) $z - w$

Solution

(a) $z + w = (5 + 7i) + (3 + 2i)$

$\qquad\quad = (5 + 3) + (7 + 2)i$

$\qquad\quad = 8 + 9i$

(b) $z - w = (5 + 7i) - (3 + 2i)$

$\qquad\quad = (5 - 3) + (7 - 2)i$

$\qquad\quad = 2 + 5i$

EXAMPLE 2

If $z_1 = 2 - \frac{1}{3}i$, $z_2 = -\frac{1}{2} - 5i$, $z_3 = \frac{10}{3}i - \frac{3}{2}$, find $z_1 + z_2 + z_3$.

Solution

$z_1 + z_2 + z_3 = 2 - \frac{1}{3}i - \frac{1}{2} - 5i + \frac{10}{3}i - \frac{3}{2} = 0 - 2i$ (Remember $i = 1i$)

ACTIVITY 6

ACTION
Adding and subtracting complex numbers

OBJECTIVE
To carry out these operations and to explore their geometric meaning

WORKED EXAMPLE Geometric meaning of adding complex numbers

1. For $z_1 = -3$ and $w = -1 + i$, draw the line joining z_1 to $z_1 + w$ on the Argand diagram.

   $z_1 = -3 + 0i$, $w = -1 + i$

   $\Rightarrow z_1 + w = -3 + 0i + (-1 + i) = -4 + 1i$

   In terms of the Argand diagram, $z_1 = -3 + 0i$ can be represented by the point $(-3, 0)$ and $z_1 + w$ by the point $(-4, 1)$.

   $z_1 \to z_1 + w$ means $(-3, 0) \to (-4, 1)$. This is the translation obtained by adding -1 to the x co-ordinate and $+1$ to the y co-ordinate.

2. For $z_2 = -2i$ and $w = -1 + i$, draw the line joining z_2 to $z_2 + w$ on the Argand diagram.

   $z_2 + w = -2i + (-1 + i) = -1 - i$

   $\therefore z_2 \to z_2 + w$

   $\Rightarrow (0, -2) \to (-1, -1)$
   Add -1 Add $+1$

   This is the same translation as before.

3. For $z_3 = 2 + 4i$ and $w = -1 + i$, draw the line joining z_3 to $z_3 + w$ on the Argand diagram.

   $z_3 + w = 2 + 4i + (-1 + i) = 1 + 5i$

   $\therefore z_3 \to z_3 + w$

   $\Rightarrow (2, 4) \to (1, 5)$
   Add -1 Add $+1$

4. For $z_4 = 2$ and $w = -1 + i$, draw the line joining z_4 to $z_4 + w$ on the Argand diagram.

   $z_4 + w = 2 + 0i + (-1 + i) = 1 + i$

   $\therefore z_4 \to z_4 + w$

   $\Rightarrow (2, 0) \to (1, 1)$
   Add -1 Add $+1$

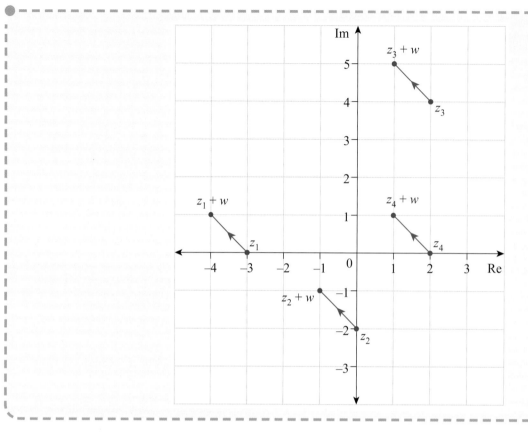

Conclusion

In geometrical terms, adding a complex number w to a given complex number z, simply translates the given number z by w.

$\therefore z \rightarrow z + w$ under the translation $0 \rightarrow w$ (where $0 = 0 + 0i$).

EXAMPLE 3

If $z = 5 - 7i$, what translation brings z to $8 - 11i$?

What is w if $z + w = 8 - 11i$?

Solution

$z \rightarrow 8 - 11i$

$\Rightarrow (5, -7) \rightarrow (8, -11)$

Add +3   Add −4

The translation is:

$(0, 0) \rightarrow (3, -4)$

$\therefore w = 3 - 4i$

EXERCISE 4

1. Simplify the following giving your answer in the form $a + bi$, $a, b \in \mathbb{R}$:

   (a) $2 + 5i + 7 + 4i$

   (b) $3 + 5i + 11 + 7i$

   (c) $6i + 7 + 2i + 7$

   (d) $(5 + 2i) + (8 + 18i)$

   (e) $3i + 2 + 9i + 1$

   (f) $3 + 11i + 5 + 7i$

   (g) $(4 + 12i) + (15 + 5i)$

   (h) $6 + 7 + 3i$

   (i) $5i + 2 + 9i$

   (j) $x + 3i + y + 2i$, $x, y \in \mathbb{R}$

2. Simplify the following giving your answer in the form $a + bi$, $a, b \in \mathbb{R}$:

(a) $3 + 5i + 7 - 6i$

(b) $-3 - 8i + 5 + 2i$

(c) $8 + 9i + 11 - 5i$

(d) $-5 + 2i - 7 - 3i$

(e) $-8 - 5i + 7i - 2$

(f) $3i - 2 - 7 + 5i$

(g) $2i + 3 + (7 - 3i)$

(h) $10 + 8i - 5 - 3i$

3. Find $z + w$ for the following giving your answer in the form $a + bi$, $a, b \in \mathbb{R}$:

(a) $z = 3 + i$, $w = 6 + 7i$

(b) $z = 4$, $w = 5i$

(c) $z = 5 - 7i$, $w = 2 - i$

(d) $z = 11 + 4i$, $w = 12 + 2i$

(e) $z = 5i$, $w = \frac{1}{2} + 2i$

(f) $z = \sqrt{3} + 2i$, $w = \sqrt{3} + 2i$

(g) $z = x + 2i$, $w = x - 4i$, $x \in \mathbb{R}$

(h) $z = 5 + xi$, $w = 4 + 3xi$, $x \in \mathbb{R}$

4. Find $z_1 + z_2 + z_3$, if:

(a) $z_1 = 2 + 3i$, $z_2 = 3 + i$, $z_3 = 5 + 3i$

(b) $z_1 = -1 + 4i$, $z_2 = 5 - 3i$, $z_3 = -2i + 7$

(c) $z_1 = -5 - 5i$, $z_2 = 3i - 6$, $z_3 = \frac{1}{2} - 4i$

(d) $z_1 = 7$, $z_2 = -3i$, $z_3 = 5 + i$

(e) $z_1 = x - 2i$, $z_2 = 4i - x$, $z_3 = y + 3i$ $(x, y \in \mathbb{R})$

5. Simplify the following giving your answer in the form $a + bi$, $a, b \in \mathbb{R}$:

(a) $(2 + 4i) - (7 + 5i)$

(b) $(3 + 5i) - (6 + 3i)$

(c) $4i - (2 - 3i)$

(d) $5 - (5 - 8i)$

(e) $(2i - 3) - (5 - 7i)$

(f) $(3 - 5i) - (-11 + 6i)$

(g) $\left(\frac{1}{2} - \frac{3}{2}i\right) - \left(-\frac{1}{2} + \frac{1}{2}i\right)$

(h) $(\sqrt{3} - 2i) - (2\sqrt{3} + i)$

(i) $(x - 2i) - (y + 4i)$, $x, y \in \mathbb{R}$

(j) $(x + yi) - (y - xi)$, $x, y \in \mathbb{R}$

6. (a) If $z = -5 + 2i$ and $z + w = 8 + 6i$, find w.

(b) If $z = -3 + 7i$, what translation maps z to $-5 + 15i$? What is w if $z + w = -5 + 15i$?

(c) If $w = 3 + 7i$, what translation maps w to $10 - 6i$? What is z if $w - z = 10 - 6i$?

(d) If $z_1 + w = -1 - i$ and $z_2 + w = 8 + 3i$, find $z_1 - z_2$.

14.2 Multiplication by a scalar

ACTIVITY 7

ACTION
Multiplying a complex number by a scalar

OBJECTIVE
To investigate the effect of multiplying complex numbers by scalars (real numbers)

KEY TERM

A **scalar** is any real number.

For example, 3, -2, $\frac{1}{2}$ and $\sqrt{3}$ are all scalars.

Therefore, a number $k + 0i$, $k \in \mathbb{R}$ is a scalar.

To multiply a complex number $a + bi$ by a scalar k, multiply the real part by k and the imaginary part by k.

▶ $3(2 + 4i) = 6 + 12i$

▶ $-2(5 - 2i) = -10 + 4i$

▶ $-\frac{1}{2}\left(4 - \frac{3}{2}i\right) = -2 + \frac{3}{4}i$

▶ $k(a + bi) = ka + kbi, \; k \in \mathbb{R}$

EXAMPLE 4

If $z = 3 + 7i$ and $w = 4 - 3i$, find:

(a) $z + 4w$

(b) $3z + 2w$

(c) $2z - 3w$

Solution

(a) $z + 4w = 3 + 7i + 4(4 - 3i)$

$\qquad\qquad = 3 + 7i + 16 - 12i = 19 - 5i$

(b) $3z + 2w = 3(3 + 7i) + 2(4 - 3i)$

$\qquad\qquad = 9 + 21i + 8 - 6i = 17 + 15i$

(c) $2z - 3w = 2(3 + 7i) - 3(4 - 3i)$

$\qquad\qquad = 6 + 14i - 12 + 9i = -6 + 23i$

WORKED EXAMPLE

Geometrical meaning of multiplication by a scalar

For the complex number $z = 2 + 4i$:

1. Plot $z_1 = 2z$ and z on the same Argand diagram. Represent z by P, z_1 by Q and the origin by O.

$z = 2 + 4i \Rightarrow z_1 = 2z = 2(2 + 4i)$

$\qquad\qquad\qquad\quad = 4 + 8i$

Slope of $OP = \frac{4}{2} = 2$

Slope of $OQ = \frac{8}{4} = 2$

This means that 0, z and z_1 are collinear.

Using the distance formula:

$\left|OP\right| = \sqrt{(2 - 0)^2 + (4 - 0)^2} = 2\sqrt{5}$

$\left|OQ\right| = \sqrt{(4 - 0)^2 + (8 - 0)^2} = 4\sqrt{5}$

$\therefore \left|OQ\right| = 2\left|OP\right|$

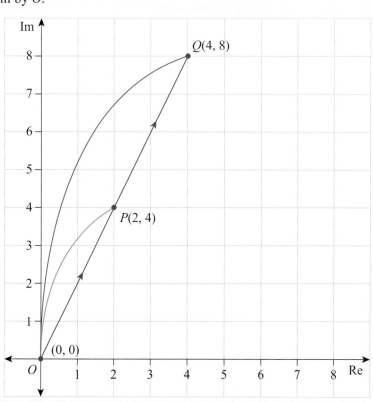

2. Plot $z_2 = -3z$ and z on the same Argand diagram.
Represent z by P, z_2 by R and the origin by O.

$z = 2 + 4i \Rightarrow z_2 = -3z = -3(2 + 4i) = -6 - 12i$

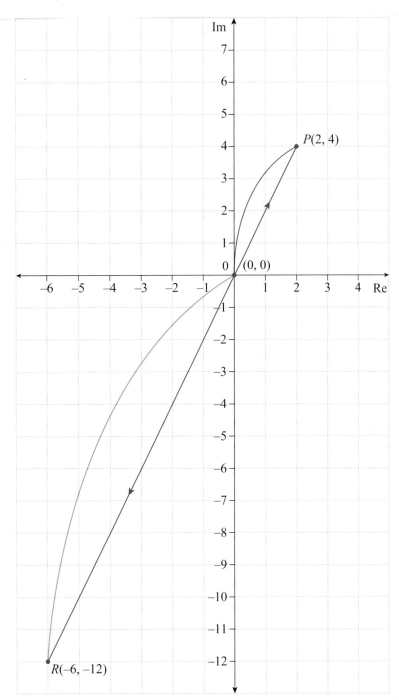

We can see that 0, z and z_2 are collinear because the slopes of OP and OR are equal.

Slope of $OP = \frac{4}{2} = 2$

Slope of $OR = \frac{-12}{-6} = 2$

$OP = \sqrt{(2 - 0)^2 + (4 - 0)^2} = 2\sqrt{5}$

$OR = \sqrt{(-6 - 0)^2 + (-12 - 0)^2} = \sqrt{36 + 144} = \sqrt{180} = 6\sqrt{5}$

$\therefore |OR| = 3|OP|$

Conclusion

Multiplying a complex number z by a scalar k gives a new complex number $w = kz$, such that $0 = 0 + 0i$, w and z are on the same straight line and the distance from 0 to w is k times the distance from 0 to z.

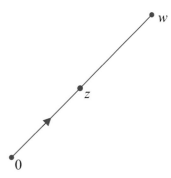

If $k > 0$, the line joining 0 to w is in the same direction as the line joining 0 to z.

If $k < 0$, the line joining 0 to w is in the opposite direction to the line joining 0 to z.

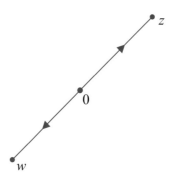

▸ $w = -\frac{1}{3}z$ means 0, w and z are collinear. However, the line joining 0 to w is in the opposite direction to the line joining 0 to z and the distance from 0 to w is $\frac{1}{3}$ of the distance from 0 to z.

EXERCISE 5

1. Simplify the following giving your answer in the form $a + bi$, $a, b \in \mathbb{R}$:

   (a) $4(3 + 2i)$

   (b) $5(11 + 10i)$

   (c) $7(6 + 2i)$

   (d) $-11(2 + 3i)$

   (e) $3(8 - 2i)$

   (f) $-5(-11 + i)$

   (g) $-5(-4 - 2i)$

   (h) $-6(-2i - 4)$

   (i) $\frac{1}{2}(-2 - 8i)$

   (j) $\frac{1}{3}(-6 + 9i)$

   (k) $5(a + bi)$, $a, b \in \mathbb{R}$

   (l) $k(1 + 2i)$, $k \in \mathbb{R}$

   (m) $k(a + bi)$, $k, a, b \in \mathbb{R}$

   (n) $3(1 + i) + 7(1 + i)$

   (o) $3(5 - i) - 7(2 + i)$

   (p) $-\frac{1}{2}(4 + 8i) - \frac{1}{4}(4i + 8)$

   (q) $2i + 3(1 - i) - 6i$

   (r) $-4i - 2(3 + 2i) - 5$

   (s) $5(2 - i) - 6(5 + 7i) - 3(4 + i)$

2. If $z = 4 + 6i$ and $w = -5 - 3i$, evaluate the following in the form $a + bi$, $a, b \in \mathbb{R}$:

   (a) $z + 2w$

   (b) $2z - w$

   (c) $3z + 2w$

   (d) $-z - w$

   (e) $-2z + 4w$

   (f) $\frac{1}{2}z - 3w$

   (g) $-\frac{1}{2}z + \frac{1}{2}w$

   (h) $3z - w$

   (i) $\frac{3}{2}z + w$

   (j) $\dfrac{z - w}{3}$

3. If $z = -5 + 12i$, write down the point P on the Argand diagram that represents z and find the distance from $O(0, 0)$ to P.

   (a) Find $2z$ and write down the distance from $O(0, 0)$ to this point.

   (b) Find $-4z$ and write down the distance from $O(0, 0)$ to this point.

   (c) Find $-\frac{1}{2}z$ and write down the distance from $O(0, 0)$ to this point.

4. $z = -4 - 2i$ is a complex number.

   (a) Draw z, $-z$, $2z$, $\frac{1}{2}z$ on an Argand diagram representing these complex numbers by points P, Q, R and S respectively.

   (b) Write down the points corresponding to each number in part **(a)**.

   (c) Find the slope of the line joining $O(0, 0)$ to each point in part **(a)** and write down the distance from $O(0, 0)$ to each of them.

5. Copy the diagram, and using your ruler,

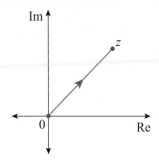

   (a) mark u on the Argand diagram if $u = 2z$,

   (b) mark v on the Argand diagram if $v = \frac{1}{2}z$.

6. If $z = 2 - 3i$ and $w = -3 + i$, find:

   (a) $3z$

   (b) $2w$

   (c) $3z + 2w$

   (d) Plot z, w, $3z$, $2w$ and $3z + 2w$ on an Argand diagram.

   (e) Show $3z + 2w$ on an Argand diagram by completing the parallelogram with sides joining 0 to $3z$ and 0 to $2w$, where $0 = 0 + 0i$.

14.3 Modulus

How big is a complex number? Is $5 + 2i$ bigger or smaller than $2 + 5i$?

The concept of the magnitude (size) of a complex number is based on the same concept as for real numbers. The number 8 is a bigger number than 4, in the sense that it is further away from 0 than 4.

KEY TERM

The **modulus of a complex number** z is its distance to the origin $O(0, 0)$.

The modulus of a complex number is denoted by $|z|$ (read as 'mod z').

TIP

Before 'taking a modulus', always write the complex number in the form $z = a + bi = \text{Re} + \text{Im } i$.

WORKED EXAMPLE Modulus of a complex number

Find $|2 + 5i|$.

This is the distance of $2 + 5i$ from $O(0, 0)$ or the distance of $(2, 5)$ from $(0, 0)$.

$|2 + 5i| = \sqrt{(2 - 0)^2 + (5 - 0)^2} = \sqrt{(2)^2 + (5)^2} = \sqrt{29}$

It is important to note the following:

1. $|z|$ is always positive.

2. $|z|$ is always real because it is a distance.

3. $|i| = |0 + 1i| = \sqrt{0^2 + 1^2} = 1$

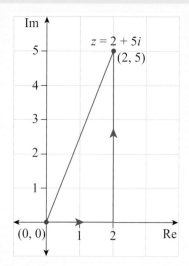

In general, for $z = a + bi$, $|z| = \sqrt{a^2 + b^2}$

$= \sqrt{(\text{Real part})^2 + (\text{Imaginary part})^2}$

$= \sqrt{(\text{Re})^2 + (\text{Im})^2}$

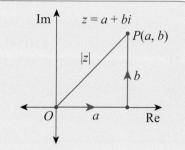

▶ $z = 2 + 0i \Rightarrow |z| = \sqrt{(2)^2 + (0)^2} = \sqrt{4} = 2$

▶ $z = 0 + 3i \Rightarrow |z| = \sqrt{(0)^2 + (3)^2} = \sqrt{9} = 3$

▶ $z = 1 + 1i \Rightarrow |z| = \sqrt{(1)^2 + (1)^2} = \sqrt{2}$

▶ $z = 3 - 2i \Rightarrow |z| = \sqrt{(3)^2 + (-2)^2} = \sqrt{9 + 4}$

   $= \sqrt{13}$ [$z = 3 - 2i$ is $\sqrt{13}$ units from $(0, 0)$]

EXAMPLE **5**

If $z = 5 + 2i$, find $|z|$.

Solution

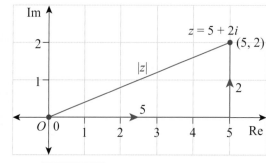

$|z| = \sqrt{(5)^2 + (2)^2} = \sqrt{29}$

ACTIVITY **8**

ACTION
Exploring the modulus of a complex number

OBJECTIVE
To find the moduli of complex numbers and to see the effects by graphing on an Argand diagram

Steps for finding the modulus of a complex number z

1. Tidy up z into a single complex number in the form $z = a + bi$.

2. Find the modulus using $|z| = \sqrt{(a)^2 + (b)^2}$.

EXAMPLE **6**

Show that $|z| = |w|$, if $z = 3 - 4i$ and $w = -3 + 4i$.

Solution

$z = 3 - 4i$: $|z| = \sqrt{(3)^2 + (-4)^2}$
$\qquad\qquad = \sqrt{9 + 16} = \sqrt{25} = 5$

$w = -3 + 4i$: $|w| = \sqrt{(-3)^2 + (4)^2}$
$\qquad\qquad = \sqrt{9 + 16} = \sqrt{25} = 5$

$$\therefore |z| = |w|$$

EXAMPLE **7**

If $z = 3 - 4i$ and $w = 15 + 8i$, find:

(a) $|z|$

(b) $|w|$

(c) $|z + w|$

(d) $|2w|$

(e) $2|w|$

(f) $|3z + w|$

(g) $|z| + |w|$

Solution

$z = 3 - 4i$, $w = 15 + 8i$

(a) $|z| = \sqrt{(3)^2 + (-4)^2} = \sqrt{9 + 16} = \sqrt{25} = 5$

(b) $|w| = \sqrt{(15)^2 + (8)^2} = \sqrt{225 + 64} = \sqrt{289} = 17$

(c) $|z + w| = |3 - 4i + 15 + 8i| = |18 + 4i|$
$\qquad\qquad = \sqrt{(18)^2 + (4)^2} = 2\sqrt{85}$

(d) $|2w| = |2(15 + 8i)| = |30 + 16i|$
$\qquad\qquad = \sqrt{(30)^2 + (16)^2} = 34$

(e) $2|w| = 2(17) = 34$

(f) $|3z + w| = |3(3 - 4i) + (15 + 8i)|$
$\qquad\qquad = |9 - 12i + 15 + 8i|$
$\qquad\qquad = |24 - 4i| = \sqrt{(24)^2 + (-4)^2} = 4\sqrt{37}$

(g) $|z| + |w| = 5 + 17 = 22$

In general, the following results can be deduced from Example 7:

1. $|z + w| \neq |z| + |w|$

2. $|kz| = k|z|$, $k \in \mathbb{R}$

EXAMPLE 8

(a) Find $|x + yi - 2 - 3i|$, $x, y \in \mathbb{R}$.

(b) What curve on the Argand diagram is represented by $|x + yi - 2 - 3i| = 4$?

Solution

(a) $|x + yi - 2 - 3i| = |(x - 2) + (y - 3)i|$

$$= \sqrt{(x - 2)^2 + (y - 3)^2}$$

(b) $\sqrt{(x - 2)^2 + (y - 3)^2} = 4$

$$(x - 2)^2 + (y - 3)^2 = 16$$

This is a circle with centre (2, 3) and radius 4.

EXAMPLE 9

If $|x + 3i| = \sqrt{13}$, find $x \in \mathbb{R}$.

Solution

$|x + 3i| = \sqrt{13} \Rightarrow \sqrt{x^2 + 9} = \sqrt{13}$

$x^2 + 9 = 13$

$x^2 = 4$

$\therefore x = \pm 2$

EXERCISE 6

1. Find $|z|$ for the following:

(a) $z = 3 + 4i$

(b) $z = 1 + 2i$

(c) $z = 4 + 5i$

(d) $z = 2 + 5i$

(e) $z = 6i + 2$

(f) $z = 1 - i$

(g) $z = -7 + 24i$

(h) $z = -2 - 3i$

(i) $z = -\sqrt{2} + \sqrt{2}\,i$

(j) $z = -\frac{1}{3} + \frac{2}{3}i$

(k) $z = \frac{\sqrt{3}}{2} - \frac{1}{2}i$

(l) $z = \frac{1}{2} + \frac{1}{4}i$

2. If $z = 3 + 4i$ and $w = 5 - 12i$, find $|z|$ and $|w|$ and then calculate each of the following:

(a) $|z + w|$ and $|z| + |w|$

(b) $|z - w|$ and $|z| - |w|$

(c) $|2z|$ and $2|z|$

(d) $|z + 3|$ and $|z| + 3$

(e) $|w + i|$ and $|w| + |i|$

(f) $|2z - w|$ and $2|z| - |w|$

(g) $\left|\frac{z}{5}\right|$ and $\frac{1}{5}|z|$

(h) $\frac{1}{13}|w|$ and $\left|\frac{w}{13}\right|$

3. Plot $0 = 0 + 0i$, $z = 3 + 4i$ and $w = 4 - 3i$ on the same Argand diagram as points O, A and B, respectively.

(a) Show that the triangle formed by these points is right-angled by finding the slopes of OA and OB.

(b) Find $|z|$ and $|w|$.

(c) Find the length of side $[AB]$ and the area of $\triangle OAB$.

4. **(a)** If $z = 3i + 7 - xi + y$, $x, y \in \mathbb{R}$, find $|z|$.

(b) If $z = x + yi - 2i + 3$, $x, y \in \mathbb{R}$, find $|z|$.

(c) If $z = x + yi$, find the equation and centre of the circle given by $|z| = 5$, $x, y \in \mathbb{R}$.

(d) If $z = -yi + 7 - 5i + x$, find the equation and centre of the circle given by $|z| = \sqrt{6}$, $x, y \in \mathbb{R}$.

5. Solve the following for $k \in \mathbb{R}$:

(a) $|k + 7i| = 25$

(b) $|2 + ki| = \sqrt{13}$

(c) $|2k - 3i| = 3\sqrt{5}$

(d) $|5\sqrt{3} - 3ki| = 10$

14.4 Conjugate

ACTIVITY 9

ACTION
Exploring the conjugate of a complex number

OBJECTIVE
To find the conjugate of complex numbers and to deduce some general results

In order to divide two complex numbers, you need to understand the idea of the conjugate of a complex number.

KEY TERM

The **conjugate** $\bar{z}$ ('z bar') of a complex number z is obtained by changing the sign of the imaginary part of z.

$$z = a \oplus bi \Rightarrow \bar{z} = a \ominus bi \quad [+bi \text{ changes to } -bi]$$

▸ $z = 3 - 2i \Rightarrow \bar{z} = \overline{3 - 2i} = 3 + 2i$

▸ $z = -\sqrt{3} + \frac{1}{2}i \Rightarrow \bar{z} = \overline{-\sqrt{3} + \frac{1}{2}i} = -\sqrt{3} - \frac{1}{2}i$

TIP

Make sure the complex number is in the form $a + bi$ before you take its conjugate.

▸ $\overline{7i - 2} = \overline{-2 + 7i} = -2 - 7i$

▸ $\overline{3} = \overline{3 + 0i} = 3 - 0i = 3$ [The conjugate of a purely real number is the number itself.]

▸ $\overline{2i} = \overline{0 + 2i} = 0 - 2i = -2i$ [The conjugate of a purely imaginary number is the negative of the number.]

▸ $z = x + iy - 2i + 3, \ x, y \in \mathbb{R}$

$z = (x + 3) + i(y - 2)$

$\bar{z} = (x + 3) - i(y - 2)$

▸ $z = -2 - i$

$3\bar{z} = 3(\bar{z}) = 3(\overline{-2 - i}) = 3(-2 + i) = -6 + 3i$

EXAMPLE 10

If $z = 3 - 2i$ and $w = 2 + 4i$, find the following in form $a + bi$:

(a) $z + \bar{z}$ **(f)** $\bar{z} + \bar{w}$

(b) $z - \bar{z}$ **(g)** $\overline{3z + 2w}$

(c) $\bar{\bar{z}}$ **(h)** $3\bar{z} + 2\bar{w}$

(d) $3\bar{z} - \bar{i}$ **(i)** $|z|$

(e) $\overline{z + w}$ **(j)** $|\bar{z}|$

Solution

$z = 3 - 2i, w = 2 + 4i$

(a) $z + \bar{z} = 3 - 2i + \overline{3 - 2i}$

$= 3 - 2i + 3 + 2i = 6 + 0i = 6$

(b) $z - \bar{z} = 3 - 2i - (\overline{3 - 2i})$

$= 3 - 2i - (3 + 2i) = 3 - 3 - 2i - 2i$

$= 0 - 4i = -4i$

(c) $\bar{\bar{z}} = \overline{\overline{3 - 2i}} = \overline{3 + 2i} = 3 - 2i \quad [\bar{\bar{z}} = z]$

(d) $3\bar{z} - \bar{i} = 3(\overline{3 - 2i}) - \bar{i}$

$= 3(3 + 2i) + i = 9 + 6i + i = 9 + 7i$

(e) $\overline{z + w} = \overline{3 - 2i + 2 + 4i}$

$= \overline{5 + 2i} = 5 - 2i$

(f) $\bar{z} + \bar{w} = \overline{3 - 2i} + \overline{2 + 4i}$

$= 3 + 2i + 2 - 4i = 5 - 2i$

(g) $\overline{3z + 2w} = \overline{3(z) + 2(w)} = \overline{3(3 - 2i) + 2(2 + 4i)}$

$= \overline{9 - 6i + 4 + 8i} = \overline{13 + 2i} = 13 - 2i$

(h) $3\bar{z} + 2\bar{w} = 3(\overline{3 - 2i}) + 2(\overline{2 + 4i})$

$= 3(3 + 2i) + 2(2 - 4i) = 9 + 6i + 4 - 8i$

$= 13 - 2i$

(i) $|z| = |3 - 2i| = \sqrt{(3)^2 + (-2)^2} = \sqrt{9 + 4} = \sqrt{13}$

(j) $|\bar{z}| = |3 + 2i| = \sqrt{(3)^2 + (2)^2} = \sqrt{9 + 4} = \sqrt{13}$

In general, the following results can be deduced from Example 10:

1. $\overline{z + w} = \overline{z} + \overline{w}$

2. $\overline{z - w} = \overline{z} - \overline{w}$

3. $\overline{\overline{z}} = z$

4. $\overline{kz + lw} = k\overline{z} + l\overline{w}, k, l \in \mathbb{R}$

5. $|\overline{z}| = |z|$

EXERCISE 7

1. Find $\overline{z}$ for the following in the form $a + bi$:

   (a) $z = 2 + 5i$

   (b) $z = 7 + 11i$

   (c) $z = 3 + 7i$

   (d) $z = \sqrt{3} + i$

   (e) $z = a + ci,$ $a, c \in \mathbb{R}$

   (f) $z = 3 - 2i$

   (g) $z = -5 - 2i$

   (h) $z = 4 + 6i$

   (i) $z = 3$

   (j) $z = -2$

   (k) $z = 5i$

   (l) $z = -7i$

   (m) $z = 3i - 2$

   (n) $z = 5i - 1$

   (o) $z = -6i + \sqrt{3}$

   (p) $z = 5 - 1i + 3 - 2i$

   (q) $z = x + 2i - 7, x \in \mathbb{R}$

   (r) $z = x + 3i - 2 + yi,$ $x, y \in \mathbb{R}$

   (s) $z = 3 + x - yi,$ $x, y \in \mathbb{R}$

   (t) $z = 4x - 3i + y - 2,$ $x, y \in \mathbb{R}$

2. If $z = 3 - 11i$, $w = -3 + 5i$ and $u = 2i$, find for the following:

   (a) $\overline{z + w}$

   (b) $\overline{z} + \overline{w}$

   (c) $\overline{2z}$

   (d) $2\overline{z}$

   (e) $\overline{z + w + u}$

   (f) $\overline{z} + \overline{w} + \overline{u}$

   (g) $\overline{z + u - w}$

   (h) $\overline{2z + 3w + 4u}$

   (i) $2\overline{z} + 3\overline{w} + 4\overline{u}$

   (j) $\overline{z - w}$

   (k) $\overline{z} - \overline{w}$

   (l) $\overline{\overline{z}}$

   (m) $\overline{\overline{w}}$

3. If $z = 5 + 7i$ and $w = -2 - 8i$, find for the following:

   (a) $3\overline{z}$

   (b) $4\overline{w}$

   (c) $\overline{3z + 4w}$

   (d) $2\overline{z} - \overline{w}$

   (e) $\overline{\dfrac{w}{2}} + z$

   (f) $2\overline{z} + w$

   (g) $\overline{z + w}$

   (h) $\overline{3z - w}$

   (i) $8\overline{z} + 7\overline{w}$

   (j) $3\overline{z} + \overline{w}$

4. (a) If $z_1 = 3 + 4i$, find $\overline{z_1}$.

   (i) Plot z_1 and $\overline{z_1}$ on an Argand diagram.

   (ii) Join z_1 and $\overline{z_1}$ with a line segment and an arrow from z_1 to $\overline{z_1}$.

   Repeat the process in part (i) and (ii) for the following and plot all complex numbers and their conjugates on the same Argand diagram:

   (b) $z_2 = -3 - 2i$

   (c) $z_3 = 1 - 3i$

   (d) $z_4 = -2 + i$

   (e) Make a conclusion regarding z and $\overline{z}$ in geometric terms.

5. (a) If $z = -15 + 8i$, find $\overline{z}$. Show that $|z| = |\overline{z}|$.

   (b) If $z = \sqrt{3} + i$, find $\overline{z}$. Show that $|z| = |\overline{z}|$.

14.5 Multiplication

To multiply complex numbers, multiply out the brackets term by term and put $i^2 = -1$ when it occurs.

▶ $i(5 - 7i) = 5i - 7i^2 = 5i + 7 = 7 + 5i$

▶ $-3i(4 + 11i) = -12i - 33i^2 = -12i + 33 = 33 - 12i$

▶ $(4 - 2i)(5 + 3i) = 4 \times 5 + 4 \times 3i - 2i \times 5 - 2i \times 3i$
$$= 20 + 12i - 10i - 6i^2 = 20 + 2i + 6 = 26 + 2i$$

EXAMPLE 11

If $z = 2 + 3i$ and $w = 5 - 4i$, find the following:

(a) zw, wz (e) $w\overline{w}$ (i) $|z||w|$

(b) $\overline{z}$ (f) $\overline{zw}$ (j) $|zw|$

(c) $\overline{w}$ (g) $\overline{z}\,\overline{w}$

(d) $z\overline{z}$ (h) $|z|$, $|w|$

Solution

(a) $zw = (2 + 3i)(5 - 4i)$ | $wz = (5 - 4i)(2 + 3i)$

$\quad = 10 - 8i + 15i - 12i^2$ | $= 10 + 15i - 8i - 12i^2$

$\quad = 10 + 7i + 12$ | $= 10 + 7i + 12$

$\quad = 22 + 7i$ | $= 22 + 7i$

$\qquad\qquad\qquad \therefore zw = wz$

(b) $\overline{z} = \overline{2 + 3i} = 2 - 3i$

(c) $\overline{w} = \overline{5 - 4i} = 5 + 4i$

(d) $z\overline{z} = (2 + 3i)(2 - 3i)$

$\quad = 4 - 6i + 6i - 9i^2 = 4 + 9 = (2)^2 + (3)^2 = 13$

(e) $w\overline{w} = (5 - 4i)(5 + 4i) = 25 + 20i - 20i - 16i^2$

$\quad = 25 - 16i^2 = 25 + 16 = (5)^2 + (4)^2 = 41$

(f) $\overline{zw} = \overline{22 + 7i} = 22 - 7i$

(g) $\overline{z}\,\overline{w} = \overline{2 + 3i}\ \overline{5 - 4i}$

$\quad = (2 - 3i)(5 + 4i) = 10 + 8i - 15i - 12i^2$

$\quad = 10 - 7i + 12 = 22 - 7i$

$\quad = \overline{zw}$

(h) $|z| = |2 + 3i|$ | $|w| = \sqrt{5 - 4i}$

$\quad = \sqrt{4 + 9} = \sqrt{13}$ | $= \sqrt{25 + 16} = \sqrt{41}$

(i) $|z||w| = \sqrt{13} \times \sqrt{41} = \sqrt{533}$

(j) $|zw| = |22 + 7i|$

$\quad = \sqrt{484 + 49} = \sqrt{533} = |z||w|$

In general, the following results can be deduced from Example 11:

1. $zw = wz$
2. $\overline{zw} = \overline{z}\,\overline{w}$
3. $|zw| = |z|\,|w|$

> **TIP**
>
> If you multiply a complex number by its conjugate, you get: (Positive value of Re)^2 + (Positive value of Im)^2.

▶ $(4 - 11i)(4 + 11i) = 16 + 44i - 44i - 121i^2$

$\qquad\qquad\qquad = 16 - 121i^2 = 16 + 121 = (4)^2 + (11)^2 = 137$

▶ $(-5 - 2i)(-5 + 2i) = 25 - 10i + 10i - 4i^2$

$\qquad\qquad\qquad = 25 - 4i^2 = 25 + 4 = (5)^2 + (2)^2 = 29$

▶ $(2 - 7i)(2 + 7i) = (2)^2 + (7)^2 = 53$

Powers of complex numbers

To find a power of a complex number, simply multiply out the brackets.

EXAMPLE 12

Expand the following:

(a) $(3 - 2i)^2$ (b) $(2 - i)^3$ (c) $(1 + i)^4$

Solution

(a) $(3 - 2i)^2 = (3 - 2i)(3 - 2i)$

$\quad = 9 - 6i - 6i + 4i^2 = 9 - 12i - 4 = 5 - 12i$

(b) $(2 - i)^3 = (2 - i)(2 - i)(2 - i)$

$\quad = (4 - 2i - 2i + i^2)(2 - i)$

$\quad = (3 - 4i)(2 - i) = 6 - 3i - 8i + 4i^2 = 2 - 11i$

(c) $(1 + i)^4 = (1 + i)(1 + i)(1 + i)(1 + i)$

$\quad = (1 + 2i + i^2)(1 + 2i + i^2)$

$\quad = (2i)(2i) = 4i^2 = -4$

Geometric interpretation of complex number multiplication

ACTIVITY 10

ACTION
Exploring the geometric effect of multiplying numbers by powers of i (1)

OBJECTIVE
To explore the effects of multiplying numbers by powers of i

WORKED EXAMPLE

The geometric effect of multiplying 1 by powers of i

1. If you multiply a real number by i once, it moves from the Re axis to the Im axis.

   $1 \times i = i \Rightarrow 1 \to i$

   $(1, 0) \to (0, 1)$

   Result: 1 has been rotated anticlockwise about the origin $(0, 0)$ through $90°$ by multiplying it by i **once**.

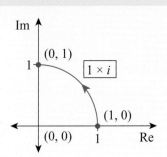

2. If you multiply a real number by i twice, it moves back on to the Re axis.

   $1 \times i \times i = i^2 = -1 \Rightarrow 1 \to -1$

   $(1, 0) \to (-1, 0)$

   Result: 1 has been rotated through $180°$ anticlockwise by multiplying it by i **twice**.

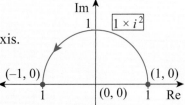

3. If you multiply a real number by i three times, it moves back on to the Im axis.

   $1 \times i \times i \times i = i^3 = -i \Rightarrow 1 \to -i$

   $(1, 0) \to (0, -1)$

   Result: 1 has been rotated through $270°$ anticlockwise by multiplying it by i **three times**.

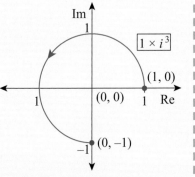

4. If you multiply a real number by i four times, it moves back on to the Re axis.

   $1 \times i \times i \times i \times i = i^4 = 1 \Rightarrow 1 \to 1$

   $(1, 0) \to (1, 0)$

   Result: 1 has been rotated through $360°$ anticlockwise by multiplying it by i **four times**.

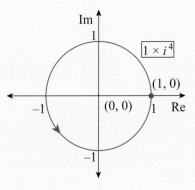

ACTIVITY **11**

ACTION
Exploring the geometric effect of multiplying numbers by powers of i (2)

OBJECTIVE
To explore more difficult examples of the effects of multiplying numbers by powers of i

WORKED **EXAMPLE**

The geometric effect of multiplying a complex number by powers of i

Consider the complex number $z = 4 + 3i$.

$iz = i(4 + 3i) = 4i + 3i^2 = -3 + 4i$

$i^2z = -1(4 + 3i) = -4 - 3i$

$i^3z = -i(4 + 3i) = -4 - 3i^2 = 3 - 4i$

$i^4z = 1(4 + 3i) = 4 + 3i$

On the Argand diagram, z, iz, i^2z, i^3z and i^4z are represented by the points A, B, C, D and E, respectively, and O is $(0, 0)$.

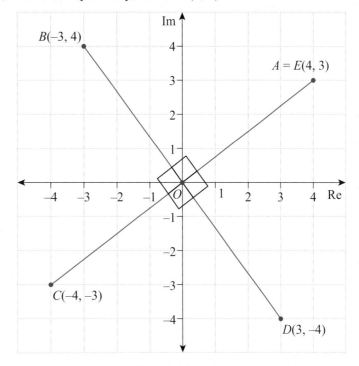

Calculate the slopes of the lines OA, OB, OC, OD and OE and the moduli of the complex numbers corresponding to the points A, B, C, D and E.

Slope of $OA = \frac{3}{4}$; $|OA| = |z| = \sqrt{4^2 + 3^2} = 5$

Slope of $OB = \frac{4}{-3} = -\frac{4}{3}$; $|OB| = |iz| = \sqrt{(-3)^2 + 4^2} = 5$

Slope of $OC = \frac{-3}{-4} = \frac{3}{4}$; $|OC| = |i^2z| = \sqrt{(-4)^2 + (-3)^2} = 5$

Slope of $OD = \frac{-4}{3} = -\frac{4}{3}$; $|OD| = |i^3z| = \sqrt{3^2 + (-4)^2} = 5$

Slope of $OE = \frac{3}{4}$; $|OE| = |i^4z| = \sqrt{4^2 + 3^2} = 5$

All the moduli are the same.

(Slope of OA) × (Slope of OB) = $\frac{3}{4} \times -\frac{4}{3} = -1 \Rightarrow OA \perp OB$

$\therefore |\angle AOB| = 90°$

Similarly, it can be shown that $OB \perp OC$, $OC \perp OD$ and $OD \perp OE$.

Conclusion

Multiplying a complex number z by i rotates it in an anticlockwise direction about $O(0, 0)$ by 90° but leaves its modulus unchanged.

Multiplying a complex number z by i^2 rotates it in an anticlockwise direction about $O(0, 0)$ by 180° but leaves its modulus unchanged.

Multiplying a complex number z by i^3 rotates it in an anticlockwise direction about $O(0, 0)$ by 270° but leaves its modulus unchanged.

Multiplying a complex number z by i^4 rotates it in an anticlockwise direction about $O(0, 0)$ by 360° but leaves its modulus unchanged.

Multiplication of a complex number z:

By	Anticlockwise rotation of the line from 0 to z through	$|z|$
i	90°	unchanged
i^2	180°	unchanged
i^3	270°	unchanged
i^4	360°	unchanged

EXERCISE 8

1. Simplify the following giving your answer in the form $a + bi$, $a, b \in \mathbb{R}$:

   (a) $2i(3 + 2i)$

   (b) $(2 + i)(3 + i)$

   (c) $(3 + 2i)(4 + 3i)$

   (d) $(-2 + 3i)(5 + i)$

   (e) $(-2 - i)(-i + 2)$

   (f) $(5 + 3i)(2 - 3i)$

   (g) $(-1 - i)(-5 - 3i)$

2. If $z = 3 + 5i$, $w = 2 - 4i$ and $u = -5 - 3i$, find the following:

   (a) zw (e) $\bar{z}\,\bar{w}$ (i) $|w|$

   (b) uz (f) $\overline{uz}$ (j) $|zw|$

   (c) $\bar{z}w$ (g) $\overline{w}\,\overline{u}$ (k) $|z||w|$

   (d) $\overline{zw}$ (h) $|z|$

3. Simplify the following giving your answer in the form $a + bi$, $a, b \in \mathbb{R}$:

   (a) $3i(2 + i) + 6i$

   (b) $3i + i(2 + 3i)$

   (c) $2i(3 + 5i) + 2(3 - 2i)$

   (d) $5 + 4i(2i + 1) - 2i$

   (e) $4i(2 - 3i) + 3i(1 + i)$

   (f) $5 - i(3 - i)$

   (g) $i(3 + i) - 4(1 + i)$

   (h) $3i + 2(5 - 2i) - i(1 + i)$

4. Write down the answers to the following:

   (a) $(1 - i)(1 + i)$ (d) $(6 - 3i)(6 + 3i)$

   (b) $(2 + 3i)(2 - 3i)$ (e) $(1 - 2i)(1 + 2i)$

   (c) $(5 - 2i)(5 + 2i)$

5. Simplify the following giving your answer in the form $a + bi$, $a, b \in \mathbb{R}$:

   (a) $(5 + 6i)^2$ (c) $(1 - i)^4$

   (b) $(1 - i)^3$ (d) $(2 + i)^2 - (2 - i)^2$

6. (a) Multiply $-8 + 6i$ by $\frac{1}{2}$.

   (b) Plot $-8 + 6i$ and $\frac{1}{2}(-8 + 6i)$ on an Argand diagram.

   (c) Calculate $|-8 + 6i|$ and $\left|\frac{1}{2}(-8 + 6i)\right|$.

   (d) What was the effect of multiplication by $\frac{1}{2}$ on $-8 + 6i$?

7. **(a)** Multiply $-8 + 6i$ by i.

   (b) Plot $-8 + 6i$ and $i(-8 + 6i)$ on an Argand diagram.

   (c) Calculate $|i(-8 + 6i)|$ and $|-8 + 6i|$.

   (d) What was the effect on $-8 + 6i$ of multiplication by i?

8. **(a)** Plot $2 + 4i$ on an Argand diagram.

   (b) Multiply $-i$ by $2 + 4i$.

   (c) Plot $-i(2 + 4i)$ on the same Argand diagram.

   (d) Calculate $|2 + 4i|$ and $\left|-i(2 + 4i)\right|$.

   (e) What was the effect of multiplication by $-i$ on $2 + 4i$?

9. Copy and complete the following statements: When a complex number:

   (a) z is multiplied by 1 it is rotated _____ by _____ degrees and its modulus is multiplied by _____.

   (b) z is multiplied by i it is rotated _____ by _____ degrees and its modulus is _____.

   (c) z is multiplied by i^2 it is rotated _____ by _____ degrees and its modulus is multiplied by _____.

   (d) z is multiplied by i^3 it is rotated _____ by _____ degrees and its modulus is _____.

10. Plot $z = 4 + i(3 - 2i)$ and $2iz$ on an Argand diagram.

11. **(a)** Plot $z = -3 + 6i$ and $w = 1 - 2i$ on an Argand diagram.

    (b) Evaluate zw.

    (c) Plot zw on the same Argand diagram.

12. **(a)** Plot $1 + 5i$ and $-1 - i$ on an Argand diagram.

    (b) Multiply $(1 + 5i)(-1 - i)$.

    (c) Plot the result of part **(b)** on the same Argand diagram.

14.6 Division

To divide one complex number by another complex number, multiply above and below by the conjugate of the number on the bottom.

EXAMPLE 13

Simplify $\dfrac{22 - 7i}{3 + 2i}$.

Solution

$$\frac{22 - 7i}{3 + 2i} = \frac{(22 - 7i)}{(3 + 2i)} \times \frac{(3 - 2i)}{(3 - 2i)}$$ [Multiply above and below by the conjugate of $(3 + 2i)$]

$$= \frac{(22 - 7i)(3 - 2i)}{(3 + 2i)(3 - 2i)}$$

$$= \frac{66 - 44i - 21i + 14i^2}{9 - 6i + 6i - 4i^2}$$

$$= \frac{66 - 65i - 14}{9 + 4} = \frac{52 - 65i}{13}$$

$$= \frac{13(4 - 5i)}{13}$$

$$= 4 - 5i$$

▶ $\dfrac{1}{i} = \dfrac{(1)}{(i)} \times \dfrac{(-i)}{(-i)} = \dfrac{-i}{-i^2} = \dfrac{-i}{1} = -i$

TIP

$\dfrac{1}{i} = -i$: Division by i is the same as multiplication by $-i$.

▶ $\dfrac{1}{-i} = i$

▶ $\dfrac{5}{i} = 5 \times (-i) = -5i$

▶ $\dfrac{2 - 3i}{i} = (2 - 3i)(-i) = -2i + 3i^2 = -3 - 2i$

Division is sometimes called multiplication by the inverse.

EXAMPLE 14

If $z = 3 + i$ and $w = 2 - i$, find:

(a) $|z|$ (e) $\dfrac{z}{w}$ (h) $\left|\dfrac{z}{w}\right|$

(b) $|w|$

(c) $\bar{z}$ (f) $\overline{\left(\dfrac{z}{w}\right)}$ (i) $\dfrac{|z|}{|w|}$

(d) $\bar{w}$ (g) $\left(\dfrac{\bar{z}}{\bar{w}}\right)$

Solution

(a) $|z| = |3 + i| = \sqrt{(3)^2 + (1)^2} = \sqrt{9 + 1} = \sqrt{10}$

(b) $|w| = |2 - i| = \sqrt{(2)^2 + (-1)^2} = \sqrt{4 + 1} = \sqrt{5}$

(c) $\bar{z} = \overline{3 + i} = 3 - i$

(d) $\bar{w} = \overline{2 - i} = 2 + i$

(e) $\dfrac{z}{w} = \dfrac{3 + i}{2 - i} = \dfrac{(3 + i)}{(2 - i)} \times \dfrac{(2 + i)}{(2 + i)}$

$= \dfrac{6 + 3i + 2i + i^2}{4 + 2i - 2i - i^2} = \dfrac{6 + 5i - 1}{4 + 1} = \dfrac{5 + 5i}{5}$

$= \dfrac{5(1 + i)}{5} = 1 + i$

(f) $\overline{\left(\dfrac{z}{w}\right)} = \overline{1 + i} = 1 - i$

(g) $\left(\dfrac{\bar{z}}{\bar{w}}\right) = \dfrac{3 - i}{2 + i} = \dfrac{(3 - i)}{(2 + i)} \times \dfrac{(2 - i)}{(2 - i)}$

$= \dfrac{6 - 3i - 2i + i^2}{4 - 2i + 2i - i^2} = \dfrac{6 - 5i - 1}{4 + 1}$

$= \dfrac{5 - 5i}{5} = \dfrac{5(1 - i)}{5} = 1 - i$

(h) $\left|\dfrac{z}{w}\right| = |1 + i| = \sqrt{1^2 + 1^2} = \sqrt{2}$

(i) $\dfrac{|z|}{|w|} = \dfrac{\sqrt{10}}{\sqrt{5}} = \sqrt{2}$

In general, the following results can be deduced from Example 14:

ACTIVITY 12

ACTION
Exploring the geometric effect of dividing complex numbers

OBJECTIVE
To explore the effects of dividing complex numbers by each other

1. $\overline{\left(\dfrac{z}{w}\right)} = \dfrac{\bar{z}}{\bar{w}}$

2. $\left|\dfrac{z}{w}\right| = \dfrac{|z|}{|w|}$

Geometric interpretation of complex number division

Division of a complex number z by powers of i

Since $\dfrac{z}{i} = -iz = i^3 z$ the division of a complex number z by i means an anticlockwise rotation of $270°$ about the origin. This is the same as a clockwise rotation of $90°$ about $(0, 0)$.

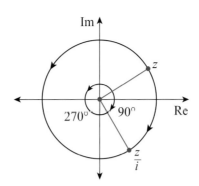

Also $\left|\dfrac{z}{i}\right| = |-iz| = |-i| \times |z| = |z|$ means dividing a complex number by i leaves its modulus unchanged.

Conclusion

The division of a complex number z:

By	Clockwise rotation of the line joining 0 to z through:	|z|
i	90°	unchanged
i^2	180°	unchanged
i^3	270°	unchanged
i^4	360°	unchanged

EXERCISE 9

1. Simplify the following giving your answer in form $a + bi$, $a, b \in \mathbb{R}$:

(a) $\dfrac{3}{i}$

(b) $\dfrac{-7}{i}$

(c) $\dfrac{5}{-i}$

(d) $\dfrac{2}{3i}$

(e) $\dfrac{3}{2 - i}$

(f) $\dfrac{4}{7 + 3i}$

(g) $\dfrac{-5}{2 - 3i}$

(h) $\dfrac{1 + i}{2 + i}$

(i) $\dfrac{3 + i}{4 + 3i}$

(j) $\dfrac{1 - 2i}{3 - 2i}$

(k) $\dfrac{-4 + 3i}{-2 + i}$

(l) $\dfrac{-3 - 5i}{-4 + 3i}$

2. If $z = 4 + 3i$ and $w = 2 - i$, find the following in the form $a + bi$, $a, b \in \mathbb{R}$:

(a) $\dfrac{z}{w}$

(b) $\dfrac{w}{z}$

(c) $\dfrac{1}{z}$

(d) $\dfrac{z}{\bar{z}}$

(e) $\dfrac{w}{\bar{w}}$

(f) $\dfrac{z}{\bar{w}}$

(g) $\dfrac{w}{\bar{z}}$

(h) $\dfrac{\bar{z}}{\bar{w}}$

(i) $\dfrac{\bar{w}}{\bar{z}}$

(j) $\overline{\left(\dfrac{z}{w}\right)}$

(k) $\left|\dfrac{z}{w}\right|$

(l) $\dfrac{|z|}{|w|}$

(m) $\left|\dfrac{z}{\bar{w}}\right|$

(n) $\dfrac{|z|}{|\bar{w}|}$

(o) $\left|\dfrac{1}{z}\right|$

14.7 Equality of complex numbers

ACTIVITY 13

ACTION
Exploring the equality of complex numbers

OBJECTIVE
To perform simple examples involving the equality of complex numbers

Two complex numbers are equal if they have the same co-ordinates on an Argand diagram.

$$a + bi = c + di \text{ means:}$$

1. $a = c$ (x co-ordinates are equal) **and** $b = d$ (y co-ordinates are equal).

or

2. Re = Re (the real parts are equal) **and** Im = Im (the imaginary parts are equal).

▶ $x + yi = 3 + 2i, x, y \in \mathbb{R}$

$\Rightarrow x = 3$ and $y = 2$

▶ $x - 3i + yi + 2 = 0, x, y \in \mathbb{R}$

$(x + 2) + i(y - 3) = 0 + 0i$ [Remember $0 = 0 + 0i$]

$x + 2 = 0$ and $y - 3 = 0$

$x = -2, y = 3$

▶ $x - yi + 2 - 3i = 2 + i, x, y \in \mathbb{R}$

$(x + 2) + i(-y - 3) = 2 + 1i$

$x + 2 = 2$ and $-y - 3 = 1$

$x = 0, y = -4$

Steps for solving complex number equations

1. Tidy up each side into the form Re + Imi.

2. Put: Re on the left = Re on the right

     and: Im on the left = Im on the right

3. Solve the resulting equations.

EXAMPLE 15

Solve for $x, y \in \mathbb{R}, i = \sqrt{-1}$

$2x + xi + yi - y = 5 + 4i$

Solution

$\underline{2x} + xi + yi \underline{- y} = 5 + 4i$

$(2x - y) + i(x + y) = 5 + 4i$

Re = Re

$2x - y = 5$ **(1)**

Im = Im

$x + y = 4$ **(2)**

$2x - y = 5$	**(1)**
$\underline{x + y = 4}$	**(2)**
$3x \quad = 9$	**(1)** + **(2)**
$x = 3$	

Into (2): $3 + y = 4$

$y = 1$

$\therefore x = 3, y = 1$

EXERCISE 10

Solve the following for $x, y \in \mathbb{R}, i = \sqrt{-1}$.

1. $x + yi = 2 + 3i$

2. $x + 7yi = -3 + 21i$

3. $2x - 3yi = -8 - 9i$

4. $x + 3 - yi = 4 + 6i$

5. $3x + y + ix = 7 + 2i$

6. $2x - 14 + 5xi = 3y - yi + 18i$

REVISION QUESTIONS

1. **(a)** If $i^2 = -1$, simplify $4(7 - 2i) - i(-3 + 2i)$ and give your answer in the form $a + bi$, $a, b \in \mathbb{R}$.

    (b) Let $z = 1 - 4i$:

    (i) plot z and $-z$ on an Argand diagram

    (ii) calculate $|z + 2|$

    (c) If $w = 7 - 2i$:

    (i) find $\overline{w}$

    (ii) find $w^2 + (\overline{w})^2$

    (iii) show that $\dfrac{53}{w} = \overline{w}$

2. **(a)** If $z = 3 + 5i$, find $\overline{z} + i$ and hence, $|\overline{z} + i|$.

    (b) (i) Show that $i^3 = -i$.

    (ii) Find the image v of $u = 2 + 7i$ under an anticlockwise rotation of $270°$ about the origin $0 = 0 + 0i$.

    (iii) Show that $|u| = |v|$.

    (c) Simplify $i(i^5 + i^6 + i^7)$ into its simplest form.

3. If $z = -3 + 5i$ and $0 = 0 + 0i$,

    (a) find:

    (i) $|z|$

    (ii) $|2z|$

    (iii) $|2iz|$

    (iv) $|-2iz|$

    (b) find the angle:

    (i) between the line joining 0 to z and the line joining 0 to $2z$,

    (ii) between the line joining 0 to z and the line joining 0 to $2iz$.

4. **(a)** If $z = 3 + 2i$ and $i = \sqrt{-1}$, express iz^2 in the form $a + bi$, $a, b \in \mathbb{R}$.

    (b) If $z = 1 + i$ and $w = 1 + 7i$, $i = \sqrt{-1}$, find:

    (i) $z + w$

    (ii) $z - w$

    (iii) $|z + w|$

    (iv) $|z - w|$

    (c) Let $u = 3 - i$:

    (i) simplify $\dfrac{20}{u}$

    (ii) if $c\left(\dfrac{20}{u}\right) - d(u + 5i) = 3 - 8i$, find $c, d \in \mathbb{R}$

5. **(a)** If $v = 1 - i$, find $\dfrac{6}{v}$ in the form $a + bi$, $a, b \in \mathbb{R}$, $i = \sqrt{-1}$.

    (b) Solve $x + 3 - 2iy = y - 6i$, $x, y \in \mathbb{R}$.

    (c) If $z = 3 - 4i$ and $w = 5 - 12i$, find $\overline{z}$ and $\overline{w}$. Show that:

    (i) $z\overline{w} + w\overline{z}$ is real

    (ii) $|z| + |w| > |z + w|$

6. **(a)** Let $z = -3 + 5i$, where $i^2 = -1$. Plot:

    (i) z on an Argand diagram

    (ii) $z + 3$ on an Argand diagram

    (b) Let $w = 1 + 2i$:

    (i) express $\dfrac{5}{w}$ in the form $a + bi$, $a, b \in \mathbb{R}$

    (ii) investigate if $|w + wi| = |wi| + |w|$

    (c) Let $u = 1 - 3i$:

    (i) find $\overline{u}$

    (ii) find $k, t \in \mathbb{R}$, if $ku + t\overline{u} = u^2$

7. **(a)** Simplify $3 + 2i(5 + 8i) - 11i$ in the form $a + bi$, $i = \sqrt{-1}$, $a, b \in \mathbb{R}$.

    (b) Let $z = (1 + 3i)(2 - i)$. Plot the following on an Argand diagram:

    (i) z

    (ii) $z - 7$

    (iii) $\overline{z}$

    (c) Find $z\overline{z}$.

    (d) Let $w = 4 - 3i$:

    (i) solve for $x, y \in \mathbb{R}$, if $x + w = 6yi$, $i = \sqrt{-1}$

    (ii) solve for $s, t \in \mathbb{R}$, if $|w|(s + ti) = \dfrac{10}{w}$, $i = \sqrt{-1}$

225

8. (a) If $z = i$, show that $z^{102} + 1 = 0$, where $i = \sqrt{-1}$.

(b) If $z_1 = 1 + i$ and $z_2 = 3 - 2i$, find:

   (i) $z_1 z_2$

   (ii) $\dfrac{z_1}{z_2}$

(c) (i) If $w = 1 + i$ is represented by the point P, plot P on an Argand diagram and find the slope of OP, where O is the origin.

   (ii) If $u = \dfrac{1 + i}{2i}$, simplify u in the form $a + bi$, $a, b \in \mathbb{R}$. If u is represented by the point Q, plot OQ on an Argand diagram, where O is the origin. Find the slope of OQ.

   (iii) Find $\dfrac{|w|}{|u|}$.

   (iv) Complete this sentence: The line joining $0 = 0 + 0i$ to w is rotated _____ through _____ degrees when w is divided by _____.

9. (a) Find the values of $k \in \mathbb{R}$, if $|k + 6i| = 10$, $i = \sqrt{-1}$.

(b) (i) If $z = \dfrac{2 + 4i}{1 - i}$, express z in the form $a + bi$, $a, b \in \mathbb{R}$, $i = \sqrt{-1}$.

   (ii) Find $|z|$ and show that $|z|^2 = z\bar{z}$.

(c) (i) If $u = -9 + 6i$, plot u on an Argand diagram. If u is represented by the point P, find the slope of OP, where O is the origin.

   (ii) Evaluate $w = \dfrac{ui}{3}$ and plot w on the same Argand diagram as u. If w is represented by the point Q, find the slope of OQ, where O is the origin.

   (iii) Show that $OP \perp OQ$ and $|w| = \dfrac{1}{3}|u|$.

10. (a) Plot $w = 1 + 1i$ on an Argand diagram on graph paper. Plot $2iw$, $3i^2 w$ and $i^4 w$ on the same Argand diagram, $i = \sqrt{-1}$.

(b) Let $z = 4 - i$, where $i = \sqrt{-1}$:

   (i) plot $z + 4i$ on an Argand diagram

   (ii) calculate $|z + 4i|$

   (iii) express $\dfrac{1}{z + 4i}$ in the form $a + bi$, $a, b \in \mathbb{R}$

(c) Evaluate $(3 + 4i)(5 - 12i)(3 - 4i)(5 + 12i)$.

SUMMARY

1. Imaginary numbers:
   (a) $i = \sqrt{-1} \Rightarrow i^2 = -1$

   (b) $i^n = \begin{cases} 1 \\ i \\ -1 \\ -i \end{cases}$ $n \in \{0, 1, 2, \dots\}$

   (c) $i^n = i^R$, where R is the remainder when n is divided by 4.

2. Complex number definition:
   $z = a + bi$, where a, $b \in \mathbb{R}$, $i = \sqrt{-1}$

   a is the real part (Re) of z.

   b is the imaginary part (Im) of z.

3. The Argand diagram:

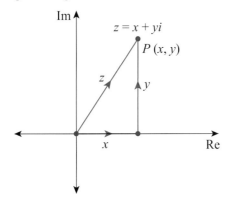

4. Addition of complex numbers:
   $(a + bi) + (c + di) = (a + c) + (b + d)i$

   Add the real parts and add the imaginary parts.

5. Multiplication of a complex number by a scalar $k \in \mathbb{R}$:
   $k(a + bi) = ka + kbi$

6. The modulus of a complex number:
   $z = a + bi \Rightarrow |z| = \sqrt{(a)^2 + (b)^2} = \sqrt{(\text{Re})^2 + (\text{Im})^2}$

7. The conjugate of a complex number:
   $z = a + bi \Rightarrow \bar{z} = a - bi$

   Change the sign between Re and Im.

8. Multiplication of complex numbers:
   $(a + bi)(c + di) = (ac - bd) + (bc + ad)i$

   Multiply out the brackets and put $i^2 = -1$.

   Conjugate multiplication:
   $(a + bi)\overline{a + bi} = (a + bi)(a - bi) = (a)^2 + (b)^2$

9. Powers of complex numbers:
   Multiply out the brackets.

10. Division of complex numbers:
    $$\frac{a + bi}{c + di} = \frac{(a + bi)(c - di)}{(c + di)(c - di)}$$

    Multiply above and below by the conjugate of the complex number on the bottom.

11. Equality of complex numbers:
    $a + bi = c + di \Rightarrow a = c$ and $b = d$

    Remember: $0 = 0 + 0i$

SECTION 7

Functions

Functions are the engines of
mathematics. They relate different
variables using mathematical
equations and are used extensively
in science, engineering, business
and finance.

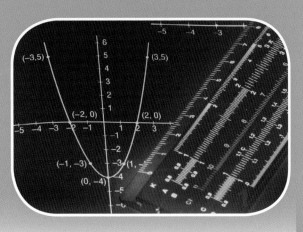

CHAPTER 15

Relations and Functions

Learning Outcomes

- To understand what a function is.
- To use function notation.
- To understand the composition of functions.
- To understand the concept of the limit of a function.

Introduction

Five students sit a test where the grades that can be awarded are A, B, C, D, E and F. The results of the test are as follows:

Anne (B)

John (C)

Mary (A)

Paul (B)

Sandra (D)

KEY TERM

The **domain** of a function is the set of values which is mapped by a function.

There is a relation between the student and the grade received. A set S of ordered pairs can be used to represent this relation.

S = {(Anne, B), (John, C), (Mary, A), (Paul, B), (Sandra, D)}

This relation can be mapped as shown:

KEY TERM

The **range** of a function is the set of images obtained by mapping the elements of the domain.

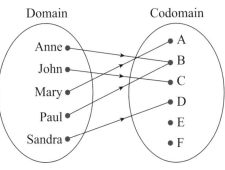

The five students form the elements of the **domain**. The grades that they can receive form the elements of the **codomain**. The **range** is the set of grades received by the students. The range is a subset of the codomain.

KEY TERM

A **function** $f(x)$ takes values of a variable x from a set called the domain and sends them to values y in a set called the codomain so that each value of x is sent to one and only one value of y.

Domain = {Anne, John, Mary, Paul, Sandra}

Codomain = {A, B, C, D, E, F}

Range = {A, B, C, D}

This relation is known as a **function** because each element of the domain maps onto one and only one value in the codomain. This makes sense as every student who sits the test receives only one grade. It would not make sense if a student got both a grade B and grade D in the test!

15.1 What is a function?

A function $f(x)$ is an operation that takes values of a variable x (inputs) and spits out values of a new variable y (outputs) so that for each value of x there is one and only one value of y. The diagram on the right shows a function, as each value of x is assigned only one value of y.

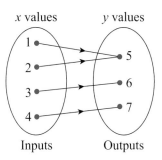

However, the next diagram does not represent a function. Each value of x does not have one and only one value of y.

You can see '1' maps onto two values: '4' and '5'.

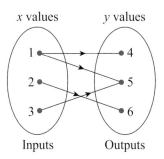

The domain of a function is the set of permissible values of the inputs. This is the set of values the function operates on (x values). The range of a function is the set of values of the outputs or images. This is the set of results that the function spits out (y values).

If any element of the domain is sent to more than one y value, then the operation is not a function. A function f can be visualised as a machine that takes a variable (or number), does an operation on it and spits out a new variable (number).

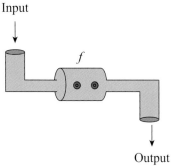

For example, in the function machine below, the outputs are obtained by 'squaring' the inputs.

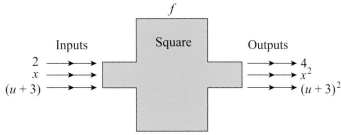

EXAMPLE 1

Find the domain and the range of the function which cubes each value of $x \in \{-2, -1, 0, 1, 2\}$.

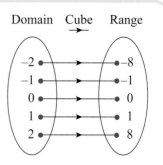

Solution

The set of values that are allowed (inputs) = domain = $\{-2, -1, 0, 1, 2\}$

The set of images = range = $\{-8, -1, 0, 1, 8\}$.

15.2 Function notation

You can be asked to find the image of a variable x in four ways.

1. Bracket notation

$f(x) = 3x - 2$ [Read as f of x]

This means the function f takes the variable x, multiplies it by 3 and subtracts 2.

EXAMPLE 2

If $f(x) = 2x^2 + 1$, find $f(-1), f(7), f(u), f(x + 1)$, $f(x) + 1, f(2p)$.

Solution

> **TIP**
>
> ↑ Put a bracket around the variable x on the right-hand side first.

$f(x) = 2(x)^2 + 1$

Then just replace the variable x on the right by whatever you see inside f to get the image $f(x)$.

$f(-1) = 2(-1)^2 + 1 = 3$

$f(7) = 2(7)^2 + 1 = 99$

$f(u) = 2(u)^2 + 1 = 2u^2 + 1$

$f(x + 1) = 2(x + 1)^2 + 1 = 2(x^2 + 2x + 1) + 1$
$\qquad\qquad = 2x^2 + 4x + 2 + 1 = 2x^2 + 4x + 3$

$f(x) + 1 = (2x^2 + 1) + 1 = 2x^2 + 2$

$f(2p) = 2(2p)^2 + 1 = 8p^2 + 1$

2. Double-dot notation

$$f: x \rightarrow \frac{x + 5}{2}, x \in \mathbb{N}$$

f sends x to $\dfrac{x + 5}{2}, x \in \mathbb{N}$

$$f: 1 \rightarrow \frac{1 + 5}{2} = 3$$

The best way to deal with double dots is to change them into bracket notation immediately.

$$f(x) = \frac{(x) + 5}{2}, x \in \mathbb{N}$$

EXAMPLE 3

Write down the domain and range of the following function:

$$f: x = \begin{cases} 1, & x \text{ even} \\ 2, & x \text{ odd} \end{cases}, x \in \mathbb{N}$$

Solution

$$f(x) = \begin{cases} 1, & x \text{ even} \\ 2, & x \text{ odd} \end{cases}, x \in \mathbb{N}.$$

The domain $\mathbb{N} = \{1, 2, 3, \ldots\}$

$f(1) = 2$ [1 is an odd number.]

$f(2) = 1$ [2 is an even number.]

$f(3) = 2$

$f(4) = 1$

The range is $\{1, 2\}$.

3. Co-ordinate notation

y is often used instead of $f(x)$ to facilitate the drawing of the graph of a function.

$$y = f(x) = x^2 - 2x + 5, x \in \mathbb{R}$$

So $y = f(x)$ is the y co-ordinate corresponding to any given x co-ordinate.

EXAMPLE 4

For the function $y = f(x) = x^2 - 2x + 5$, find $f(-1), f(0), f(1), f(2)$ and $f(3)$. Plot a graph of the function.

Solution

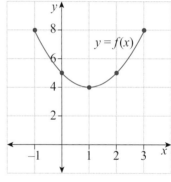

$y = f(x) = (x)^2 - 2(x) + 5$

$f(-1) = (-1)^2 - 2(-1) + 5 = 8$ $(-1, 8)$ is a point on the graph.

$f(0) = (0)^2 - 2(0) + 5 = 5$ $(0, 5)$ is a point on the graph.

$f(1) = (1)^2 - 2(1) + 5 = 4$ $(1, 4)$ is a point on the graph.

$f(2) = (2)^2 - 2(2) + 5 = 5$ $(2, 5)$ is a point on the graph.

$f(3) = (3)^2 - 2(3) + 5 = 8$ $(3, 8)$ is a point on the graph.

If you plot the points $(x, y) = (x, f(x))$, you generate the graph of the function $y = f(x)$.

4. Graphical approach

A function $y = f(x)$ can be plotted as a graph with the values in the domain on the x-axis and the values in the range (the images) on the y-axis.

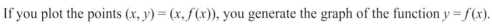

EXAMPLE 5

Using the graph shown of $y = f(x)$, find the values for $f(-1)$ and $f(0.5)$.

Solution

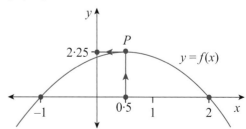

$f(-1) =$ the value of the y co-ordinate when the $x = -1$.

$f(-1) = 0$

$f(0.5) =$ the value of the y co-ordinate when x is 0.5.

This can be read off the graph by drawing the line $x = 0.5$ to intersect the graph at the point P and reading off the y co-ordinate of this point from the y-axis.

$f(0.5) = 2.25$

ACTIVITY 1

ACTION
Determining if curves
are functions

OBJECTIVE
*To use the vertical line
test to determine if
curves are functions*

Vertical line test for a function

FUNCTION TEST

$y = f(x)$ is a function if all lines drawn parallel to the y-axis through all points in the domain intersect the graph of $y = f(x)$ **once and only once**.

The function $y = f(x)$, $x \in \mathbb{R}$, shown below is a function because it passes the vertical line test. The vertical lines intersect the graph $y = f(x)$ once and only once.

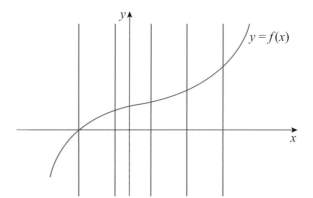

However, the graph of the function
$y = g(x)$, $x \geq 0$, $x \in \mathbb{R}$, as shown, is not a function.

The curve described by $y = g(x)$ is not a function as each value of $x > 0$ gives two values of y.

At $x = a$: $y = b_1$ and b_2

Vertical lines from points in the domain intersect the graph of $y = g(x)$ at one or two points.

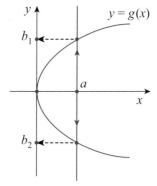

Using other letters

Although x, y and $f(x)$ are generally used when dealing with functions, other letters can be used.

EXAMPLE 6

If $h(s) = 3s^2 - 2$, find:

(a) $h(3)$

(b) $h(x)$

(c) $h(s + 2)$

Solution

$h(s) = 3(s)^2 - 2$

(a) $h(3) = 3(3)^2 - 2 = 25$

(b) $h(x) = 3(x)^2 - 2 = 3x^2 - 2$

(c) $h(s + 2) = 3(s + 2)^2 - 2$
$$= 3(s^2 + 4s + 4) - 2$$
$$= 3s^2 + 12s + 12 - 2$$
$$= 3s^2 + 12s + 10$$

EXERCISE 1

1. **(a)** Write down the relations described by the diagrams below as a set of ordered pairs S.

   (b) Write down the domain D and range I of each relation.

   (c) Say whether or not the relation is a function.

   (i)

   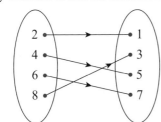

   (ii)

   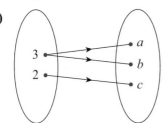

   (iii)

   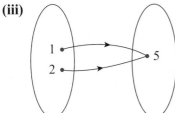

   (iv)

   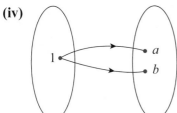

   (v)

   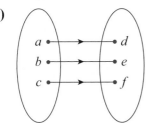

2. Draw the mapping of the relations below. State if the relations S are functions, giving a reason for your answer. Write down the domain D and range I of the relation in each case:

   (a) $S = \{(a, 1), (b, 1) (c, 1)\}$

   (b) $S = \{(1, a), (1, b), (2, a)\}$

   (c) $S = \{(1, 1), (2, 4), (3, 9), (4, 16)\}$

   (d) $S = \{(1, 1), (1, -1), (4, 2), (4, -2)\}$

   (e) $S = \{(1, 0), (2, 0), (3, 0), (4, 0)\}$

3. Evaluate the given functions at the given values of the variable:

   (a) $f : x \rightarrow 2x - 7$ at:

      (i) $x = 3$

      (ii) $x = -1$

      (iii) $x = \frac{1}{2}$

   (b) $f(x) = x^2$ at:

      (i) $x = 2$

      (ii) $x = -3$

      (iii) $x = 0 \cdot 5$

   (c) $f(x) = 3x^2 + 5x - 18$ at:

      (i) $x = 1$

      (ii) $x = -1$

      (iii) $x = 4$

   (d) $f(x) = -4x^2 + 2x - 8$ at:

      (i) $x = 1$

      (ii) $x = -1$

      (iii) $x = \frac{1}{2}$

   (e) $f(x) = x^3$ at:

      (i) $x = 2$

      (ii) $x = -2$

      (iii) $x = 2\frac{1}{2}$

4. Evaluate the given function at the given value of the variable:

   (a) $f(x) = 3x + 2$ at $x = 5$

   (b) $f(x) = \dfrac{x - 8}{3}$ at $x = -4$

   (c) $g(2)$ if $g(x) = \dfrac{3}{x^2 - 2}$

   (d) $h(1)$ if $h(s) = 2s^2 - 3s + 4$

   (e) $f(\sqrt{2})$ if $f(x) = 3x^2 - \dfrac{1}{x^2}$

   (f) $g(-2)$ if $g(p) = (p - 1)(p + 3)$

   (g) $h(0 \cdot 5)$ if $h(t) = t + \dfrac{1}{t}$

   (h) $g\left(\dfrac{2}{3}\right)$ if $g(x) = 9x^2 - 6x + 1$

5. **(a)** If $f: x \to 2x - 1$, $x \in \mathbb{R}$, find $f(3)$, $f(5)$, $f\left(-\dfrac{3}{2}\right)$.

(b) If $h: s \to \dfrac{1}{s}$, $s \in \mathbb{R}$, find $h(1)$, $h(2)$, $h\left(\dfrac{1}{2}\right)$, $h\left(-\dfrac{1}{3}\right)$.

(c) If $g(n) = \begin{cases} 2^n, & n \text{ odd}, n \in \mathbb{N} \\ \dfrac{1}{n}, & n \text{ even}, n \in \mathbb{N} \end{cases}$

find $g(3)$, $g(2)$, $g(8) + g(1)$.

(d) If $y = 2x^2 - 5x + 11$, find the value of y when (i) $x = -3$, (ii) $x = \dfrac{1}{2}$.

(e) Find $f(-3)$, $f(2)$ and $f(0)$ from the graph shown.

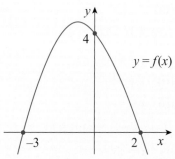

(f) If $g: s \to \dfrac{s^2}{3s + 5}$, $s \in \mathbb{R}$, find $g\left(\dfrac{1}{3}\right)$, $g(-2)$.

(g) If $h(x)$ is described by the graph below, find $h\left(\dfrac{1}{2}\right)$, $h(1)$, $h(2 \cdot 5)$, $h(3)$.

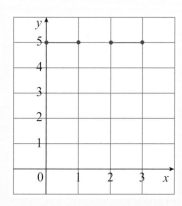

(h) If $f(x) = 3^{x-1}$, find $f(1)$ and $f(2)$.

6. **(a)** If $f(x) = 2x + 7$, find $f(2)$, $f(x + 1)$ and $f(3 - 2x)$.

(b) If $g(t) = 4 - t^2$, find $g(-2)$ and $g(2t)$.

(c) If $h(s) = \dfrac{3}{s + 1}$, find $h(2)$ and $h(x + 3)$.

(d) If $h(s) = s^2 + 4$, find $h(-3)$, $h(\sqrt{s})$ and $h(s - 1)$.

(e) If $f(x) = 3x^2 - 2x + 1$, find $f\left(\dfrac{1}{2}\right)$ and $f(1 - 2p)$.

(f) If $g(p) = 3 \times 2^p$, find $g(2)$ and $g(3x - 1)$.

7. **(a)** If $f(x) = 2x + 1$, find x when $f(x) = 3$.

(b) If $h(t) = \dfrac{4}{5}t - 3$, find t when $h(t) = 9$.

(c) If $g(x) = x^2 - 7x + 2$, find the values of x for which $g(x) = -4$.

(d) If $f(n) = 2^n$, find the value of n for which $f(n) = 16$.

(e) If $g(x) = 3 - kx$ and $g(-4) = 19$, find $k \in \mathbb{R}$.

(f) If $f(x) = \sqrt{x} + 1$, find x when $f(x) = 3$.

(g) If $f(x) = 2x^2 + 4x - 9$, find x when $f(x) = 7$.

(h) If $h(t) = t^3 + t^2 - 2t - 10$, find t when $h(t) = -10$.

8. **(a)** If $f(x) = 4x + k$, find k if $f(5) = 0$, $k \in \mathbb{R}$.

(b) If $f(x) = 5 + 4x$ and $g(x) = 3x + 2$, find t if $g(t) = f(t)$.

(c) If $f(x) = 3x + 5$, for what value of x is $f(x + 1) = f(2x - 3)$?

(d) If $f(x) = x^2 + 4x$ and $g(x) = 2x + 3$, for what values of x is $f(x) = g(x)$?

(e) If $f(x) = x^2 + ax + k$, find a and $k \in \mathbb{R}$, if $f(2) = 0$ and $f(-2) = f(3)$.

(f) If $f(x) = x^3 + ax^2 + bx - 8$, find a, $b \in \mathbb{R}$, if $f(-2) = 0$ and $f(1) = 0$.

15.3 Composition of functions (a function of a function)

WORKED EXAMPLE Explaining the idea of a function of a function

An €80 pair of shoes is on sale for 25% off the price. However, on the final day of the sale the shop offers an additional 10% off the sale price. What is the price of these shoes on the final day of the sale? You might think that all you have to do is to decrease €80 by 35% to get €52. This is incorrect. It is a two-stage process of two functions, g and f.

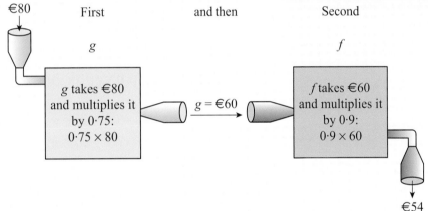

€80   First   and then   Second

g f

g takes €80 and multiplies it by 0·75: $0·75 \times 80$ → $g = €60$ → f takes €60 and multiplies it by 0·9: $0·9 \times 60$

€54

Therefore, the final-day price is €54. f is done **after** g.
Mathematically, 'f after g' acting on x is written as $(f_O\, g)(x)$ or $f(g(x))$.

'after'

In general:

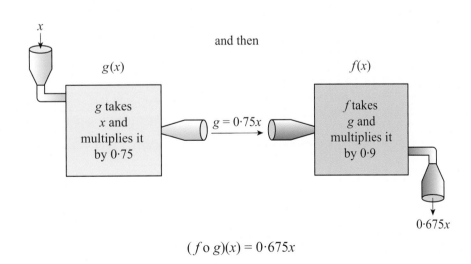

x and then

$g(x)$ $f(x)$

g takes x and multiplies it by 0·75   → $g = 0·75x$ → f takes g and multiplies it by 0·9

$0·675x$

$$(f \circ g)(x) = 0·675x$$

or

$$f(g(x)) = 0·675x$$

Method for finding the composition of functions

To find $(f \circ g)(x)$ or $f(g(x))$:

1. Evaluate $g(x)$ for the value of x and call the answer u.

2. Evaluate f at the value $g(x) = u$.

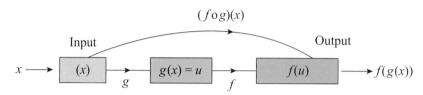

$(f \circ g)(x)$

Input   Output

$x \longrightarrow \boxed{(x)} \xrightarrow{g} \boxed{g(x) = u} \xrightarrow{f} \boxed{f(u)} \longrightarrow f(g(x))$

3. Write $f(u)$ in terms of x.

EXAMPLE 7

If $f(x) = 2x + 1$ and $g(x) = x^2 - 3$, find:

(a) $f(g(x))$ (c) $(f \circ f)(x)$

(b) $(g \circ f)(x)$ (d) $g(g(x))$

Solution

TIP

Always do the function on the extreme right first.

(a) $g(x) = (x^2 - 3) = u$

$f(g(x)) = f(u) = 2u + 1$

$f(g(x)) = 2(x^2 - 3) + 1 = 2x^2 - 5$

(b) $f(x) = (2x + 1) = u$

$g(f(x)) = g(u) = u^2 - 3 = (2x + 1)^2 - 3$

$g(f(x)) = 4x^2 + 4x - 2$

(c) $f(x) = (2x + 1) = u$

$f(f(x)) = f(u) = 2u + 1 = 2(2x + 1) + 1$

$= 4x + 3$

(d) $g(x) = (x^2 - 3) = u$

$g(g(x)) = g(u) = u^2 - 3 = (x^2 - 3)^2 - 3$

$= x^4 - 6x^2 + 6$

EXAMPLE 8

If $f(x) = 2^x$, $g(x) = x + 1$ and $h(x) = x^2$, find:

(a) $f(g(x))$ (c) $g(h(x))$

(b) $(h \circ f)(x)$ (d) $(f \circ (g \circ h))(x)$

Solution

(a) $g(x) = (x + 1) = u$

$f(g(x)) = f(u) = 2^u = 2^{x+1}$

(b) $f(x) = (2^x) = u$

$h(f(x)) = h(u) = u^2 = (2^x)^2 = 2^{2x}$

(c) $h(x) = x^2 = u$

$g(h(x)) = g(u) = (u) + 1 = x^2 + 1$

(d) $h(x) = x^2 = u$

$g(h(x)) = g(u) = u + 1 = v$

$f(g(h(x))) = f(v) = 2^v = 2^{(u)+1} = 2^{x^2+1}$

EXERCISE 2

1. If $f(x) = 2x - 1$ and $g(x) = 3x + 2$, find the following:

   (a) $f(g(2))$

   (b) $g(f(-1))$

   (c) $(f \circ f)\left(\dfrac{1}{2}\right)$

   (d) $(g \circ g)\left(-\dfrac{2}{3}\right)$

2. Find $f(g(x))$ and $g(f(x))$ for the following:

   (a) $f(x) = 1 - x^2$, $g(x) = 2x + 3$

   (b) $f(x) = 4x$, $g(x) = \sqrt{2x + 4}$

   (c) $f(x) = \dfrac{1}{x}$, $g(x) = 2x + 5$

   (d) $f(x) = 3^x$, $g(x) = \sqrt{x}$

   (e) $f(x) = \dfrac{x - 1}{3}$, $g(x) = x^2$

   (f) $f(x) = x^3$, $g(x) = \dfrac{1}{x}$

   (g) $f(x) = \sqrt{x}$, $g(x) = x^2$

3. **(a)** If $f(x) = 3x + 2$ and $g(x) = ax + 4$, find a if $(f \circ g)(-1) = 3$.

   (b) If $f(x) = x^2 - 2x$, find k, b, if $g(x) = kx + b$, $k > 0$, and if $(f \circ g)(x) = 4x^2 + 8x + 3$.

15.4 The concept of limits

WORKED EXAMPLE — Introducing limits

The speed limit on Irish motorways is 120 km/h. This means a driver can get closer and closer to 120 km/h but should never go above it. With this in mind, consider

the function $y = 1 - \left(\dfrac{1}{2}\right)^x$, and work out the value of

y as x gets bigger and bigger.

x	1	2	3	4	5	$\to$ Infinity (∞)
y	$\dfrac{1}{2}$	$\dfrac{3}{4}$	$\dfrac{7}{8}$	$\dfrac{15}{16}$	$\dfrac{31}{32}$	$\to 1$

Clearly, as x gets bigger and bigger, y gets closer and closer to 1.

y approaches 1 as x goes to infinity: $y \to 1$ as $x \to \infty$

This is stated as: the limit of y as x approaches ∞ is 1. Stated mathematically: $\lim\limits_{x \to \infty} y = 1$

Evaluating a limit

To evaluate the limit of a function $y = f(x)$, all you need do is take values of x closer and closer to the specified value of x and work out the corresponding values of y on the calculator until a pattern emerges.

EXAMPLE 9

Evaluate $\lim\limits_{x \to -2} (3x + 5)$.

Solution

x	$-1{\cdot}9$	$-1{\cdot}99$	$-1{\cdot}999$	$-1{\cdot}9999$	$\to -2$
$3x + 5$	$-0{\cdot}7$	$-0{\cdot}97$	$-0{\cdot}997$	$-0{\cdot}9997$	$\to -1$

$\therefore \lim\limits_{x \to -2} (3x + 5) = -1$

EXAMPLE 10

Evaluate $\lim\limits_{x \to 2}\left(\dfrac{x-2}{x^2-4}\right)$.

Solution

x	1·9	1·99	1·999	1·9999	$\to 2$
$\dfrac{x-2}{x^2-4}$	0·256	0·2506	0·25006	0·250006	$\to 0·25$

$\therefore \lim\limits_{x \to 2}\left(\dfrac{x-2}{x^2-4}\right) = 0·25 = \dfrac{1}{4}$

EXERCISE 3

Copy the following tables and evaluate each limit:

1. $\lim\limits_{x \to 7}(x + 2)$

x	6·9	6·99	6·999	6·9999	$\to 7$
$x + 2$					$\to ?$

2. $\lim\limits_{x \to 0}(3x - 2)$

x	0·1	0·01	0·001	0·0001	$\to 0$
$3x - 2$					$\to ?$

3. $\lim\limits_{x \to -3}(4x^2 + 1)$

x	−2·9	−2·99	−2·999	−2·9999	$\to -3$
$4x^2 + 1$					$\to ?$

4. $\lim\limits_{x \to \infty}\left(\dfrac{1}{x}\right)$

x	100	1000	10000	100000	$\to \infty$
$\dfrac{1}{x}$					$\to ?$

5. $\lim\limits_{x \to 3}\left(\dfrac{x^2-9}{x-3}\right)$

x	2·9	2·99	2·999	2·9999	$\to 3$
$\dfrac{x^2-9}{x-3}$					$\to ?$

6. $\lim\limits_{x \to \infty}\left(\dfrac{2x+1}{x+1}\right)$

x	10	100	1000	10000	$\to \infty$
$\dfrac{2x+1}{x+1}$					$\to ?$

7. $\lim\limits_{x \to \frac{1}{2}}(4x - 2)$

x	0·49	0·499	0·4999	0·49999	$\to 0·5$
$4x - 2$					$\to ?$

8. $\lim\limits_{x \to 0}\dfrac{2}{x+1}$

x	0·1	0·01	0·001	0·0001	$\to 0$
$\dfrac{2}{x+1}$					$\to ?$

9. $\lim\limits_{x \to 2}\dfrac{x+2}{x+4}$

x	1·9	1·99	1·999	1·9999	$\to 2$
$\dfrac{x+2}{x+4}$					$\to ?$

10. $\lim\limits_{x \to \infty}\left[3 - \left(\dfrac{1}{3}\right)^x\right]$

x	1	2	3	4	5	$\to \infty$
$3 - \left(\dfrac{1}{3}\right)^x$						$\to ?$

Linear Functions

CHAPTER 16

Learning Outcomes

- To recognise a linear function.
- To be able to use both forms of an equation of a straight line: $y = mx + c$ and $(y - y_1) = m(x - x_1)$.
- To be able to find the equation of a straight line from its graph.
- To be able to find the intercepts of a straight line on the axes.
- To recognise the equations of straight lines that are parallel to the axes.
- To plot intersecting linear functions finding where they intersect both graphically and algebraically.
- To use linear functions to solve real-life problems.

16.1 What is a linear function?

A linear function is a relation between two variables x and y that can be written in the form: $y = f(x) = mx^1 + c$ or $y = f(x) = ax + b$, where $m, c, a, b \in \mathbb{R}$ are constant real numbers. The equations are both forms of the equation of a straight line and so the graph of y against x is a straight-line graph.

m (or a) is called the coefficient of x.

c (or b) is called the constant term.

EXAMPLE 1

Write the following in the form $y = mx + c$ and hence write down the values of m and c:

(a) $3y = 7x - 11$ (b) $2x + y = 0$

(b) $2x + y = 0$

$y = -2x + 0$

$m = -2, c = 0$

Solution

(a) $3y = 7x - 11$

$y = \frac{7}{3}x - \frac{11}{3}$

$m = \frac{7}{3}, c = -\frac{11}{3}$

> m is the slope of the line and c is its intercept on the y-axis.

16.2 Plotting graphs of linear functions

ACTIVITY 2

ACTION
Plotting linear functions

OBJECTIVE
To plot a number of linear functions in a given domain

EXAMPLE 2

Plot the graph of $y = -2x + 1$, $-3 \le x \le 4$, $x \in \mathbb{R}$.

Solution

x	−3	−2	−1	0	1	2	3	4
y	7	5	3	1	−1	−3	−5	−7

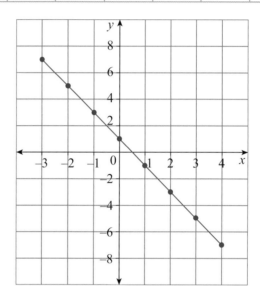

Because graphs of linear functions are straight lines, you need only **two points** to plot the straight line.

EXAMPLE 3

Plot the graph of $2y = 3x - 2$, $-2 \le x \le 4$, $x \in \mathbb{R}$.

Solution

$2y = 3x - 2$

$y = \frac{3}{2}x - 1$

Take the extreme values of $x = -2$ and $x = 4$ in the domain to evaluate the corresponding y values.

$x = -2$: $y = \frac{3}{2}(-2) - 1 = -4$

$x = 4$: $y = \frac{3}{2}(4) - 1 = 5$

x	−2	4
y	−4	5

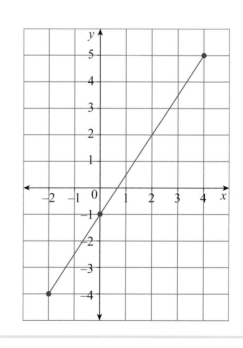

16.3 Finding the equation of a straight line from its graph

Method

1. Find the slope $m = \dfrac{y_2 - y_1}{x_2 - x_1}$ using two points (x_1, y_1), (x_2, y_2) on the straight line.

2. Find the equation from the equation of a line formula:

$$(y - y_1) = m(x - x_1)$$

$$or$$

$y = mx + c$, where c is the y-intercept.

EXAMPLE 4

Find the equation of the straight line l shown below.

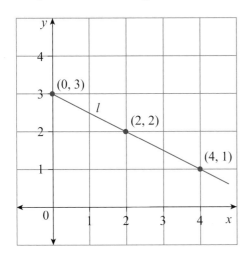

Solution

Find the slope using any two points on the line, say $(2, 2)$ and $(4, 1)$.

Slope $m = \dfrac{2 - 1}{2 - 4} = -\dfrac{1}{2}$

Using the slope and any point, find the equation of the line using $(y - y_1) = m(x - x_1)$.

Point: $(x_1, y_1) = (2, 2)$

$$y - 2 = -\frac{1}{2}(x - 2)$$

$$y - 2 = -\frac{x}{2} + 1$$

$$y = -\frac{1}{2}x + 3$$

$$or$$

Using the slope and the y-intercept, find the equation of the line using $y = mx + c$.

Slope $m = -\dfrac{1}{2}$

y-intercept: $c = 3$

$$y = -\frac{1}{2}x + 3$$

This is the equation of the line l. All points on this line satisfy this equation.

16.4 Properties of linear functions

1. Lines parallel to the axes

(a) Parallel to the x-axis

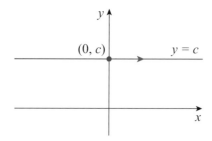

- A line parallel to the x-axis has a slope of 0.

  So $m = 0$ in $y = mx + c$ means

  $y = c$ (constant) for all values of x.

- Every point on this line has the same y co-ordinate.

- $y = c$ is the equation of a line parallel to the x-axis through $(0, c)$.

- Therefore, the equation of the x-axis is $y = 0$ as it passes through $(0, 0)$.

(b) Parallel to the y-axis

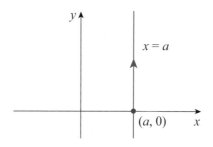

- A line parallel to the y-axis has a slope of infinity (∞).

- Every point on this line has the same x co-ordinate.

- $x = a$ is the equation of a line parallel to the y-axis through $(a, 0)$.

- Therefore, the equation of the y-axis is $x = 0$ as it passes through $(0, 0)$.

EXAMPLE 5

Write down the equations of the lines h, k, l, x, y.

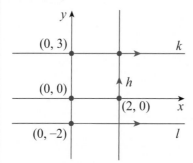

Solution

$h : x = 2$

$k : y = 3$

$l : y = -2$

$x : y = 0$

$y : x = 0$

2. Crossing the axes

(a) The x-axis has equation $y = 0$

Putting $y = 0$ in $y = mx + c$:

$0 = mx + c$

$x = -\dfrac{c}{m}, \; m \neq 0$

If $m \neq 0$, every linear function crosses the x-axis at exactly one point, $P\left(-\dfrac{c}{m}, 0\right)$.

(b) The y-axis has equation $x = 0$

Putting $x = 0$ in $y = mx + c$:

$y = c$

Therefore, every linear function crosses the y-axis at exactly one point $Q(0, c)$.

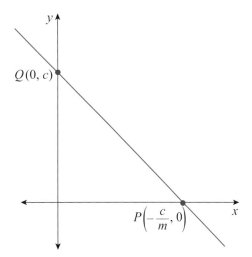

EXAMPLE 6

Find where $y = 3x - 4$ crosses the axes.

Solution

x-axis: $y = 0$

$3x - 4 = 0$

$x = \dfrac{4}{3}$

The line crosses the x-axis at $\left(\dfrac{4}{3}, 0\right)$.

y-axis: $x = 0$

$y = -4$

The line crosses the y-axis at $(0, -4)$.

16.5 Intersecting linear functions

ACTIVITY 3

ACTION
Intersecting linear functions

OBJECTIVE
To plot two linear functions and find their point of intersection both graphically and geometrically

EXAMPLE 7

Using the same grid, graph the linear functions $f(x) = x + 1$ and $g(x) = 2x - 3$ in the domain $-1 \leq x \leq 5, x \in \mathbb{R}$.

Use the graph to solve the $f(x) = g(x)$. Verify your answer algebraically.

Solution

As the functions are linear, you need just get two points on each line. Choose the extreme x values of the domain.

x	−1	5
$f(x)$	0	6
$g(x)$	−5	7

Graph:

$f(x) = g(x)$ at $x = 4$

Algebra:

$$f(x) = g(x)$$
$$x + 1 = 2x - 3$$
$$1 + 3 = 2x - x$$
$$4 = x$$

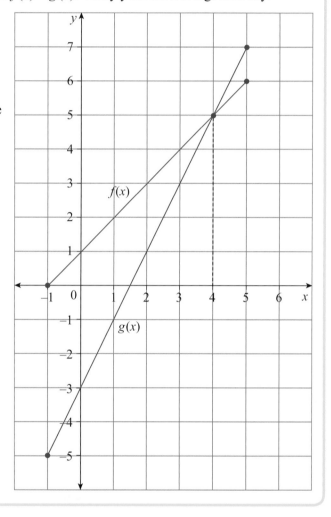

EXERCISE 4

1. Draw the following linear functions on graph paper in the given domain for $x \in \mathbb{R}$:

   Note: This is also Activity 2. The activity supplies you with the appropriate grids.

   (a) $f(x) = x + 1, -1 \leq x \leq 5$

   (b) $f(x) = x - 3, -2 \leq x \leq 6$

   (c) $f(x) = 2x + 1, -2 \leq x \leq 4$

   (d) $f(x) = 4x - 3, -1 \leq x \leq 3$

   (e) $f(x) = \frac{1}{2}x + 3, -2 \leq x \leq 5$

2. Write the following in the form $y = mx + c$:

(a) $3(x + y) = 7$

(b) $4x - 3y = 9$

(c) $y - 0·2 = 7(x - 0·1)$

(d) $y = 5$

(e) $x + y = 8$

3. Say which functions are linear. If they are linear, write them in the form $y = mx + c$, using the given variable as x:

(a) $f(x) = \dfrac{-1 - 2x}{3}$

(b) $h(x) = \dfrac{3}{5}x + 4$

(c) $C(r) = 2\pi r$

(d) $f(x) = 3x^2 - 7$

(e) $F(p) = 13 - \left(\dfrac{2^{-3}}{8}\right)p$

4. Write in the form $y = mx + c$ equations for the linear functions with the following properties:

(a) Slope 3, y-intercept -2

(b) Slope -2, x-intercept 5

(c) Slope $-\dfrac{2}{5}$, through the point $(2, 3)$

(d) $f(1) = 2$, $f(-2) = 3$, if $y = f(x)$

(e) Passing through $(1, 4)$ and $(2, -3)$

5. Write down a formula in the form $y = mx + c$ for the linear functions described by the tables and graphs below, using the variables, respectively, in the question for x and y:

(a)

Time t in years	0	1	2
Value V of computer in €	500	320	140

(b)

Temperature T (°C)	0	5	20
Temperature θ (°F)	32	41	68

(c)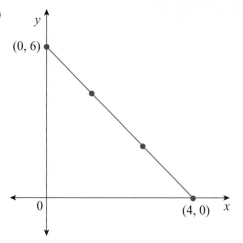

(d)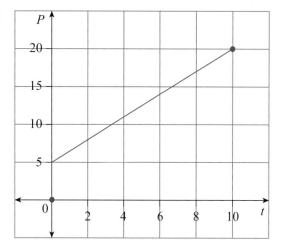

6. Using the same grid, graph the following linear functions in the given domain. Use the graph to solve $f(x) = g(x)$. Verify your answer algebraically.

> **Note:** This is also Activity 3. The activity supplies you with the appropriate grids.

(a) $f(x) = x + 1$ and $g(x) = 3x - 2$, $-2 \le x \le 2$, $x \in \mathbb{R}$

(b) $f(x) = 3x + 1$ and $g(x) = 3 - x$, $-2 \le x \le 4$, $x \in \mathbb{R}$

(c) $f(x) = 3$ and $g(x) = \dfrac{1}{2}x + 2$, $-2 \le x \le 3$, $x \in \mathbb{R}$

(d) $f(x) = 4x + 1$ and $g(x) = 3x - 2$, $-4 \le x \le 1$, $x \in \mathbb{R}$

16.6 Contexts and applications

EXAMPLE 8

The price P in euro of a stock t months after its launch on the stock market is described by the linear function on the graph shown. The launch price is €1·50.

Find a formula relating P to t and use it to find P when $t = 3·5$ months.

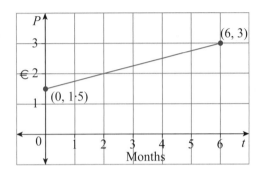

The equation: $P = \frac{1}{4}t + 1·5$ $[y = mx + c]$

When **$t = 3·5$**: $P = \frac{3·5}{4} + 1·5 = €2·375$

Solution

Two points on the line: $(0, 1·5)$, $(6, 3)$

Slope $m = \dfrac{3 - 1·5}{6 - 0} = \dfrac{1·5}{6} = \dfrac{1}{4}$

EXAMPLE 9

As a diver descends in the ocean, the pressure P in Pascals (Pa) increases linearly with depth h in metres (m) from its pressure at the surface. If the pressure at the surface is 1×10^5 Pa and is $1·98 \times 10^5$ Pa at a depth of 10 m, find the equation of the straight line connecting P and h.

(a) Find the pressure at a depth of 20 m.

(b) The safe depth to which a diver can descend is the depth at which the pressure is $3·75 \times 10^5$ Pa. What is this depth, correct to two decimal places?

Solution

Surface $P = 1 \times 10^5$ Pa

$h = 10$ m

$P = 1·98 \times 10^5$ Pa

A graph of P ($\times 10^5$ Pa) against h(m) is shown.

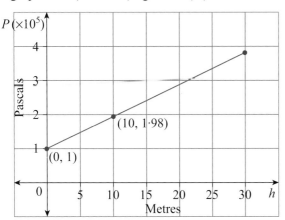

The slope m of the straight line is

$$m = \frac{(1 \cdot 98 - 1) \times 10^5}{10 - 0} = 0 \cdot 98 \times 10^4 = 9800$$

The y-intercept is $c = 1 \times 10^5$.

The equation of the straight line is

$$P = 9800h + 1 \times 10^5 \quad [y = mx + c]$$

(a) The pressure at a depth of 20 m is:
$$P = 9800 \times 20 + 1 \times 10^5 = 2 \cdot 96 \times 10^5 \text{ Pa}$$

(b) The safe depth to which a diver can descend is the depth at which the pressure is $3 \cdot 75 \times 10^5$ Pa. The depth at which this occurs is given by:
$$3 \cdot 75 \times 10^5 = 9800h + 1 \times 10^5$$
$$2 \cdot 75 \times 10^5 = 9800 \, h$$
$$h = \frac{2 \cdot 75 \times 10^5}{9800} = 28 \cdot 06 \text{ m}$$

The point of intersection of two linear functions can be found graphically or by solving their equations simultaneously.

EXAMPLE 10

Two companies, Awed and Bliss, produce wedding invitations. The cost equations for their invitations are set out below:

Awed: $C = 60 + 0 \cdot 8x$

Bliss: $C = 1 \cdot 2x$

x is the number of invitations and C is the cost in euro. Plot graphs of these two functions on the same diagram. Use your graphs to find the number of invitations for which the price charged by the two companies is the same, and what that price is. Verify your answers algebraically.

Solution

To plot the graphs of these, you need two points on each graph.

Awed: $x = 0 \Rightarrow C = 60$: $(0, 60)$

$x = 150 \Rightarrow C = 180$: $(150, 180)$

Bliss: $x = 0 \Rightarrow C = 0$: $(0, 0)$

$x = 200 \Rightarrow C = 240$: $(200, 240)$

The graphs are plotted below:

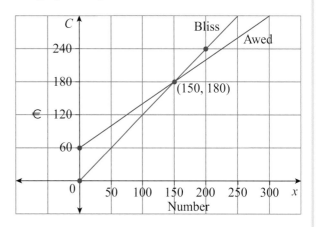

For $x > 150$, Awed is cheaper than Bliss.

They are equally expensive for $x = 150$.

You can verify this by solving the equations simultaneously:

$$60 + 0 \cdot 8x = 1 \cdot 2x$$
$$60 = 0 \cdot 4x$$
$$x = 150 \text{ and } C = 1 \cdot 2 \times 150 = 180$$

EXERCISE 5

1. The value V in euro of a car t years after its purchase is shown by the linear graph below:

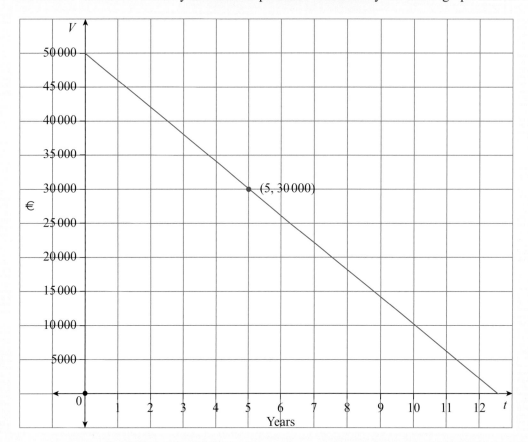

If it cost €50 000 new and its value after 5 years was €30 000, find:

   (a) the relationship between V and t,

   (b) when its value was €20 000,

   (c) when its value was €0.

2. A cable car starts its journey at 6000 m above the ground. It descends at 300 m per minute. Find an expression for its distance s in metres above the ground after t minutes. Use this expression to find how long it takes to reach the ground.

3. For the points (x, y) given in the table below, investigate if y is a linear function of x.

x	–8	–4	0	4	8
y	0	0·5	1	1·5	2

   If it is linear, find a formula for this relationship.

4. The populations of two countries A and B in millions from 1950 to 2000 are shown in the table below.

	1950	1960	1970	1980	1990	2000
A	8·2	9·9	12·8	16·2	18·3	24·9
B	7·6	10·0	12·4	14·8	17·2	19·6

One country experienced linear growth from 1950 to 2000.

(a) Which country experienced linear growth in its population?

(b) For the country which experienced linear growth:

  (i) write down a formula relating its population P to the time t years after 1950,

  (ii) find the population of this country in 2020.

(c) For the non-linear growth country, find the average rate of change of its population from 1950 to 2000.

5. In a golf club a fixed fee is paid for membership and then each round of golf is charged on top of the fixed fee. Twenty rounds of golf cost €850 and 32 rounds of golf cost €1210.

(a) Find the membership fee and the cost per round.

(b) Write down a formula for the cost C in euro of playing golf in terms of the number n of rounds played.

(c) Find the cost for 50 rounds.

(d) How many rounds of golf can a member get for €1000?

6. The number N of cases of a flu epidemic in a country t days after the discovery of its outbreak was given by $N = 80 + 30t$.

(a) Plot a graph of N against t for $0 \leq t \leq 4$.

(b) Find the number of cases 2 weeks after the outbreak if no action was taken.

(c) If after 4 days a massive inoculation programme was initiated so that the number n of cases decreased at a steady rate of five per day, find a formula for n, in terms of t, for $t > 4$. How long, after the start of the inoculation programme, does it take for the epidemic to be eradicated?

Quadratic Functions

Learning Outcomes

- To recognise a quadratic function: $y = f(x) = ax^2 + bx + c$.
- To be able to plot a graph of a quadratic function.
- To be able to find properties of quadratic functions (crossing axes, vertices, axis of symmetry).
- To work with intersecting quadratic functions.
- To use quadratic functions to solve real-life problems.

17.1 What is a quadratic function?

A quadratic function is a relationship between two variables x and y that can be written in the form $y = f(x) = ax^2 + bx + c$, where a, b, c are constant real numbers, $a \neq 0$.

a is called the coefficient of x^2.

b is called the coefficient of x.

c is called the constant term.

They have many applications in areas such as architecture (arches), economics, engineering, mechanics and physics.

▶ The trajectory (path) of a javelin is described by a quadratic function, as shown:

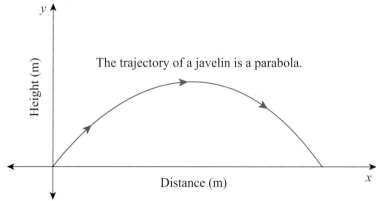

The trajectory of a javelin is a parabola.

Height (m)

Distance (m)

EXAMPLE 1

(a) If $y = 2x^2 - 5x + 7$, find y when $x = -2$.

(b) If $f(x) = -3x^2 + 7x - 1$, find $f\left(\frac{1}{2}\right)$.

Solution

(a) $x = -2$: $y = 2(-2)^2 - 5(-2) + 7 = 25$

(b) $f\left(\frac{1}{2}\right) = -3\left(\frac{1}{2}\right)^2 + 7\left(\frac{1}{2}\right) - 1 = \frac{7}{4}$

17.2 Plotting graphs of quadratic functions

ACTIVITY 4

ACTION
Plotting quadratic graphs

OBJECTIVE
To plot quadratic functions given their domain

Method

To plot a graph of a quadratic function:

1. Isolate y on one side of the equation.

2. Substitute the values of x in the domain to find the corresponding values of y.

3. Plot the y (dependent variable) values on the vertical axis against the x (independent variable) values on the horizontal axis.

EXAMPLE 2

Plot $y = 2x^2 - 3x - 12$ in the domain $-3 \le x \le 3$, $x \in \mathbb{R}$.

Solution

$y = 2x^2 - 3x - 12$

$x = -3$: $y = 2(-3)^2 - 3(-3) - 12 = 15$

$x = -2$: $y = 2(-2)^2 - 3(-2) - 12 = 2$

$x = -1$: $y = 2(-1)^2 - 3(-1) - 12 = -7$

$x = 0$: $y = 2(0)^2 - 3(0) - 12 = -12$

$x = 1$: $y = 2(1)^2 - 3(1) - 12 = -13$

$x = 2$: $y = 2(2)^2 - 3(2) - 12 = -10$

$x = 3$: $y = 2(3)^2 - 3(3) - 12 = -3$

x	-3	-2	-1	0	1	2	3
y	15	2	-7	-12	-13	-10	-3

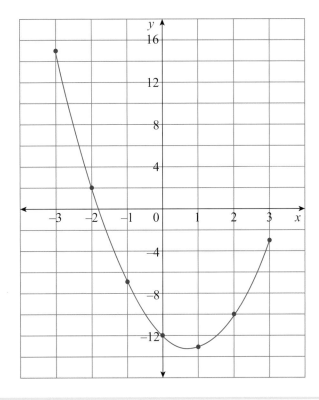

EXAMPLE 3

A rocket is launched into the air. Its height h above the ground is given by $h = 8x - 2x^2$, where h is its height in hundreds of metres and x is its distance horizontally from the launch site in hundreds of metres. Plot h against x in the domain $0 \leq x \leq 4, x \in \mathbb{R}$.

Solution

$h = 8(x) - 2(x)^2$

x	0	1	2	3	4
h	0	6	8	6	0

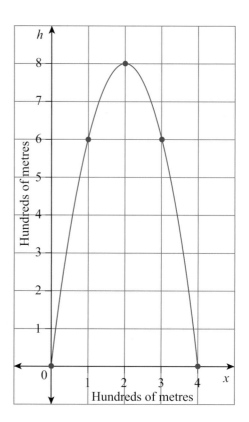

General shape of quadratic functions

The general shape of all quadratic functions, $y = ax^2 + bx + c$, is either:

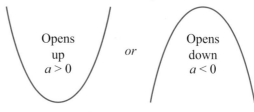

Opens up $a > 0$ *or*   Opens down $a < 0$

If $a > 0$, the curve opens up $\cup$ like a cup.

▸ $y = 4x^2 - x$ has a $\cup$ shape.

If $a < 0$, the curve opens down $\cap$ like a cap.

▸ $y = -x^2 + 5x - 57$ has a $\cap$ shape.

You will see why quadratic functions have this shape in Section 8: Differentiation.

In general, if you want to find where a quadratic function intersects a straight line, solve the equation of the quadratic function $y = f(x) = ax^2 + bx + c$ with the equation of the straight line l.

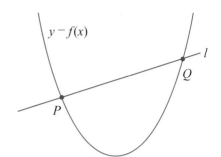

1. Finding where the quadratic function crosses the y-axis

The equation of a quadratic function is $y = ax^2 + bx + c$.

The equation of the y-axis is $x = 0$.

Solving the quadratic function $y = ax^2 + bx + c$ and $x = 0$ gives:

$$y = 0 + 0 + c$$

$$y = c$$

The graph of the quadratic function crosses the y-axis at $(0, c)$.

EXAMPLE 4

Find where the following quadratic functions cross the y-axis:

(a) $y = 2x^2 + 5x - 7$

(b) $y = 2x + 8 - x^2$

Solution

(a) $y = 2x^2 + 5x - 7$

$x = 0$: $y = 2(0)^2 + 5(0) - 7 = -7$

It crosses the y-axis at $(0, -7)$.

(b) $y = 2x + 8 - x^2$

$x = 0$: $y = 2(0) + 8 - (0)^2 = 8$

It crosses the x-axis at $(0, 8)$.

2. Finding where the quadratic function crosses the x-axis

The equation of the x-axis is $y = 0$.

The equation of the quadratic function is $y = ax^2 + bx + c$.

Solving simultaneously: $ax^2 + bx + c = 0$

The point(s) where the graph of the quadratic function crosses the x-axis are the solutions of the quadratic equation $ax^2 + bx + c = 0$.

These solutions are given by:

$$x = \frac{-b \pm \sqrt{b^2 - 4ac}}{2a}$$

Three situations arise:

(a) $b^2 - 4ac > 0 \Rightarrow b^2 > 4ac$

This means there are **two different roots**. As a result, the graph of $y = ax^2 + bx + c$ crosses the x-axis at two different points, $P(p, 0)$ and $Q(q, 0)$.

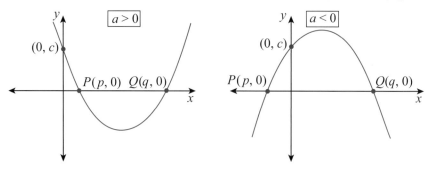

EXAMPLE 5

Find where the following curves cross the axes:

(a) $y = 2x^2 - x - 2$ **(b)** $y = 6x^2 - x - 12$

Solution

(a) $y = 2x^2 - x - 2$

$b^2 - 4ac = 1 + 16 = 17 > 0$

$\therefore b^2 > 4ac$ [Two different roots]

Crosses y-axis: $x = 0$

$y = -2$

It crosses the y-axis at $(0, -2)$.

Crosses x-axis: $y = 0$

$2x^2 - x - 2 = 0$

$x = \dfrac{1 \pm \sqrt{17}}{4} = -0{\cdot}78,\ 1{\cdot}28$

It crosses the x-axis at $P(-0{\cdot}78, 0)$ and $Q(1{\cdot}28, 0)$.

(b) $y = 6x^2 - x - 12$

$b^2 - 4ac = 1 + 288 = 289 > 0$

$\therefore b^2 > 4ac$ [Two different roots]

As $289 = 17^2$, the quadratic factorises.

Crosses y-axis: $x = 0$

$y = -12$

It crosses the y-axis at $(0, -12)$.

Crosses x-axis: $6x^2 - x - 12 = 0$

$(3x + 4)(2x - 3) = 0$

$x = -\dfrac{4}{3}, \dfrac{3}{2}$

It crosses the x-axis at $P\left(-\dfrac{4}{3}, 0\right)$ and $Q\left(\dfrac{3}{2}, 0\right)$.

(b) $b^2 - 4ac = 0 \Rightarrow b^2 = 4ac$

This means there are **two equal roots**. As a result, the graph of $y = ax^2 + bx + c$ crosses the x-axis at only one point $P(p, 0)$.

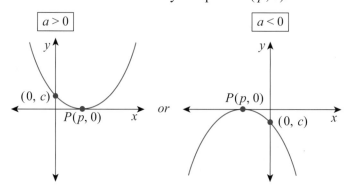

ACTIVITY 5

ACTION
Sketching graphs given quadratic functions

OBJECTIVE
To draw a quadratic graph by looking at the equation

EXAMPLE 6

Find the points where the following quadratic functions cross the axes:

(a) $y = 3x^2 + 12x + 12$

(b) $y = 3(2x - 1)^2$

Solution

(a) $y = 3x^2 + 12x + 12$

$b^2 - 4ac = 144 - 144 = 0$

$b^2 = 4ac$ [Two equal roots]

Crosses y-axis: $x = 0$

$y = 12$

It crosses the y-axis at $(0, 12)$.

Crosses x-axis: $y = 0$

$3x^2 + 12x + 12 = 0$

$x^2 + 4x + 4 = 0$

$(x + 2)(x + 2) = 0$

$x = -2, -2$

It crosses the x-axis at $P(-2, 0)$.

(b) $y = 3(2x - 1)^2$

As this is already factorised, do not multiply it out.

Crosses y-axis: $x = 0$

$y = 3(0 - 1)^2 = 3$

It crosses the y-axis at $(0, 3)$.

Crosses x-axis: $y = 0$

$3(2x - 1)(2x - 1) = 0$

$x = \frac{1}{2}, \frac{1}{2}$

It crosses the x-axis at $P\left(\frac{1}{2}, 0\right)$.

EXAMPLE 7

An underground geyser at $x = 0$ projects a jet of hot water along a path described by the equation $y = (8 - x)(x - 2)$, where x and y are in tens of metres and $y = 0$ is the horizontal ground.

(a) Find the depth of the geyser below the ground.

(b) Find the points where the waterjet hits the ground.

(c) Plot its trajectory for $0 \leq x \leq 8$.

Solution

$y = (8 - x)(x - 2)$

(a) $x = 0: y = (8)(-2) = -16$

It crosses the y-axis at $(0, -16)$. -16 is the y-intercept.

The launch point is 160 m below the ground.

(b) $y = 0: (8 - x)(x - 2) = 0$

$x = 8, 2$

$(8, 0)$ and $(2, 0)$ means the x-intercepts at 20 m and 80 m from $x = 0$.

(c)

x	0	2	4	6	8
y	-16	0	8	8	0

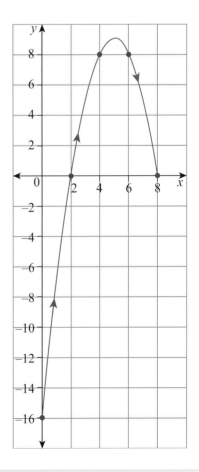

(c) $b^2 - 4ac < 0 \Rightarrow b^2 < 4ac$

This means there are **no real roots**. (They are complex.) The graph of $y = ax^2 + bx + c$ does **not** cross the x-axis at any point.

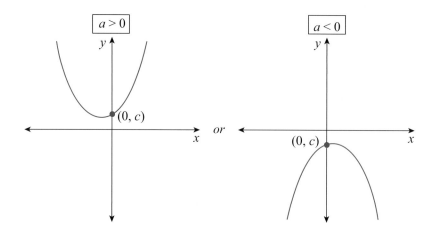

▶ $y = 2x^2 - 4x + 5$

$b^2 - 4ac = 16 - 40 = -24 < 0$

Beacause $b^2 < 4ac$, the graph of the function does not cross the x-axis.

It crosses the y-axis at $(0, 5)$.

3. Finding the maximum and minimum points (vertices or turning points) of a quadratic function

Given the quadratic function $y = ax^2 + bx + c$, the maximum or minimum values of the function occur at $x = -\dfrac{b}{2a}$. You will see why this is the case in Section 8: Differentiation.

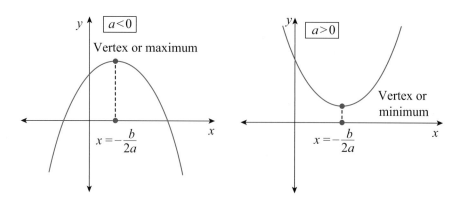

The vertex is the most important point on a quadratic graph.

EXAMPLE 8

Find the co-ordinates of the point V which gives $y = 3x^2 - 12x + 5$ its minimum value.

Solution

$y = 3x^2 - 12x + 5$

$a = 3, b = -12, c = 5$

Vertex V

As $a > 0$, the quadratic graph is cup-shaped and so the vertex is the point at which the minimum value of the function occurs. The minimum value of the function is the value of the y co-ordinate at this point.

At the vertex: $x = -\dfrac{b}{2a} = \dfrac{-(-12)}{6} = 2$

$x = 2$: $y = 3(2)^2 - 12(2) + 5 = -7$

Therefore, the co-ordinates of the vertex are $V(2, -7)$.

EXAMPLE 9

Find the co-ordinates of the point V which gives $y = -2x^2 - x + 7$ its maximum value.

Solution

Vertex V

$y = -2x^2 - x + 7$

$a = -2, b = -1, c = 7$

As $a < 0$, the quadratic graph is cap-shaped and so the vertex is the point at which the maximum value of the function occurs. The maximum value of the function is the value of the y co-ordinate at this point.

At the vertex: $x = -\dfrac{b}{2a} = \dfrac{-(-1)}{2(-2)} = -\dfrac{1}{4}$

$x = -\dfrac{1}{4}$: $y = -2\left(-\dfrac{1}{4}\right)^2 - \left(-\dfrac{1}{4}\right) + 7 = \dfrac{57}{8}$

Therefore, the co-ordinates of the vertex are $V\left(-\dfrac{1}{4}, \dfrac{57}{8}\right)$.

The maximum value of the function is $\dfrac{57}{8}$.

EXAMPLE 10

A ball is projected vertically upwards from the top of a 13 m high cliff. The ball's height h, in metres above the ground, t seconds after it is launched is given by: $h = -10t^2 + 20t + 13$

(a) Find its maximum height above the ground.

(b) Find when it hits the ground, correct to two decimal places.

Solution

$h = -10t^2 + 20t + 13$

$a = -10, b = 20, c = 13$

V

As $a = -10 < 0$, the quadratic graph is cap-shaped.

(a) The maximum height occurs when:

$t = -\dfrac{b}{2a} = \dfrac{-20}{2(-10)} = 1$

$t = 1$: $h = (-10)(1)^2 + 20(1) + 13 = 23$ m

(b) $h = 0$: $-10t^2 + 20t + 13 = 0$

$10t^2 - 20t - 13 = 0$

$t = \dfrac{20 \pm \sqrt{(-20)^2 - 4 \times 10 \times (-13)}}{20}$

$= 2 \cdot 52$ or $-0 \cdot 52$ [Reject the negative value.]

$\therefore t = 2 \cdot 52$ s

It hits the ground after $2 \cdot 52$ s.

4. Finding the axis of symmetry

The axis of symmetry of a quadratic function $y = ax^2 + bx + c$ is the line through the vertex V parallel to the y-axis.

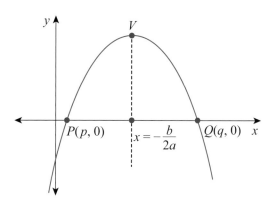

The equation of the axis of symmetry is $x = -\dfrac{b}{2a}$.

This means the roots of $ax^2 + bx + c = 0$ are symmetrical about $x = -\dfrac{b}{2a}$.

$$P(p, 0) \qquad V\left(-\dfrac{b}{2a}, 0\right) \qquad Q(q, 0)$$

$\left(-\dfrac{b}{2a}, 0\right)$ is the midpoint of $P(p, 0)$ and $Q(q, 0)$.

EXAMPLE 11

For the quadratic function $y = x^2 - 2x - 8$, find the point V which gives the function its minimum value. Find the roots of $x^2 - 2x - 8 = 0$ and show they are symmetrical about the x co-ordinate of V.

Solution

$y = x^2 - 2x - 8$

$a = 1, b = -2, c = -8$

Vertex V: $x = \dfrac{-b}{2a} = \dfrac{2}{2} = 1$

$x = 1$: $y = (1)^2 - 2(1) - 8 = -9$

Therefore, the x co-ordinate of the vertex $V(1, -9)$ is 1.

Roots: $x^2 - 2x - 8 = 0$

$(x + 2)(x - 4) = 0$

$x = -2, 4$

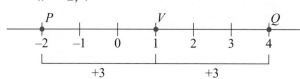

1 is the midpoint of the roots.

EXAMPLE 12

Find where the function with equation $y = -2x^2 + 5x + 3$, $x \in \mathbb{R}$, crosses the axes. Find the co-ordinates of its vertex and the equation of its axis of symmetry.

Solution

$y = -2x^2 + 5x + 3$, $x \in \mathbb{R}$

$a = -2$, $b = 5$, $c = 3$

Crosses y-axis: $x = 0$

$y = 3$

It crosses the y-axis at $(0, 3)$.

Crosses x-axis: $y = 0$

$2x^2 - 5x - 3 = 0$

$(2x + 1)(x - 3) = 0$

$x = -\dfrac{1}{2}, 3$

It crosses the x-axis at $\left(-\dfrac{1}{2}, 0\right)$ and $(3, 0)$.

Vertex V: $x = \dfrac{3 + \left(-\dfrac{1}{2}\right)}{2} = \dfrac{5}{4}$ [Using the midpoint formula]

or

$x = -\dfrac{b}{2a} = -\dfrac{5}{2(-2)} = \dfrac{5}{4}$

$\mathbf{x = \dfrac{5}{4}}$: $y = -2\left(\dfrac{5}{4}\right)^2 + 5\left(\dfrac{5}{4}\right) + 3 = \dfrac{49}{8}$

$\therefore V\left(\dfrac{5}{4}, \dfrac{49}{8}\right)$

Equation of the axis of symmetry:

$$x = \dfrac{5}{4}$$

or $4x - 5 = 0$

EXERCISE 6

1. Draw the following quadratic functions on graph paper in the given domain for $x \in \mathbb{R}$:

   > **Note:** This is also Activity 4. The activity supplies you with the appropriate grids.

   (a) $f(x) = 2x^2 - 5x + 1$, $-1 \leq x \leq 3$

   (b) $f(x) = -2x^2 + 3x + 4$, $-2.5 \leq x \leq 3$

   (c) $f(x) = x^2 - 2x + 1$, $-1 \leq x \leq 3$

   (d) $f(x) = -4x^2 + 4x - 1$, $-1 \leq x \leq 1$

   (e) $f(x) = 2x^2 + 3x + 2$, $-2.5 \leq x \leq 1$

   (f) $f(x) = -x^2 + 2x - 3$, $-1 \leq x \leq 3$

2. Find the points at which the following quadratic functions cross the axes. Give all answers as rational or irrational numbers. If the curve does not cross the x-axis, say so.

   (a) $y = x^2 - 1$ **(f)** $y = -3x^2 + 8x - 4$

   (b) $y = 3x^2 + 1$ **(g)** $y = 4 - (x - 1)^2$

   (c) $y = x^2 - 5x + 6$ **(h)** $y = 4(x - 2)^2 - 9$

   (d) $y = (2 - x)(x - 1)$ **(i)** $y = x^2 - 5x + 7$

   (e) $y = 2(2x - 1)^2$ **(j)** $y = 2x^2 + 7x - 11$

3. For all the functions in Question 2, find the co-ordinates of the maximum or minimum value of the quadratic function and the equation of the axis of symmetry.

4. By calculating $b^2 - 4ac$, state for each quadratic function, $y = ax^2 + bx + c$, whether the function crosses the x-axis at one point or at two different points:

   (a) $y = x^2 - 5$

   (b) $y = x^2 - 7x + 12$

   (c) $y = 15 + 14x - 8x^2$

   (d) $y = 4(3x - 2)^2$

   (e) $y = 4x^2 - 1$

   (f) $y = 4x^2 - 7x - 1$

   (g) $y = (2x - 1)(3x + 5)$

   (h) $y = 3(2 - 3x)^2$

17.4 Intersecting quadratic functions

In general, to find where two functions f and g intersect, equate their y co-ordinates and solve.

or

Plot the functions on the same diagram and read off their points of intersection.

Finding the points(s) of intersection

1. Algebraically: Equate the y co-ordinates and solve the resulting equation.

2. Graphically: Plot the functions on the same graph paper and read off their points of intersection.

ACTIVITY 6

ACTION
Intersecting quadratic functions

OBJECTIVE
To plot two functions (either a linear and quadratic or two quadratics) and to find their points of intersection both graphically and geometrically

EXAMPLE 13

A road with equation $y = f(x) = x^2 - 5x + 7$ is passing through a town. The road that bypasses the town is a motorway with equation $y = g(x) = x + 2$. Find the points where the road intersects the motorway. If all of the distances are in kilometres (km) and the speed limit is 120 km/h, find the least time a car can travel between these points. Put the time in minutes correct to one decimal place.

Solution

$y = g(x) = x + 2$

$y = f(x) = x^2 - 5x + 7$

$x + 2 = x^2 - 5x + 7$

$x^2 - 6x + 5 = 0$

$(x - 1)(x - 5) = 0$

$x = 1, 5$

Substituting into g: $y = 3, 7$

$\therefore A(1, 3) \ B(5, 7)$

$|AB| = \sqrt{16 + 16} = \sqrt{32}$ km

$v = \dfrac{s}{t} \Rightarrow t = \dfrac{s}{v} = \dfrac{\sqrt{32}}{120} = \dfrac{\sqrt{2}}{30}$ s

$t = \dfrac{\sqrt{2}}{30} \times 60$ minutes

$= 2\sqrt{2}$ minutes

$= 2 \cdot 8$ minutes

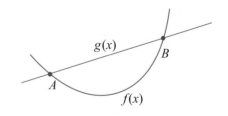

EXAMPLE 14

Plot the graph of $f(x) = x^2 - x - 6, -3 \leq x \leq 4, x \in \mathbb{R}$.

(a) Use the graph to solve $f(x) = 0$ and to find the y-intercept. Verify the results algebraically.

(b) Use the graph to solve $f(x) = 2$. Verify the results algebraically.

Give all the answers correct to one decimal place.

Solution

x	-3	-2	-1	0	1	2	3	4
f	6	0	-4	-6	-6	-4	0	6

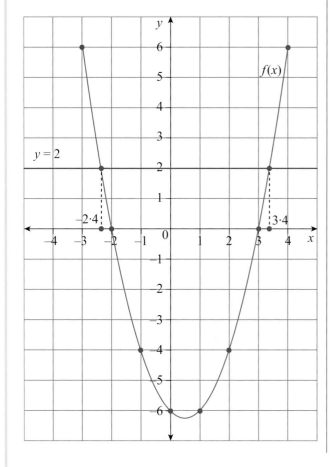

(a) Graph: $y = 0$:

$x = -2, 3$ [The roots are where the graph cuts the x-axis.]

y-intercept: $y = -6$

Algebra: $f(x) = 0$:

$x^2 - x - 6 = 0$

$(x + 2)(x - 3) = 0$

$x = -2, 3$

y-intercept: $f(0) = (0)^2 - (0) - 6 = -6$

(b) Draw the line $y = 2$.

Graph: $f(x) = 2$:

$x = -2{\cdot}4, 3{\cdot}4$

Algebra: $f(x) = 2$:

$x^2 - x - 6 = 2$

$x^2 - x - 8 = 0$

Use the quadratic formula: $a = 1, b = -1, c = -8$

$$x = \frac{-(-1) \pm \sqrt{(-1)^2 - 4(1)(-8)}}{2(1)}$$

$$= \frac{1 \pm \sqrt{1 + 32}}{2}$$

$$= \frac{1 \pm \sqrt{33}}{2}$$

$$= -2{\cdot}4, 3{\cdot}4$$

EXAMPLE 15

Using the table below, plot graphs of f and g on the same diagram for $-2 \le x \le 4$, $x \in \mathbb{R}$, where $f(x) = x^2 - 2x - 7$ and $g(x) = x - 6$.

x	-2	-1	0	1	2	3	4
f							
g							

(a) Use your graphs to solve $x^2 - 3x - 1 = 0$, correct to one decimal place.

(b) Solve $x^2 - 3x - 1 = 0$ algebraically, correct to one decimal place.

Solution

x	-2	-1	0	1	2	3	4
f	1	-4	-7	-8	-7	-4	1
g	-8	-7	-6	-5	-4	-3	-2

(a) $f(x) = g(x)$

$x^2 - 2x - 7 = x - 6$

$x^2 - 3x - 1 = 0$

$x = -0.3, \ 3.3$

(b) $x^2 - 3x - 1 = 0$

Use the quadratic formula: $a = 1, b = -3, c = -1$

$$x = \frac{-b \pm \sqrt{b^2 - 4ac}}{2a}$$

$$= \frac{-(-3) \pm \sqrt{(-3)^2 - 4(1)(-1)}}{2(1)}$$

$$= \frac{3 \pm \sqrt{9+4}}{2} = \frac{3 \pm \sqrt{13}}{2}$$

$$= -0.3, \ 3.3$$

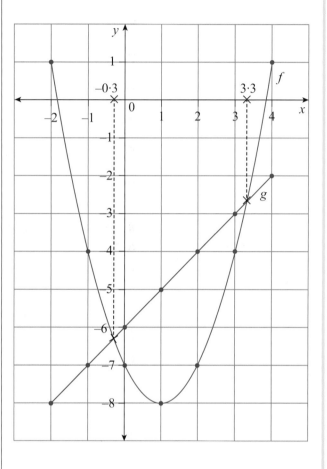

EXAMPLE 16

A plane flying along the curve $y = f(x) = x^2$, $x \ge 0$, $x \in \mathbb{R}$, is struck by a bird flying along the curve $y = g(x) = 9 - x^2$, $x \ge 0$, $x \in \mathbb{R}$. Plot the functions f and g on the same diagram and use it to estimate their point of intersection. By solving $f(x) = g(x)$, verify your estimate.

Solution

x	0	1	2	3
f	0	1	4	9
g	9	8	5	0

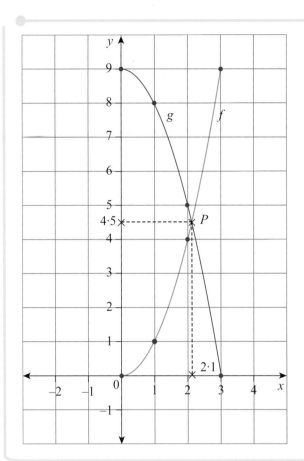

Graph: Co-ordinates of P: $x = 2\cdot1$, $y = 4\cdot5$

Algebra: $x^2 = 9 - x^2$

$2x^2 = 9$

$x^2 = \dfrac{9}{2}$

$x = \pm\dfrac{3}{\sqrt{2}} = \pm\dfrac{3\sqrt{2}}{2}$

$y = \dfrac{9}{2}$

Co-ordinates of $P\left(\dfrac{3\sqrt{2}}{2}, \dfrac{9}{2}\right) = (2\cdot1, 4\cdot5)$ on your calculator.

EXERCISE 7

1. Using the same grid, graph the following functions in the given domain for $x \in \mathbb{R}$. Use the graphs to solve $f(x) = g(x)$ for x, correct to one decimal place. Verify your answer algebraically.

> **Note:** This is also Activity 6. The activity supplies you with the appropriate grids.

   (a) $f(x) = 2x^2 + 3x - 2$ and $g(x) = 2$, $-3 \leq x \leq 1$

   (b) $f(x) = -x^2 + 2x + 5$ and $g(x) = -1$, $-2 \leq x \leq 4$

   (c) $f(x) = -x^2 - 2x + 2$ and $g(x) = x + 1$, $-4 \leq x \leq 1$

   (d) $f(x) = 3x^2 - 7x - 1$ and $g(x) = -2x + 3$, $-1 \leq x \leq 3$

   (e) $f(x) = x^2 - 6$ and $g(x) = -x^2 + 4x + 5$, $-4 \leq x \leq 1$

   (f) $f(x) = x^2 + 3$ and $g(x) = 3x^2 - x$, $-1\cdot5 \leq x \leq 2$

2. Given $f(x) = 2x^2 + 5x - 3$, $x \in \mathbb{R}$:

   (a) Find:

       (i) the co-ordinates of the point where f crosses the y-axis,

       (ii) the co-ordinates of the points where f crosses the x-axis,

       (iii) the minimum point of f.

   (b) Sketch it roughly on graph paper using the information in part **(a)**.

3. Temperatures T in degrees Celsius (°C) are recorded over a 6-hour period.

   The table below shows the temperature T at various times t in hours.

Time t (hours)	0	1	2	3	4	5	6
Temperature T (°C)	7	2	−1	−2	−1	2	7

   (a) Plot a graph of T against t on graph paper.

   (b) Use the graph to estimate:

   (i) the temperature when $t = 3\cdot5$ hours, correct to one decimal place,

   (ii) the difference between the highest and lowest temperatures for $0 \le t \le 6$,

   (iii) how long in hours, correct to one decimal place, the temperature was above $2\cdot5$ °C,

   (iv) when in hours the temperature is 0 °C, correct to one decimal place.

   (c) If $T = at^2 + bt + c$, use the results in the table to find a, b, c.

4. The path of a jet of water from a high-powered hose is given by $h = -x^2 + 40x,\ 0 \le x \le 40,\ x \in \mathbb{R}$, where h is the height above the ground in centimetres and x is the horizontal distance from the nozzle in centimetres.

   (a) Plot a graph of h against x using the table below.

x (cm)	0	10	20	30	40
h (cm)					

   (b) Use your graph to find:

   (i) the height of the jet when $x = 25$ cm,

   (ii) the horizontal distances the jet is from the nozzle when its height is 35 cm,

   (iii) the maximum height of the jet.

   Give all answers correct to the nearest whole number.

5. The height h in metres of a model rocket in flight can be approximated by $h = -5t^2 + 24t + 1$, where t is the time in seconds.

   (a) By copying and completing the table below, plot a graph of h against t on graph paper.

t (s)	0	1	2	3	4
h (m)					

   (b) Use your graph to find:

   (i) the height of the rocket after $3\cdot5$ s, correct to the nearest metre,

   (ii) when the rocket is at 18 m, correct to one decimal place,

   (iii) the maximum height of the rocket, correct to the nearest metre.

   (c) Find the maximum height by calculation.

   (d) Find the percentage error in the maximum height read off the graph as a percentage of the calculated value, correct to one decimal place.

6. A hang glider takes off from a point above horizontal ground. Its height h in hundreds of metres is given by $h = f(x) = -0.225x^2 + 1.35x + 4$, where x is its horizontal distance in hundreds of metres from its starting point. It lands on sloping ground with equation $y = g(x) = 0.2x$.

   (a) Using the table below, plot graphs of f and g on the same diagram, giving all answers correct to two significant figures.

x	0	1	2	3	4	5	6
f							
g							

   (b) Use the graph to find:

   (i) the maximum height in metres of the hang glider above horizontal ground,

   (ii) its height in metres above the ground when it lands on the sloping ground.

   Give both answers correct to two significant figures.

7. The price P_1 in euro per share of a banking stock varies over a 12-year period, according to the equation $P_1 = -x^2 + 15x + 12$. The price P_2 in euro per share of another banking stock varied over the same period, according to the equation $P_2 = 3x + 32$. x is the number of years after the year 2000.

   (a) For what values of x are the two stock prices the same?

   (b) For what values of x is $P_1 > P_2$?

8. The demand d for an item is given by $d = 125 - 5x$, where €x is the selling price of the item.

   (a) Write down an inequality satisfied by x.

   (b) The revenue R in euro for a selling price of €x per item is given by $R = x(125 - 5x)$. Plot R and d against x on the same graph for $0 \le x \le 25$, $x \in \mathbb{R}$ by copying and completing the table below:

x	0	5	10	15	20	25
R						
d						

   (c) Use your graphs to find:

   (i) the maximum revenue, correct to two significant figures,

   (ii) the value of x that gives this maximum revenue, correct to one decimal place,

   (iii) x when $R = 600$, correct to the nearest whole number.

   (iv) d when $R = 500$, correct to the nearest whole number.

   (d) Calculate the maximum value of R.

9. The graphs of $f(x) = px^2 + qx + r$ and $g(x) = -2x + 6$ are sketched below. (1, 12) are the co-ordinates of the maximum value of f. g crosses the x-axis at B.

(a) Find B.

(b) Find C.

(c) Find A.

(d) Find p, q and r.

(e) Find D.

(f) Find P.

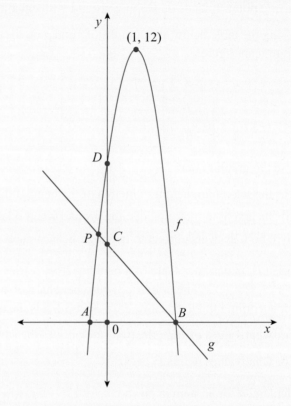

Cubic Functions

CHAPTER 18

Learning Outcomes

- To recognise a cubic function: $y = f(x) = ax^3 + bx^2 + cx + d$.
- To be able to plot a graph of a cubic function and recognise the various shapes of cubic graphs.
- To be able to find properties of cubic functions (crossing axes).
- To work with intersecting cubic functions.
- To use cubic functions to solve real-life problems.
- To understand how to transform functions.

18.1 What is a cubic function?

A cubic function is a relationship between two variables x and y which can be written in the form $y = f(x) = ax^3 + bx^2 + cx + d$, where a, b, c, d are constant real numbers, $a \neq 0$.

a is called the coefficient of x^3.

b is called the coefficient of x^2.

c is called the coefficient of x.

d is called the constant term.

EXAMPLE 1

(a) If $y = 2x^3 - 5x^2 + 7x - 1$, find y when $x = 2$.

(b) If $f(x) = -3x^3 + 5x^2 - x - 3$, find $f(-3)$.

Solution

(a) $x = 2$: $y = 2(2)^3 - 5(2)^2 + 7(2) - 1 = 9$

(b) $f(-3) = -3(-3)^3 + 5(-3)^2 - (-3) - 3 = 126$

18.2 Plotting graphs of cubic functions

Method

To plot a graph of a cubic function:

1. Isolate y on one side of the equation.

2. Substitute the values of x in the domain to find the corresponding values of y.

3. Plot the y values on the vertical axis against the x values on the horizontal axis.

EXAMPLE 2

Plot $y = x^3 + 4x^2 + x - 6$ in the domain $-4 \leq x \leq 2, x \in \mathbb{R}$.

Solution

x	−4	−3	−2	−1	0	1	2
y	−10	0	0	−4	−6	0	20

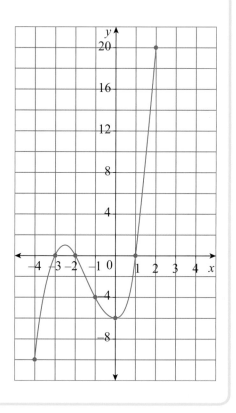

General shape of cubic functions

The sign of a in the cubic function $y = f(x) = ax^3 + bx^2 + cx + d$ tells you the general shape of the cubic graph.

▶ $y = 4x^3 - 9x^2 + 11x - 2$

$a = 4 > 0$

Shape: $a > 0$

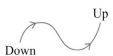

Down   Up

▶ $y = -x^3 + 7x^2 - 5$

$a = -1 < 0$

Shape: $a < 0$

Up   Down

ACTIVITY 7

ACTION
Plotting cubic functions

OBJECTIVE
To draw a number of cubic functions

18.3 Properties of cubic functions

1. Finding where a cubic function crosses the y-axis

Solving the equation of the y-axis ($x = 0$) with the equation of the cubic function $y = ax^3 + bx^2 + cx + d$ gives $y = d$.

The graph of the cubic function crosses the y-axis at $(0, d)$.

EXAMPLE 3

Find where the following cubic functions cross the y-axis:

(a) $y = -2x^3 + 3x^2 - 5x - 7$

(b) $y = x^3 + 11x^2 - 3x + 4$

Solution

(a) $y = -2x^3 + 3x^2 - 5x - 7$

$x = 0$: $y = -7$

It crosses the y-axis at $(0, -7)$.

(b) $y = x^3 + 11x^2 - 3x + 4$

$x = 0$: $y = 4$

It crosses the y-axis at $(0, 4)$.

2. Finding where a cubic function crosses the x-axis

Solving the equation of the x-axis ($y = 0$) with the cubic function $y = ax^3 + bx^2 + cx + d$ gives $ax^3 + bx^2 + cx + d = 0$.

The point(s) where the graph crosses the x-axis are the solutions of the cubic equation $ax^3 + bx^2 + cx + d = 0$.

EXAMPLE 4

Draw a sketch of $y = (2x + 1)(x - 3)(x - 1)$, $x \in \mathbb{R}$, by finding where it crosses the axes.

Solution

$y = (2x + 1)(x - 3)(x - 1)$

Crosses x-axis: $y = 0$:

$(2x + 1)(x - 3)(x - 1) = 0$

$x = -\frac{1}{2}, 1, 3$

Crosses y-axis: $x = 0$:

$y = (+1)(-3)(-1) = +3$

It crosses the y-axis at $(0, 3)$.

If you multiply out the brackets, you get $+2x^3$ as the first term in the cubic function.

$a = +2 > 0$ [This gives us the general shape.]

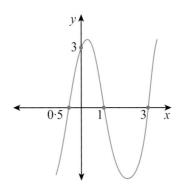

271

18.4 Intersecting cubic functions

To find where two functions intersect, equate their y co-ordinates and solve the resulting equation *or* plot them on the same diagram and read off their points of intersection.

ACTIVITY 8

ACTION
Intersecting cubic functions

OBJECTIVE
To plot two functions (where at least one is cubic) and find their points of intersection

EXAMPLE 5

Plot $y = f(x) = x^3 + x^2 - 6x$ and $y = g(x) = -2x + 2$, $-3 \le x \le 2$, $x \in \mathbb{R}$, on the same diagram. Use your graphs to solve $x^3 + x^2 - 4x - 2 = 0$, correct to one decimal place.

Solution

x	−3	−2	−1	0	1	2
$f(x)$	0	8	6	0	−4	0
$g(x)$	8	6	4	2	0	−2

Solving: $f(x) = g(x)$

$x^3 + x^2 - 6x = -2x + 2$

$x^3 + x^2 - 4x - 2 = 0$

The points of intersection of the functions are the solutions of $x^3 + x^2 - 4x - 2 = 0$.

Solutions: $x = -2 \cdot 3,\ -0 \cdot 5,\ 1 \cdot 8$

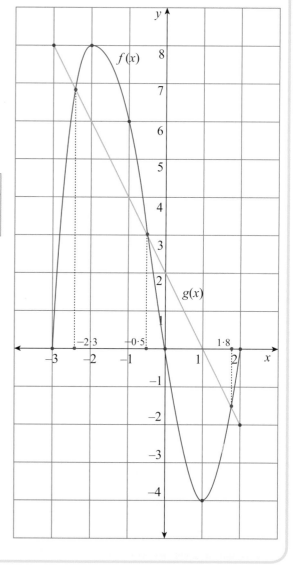

EXAMPLE 6

Plot $f(x) = -x^3 + 4x^2 + x - 4$ and $g(x) = x^2 - 2x - 3$, $-1 \le x \le 4$, $x \in \mathbb{R}$, on the same diagram. Use your graphs to solve $x^3 - 3x^2 - 3x + 1 = 0$, correct to one decimal place.

Solution

x	−1	0	1	2	3	4
$f(x)$	0	−4	0	6	8	0
$g(x)$	0	−3	−4	−3	0	5

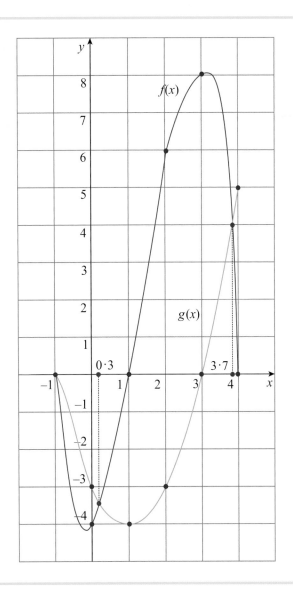

$f(x) = g(x)$

$-x^3 + 4x^2 + x - 4 = x^2 - 2x - 3$

$x^3 - 3x^2 - 3x + 1 = 0$

Graphically: $x = -1,\ 0{\cdot}3,\ 3{\cdot}7$

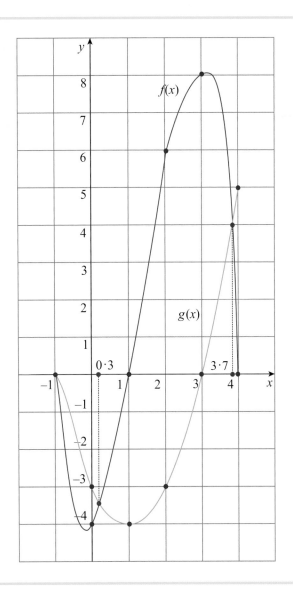

EXERCISE 8

1. Draw the following cubic functions on graph paper in the given domain for $x \in \mathbb{R}$. In each case, write down the roots correct to one decimal place and the point at which the curve crosses the y-axis:

> **Note:** This is also Activity 7. The activity supplies you with the appropriate grids.

   (a) $f(x) = x^3 - 4x - 1,\ -2{\cdot}5 \le x \le 2{\cdot}5$

   (b) $f(x) = -x^3 - 5x^2 - x + 8,\ -5 \le x \le 1{\cdot}5$

   (c) $f(x) = x^3 - 3x - 2,\ -2 \le x \le 2{\cdot}5$

   (d) $f(x) = -x^3 - x^2 + 5x - 3,\ -3 \le x \le 2$

   (e) $f(x) = x^3 - 2x^2 - x - 2,\ -1{\cdot}5 \le x \le 3$

2. Plot the following cubic functions in the given domain for $x \in \mathbb{R}$ and state how many real roots exist:

   (a) $y = -x^3 + 2x^2 - x + 2,\ -1 \le x \le 3$

   (b) $y = (x + 3)^2(x - 2),\ -4 \le x \le 2$

   (c) $y = x^3 - 2x^2 - 5x + 6,\ -3 \le x \le 4$

   (d) $y = x^3 - 2x^2 + 3,\ -1 \le x \le 3$

3. Find the co-ordinates of the points at which the following cubic functions cross the axes:

   (a) $y = (x + 2)(x - 1)(x - 2)$

   (b) $y = -3x(2x - 1)(x + 2)$

   (c) $y = x(x - 1)^2$

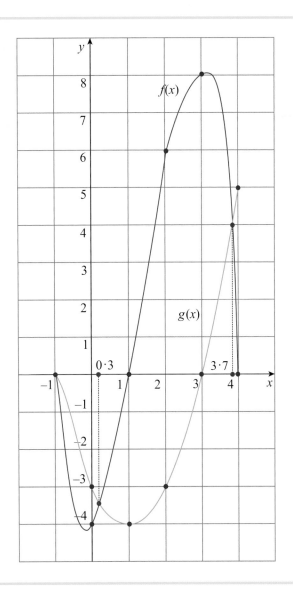

(d) $y = 3x(x^2 + 1)$

(e) $y = 2(x - 2)(x^2 - 3x - 1)$

(f) $y = (4 - x)(x^2 - 5x + 6)$

(g) $y = (3x^2 - 2)(x + 1)$

(h) $y = x^2(3x - 2)$

(i) $y = (4x - 3)(x + 1)(5x - 2)$

(j) $y = -2(x + 5)(4x^2 - x + 1)$

4. The number M of tonnes of household waste recycled in a city t years after 2000 is given by $M = 3t^3 - 19t^2 + d$.

(a) If the number of tonnes recycled in 2000 was 800, find d.

(b) Use the table below to plot a graph of M against t. Give the values of M to the nearest 10 tonnes.

t (years)	0	2	4	6	8
M (tonnes)					

(c) Use your graph to find:

   (i) the mass recycled in 2005 correct to two significant figures,

   (ii) the year in which the minimum number of tonnes was recycled,

   (iii) during what year the mass recycled exceeded 1000 tonnes.

5. Using the same grid, graph the following functions in the given domain for $x \in \mathbb{R}$. Use the graph to solve $f(x) = g(x)$ for x, correct to one decimal place.

> **Note:** This is also Activity 8. The activity supplies you with the appropriate grids.

(a) $f(x) = 2x^3 + 5x^2 - 1$ and $g(x) = 2$, $-3 \le x \le 1$

(b) $f(x) = -x^3 + 3x^2 + 2x - 1$ and $g(x) = -2$, $-1 \le x \le 4$

(c) $f(x) = -x^3 + 2x^2 + 2x$ and $g(x) = -2x$, $-1 \cdot 5 \le x \le 3 \cdot 5$

(d) $f(x) = x^3 - 4x^2 - x + 3$ and $g(x) = x + 1$, $-1 \cdot 5 \le x \le 4 \cdot 5$

(e) $f(x) = x^3 + 2x^2 - 5x - 6$ and $g(x) = x^2 - 4$, $-4 \le x \le 3$

(f) $f(x) = -x^3 - 3x^2 + 2$ and $g(x) = x^2 + 3x - 3$, $-4 \le x \le 2$

(g) $f(x) = x^3 + x^2 - 5x$ and $g(x) = x^2 + x - 2$, $-4 \le x \le 3$

6. $f : x \to x^3 - 9x^2 + 24x - 18$ and $g : x \to 2 - \frac{2}{3}x$ are two functions defined for $x \in \mathbb{R}$.

(a) Copy and complete the table below and use it to draw the graph of $f(x) = x^3 - 9x^2 + 24x - 18$ in the domain $1 \le x \le 5$.

x	1	2	3	4	5
$f(x)$	-2				2

(b) By finding where $g(x) = 2 - \frac{2}{3}x$ crosses the axes, plot it on the same diagram as $f(x)$.

(c) Use your graphs to solve $f(x) = g(x)$, correct to one decimal place.

7. Two functions f and g are defined for $x \in \mathbb{R}$ as follows:

$f : x \to -x^3 + 2x^2 - x + 2$

$g : x \to 3 - x$

(a) Copy and complete the table below and use it to draw the graphs of f and g for $-1 \le x \le 2$, giving all answers correct to one decimal place.

x	-1	$-0 \cdot 5$	0	$0 \cdot 5$	1	$1 \cdot 5$	2
$f(x)$							
$g(x)$							

(b) Use your graphs to estimate the values for which $x^3 - 2x^2 + 1 = 0$, correct to one decimal place.

8. Two functions f and g are defined for $x \in \mathbb{R}$ as follows:

$f : x \to x^3$

$g : x \to 3 - 3x^2$

(a) Copy and complete the table below and use it to draw the graphs of f and g for $-1 \cdot 5 \le x \le 1 \cdot 5$, giving all answers correct to one decimal place.

x	$-1 \cdot 5$	-1	$-0 \cdot 5$	0	$0 \cdot 5$	1	$1 \cdot 5$
$f(x)$							
$g(x)$							

(b) Use your graphs to estimate the values for which $x^3 + 3x^2 = 3$, $-1 \cdot 5 \le x \le 1 \cdot 5$, correct to one decimal place.

(c) Write down the value of the maximum value of $g(x)$.

18.5 Transformations of functions (vertical and horizontal shift)

ACTIVITY 9

ACTION
Transforming functions

OBJECTIVE
To transform (shift) various functions

Vertical shift

If a constant v is added to each y co-ordinate of a graph, the effect is to shift the whole graph vertically up or down by v units.

WORKED EXAMPLE Vertical shift

Consider the functions $f(x) = x^2$ and $f(x) + 2$, $-2 \le x \le 2$, $x \in \mathbb{R}$.

x	-2	-1	0	1	2
$f(x) = x^2$	4	1	0	1	4
$f(x) + 2 = x^2 + 2$	6	3	2	3	6

The shape of the graph remains unchanged but the whole graph has been translated **vertically upwards** by two units.

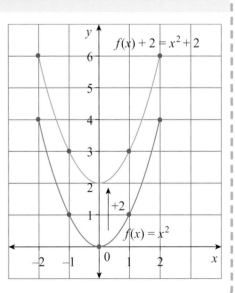

Horizontal shift

If a constant h is added to each x co-ordinate of a graph, the effect is to shift the whole graph horizontally left or right by a factor of h.

WORKED EXAMPLE

Horizontal shift

Consider $f(x) = x^2$, $-2 \leq x \leq 2$, and $f(x + 2)$, $-4 \leq x \leq 0$, $x \in \mathbb{R}$.

x	-2	-1	0	1	2
$f(x) = x^2$	4	1	0	1	4

x	-4	-3	-2	-1	0
$f(x + 2) = (x + 2)^2$	4	1	0	1	4

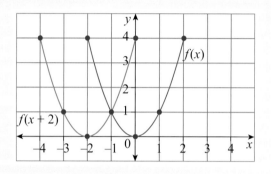

The shape of the graph remains unchanged but the whole graph has been translated **backwards** (to the left) by two units.

Vertical and horizontal shifts

If $y = f(x)$, then:

1. $f(x) + v$ shifts $f(x)$ vertically up by v units, if $v > 0$.

2. $f(x) - v$ shifts $f(x)$ vertically down by v units, if $v > 0$.

3. $f(x + h)$ shifts $f(x)$ horizontally left by h units, if $h > 0$.

4. $f(x - h)$ shifts $f(x)$ horizontally right by h units, if $h > 0$.

EXERCISE 9

1. The graph of $y = f(x)$ is shown on the grids. Copy each function onto your graph paper and sketch the required function.

   (a) Sketch the graph of $y = f(x) - 2$.

   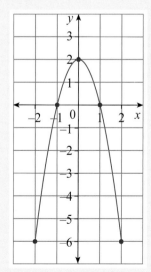

   (b) Sketch the graph of $y = f(x + 4)$.

   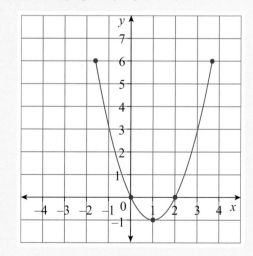

2. The green-coloured graph is a transformation of the red-coloured graph whose equation is shown. Write down the equation of the transformed graph.

(a)

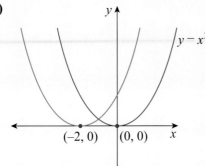

$y = x^2$

$(-2, 0)$ $\quad$ $(0, 0)$ $\quad$ x

(b)

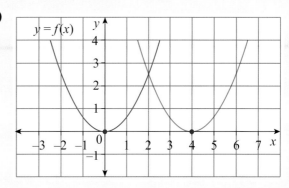

$y = f(x)$

(c)

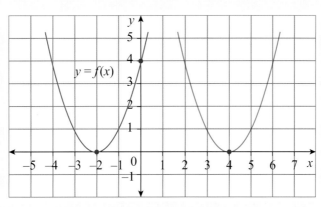

$y = f(x)$

(d)

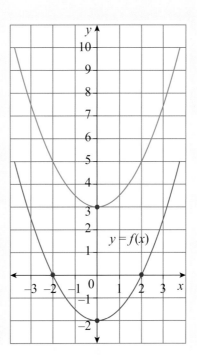

$y = f(x)$

19 Exponential Functions

Learning Outcomes

- To recognise an exponential function: $y = ka^{bx}$.
- To be able to plot a graph of an exponential function.
- To know the properties of exponential functions of the type $y = ka^{bx}$.
- To work with problems of intersecting functions involving an exponential function.
- To use exponential functions to solve real-life problems.

19.1 What is an exponential function?

ACTIVITY 10

ACTION
Plotting exponential functions

OBJECTIVE
To rewrite exponential functions in a particular format and to plot their graphs

The mathematics of uncontrolled growth (decay) is frightening. A single bacterium such as an *E. coli* cell can multiply rapidly (exponentially) under favourable circumstances.

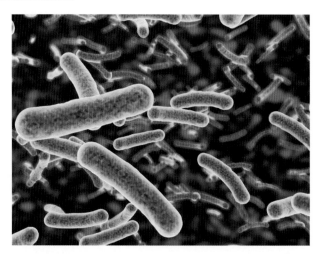

An exponential function is a relation between two variables, x and y, which can be written in the form $y = ka^{bx}$, where k, a, b are constants with $a, b \in \mathbb{R}, a > 0, k \in \mathbb{N}$.

▸ $y = 3 \times 2^{4x}$: $k = 3, a = 2, b = 4$

▸ $y = 2^{-3x}$: $k = 1, a = 2, b = -3$

The rules of powers can be applied as normal.

EXAMPLE 1

Show that $y = 3^{x+5}$ can be written in the form $y = ka^{bx}$.

Solution

$y = 3^{x+5}$

$\quad = 3^x \times 3^5$

$\quad = 243 \times 3^x$

$\therefore k = 243, a = 3, b = 1$

19.2 Plotting graphs of exponential functions

Method

Substitute the values in the domain for x and calculate the corresponding value of y.

EXAMPLE 2

Plot $y = 2^x$, $-2 \le x \le 3$, $x \in \mathbb{R}$.

Solution

x	−2	−1	0	1	2	3
y	$\frac{1}{4}$	$\frac{1}{2}$	1	2	4	8

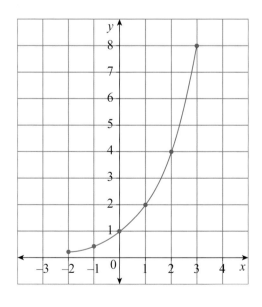

EXAMPLE 3

Show that $2(\sqrt{3})^x$ can be written as $2 \times 3^{\frac{1}{2}x}$ and hence plot $y = 2(\sqrt{3})^x$ in the domain $-2 \le x \le 2$, $x \in \mathbb{R}$.

Solution

$2(\sqrt{3})^x = 2 \times \left(3^{\frac{1}{2}}\right)^x = 2 \times 3^{\frac{1}{2}x}$

$\therefore y = 2(\sqrt{3})^x = 2 \times 3^{\frac{1}{2}x}$

x	−2	−1	0	1	2
y	$\frac{2}{3}$	1·2	2	3·5	6

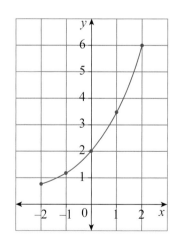

EXAMPLE 4

Plot $y = 3\left(\dfrac{1}{2}\right)^{x}$, $-2 \leq x \leq 2$, $x \in \mathbb{R}$.

Solution

$$y = 3\left(\dfrac{1}{2}\right)^{x} = 3 \times (2^{-1})^{x} = 3 \times 2^{-x}$$

x	-2	-1	0	1	2
y	12	6	3	1·5	0·75

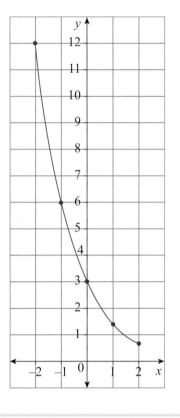

19.3 Properties of exponential functions

We are dealing with exponential functions of the form $y = ka^{bx}$, where k, a, b are constants with $k \in \mathbb{N}$, $a, b \in \mathbb{R}$, $a > 0$ and x, y are variables.

1. Exponential curves of this form never cross the x-axis. They have no real roots.

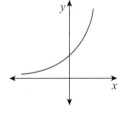

2. They always cross the y-axis.

    $x = 0$: $y = ka^{0} = k$

    $\therefore$ $(0, k)$ is the point at which such curves cross the y-axis.

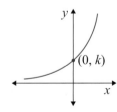

3. The curves are always increasing or decreasing.

EXERCISE 10

1. **(a)** Copy and complete the table below and draw the graph of the curve $y = 2^x$ in the domain $-2 \leq x \leq 2, x \in \mathbb{R}$.

x	-2	-1	0	1	2
y					

(b) Use the graph to solve $2^x = 3$, correct to one decimal place.

(c) Use the graph to find $2^{0.5}$, correct to one decimal place.

2. The diagram shows the graph of $y = ka^x$. Find k and a, $a > 0$.

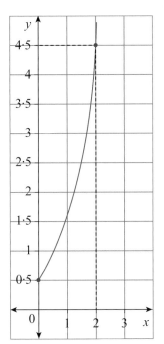

3. The population P of bees in a hive, t days after it was established, is given by $P = 20\,000(1 \cdot 15)^t$.

(a) How many bees were initially in the hive?

(b) How many bees were in the hive, correct to three significant figures:

   (i) after 10 days,

   (ii) after 20 days?

(c) Using the table below, plot a graph of P against t on graph paper. Give all answers in the table correct to three significant figures.

t	0	5	10	15	20
P					

(d) Use your graph to estimate when the population becomes 120 000, correct to the nearest day.

4. The number N of bacteria in a sample, t hours after starting an experiment, is given by $N = 60\,(3)^{0 \cdot 04t}$.

(a) Find the number of bacteria in the sample at the start of the experiment.

(b) Find the number of bacteria in the sample 3 hours after starting the experiment.

(c) Plot a graph of N against t on graph paper using the table below, giving each value of N correct to three significant figures.

t	0	4	8	12	16	20	24
N							

(d) Use your graph to estimate when $N = 100$, correct to one decimal place.

5. The value V in euro of a mobile phone after

t years is given by $V = k\left(\dfrac{1}{2}\right)^t$, k is a constant.

(a) Find k if the mobile phone is worth € 80 after 4 years.

(b) Find its value after 5 years.

(c) After how many years is it worth € 5?

(d) Plot a graph of V against t by copying and completing the following table:

t	0	1	2	3	4	5
V						

19.4 Intersecting exponential functions

ACTIVITY 11

ACTION
Intersecting exponential functions

OBJECTIVE
To plot two functions (where at least one is exponential) and to find their points of intersection

To find where two functions intersect, equate their y co-ordinates and solve for x *or* plot them on the same diagram and read off their points of intersection.

EXAMPLE 5

Two functions f and g are defined as:

$f : x \rightarrow 2^x$, $x \in \mathbb{R}$

$g : x \rightarrow 2x + 1$, $x \in \mathbb{R}$

(a) Complete the table below and use it to draw graphs of f and g for $0 \le x \le 3$ on the same diagram.

x	0	0·5	1	1·5	2	2·5	3
f							
g							

(b) Use the graphs to estimate the values of x for which $2^x - 2x - 1 = 0$, correct to one decimal place.

(c) If $2^k = 5$, use the graphs to estimate k and $g(k)$, correct to one decimal place.

Solution

$f(x) = 2^x$

$g(x) = 2x + 1$

(a)

x	0	0·5	1	1·5	2	2·5	3
f	1	1·4	2	2·8	4	5·7	8
g	1	2	3	4	5	6	7

(b) The points of intersection of the curves are the solutions of:

$$f(x) = g(x)$$
$$2^x = 2x + 1$$
$$2^x - 2x - 1 = 0$$

Using the graph, the solutions to $2^x - 2x - 1 = 0$ are $x = 0$ and $x = 2\cdot6$.

(c) $f(x) = 5$: $2^k = 5 \Rightarrow k = 2\cdot3$
and $g(k) = 5\cdot6$

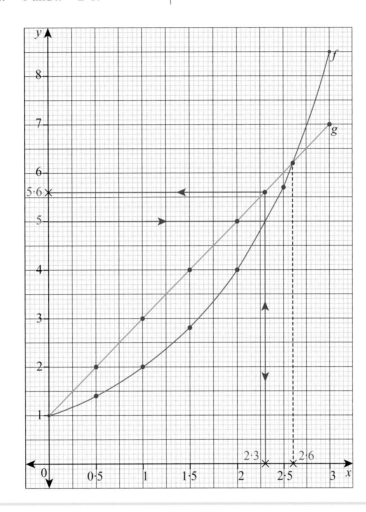

EXAMPLE 6

A missile is fired from a point A. Its height, in tens of metres above the ground, t seconds after being fired, is given by $h_1 = 2^t$, $t \geq 0$. The instant it is fired, another missile is fired from a drone at point B. Its height h_2, in tens of metres above the ground, t seconds after being fired, is given by $h_2 = 10 - t^2$, $t \geq 0$.

(a) Find the initial height of each missile above the ground.

(b) Use the table below to plot graphs of h_1 and h_2 against t on graph paper.

t	0	0·5	1	1·5	2	2·5	3
h_1							
h_2							

(c) Use your graph to estimate when the missiles collide and how high above the ground the collision occurs.

Solution

$h_1 = 2^t$

$h_2 = 10 - t^2$

(a) $t = 0 \Rightarrow h_1 = 1$. The initial height of the first missile is 10 m above the ground.

$t = 0 \Rightarrow h_2 = 10$. The initial height of the second missile is 100 m above the ground.

(b)

t	0	0·5	1	1·5	2	2·5	3
h_1	1	1·4	2	2·8	4	5·7	8
h_2	10	9·8	9	7·8	6	3·8	1

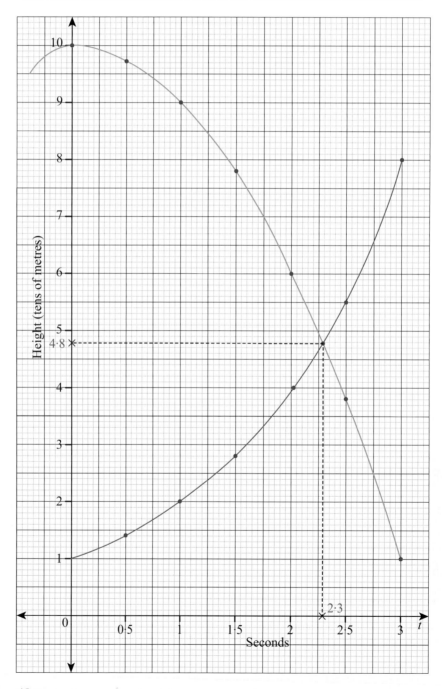

(c) $t = 2·3$ s at $h = 48$ m

EXERCISE 11

1. A clay pigeon is released from a trap at *B*. The equation of its path is given by $f(x) = 2^x$, where *x* is in metres. At the same instant a gun is fired from *C* and the shot travels along a straight line with equation $g(x) = -x + 4$.

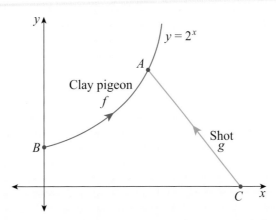

   (a) Use the table below to plot *f* and *g* on the same diagram. Give all answers in the table correct to one decimal place.

x	0	0·5	1	1·5	2	2·5	3
f							
g							

   (b) Use the graphs to find the co-ordinates of the point *A* at which the shot hits the clay pigeon, correct to one decimal place.

2. Two functions *f* and *g* are defined for $x \in \mathbb{R}$ as follows:
   $$f: x \to x^3 - 4x^2 + x + 6$$
   $$g: x \to \tfrac{3}{2}(2^x)$$

   (a) Complete the table below and use it to draw the graphs of *f* and *g* for $-1 \leq x \leq 3$.

x	−1	0	1	2	3
f(x)					
g(x)					

   (b) Use your graphs to estimate the values of *x* for which $x^3 - 4x^2 + x + 6 - \tfrac{3}{2}(2^x) = 0$, correct to one decimal place.

3. The populations of two colonies of insects vary with time *t* in days, according to the equations:
   Colony 1: $P_1 = 75t - t^3 + 10, \ 0 \leq t \leq 7$
   Colony 2: $P_2 = 30 \times (1\cdot5)^t, \ 0 \leq t \leq 7$
   where:
   P_1 is the population of colony 1 in thousands.
   P_2 is the population of colony 2 in thousands.

(a) By copying and completing the table below, plot graphs of P_1 against t and P_2 against t on the same diagram. Give all answers correct to the nearest whole number.

t	0	1	2	3	4	5	6	7
P_1								
P_2								

(b) Use your graphs to find the times in days at which the two populations are equal, correct to one decimal place.

4. Let $f: x \to 3^x$ and $g: x \to \left(\dfrac{1}{3}\right)^x$.

(a) By copying and completing the table below, draw graphs of f and g on the same diagram for $-2 \leq x \leq 2, x \in \mathbb{R}$.

x	−2	−1	0	1	2

(b) Write down the co-ordinates of their only point of intersection.

(c) Use your graphs to solve:

(i) $3^x = 4 \cdot 5$, correct to one decimal place,

(ii) $2\left(\dfrac{1}{3}\right)^x = 13$, correct to one decimal place.

5. The functions $f(x) = 4(\sqrt{2})^x$ and $g(x) = a - (x - 2)^2$ are shown in the diagram. The graphs intersect at A on the y-axis and at B, the point at which $g(x)$ has its maximum value.

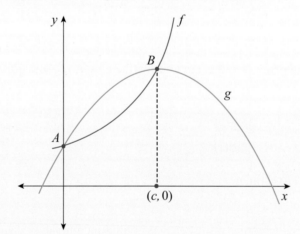

(a) Find the co-ordinates of A. Find a.

(b) Find c, the x co-ordinate of the maximum value of g.

(c) Find the co-ordinates of B.

REVISION QUESTIONS

1. Two bodies A and B move along a straight line. At time t, in seconds, the distance s that body A is from the fixed point is given by $s = t^3 - 10t^2 + 24t$. The distance d that body B is from the same fixed point at time t seconds is given by $d = 4 - t$, where s and d are in metres.

   (a) Copy and complete the table below.

t	0	1	2	3	4	5	6
s							
d							

   (b) Plot graphs of s against t and d against t on the same diagram for $0 \leq t \leq 6$, correct to one decimal place.

   (c) Use your graph to find when body A is 8 m from the fixed point, correct to one decimal place.

   (d) Use your graph to find the maximum distance body A is from the fixed point to the nearest metre.

   (e) Use your graphs to find the times at which the bodies are the same distance from the fixed point, correct to one decimal place.

2. The rate R of flow of fluids in a tree over a 24-hour period is given by:

   $$R = \begin{cases} 2t^2 - 192, & 0 \leq t \leq 12 \\ 96, & 12 \leq t \leq 18 \\ -12t + 312, & 18 \leq t \leq 24 \end{cases}$$

   where R is in cm³/hour and t is in hours.

   (a) Copy and complete the table below.

t	0	3	6	9	12	15	18	21	24
R									

   (b) Copy and complete the grid below and use the results in the table to draw a graph of R against t on it.

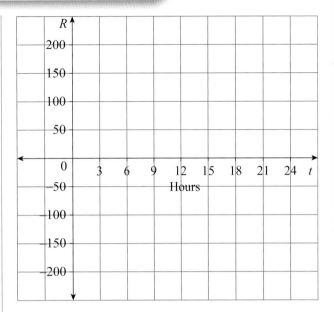

   (c) Use your graph to find:

      (i) the rate of flow at $t = 16$ hours,

      (ii) the rate of flow at $t = 20$ hours, correct to the nearest whole number,

      (iii) the times at which the rate of flow is 50 cm³/hour, correct to the nearest hour,

      (iv) the average rate of flow over the 24-hour period.

3. The graphs of $f(x) = -x^2 + 5x + 6$ and $g(x) = -2x + 12$ are sketched below.

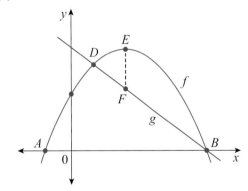

   f and g intersect at D and B. A and B are the intercepts of f on the x-axis.

   (a) Find the co-ordinates of A and B.

   (b) Find the co-ordinates of D.

   (c) Find the co-ordinates of E, the maximum point on f.

287

(d) If *EF* is parallel to the *y*-axis, find the co-ordinates of *F*.

(e) Find |*EF*|.

4. When a games console is switched off, the current *I* in amps (A) dies away according to the formula $I = 5(0·6)^t$, where *t* is the time in seconds.

(a) Find the current at the instant the console is switched off.

(b) Copy and complete the table below, giving the *I* values correct to one decimal place.

t (s)	0	1	2	3	4	5
I (A)						

(c) Plot *I* against *t* on graph paper.

(d) Use the graph to find:

  (i) the current after 2·5 s, correct to one decimal place,

  (ii) the time it takes the current to reach 0·5 A, correct to one decimal place.

(e) Evaluate $(0·6)^4$ as a rational number and hence calculate the time for the current to become 0·648 A.

5. In a certain country, income tax *T* in € is levied as follows. For an income over €20 000, the tax payable is €800 plus 6% of earnings over €20 000.

(a) If a person's income is €*x*, *x* > 20 000, write down a linear function connecting *T* and *x*.

(b) Use the function to find the tax on an income of €45 000.

(c) Use the function to find the income that will give a tax of €1100.

6. (a) Write 20% as a decimal.

(b) Increase 1000 by 20%.

(c) A population of 1000 organisms increases by 20% every day. Copy and complete the table below for the population *P* after *t* days. Give the *P* values correct to three significant figures.

t (days)	0	1	2	3	4	5	6	7
P	1000							

(d) Draw a graph of *P* against *t* on graph paper.

(e) Use your graph to find:

  (i) the population after 4·5 days, correct to the nearest hundred,

  (ii) the number of days it takes the population to reach 3300, correct to one decimal place.

(f) Find an equation relating *P* to *t*.

7. A chessboard has 64 squares.

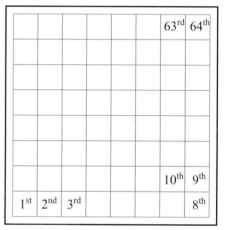

You place a 1-cent coin on the first square, two 1-cent coins on the second square, four 1-cent coins on the third square, always doubling the number of coins on the previous square.

(a) Copy and complete the table.

Square number *R*	1	2	3	4	5	6	7	8
Number *N* of 1-cent coins on the square	2^0		2^3			2^6		

(b) How many coins are there on:

  (i) the 20th square,

  (ii) the 64th square?

(c) Write down a formula relating *N* to *R*.

(d) If a 1-cent coin is 1 mm thick, how high will the pile of cents on the 64th square be in metres? Give your answer in the form $a \times 10^n$, $1 \le a \le 10$, where *a* is given correct to one decimal place.

(e) The distance from the Earth to the Sun is 150 million km. Express this in metres in the form $a \times 10^n$, $1 \le a \le 10$.

(f) Find the ratio of the height of the pile of coins in part **(d)** to the Earth–Sun distance, correct to the nearest whole number.

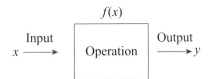

SUMMARY

1. Function:

A function $f(x)$ takes values of a variable x from a set called the domain and sends them to values y in a set called the codomain so that each value of x is sent to one and only one value of y.

$$f(x)$$

$$\text{Input } x \longrightarrow \boxed{\text{Operation}} \xrightarrow{\text{Output}} y$$

2. Domain and range:

Domain: The domain of a function is the set of values which is mapped by a function.

Range: The range of a function is the set of images obtained by mapping the elements of the domain.

3. Test for a function (vertical line test):

$y = f(x)$ is a function if all lines drawn parallel to the y-axis through all points in the domain of $f(x)$ intersect the graph of $y = f(x)$ **once and only once.**

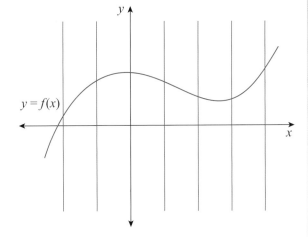

4. Combining functions:

$$f(g(x)) = (f \circ g)(x)$$

$$u = g(x) \Rightarrow f(g(x)) = f(u)$$

5. Linear functions:

(a) Equation: $y = mx + c$

(b) Shape:

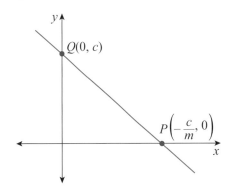

(c) Forms of the equation of a straight line:

$$(y - y_1) = m(x - x_1)$$

or

$$y = mx + c$$

or

$$ax + by + c = 0$$

6. Quadratic functions:

(a) Equation: $y = ax^2 + bx + c$

(b) Shapes:

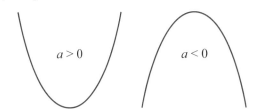

$a > 0 \qquad a < 0$

(c) Roots:

(i) $b^2 > 4ac \Rightarrow$ 2 different real roots:

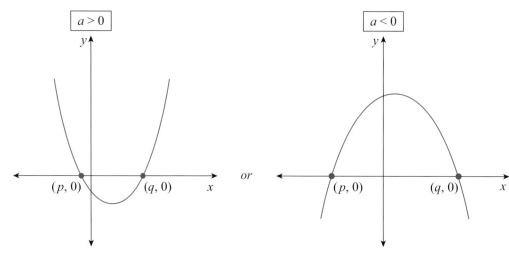

or

(ii) $b^2 = 4ac \Rightarrow$ 2 equal real roots:

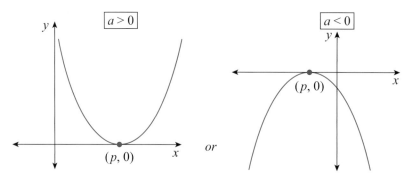

or

(iii) $b^2 < 4ac \Rightarrow$ no real roots:

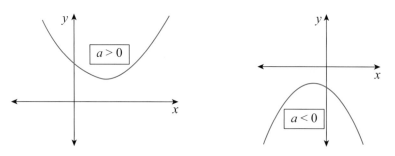

(d) Vertex and axis of symmetry:

(i) Vertex:

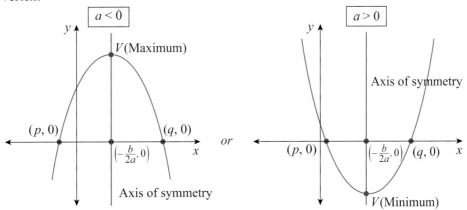

For two different roots: $\left(-\dfrac{b}{2a}, 0\right)$ is the midpoint of $(p, 0)$ and $(q, 0)$ and is the x co-ordinate of the vertex.

For two equal roots: $\left(-\dfrac{b}{2a}, 0\right)$ is the vertex.

(ii) Equation of the axis of symmetry $x = -\dfrac{b}{2a}$

7. Cubic functions:

(a) Equation: $y = ax^3 + bx^2 + cx + d$

(b) Shapes:

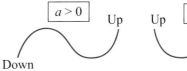
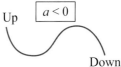

8. Transformations of functions:

Vertical and horizontal shifts

If $y = f(x)$, then:

1. $f(x) + v$ shifts $f(x)$ vertically up by v units, if $v > 0$.

2. $f(x) - v$ shifts $f(x)$ vertically down by v units, if $v > 0$.

3. $f(x + h)$ shifts $f(x)$ horizontally left by h units, if $h > 0$.

4. $f(x - h)$ shifts $f(x)$ horizontally right by h units, if $h > 0$.

9. Exponential functions:

(a) Equation: $y = ka^{bx}$, $a, b \in \mathbb{R}$, $a > 0$, $k \in \mathbb{N}$

(b) Shapes:

They always cross the y-axis at $(0, k)$.

They never cross the x-axis.

They are always increasing or decreasing.

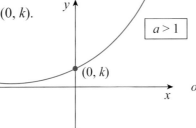
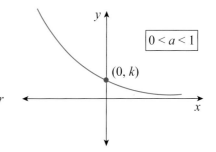

Differentiation

Differential calculus is the mathematics of change. Two great mathematicians devised differential calculus:

Newton who thought of differentiation in terms of the slope of the tangent to a curve and motion and **Leibniz** who thought of $\frac{dy}{dx}$ as a limit.

🎧 Gottfried Wilhelm Leibniz

🎧 Sir Isaac Newton

CHAPTER 20

Techniques of Differentiation

Learning Outcomes

- To understand how an instantaneous rate of change is found from an average rate of change.
- To find the tangent to a curve.
- To understand the techniques of differentiation.
- To be able to find the second derivative of a function.

20.1 Average rate of change

The average rate of change of distance s with respect to time t is called average speed.

$$\text{Average speed} = \frac{\text{Distance}}{\text{Time}}$$

Consider the journey shown below between four towns in the USA.

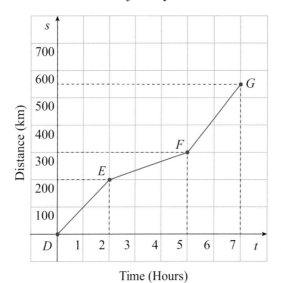

Time (Hours)

Town	Time (h)	Distance (km)
Dublin	0	0
Evesham	2	200
Fresno	5	300
George	7	550

The average speed from D to $E = \dfrac{200 - 0}{2 - 0} = 100$ km/h = slope of DE.

The average speed from E to $F = \dfrac{300 - 200}{5 - 2} = \dfrac{100}{3} = 33\frac{1}{3}$ km/h = slope of EF.

The average speed from F to $G = \dfrac{550 - 300}{7 - 5} = \dfrac{250}{2} = 125$ km/h = slope of FG.

The average speed between two points on the distance-time graph shown is the slope of the line joining the two points.

But what if the graph of distance against time is a curve rather than a series of straight lines?

WORKED EXAMPLE

Dropping a stone

A stone drops from the top of a building at time $t = 0$. Its distance s in metres, t seconds after it drops, is given by $s = 4\cdot9t^2$. Find its average speed between $t = 2$ and $t = 5$.

t (s)	0	1	2	3	4	5
s (m)	0	4·9	19·6	44·1	78·4	122·5

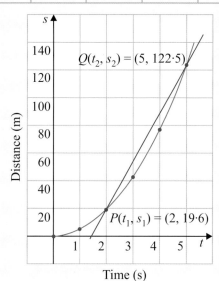

Average speed $= \dfrac{\text{Distance}}{\text{Time}} = \dfrac{s_2 - s_1}{t_2 - t_1} = \dfrac{122\cdot5 - 19\cdot6}{5 - 2} = 34\cdot3$ m/s

The average speed $= \dfrac{s_2 - s_1}{t_2 - t_1} =$ the slope of the line PQ.

In the worked example above, as in most realistic situations, the stone's speed is changing continuously as it moves from point to point. The question arises as to what is the exact speed at any point. In other words, what is the instantaneous speed?

Instantaneous rate of change

The instantaneous rate of change of distance with respect to time is called instantaneous speed. The instantaneous speed of a body is its speed v at any instant of time t.

Instantaneous rate of change is usually just called rate of change. It is the slope m of the tangent k to the curve at any point on the curve where $m = \dfrac{\text{Rise}}{\text{Run}}$ at that point.

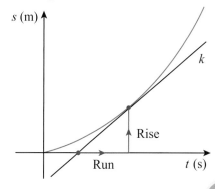

WORKED EXAMPLE ## Slopes of tangents by drawing 1

Find the slope of the tangent to the curve $s = t^2$ at $A(1, 1)$, $B(2, 4)$ and $C(3, 9)$ on the curve.

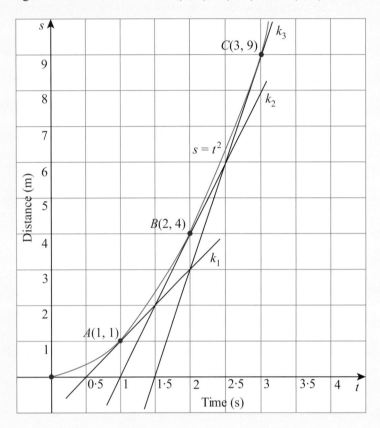

1. The slope of the tangent at $A(1, 1) = \dfrac{\text{Rise}}{\text{Run}} = \dfrac{1}{\frac{1}{2}} = 2 \times (1) = 2$ multiplied by the value of t at A.

2. The slope of the tangent at $B(2, 4) = \dfrac{\text{Rise}}{\text{Run}} = \dfrac{4}{1} = 2 \times (2) = 2$ multiplied by the value of t at B.

3. The slope of the tangent at $C(3, 9) = \dfrac{\text{Rise}}{\text{Run}} = \dfrac{9}{\frac{3}{2}} = 2 \times (3) = 2$ multiplied by the value of t at C.

There seems to be a pattern here. The slope of the tangent at a point (t, s) on the curve $s = t^2$ is equal to 2 multiplied by the value of t at the point $= 2t$.

The **slope of the tangent** at a point on a curve of s against t is called $\dfrac{ds}{dt}$ and stands for:

$$\frac{\text{Difference } (d) \text{ in } s}{\text{Difference } (d) \text{ in } t}$$

It is pronounced 'Dee s Dee t'.

$\dfrac{ds}{dt}$ is the slope of the tangent at any point on the curve.

For: $s = t^2$

$$\frac{ds}{dt} = 2t$$

This is a very powerful result as it enables you to find the slope of the tangent at any point on the curve.

EXAMPLE 1

If the distance s in metres travelled by a body from a fixed point O, after time t in seconds, is given by $s = t^2$, find:

(a) the slope of the tangent to the curve $s = t^2$ at $t = 3 \cdot 2$

(b) the rate of change of distance with respect to time at $t = 3 \cdot 2$

(c) the instantaneous speed of the body at $t = 3 \cdot 2$

Solution

$$s = t^2$$
$$\frac{ds}{dt} - 2t$$

(a) The slope of the tangent
$m = \dfrac{ds}{dt}$ at $t = 3 \cdot 2$ is $2(3 \cdot 2) = 6 \cdot 4$ m/s

(b) The rate of change of s with t at
$t = 3 \cdot 2$ is $\dfrac{ds}{dt}$ at $t = 3 \cdot 2$ which is $2(3 \cdot 2) = 6 \cdot 4$ m/s

(c) The instantaneous speed v at
$t = 3 \cdot 2$ is $\dfrac{ds}{dt}$ at $t = 3 \cdot 2$ which is $2(3 \cdot 2) = 6 \cdot 4$ m/s

Rate of change for any curve with equation $y = f(x)$

Average rate of change

The average rate of change of y with respect to x on the curve $y = f(x)$ between

the points $P(x_1, y_1)$ and $Q(x_2, y_2) = \dfrac{y_2 - y_1}{x_2 - x_1} = $ slope of line $PQ = \dfrac{f(x_2) - f(x_1)}{x_2 - x_1}$.

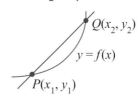

Instantaneous rate of change

The (instantaneous) rate of change of y with respect to x at a point $P(x, y)$ on the

curve $y = f(x)$ is the slope of the tangent k to the curve at this point $= \dfrac{dy}{dx}$.

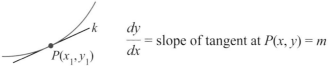

$\dfrac{dy}{dx} = $ slope of tangent at $P(x, y) = m$

The process of finding the (instantaneous) rate of change of y with respect to x where $y = f(x)$ is called:

1. differentiation

or

2. finding the derivative of the function

or

3. finding $\dfrac{dy}{dx}$

or

4. finding $f'(x)$ [pronounced 'f dash x']

or

5. finding the rate of change of y with respect to x

or

6. finding the slope of the tangent to the curve $y = f(x)$ at a point on the curve

All of these simply mean to find $\dfrac{dy}{dx}$. [pronounced 'Dee y Dee x']

WORKED EXAMPLE

Slopes of tangents by drawing 2

Find the slope of the tangent to the curve $y = x^3$ at the point $D(2, 8)$.

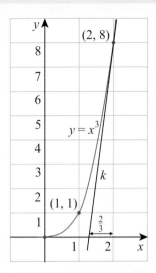

The slope of the tangent at $D(2, 8)$

$= \dfrac{8}{\frac{2}{3}} = 12 = 3 \times 4 = 3 \times (2)^2 = 3$ multiplied by the square of the value of x at the point D.

If $y = x^3$ then $\dfrac{dy}{dx}$ at $(2, 8) = 12 = $ slope of the tangent to the curve at $D(2, 8)$.

EXERCISE 1

1. Find the following from the graph:

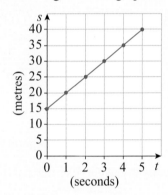

   (a) the average rate of change of s with respect to t from $t = 2$ to $t = 5$,

   (b) the instantaneous rate of change of s with respect to t at $t = 3$,

   (c) why these two results are the same.

2. If k is the tangent to the graph shown at $(5, 75)$, find the following from the graph:

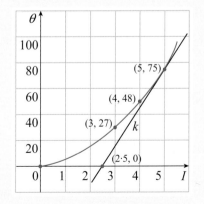

   (a) the average rate of change of θ with respect to I from $I = 4$ to $I = 5$,

   (b) $\dfrac{d\theta}{dI}$ at $I = 5$.

3. If k is the tangent to the graph shown at $(2, 5)$, find the following from the graph:

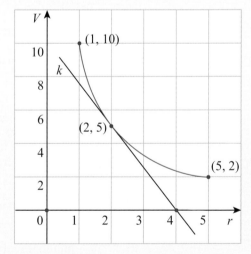

   (a) the average rate of change of V with respect to r from (i) $r = 1$ to $r = 5$, (ii) $r = 2$ to $r = 5$,

   (b) the instantaneous rate of change of V with respect to r at $r = 2$. Why is this negative?

   (c) $\dfrac{dV}{dr}$ at $r = 2$.

4. If k is the tangent to the graph shown at $x = 1$, find the following from the graph:

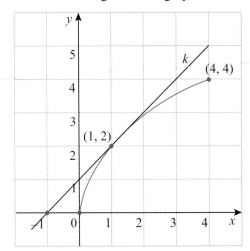

    (a) the average rate of change of y with respect to x from $x = 1$ to $x = 4$,

    (b) the instantaneous rate of change of y with respect to x at $x = 1$,

    (c) the slope of the tangent to the curve at $x = 1$,

    (d) $\dfrac{dy}{dx}$ at $x = 1$.

5. The current I, in milliamps (mA), in a semiconducting device is described by the graph shown.

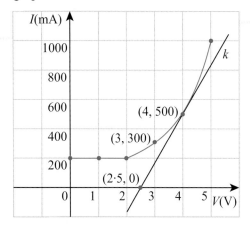

Find the following if k is the tangent to the curve shown at (4, 500):

    (a) the average rate of change of the current with voltage, measured in volts (V), from $V = 3$ to $V = 4$,

    (b) the instantaneous rate of change of the current with voltage at $V = 4$.
    What notation is used to describe the instantaneous rate of change of the current with respect to voltage?

20.2 Differentiation by rule

Finding the slope of the tangent to the curve of a function $y = f(x)$ by drawing is tedious and inaccurate. There is a quicker and more accurate method to differentiate a function $y = f(x)$.

The basic rule of differentiation

For $s = t^2$ we found $\dfrac{ds}{dt} = 2t^1$.

For $y = x^3$ we found $\dfrac{dy}{dx} = 3x^2$.

For $y = x^1$ we know $\dfrac{dy}{dx} = 1 = 1x^0$ because $y = x$ is a straight line of slope 1. $[y = 1x + 0]$
You can see that there is a pattern here:

$$y = x^n \Rightarrow \frac{dy}{dx} = nx^{n-1}$$

This is the basic rule of differentiation and holds for all powers n.

> **The rule in words:** To differentiate $y = x^n$ with respect to x, multiply down by the power and subtract 1 from the power.

Conclusion

$y = f(x)$	x	x^2	x^3
$\dfrac{dy}{dx} = f'(x)$	$1x^0$	$2x$	$3x^2$

The process of finding the slope of the tangent to a curve $y = f(x)$ at **any point** (x, y) on the curve is called differentiation.

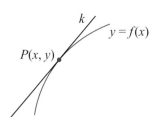

The slope m of the tangent at any point $P(x, y)$ on the curve $y = f(x)$ is given by $\dfrac{dy}{dx}$ or $f'(x)$ (f dash x).

$$m = \frac{dy}{dx} = f'(x)$$

TIP

To find $\dfrac{dy}{dx}$ at a particular point (x_1, y_1) on a curve, always differentiate first and then substitute in the value of x_1 for x.

EXAMPLE 2

Find the slope of the tangent to the curve $y = x^3$ at $(-2, -8)$.

Solution

$y = x^3$

$\dfrac{dy}{dx} = 3x^2$ [Differentiate first]

At $x = -2$: $\dfrac{dy}{dx} = 3(-2)^2 = 12 = m$ [Substitute in the value for x second.]

WORKED EXAMPLE — Equation of a tangent to a curve

Find the equation of the tangent to the curve $y = x^2$ at $(-3, 9)$.

1. Draw a rough picture.

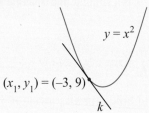

$(x_1, y_1) = (-3, 9)$

k

2. Do $\dfrac{dy}{dx}$ first.

$y = x^2$

$\dfrac{dy}{dx} = 2x$

3. Put the value of x into $\dfrac{dy}{dx}$.

$x = -3$: $\dfrac{dy}{dx} = 2(-3) = -6 = m$

4. Use the formula for the equation of a straight line, $(y - y_1) = m(x - x_1)$, to get the equation of the tangent k.

$(x_1, y_1) = (-3, 9)$, $m = -6$

$(y - 9) = -6(x + 3)$

$k: 6x + y + 9 = 0$

ACTIVITY 1

ACTION
Separating out
constant coefficients
from terms

OBJECTIVE
*To separate out the
constant coefficients
from each term in an
algebraic expression*

Some other rules of differentiation

There are a few other rules of differentiation that enable you to differentiate more difficult functions.

1. Multiplication by a constant rule

> To differentiate a function that is **multiplied by a constant**, just multiply the constant by the differentiated function.

▸ $y = 2x^2$

$\dfrac{dy}{dx} = 2(2x) = 4x$

▸ $y = 5x^4$

$\dfrac{dy}{dx} = 5(4x^3) = 20x^3$

▸ $y = \dfrac{x^3}{3} = \dfrac{1}{3}x^3$

$\dfrac{dy}{dx} = \dfrac{1}{3}(3x^2) = x^2$

▸ $y = \dfrac{-5x^2}{2} = -\dfrac{5}{2}x^2$

$\dfrac{dy}{dx} = -\dfrac{5}{2}(2x) = -5x$

2. The constant rule

The graph of $y = $ constant $= c, c \in \mathbb{R}$, is a line parallel to the x-axis.

Therefore, its slope is 0.

$y = c \Rightarrow \dfrac{dy}{dx} = 0, c$ a constant.

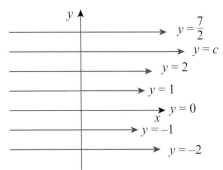

> When you differentiate a **constant on its own**, you get 0.

▸ $y = -3$

$\dfrac{dy}{dx} = 0$

▸ $y = +\dfrac{3}{2}$

$\dfrac{dy}{dx} = 0$

 ## 3. The sum rule

> To differentiate a **sum** of functions, you just differentiate each function individually.

▸ $y = x^2 + x^3$

$\dfrac{dy}{dx} = 2x + 3x^2 = x(2 + 3x)$

▶ $y = 3x^2 + 5x^1 - 7$

$$\frac{dy}{dx} = 3(2x) + 5(1x^0) - 0 = 6x + 5$$

▶ $y = \dfrac{x^3}{3} - \dfrac{5x^2}{2} + 4x - 3$

$$y = \frac{1}{3}x^3 - \frac{5}{2}x^2 + 4x^1 - 3$$

$$\frac{dy}{dx} = \frac{1}{3}(3x^2) - \frac{5}{2}(2x) + 4(1x^0) - 0 = x^2 - 5x + 4$$

Steps for differentiating linear, quadratic and cubic functions

1. Simplify the function, if possible, by multiplying out brackets or by dividing (factors).

▶ $y = (3x - 2)^2 = 9x^2 - 12x + 4$

▶ $\dfrac{4x^2 - 1}{2x - 1} = \dfrac{(2x - 1)(2x + 1)}{(2x - 1)} = 2x + 1$

2. Separate out the constants in front of the variable.

▶ $\dfrac{x}{3} = \dfrac{1}{3}x, \ \dfrac{5x^3}{2} = \dfrac{5}{2}x^3$

3. Differentiate each term in the expression.

4. Tidy up the final expression.

5. Substitute a value if asked.

▶ $y = (3x - 2)^2 = 9x^2 - 12x^1 + 4$

$$\Rightarrow \frac{dy}{dx} = 9(2x) - 12(1x^0) + 0 = 18x - 12 = 6(3x - 2)$$

EXAMPLE 3

In a mountain stage of the Tour de France, the height h in metres of a cyclist above sea level t minutes after starting the climb is given by $h = 4t^3 - 30t^2 + 250t + 130$. Find the rate of change of the cyclist's height above sea level with respect to time after 5 minutes.

Solution

$h = 4t^3 - 30t^2 + 250t^1 + 130$

$\dfrac{dh}{dt} = 4(3t^2) - 30(2t) + 250(1t^0) + 0 = 12t^2 - 60t + 250$

$t = 5: \dfrac{dh}{dt} = 12 \times 25 - 60 \times 5 + 250 = 250$ m/min

EXAMPLE 4

A rocket has a trajectory (path) described by the equation $y = f(x) = 100x(6 - x)$.

Find the slope of the tangent to the curve at:

(a) $x = 1$

(b) $x = 3$

(c) $x = 5$

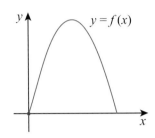

Solution

$y = 100x(6 - x) = 600x - 100x^2$

$\Rightarrow \dfrac{dy}{dx} = 600 - 200x$

(a) $x = 1$: $\dfrac{dy}{dx} = 600 - 200 = 400$

(b) $x = 3$: $\dfrac{dy}{dx} = 600 - 600 = 0$

(c) $x = 5$: $\dfrac{dy}{dx} = 600 - 1000 = -400$

Can you explain these answers by reference to the diagram?

EXAMPLE 5

If $f(x) = \left(\dfrac{5x}{2} - 3\right)^2$, find $f'(4)$.

Solution

$f(x) = \left(\dfrac{5x}{2} - 3\right)^2 = \dfrac{25x^2}{4} - 15x + 9 = \dfrac{25}{4}x^2 - 15x^1 + 9$

Differentiate first.

$f'(x) = \dfrac{25}{4}(2x) - 15(1x^0) + 0$

$f'(x) = \dfrac{25x}{2} - 15$

Now substitute 4 for x:

$f'(4) = \dfrac{25 \times 4}{2} - 15 = 35$

EXAMPLE 6

Find the derivative of $y = \dfrac{(x^2 - 9)(x + 1)}{x + 3}$.

Solution

Simplify first.

$y = \dfrac{(x^2 - 9)(x + 1)}{x + 3} = \dfrac{(x - 3)(x + 3)(x + 1)}{(x + 3)}$

$y = (x - 3)(x + 1) = x^2 - 2x - 3$

$\dfrac{dy}{dx} = 2x - 2(1x^0) - 0 = 2x - 2 = 2(x - 1)$

ACTIVITY 2

ACTION
Differentiating algebraic expressions

OBJECTIVE
To differentiate algebraic expressions and then to differentiate them again (second order differentiation)

Higher order differentiation

A function may be differentiated many times.

Consider $y = f(x) = x^3$.

The first derivative: $\dfrac{dy}{dx} = f'(x) = 3x^2$ is obtained by differentiating $f(x) = x^3$.

The second derivative: $\dfrac{d^2y}{dx^2} = f''(x) = 6x$ is obtained by differentiating $f'(x) = 3x^2$, and so on.

$\dfrac{d^2y}{dx^2}$ is pronounced 'Dee 2 y Dee x squared'.

f'' is pronounced 'f double dash x'.

The slope m of a tangent to a curve is obtained by differentiating the equation

of the curve once: Slope $= m = \dfrac{dy}{dx}$

This means that $\dfrac{d^2y}{dx^2}$ is obtained by differentiating the slope m once: $\dfrac{d^2y}{dx^2} = \dfrac{dm}{dx}$.

$$\frac{dy}{dx} = f'(x) = m \text{ means differentiate } y = f(x) \text{ once.}$$

$$\frac{d^2y}{dx^2} = f''(x) = \frac{dm}{dx} \text{ means differentiate } y = f(x) \text{ twice.}$$

EXAMPLE 7

If $y = \dfrac{x^3}{3} - \dfrac{5x^2}{2} + 7x - 9$, find:

(a) $\dfrac{dy}{dx}$ at $x = 1$ **(b)** $\dfrac{d^2y}{dx^2}$ at $x = -3$

Solution

$$y = \tfrac{1}{3}x^3 - \tfrac{5}{2}x^2 + 7x - 9$$

$$\frac{dy}{dx} = \tfrac{1}{3}(3x^2) - \tfrac{5}{2}(2x) + 7(1x^0) - 0 = x^2 - 5x + 7$$

$$\frac{d^2y}{dx^2} = 2x - 5$$

(a) $x = 1$: $\dfrac{dy}{dx} = (1)^2 - 5(1) + 7 = 3$

(b) $x = -3$: $\dfrac{d^2y}{dx^2} = 2(-3) - 5 = -11$

EXAMPLE 8

If $f(x) = x^3 - 6x^2 + 12x - 1$, find $f''(2)$.

Solution

$$f(x) = x^3 - 6x^2 + 12x - 1$$

$$\begin{aligned} f'(x) &= 3x^2 - 6(2x) + 12(1x^0) - 0 \\ &= 3x^2 - 12x + 12 \end{aligned}$$

$$f''(x) = 3(2x) - 12(1) = 6x - 12$$

$$f''(2) = 6(2) - 12 = 0$$

EXERCISE 2

1. Differentiate the following with respect to x:

(a) $y = x^2$ **(f)** $y = -5x^3$

(b) $y = 2x^3$ **(g)** $y = \dfrac{x^2}{5}$

(c) $y = 4x$ **(h)** $y = \dfrac{x^3}{3}$

(d) $y = 6x^2$ **(i)** $y = \dfrac{2x^2}{5}$

(e) $y = -x^3$ **(j)** $y = -\dfrac{3x^3}{4}$

2. Differentiate the following with respect to x:

(a) $y = 2x + 7$

(b) $y = ax + b$, a, b constants

(c) $y = 3x^2 - 5x + 4$

(d) $y = ax^2 + bx + c$, a, b, c constants

(e) $y = 4x^3 - 5x^2 + 6x - 9$

(f) $y = ax^3 + bx^2 + cx + d$, a, b, c, d constants

(g) $y = \dfrac{x^3}{3} - 5x^2 + 2x - 1$

(h) $y = \dfrac{4x^2}{3} - \dfrac{2}{5}x + 7$

(i) $y = 5x^3 - \dfrac{3x^2}{5} + \dfrac{4x}{3} - 1$

(j) $y = x^3 - x^2 + \dfrac{x}{3} - \dfrac{1}{2}$

3. Differentiate the following with respect to x:

(a) $y = 5 - \dfrac{x^2}{2}$

(b) $y = 4x + \dfrac{x^2}{3} - x^3$

(c) $y = -x^3 + \dfrac{2x^2}{5} - x + \dfrac{1}{2}$

(d) $y = 4(6 - x - x^3)$

(e) $y = \dfrac{(x - x^2 + 2)}{5}$

4. (a) Find $\dfrac{dy}{dx}$ if $y = (x - 1)(x + 2)$.

(b) Find $\dfrac{dy}{dx}$ if $y = (2x - 3)(4x + 5)$.

(c) Find $\dfrac{dy}{dx}$ if $y = x(x - 1)(2x + 1)$.

(d) Find $\dfrac{ds}{dt}$ if $s = (t - 1)(t + 1)t$.

(e) Find $\dfrac{dp}{dv}$ if $p = (3v - 2)^2$.

(f) Find $\dfrac{dl}{dr}$ if $l = \dfrac{r^2 - 1}{r - 1}$.

5. (a) If $y = x^2 + 5x$, find $\dfrac{dy}{dx}$ at $x = -2$.

(b) If $s = 2t^2 + 7t - 3$, find $\dfrac{ds}{dt}$ at $t = 3$.

(c) If $f(x) = \dfrac{x^2}{4} - 2x + 1$, find $f'(8)$.

(d) If $y = x^3 - 4x^2 + 5x - 2$, find $\dfrac{dy}{dx}$ and $\dfrac{d^2y}{dx^2}$.

(e) If $f(x) = 5x^3 - 4x^2 + 7x - 3$, find $f'(2)$ and $f''(-1)$.

(f) Find $\dfrac{dy}{dx}$ at $x = -2$ and $\dfrac{d^2y}{dx^2}$ at $x = -2$ if $y = 3x^3 - 5x^2 + 4x - 2$.

6. (a) Find the rate of change of y with respect to x at $x = \frac{1}{2}$ if $y = 4x^2 - 6x + 1$.

(b) Find the slope and the equation of the tangent to the curve $y = x^2 - 5x + 1$ at $x = 2$.

(c) Find the slope and the equation of the tangent to the curve $y = f(x) = x^3 - 2x^2 + 3x - 2$ at $x = -1$.

7. The air resistance R in Newtons (N) to a body moving with speed v in metres/second is given by $R = \dfrac{3v^2}{70}$. Find the rate of change of R with respect to v when $v = 7$ m/s.

8. (a) For $f(x) = 3x^2 - 5x + 7$, find x if $f'(x) = 1$.

(b) If $g(x) = x^3 - 12x + 7$, find x for which $g'(x) = 0$.

(c) If $y = \dfrac{x^3}{3} - \dfrac{x^2}{2} + x$, solve $\dfrac{dy}{dx} = 3$.

9. On a certain day, the temperature T in $0\,°C$ in an arid region was given by

$T = \dfrac{5t(24 - t)}{24}$, where t is the time in hours

and $t = 0$ corresponds to midnight, $0 \le t < 24$.

Find:

(a) the temperature at 2 a.m., correct to one decimal place,

(b) the temperature at 3 p.m., correct to one decimal place,

(c) the time at which the temperature was $0\,°C$,

(d) the rate of change of the temperature with time at 4 p.m., correct to two decimal places,

(e) the time at which the rate of change is $0\,°C$/h.

10. A spherical balloon is being blown up. Find the rate of change of the volume V (m^3) with respect to the radius r (m) when $r = 3$, if $V = \frac{4}{3}\pi r^3$.

11. (a) Find a if the slope of the tangent to $y = x^2 - ax + 7$ at $x = -4$ is 12.

(b) Find the slope of the tangent to the curve $y = x^3 - 7x^2 + x - 3$ at $x = 1$.

(c) Find a and c if $y = ax + c$ is a tangent to the curve $y = -x^3 + 3x - 2$ at $x = 2$.

CHAPTER 21

Applications of Differentiation

Learning Outcomes

- To understand the nature of curves. To know when a curve is increasing and decreasing.
- To find local maxima and minima.
- To sketch different types of curves.
- To work out rate of change problems.
- To solve modelling and optimisation problems.

21.1 Curves

ACTIVITY 3

ACTION
Understanding the nature of slopes (1)

OBJECTIVE
To draw tangents to curves and explore the geometrical meaning of differentiating curves

When you draw the curve that describes a function $y = f(x)$, you always read the curve from left to right.

This means that the x co-ordinate is **always** increasing: $x_2 - x_1 = 3 - 1 = +2$.

Imagine that you go for a walk in the hills, starting at A, in the graph below.

As you go from A to B, the value of the y co-ordinate is increasing (I) as you are getting higher. The curve then flattens out at B (stationary point). As you go downhill from B to C, the value of the y co-ordinate decreases (D). Now that you are getting lower, the curve flattens out again at C (stationary point). Climbing from the bottom of the valley from C to E, the value of y increases (I) again.

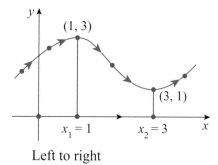

Left to right

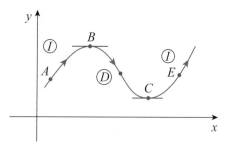

Tangents

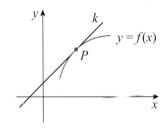

The slope of the tangent at a point on a curve can be found by differentiation.

$$\frac{dy}{dx} = m = \text{the slope of the tangent to the curve } y = f(x)$$

at **any** point P on the curve.

▸ The slope of the tangent to the curve $y = x^3 - 5x^2 + 1$ at any point P **on** the curve is given by $\frac{dy}{dx} = 3x^2 - 10x$.

EXAMPLE 1

Verify that the point $P(1, 5)$ is on the curve $y = 2x^2 + 5x - 2$. Find the slope of the tangent at this point.

Solution

Call the curve f.

$f: y = 2x^2 + 5x - 2$

Is $P(1, 5)$ on f? Substitute the co-ordinates of P into f to see if it satisfies the equation of the curve.

$2(1)^2 + 5(1) - 2 = 2 + 5 - 2 = 5$

$\therefore (1, 5)$ is on f

$\frac{dy}{dx} = 4x + 5$

Always differentiate before substituting values.

$x = 1: \frac{dy}{dx} = 4(1) + 5 = 9$

$m = 9$ is the slope of the tangent at $(1, 5)$.

EXAMPLE 2

At what points on the curve $y = x^3 + x$ do the tangents have a slope of 13?

Solution

$y = x^3 + x$

$\frac{dy}{dx} = 3x^2 + 1$

Slope $= 13 \Rightarrow 3x^2 + 1 = 13$

$3x^2 = 12$

$x^2 = 4$

$\therefore x = \pm 2$

To find the corresponding y co-ordinates, substitute these values back into $y = x^3 + x$ as they are on the curve.

$x = 2$: $y = (2)^3 + 2 = 10$

$x = -2$: $y = (-2)^3 + (-2) = -10$

The points are $(-2, -10)$ and $(2, 10)$. The tangents are parallel at these points. [Same slope]

Point of contact

The point P where a curve and a tangent k touch is called the point of contact and so satisfies **both** the equation of the curve **and** the equation of the tangent.

EXAMPLE 3

If $k: 4x - y - 4 = 0$ is the tangent to the curve $y = x^2$ at the point $P(2, 4)$, show that P is on the curve $y = x^2$ and on the tangent k.

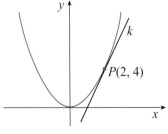

Solution

(a) Is $P(2, 4)$ on $y = x^2$?

Substituting $x = 2$ into $y = x^2$: $2^2 = 4$. Yes.

(b) Is $P(2, 4)$ on k?

Substituting $x = 2$ into $4x - y - 4$: $4(2) - (4) - 4 = 0$. Yes.

$(2, 4)$ satisfies both equations.

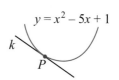

EXAMPLE 4

Find the point of contact of the tangent $k : x + y + 3 = 0$ to the curve $f : y = x^2 - 5x + 1$.

Solution

$k : x + y + 3 = 0$	$(x - 2)(x - 2) = 0$
$y = (-3 - x)$	$x = 2$
Substituting y into f gives: $-3 - x = x^2 - 5x + 1$	$y = -3 - 2 = -5$
$x^2 - 4x + 4 = 0$	$P(2, -5)$ is the point of contact.

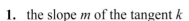

The equation of the tangent

To find the equation of a tangent k to a curve at a point on the curve you need two things:

1. the slope m of the tangent k
2. the point of contact $P(x_1, y_1)$ of the tangent to the curve

Steps for finding the equation of the tangent to a curve at a point $P(x, y)$ on the curve

1. Find $\dfrac{dy}{dx}$ at the point whose x co-ordinate is given. This is the slope m.

2. Find the point of contact $P(x_1, y_1)$ by substituting the x value given into the equation of the curve.

3. Use $(y - y_1) = m(x - x_1)$ to find the equation of the tangent.

EXAMPLE 5

Find the equation of the tangent to the curve $y = x^3 - 2x^2 + 5x - 6$ at $x = 2$.

Solution

1. $y = x^3 - 2x^2 + 5x - 6$

$\dfrac{dy}{dx} = 3x^2 - 4x + 5$

$x = 2 : \dfrac{dy}{dx} = 3(2)^2 - 4(2) + 5 = 9 = m$

2. $x = 2 : y = (2)^3 - 2(2)^2 + 5(2) - 6 = 4$

$(2, 4) = (x_1, y_1)$

3. $(y - y_1) = m(x - x_1)$

$(y - 4) = 9(x - 2)$

$9x - y - 14 = 0$

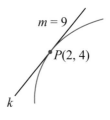

EXERCISE 3

1. Find the slope of the tangent to the curve with the given equation:

   (a) $y = x^2 - x - 2$ at $(2, 0)$

   (b) $y = -2x^2 + 5x - 3$ at $(1, 0)$

   (c) $y = x^3 - 2x^2 + 3x - 2$ at $x = -1$

   (d) $y = 3x^3 - 4x^2 + 5x - 1$ at $x = 1$

   (e) $y = x^3 + x^2 - 1$ at $x = -\dfrac{1}{2}$

2. Find the equation of the tangent to the curve for each of the following:

   (a) $y = x^2 - 3x + 5$ at $x = 1$

   (b) $y = x^3 - 5x^2 + 2x - 3$ at $x = -1$

   (c) $y = 3x^2 - 7x + 2$ at $x = 2$

   (d) $y = 4x^3 - 6x^2 + 5x - 2$ at $x = -2$

   (e) $y = (x + 3)^3$ at $(-1, 8)$

3. Find the point of contact of the tangent k and the curve f for each of the following:

   (a) $k: 2x + y + 1 = 0$

   $f: y = x^2$

   (b) $k: x + y + 2 = 0$

   $f: y = x^2 - 5x + 2$

   (c) $k: 3x - y - 8 = 0$

   $f: y = x^2 - 3x + 1$

   (d) $k: 11x + y - 5 = 0$

   $f: y = 3 - 7x - 2x^2$

4. **(a)** Find the point on the curve $y = x^2 - 3x + 1$ at which the slope of the tangent is -1.

   (b) Find the point on the curve $y = 2x^2 + 12x + 4$ at which the slope of the tangent is 8.

   (c) Find the co-ordinates of the points on the curve $y = 2x^3 - 3x^2 - 6x - 1$ at which the slope of the tangent is 6.

   (d) Find the co-ordinates of the points on the curve $y = (x^2 - 1)(2x + 3)$ at which the slope of the tangent is 10.

5. **(a)** Find the co-ordinates of the point on the curve $y = x^2 - x + 11$ at which the tangent is parallel to the line $l: 3x - y + 4 = 0$.

   (b) Find the co-ordinates of the points on the curve $y = 2x^3 + 3x^2 - 30x - 50$ at which the tangents are perpendicular to the line $l: x + 6y - 1 = 0$.

   (c) Find the co-ordinates of the points on the curve $y = x^3 + 4x^2 + 5x - 7$ at which the tangent makes an angle of $45°$ with the $+x$-axis.

   (d) Find the co-ordinates of the point on the curve $y = 2x^2 - 12x + 3$ at which the tangent is parallel to the x-axis.

   (e) If $y = f(x) = x^3 - 6x^2 + 12$, find $f'(x)$. If (x_1, y_1) and (x_2, y_2) are the two points on the curve $y = f(x)$ at which the tangents are parallel to the x-axis, show that:

   (i) $x_2 - x_1 = 4$, if $x_2 > x_1$

   (ii) $y_2 = y_1 - 32$

⚡ Increasing and decreasing functions

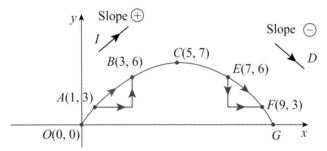

Increasing (I): As you walk from O to C along the curve shown, the y co-ordinate **increases** as the x co-ordinate increases between the two points.

Consider the walk from A to B:

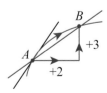

The slope of the line AB = the average rate of change of y with respect to x from A to $B = \dfrac{+3}{+2} = +1·5$.

The slope is positive in this increasing part of the curve. This means the instantaneous rate of change of y with respect to x is also positive (sloping upwards) because the slope of the tangent at every point in this 'increasing' region is positive.

ACTIVITY 4

ACTION
Understanding the nature of slopes (2)

OBJECTIVE
To further explore the geometrical meaning of differentiating curves

So, $\dfrac{dy}{dx} > 0$ for all points in an increasing part of a curve.

This is true for all points from O to C.

> A curve is increasing at a point P on a curve if $\dfrac{dy}{dx} > 0$ at this point.

This simply means that the slope of the tangent at any point of an increasing region is positive.

Decreasing (D): As you walk from C to G along the curve, the y co-ordinate **decreases** as the x co-ordinate increases between any two points.

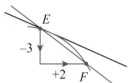

Consider the walk from E to F:

The slope of the line EF = the average rate of change of y with respect to

x from E to $F = \dfrac{-3}{+2} = -1{\cdot}5$.

The slope is negative in this decreasing part of the curve. This means the instantaneous rate of change of y with respect to x is also negative (sloping downwards) because the slope of the tangent at every point in this 'decreasing' region is negative.

So, $\dfrac{dy}{dx} < 0$ for all points in a decreasing part of a curve.

> A curve is decreasing at a point P on a curve if $\dfrac{dy}{dx} < 0$ at this point.

This is true for all points from C to G.

EXAMPLE 6

Show that the point $(2, -3)$ is on the curve $y = x^3 - 5x^2 + 7x - 5$ and investigate if the curve is increasing or decreasing at this point.

Solution

$x = 2$: $y = x^3 - 5x^2 + 7x - 5$

$\qquad = (2)^3 - 5(2)^2 + 7(2) - 5$

$\qquad = 8 - 20 + 14 - 5 = -3$

$(2, -3)$ is on the curve.

$\dfrac{dy}{dx} = 3x^2 - 10x + 7$

$x = 2$: $\dfrac{dy}{dx} = 3(2)^2 - 10(2) + 7$

$\qquad = -1 < 0$

Therefore, the curve is decreasing at $x = 2$.

EXAMPLE 7

Find the range of values of x, $x \in \mathbb{R}$, for which $y = 3x^2 - 12x + 1$ is increasing.

Solution

$y = 3x^2 - 12x + 1$

$\dfrac{dy}{dx} = 6x - 12$

Increasing: $\dfrac{dy}{dx} > 0$

$6x - 12 > 0$

$6x > 12$

$x > 2, x \in \mathbb{R}$

ACTIVITY 5

ACTION
Understanding the nature of slopes (3)

OBJECTIVE
To continue exploring the geometrical meaning of differentiating curves

EXAMPLE 8

The volume V (cm^3) of water in a tank after time t (hours) is given by $V = 3t(5t - 12)$.

Investigate if the volume V is increasing or decreasing at:

(a) $t = 1$

(b) $t = 2$

Solution

$$V = 3t(5t - 12) = 15t^2 - 36t$$
$$\frac{dV}{dt} = 30t - 36$$

(a) $t = 1$: $\frac{dV}{dt} = -6 < 0$

After 1 hour, the volume of water is decreasing.

(b) $t = 2$: $\frac{dV}{dt} = 60 - 36 = 24 > 0$

After 2 hours, the volume of water is increasing.

EXERCISE 4

1. Show that $y = 3x - 2$ is increasing for all $x \in \mathbb{R}$.

2. Show that $(-1, 3)$ is on the curve $y = 3x^2 + 7x + 7$ and that it is increasing at this point.

3. Show that $y = x^3$ is increasing for all $x \in \mathbb{R}$.

4. If $f(x) = x^2 - 4$, find the range of values of $x \in \mathbb{R}$ for which $f(x)$ is decreasing.

5. If $y = x^2 - 8x - 3$, find the range of values of $x \in \mathbb{R}$ for which y is increasing.

6. The speed v of a particle in m/s moving in a straight line at time t, in seconds, is given by $v = 5 - 3t + 4t^2 - t^3$. Investigate if the speed is increasing at:

    (a) $t = 1$ **(b)** $t = 2$ **(c)** $t = 3$

Can you interpret these results?

7. The temperature T (°C) at time t in hours on a given day is $T = \frac{1}{6}t(24 - t)$, $0 \le t < 24$.

($t = 0$ is midnight.) Investigate if the temperature is increasing or decreasing at:

    (a) $t = 3$ **(c)** $t = 15$

    (b) $t = 11$ **(d)** $t = 20$

8. The percentage efficiency E of a car engine is given by $E = 0 \cdot 78v - 0 \cdot 00005v^3$, where v is the speed of a car in km/h. Investigate if the efficiency is increasing or decreasing at:

    (a) $v = 40$ **(b)** $v = 60$ **(c)** $v = 120$

Local maxima and local minima
Local maximum (L Max)

As you walk from A to B and then to C around the hill with equation $y = 8x - x^2$, the slope m of the tangent to the curve is **decreasing** as x **increases.** The slope changes from positive values from A to B, to 0 at B, and then to negative values from B to C.

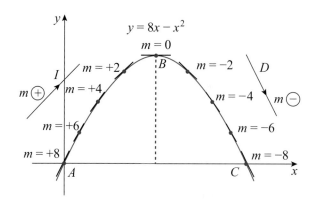

> The slope of the tangent to the curve at every point on this curve is decreasing.

The actual values for the slopes are obtained by differentiation:

$$y = 8x - x^2$$

$$\frac{dy}{dx} = 8 - 2x = m$$

x	0	1	2	3	4	5	6	7	8
m	8	6	4	2	0	-2	-4	-6	-8

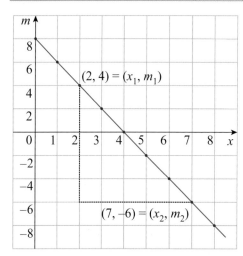

$$\frac{dm}{dx} = \frac{m_2 - m_1}{x_2 - x_1}$$

$$= \frac{-6 - 4}{7 - 2}$$

$$= -2 < 0$$

The slope m is **decreasing** for all values of $x \Rightarrow \dfrac{dm}{dx} < 0$ for all $x \in \mathbb{R}$.

> $$\frac{dm}{dx} = \frac{d^2y}{dx^2} < 0 \text{ for all points on this curve.}$$

There are many points on this curve but there is only one point at which the curve flattens out. This point is the top of the hill (point B). It is known as a **local maximum** point of the curve. At B, the slope of the tangent is 0 as the curve flattens out. At a local maximum point of a curve, two conditions hold:

> **1.** $\dfrac{dy}{dx} = 0$ at the point   [slope = 0]
>
> **2.** $\dfrac{d^2y}{dx^2} < 0$ at the point   [slope m is decreasing from $m(+)$ to $m(-)$]

ACTIVITY **6**

ACTION
Sketching graphs
of first and second
derivatives

OBJECTIVE
*To sketch the graphs
of the first and second
derivatives of functions*

Local minimum (L Min)

As you walk from A to B and then to C around the valley with equation $y = x^2 - 4x + 8$, the slope m of the tangent is **increasing** as x **increases**. The slope changes from negative values from A to B, to 0 at B, and then to positive values from B to C.

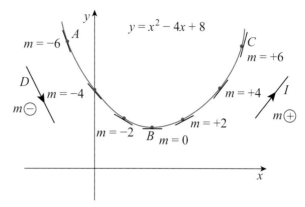

> The slope of the tangent to the curve at every point on this curve is increasing.

The actual values for the slopes are obtained by differentiation:

$y = x^2 - 4x + 8$

$\dfrac{dy}{dx} = 2x - 4 = m$

x	-1	0	1	2	3	4	5
m	-6	-4	-2	0	2	4	6

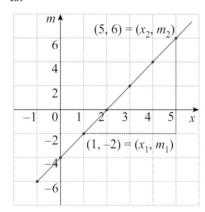

$\dfrac{dm}{dx} = \dfrac{m_2 - m_1}{x_2 - x_1}$

$= \dfrac{6 + 2}{5 - 1}$

$= +2$

The slope m is increasing for all values of $x \Rightarrow \dfrac{dm}{dx} > 0$ for all $x \in \mathbb{R}$.

> $\dfrac{dm}{dx} = \dfrac{d^2y}{dx^2} > 0$ for all points on this curve.

There are many points on this curve but there is only one point at which the curve flattens out. This point is the bottom of the valley (point B). It is known as a **local minimum** point of the curve. At B, the slope of the tangent is 0 as the curve flattens out. At a local minimum point of a curve, two conditions hold:

> **1.** $\dfrac{dy}{dx} = 0$ at the point   [slope = 0] $m\ominus \searrow \nearrow m\oplus$
>
> **2.** $\dfrac{d^2y}{dx^2} > 0$ at the point   [slope m is increasing from $m(-)$ to $m(+)$]

ACTION
Increasing and
decreasing regions

OBJECTIVE
*To mark in the increasing
and decreasing regions
of various curves*

Stationary points

In general, a curve may have several local maxima and local minima.

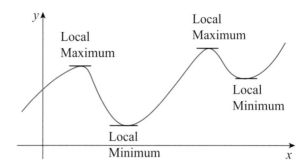

These points all have one thing in common. At every one of them, the curve flattens out. The slope of the tangent at these points is 0.

These points are collectively known as stationary points.

> A point on any curve at which $\dfrac{dy}{dx} = 0$ is known as a stationary point (SP).

WORKED EXAMPLE — Stationary points

A curve $y = f(x)$ is plotted in the domain $0 \le x \le 6$.

$(2, 8)$ is a stationary point as $\dfrac{dy}{dx} = 0$ at this point and is a local

maximum as the slope is decreasing at $(2, 8)$.

$(4, 2)$ is a stationary point as $\dfrac{dy}{dx} = 0$ at this point and is a local

minimum as the slope is increasing at $(4, 2)$.

0 is the minimum value of y in the domain.

9 is the maximum value of y in the domain.

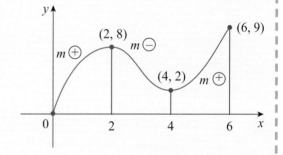

> To find the stationary points of a curve, simply put $\dfrac{dy}{dx} = 0$ and solve for x and then for y.

EXAMPLE 9

Find the stationary point of the curve
$y = -3x^2 + 18x - 5$.

Solution

$y = -3x^2 + 18x - 5$

$\dfrac{dy}{dx} = -6x + 18$

Stationary point: $\dfrac{dy}{dx} = 0$

$-6x + 18 = 0$

$x = 3$ [There is only one stationary point.]

$\boldsymbol{x = 3}$: $y = -3(3)^2 + 18(3) - 5 = 22$ [Put x into the
equation of the
curve.]

Therefore, $(3, 22)$ is the stationary point.

EXAMPLE 10

Find the stationary points of the curve
$y = 4x^3 - 6x^2 - 24x - 14$.

Solution

$y = 4x^3 - 6x^2 - 24x - 14$

$\dfrac{dy}{dx} = 12x^2 - 12x - 24$

Stationary point: $\dfrac{dy}{dx} = 0$

$12x^2 - 12x - 24 = 0$

$x^2 - x - 2 = 0$

$(x + 1)(x - 2) = 0$

$x = -1, 2$ [There are two stationary points.]

$\boldsymbol{x = -1}$: $y = 4(-1)^3 - 6(-1)^2 - 24(-1) - 14 = 0$

$\boldsymbol{x = 2}$: $y = 4(2)^3 - 6(2)^2 - 24(2) - 14 = -54$

Therefore, $(-1, 0)$ and $(2, -54)$ are the stationary points of this curve.

EXAMPLE 11

Find k if $y = 2x^2 + kx - 1$ has a stationary point at $x = -2$, $k \in \mathbb{R}$.

Solution

$y = 2x^2 + kx - 3$

$\dfrac{dy}{dx} = 4x + k$

At $\boldsymbol{x = -2}$: $\dfrac{dy}{dx} = -8 + k = 0$

$k = 8$

ACTIVITY 8

ACTION
Exploring turning points

OBJECTIVE
To explore the properties of the stationary points of curves

Finding the local maxima and local minima of a function

Conditions for a local maximum

Top $\frown$ Slope = 0 Flat	$\dfrac{dy}{dx} = 0$
$\oplus$ $\ominus$ Slope decreasing	$\dfrac{d^2y}{dx} < 0$

Conditions for a local minimum

$\smile$ Bottom Slope = 0 Flat	$\dfrac{dy}{dx} = 0$
$\ominus$ $\oplus$ Slope increasing	$\dfrac{d^2y}{dx^2} > 0$

Steps for finding local maxima and minima:

1. Find $\dfrac{dy}{dx}$.

2. Solve $\dfrac{dy}{dx} = 0$ to get all the stationary points.

3. Find $\dfrac{d^2y}{dx^2}$.

4. Test each stationary point in $\dfrac{d^2y}{dx^2}$ to decide if it is a local maximum or a local minimum.

5. Evaluate the y co-ordinates of each stationary point by substituting back into the equation of the function.

If there is only one stationary point of a function in a domain, then not only is it a local maximum or a local minimum, it is also the maximum or minimum value of the function in the domain.

> Local maxima and local minima are collectively known as turning points.

EXAMPLE 12

Find the local maxima and local minima, if any, of $y = 6 - 4x - x^2$, $x \in \mathbb{R}$.

Solution

$y = 6 - 4x - x^2$

1. $\boxed{\dfrac{dy}{dx} = -4 - 2x}$

2. $\dfrac{dy}{dx} = 0$

   $-4 - 2x = 0$

   $x = -2$ [There is only one stationary point.]

3. $\dfrac{d^2y}{dx^2} = -4$

4. $-4 < 0$ means that the stationary point is a local maximum.

5. $x = -2$: $y = 6 - 4(-2) - (-2)^2 = 6 + 8 - 4 = 10$

   The local maximum is at $(-2, 10)$.

   Only one stationary point means that $y = 10$ is the maximum value of this function.

EXAMPLE 13

Find the local maxima and local minima, if any, of the function $y = 2 - 9x + 6x^2 - x^3$, $x \in \mathbb{R}$.

Solution

$y = 2 - 9x + 6x^2 - x^3$

1. $\boxed{\dfrac{dy}{dx} = -9 + 12x - 3x^2}$

2. $-9 + 12x - 3x^2 = 0$

   $x^2 - 4x + 3 = 0$

   $(x - 3)(x - 1) = 0$

   $x = 1, 3$

3. $\dfrac{d^2y}{dx^2} = 12 - 6x$

4. $x = 1$: $\dfrac{d^2y}{dx^2} = 12 - 6 = 6 > 0$

   Therefore, there is a local minimum at $x = 1$.

   $x = 3$: $\dfrac{d^2y}{dx^2} = 12 - 18 = -6 < 0$

   Therefore, there is a local maximum at $x = 3$.

5. $x = 1$: $y = 2 - 9 + 6 - 1 = -2$

   $x = 3$: $y = 2 - 9(3) + 6(3)^2 - (3)^3 = 2$

   Therefore, the local minimum is $(1, -2)$ and the local maximum is $(3, 2)$.

In curve sketching, you will see that quadratic functions, $y = ax^2 + bx + c$, always have a local maximum *or* a local minimum but cubic functions, $y = ax^3 + bx^2 + cx + d$, normally have a local maximum *and* a local minimum.

EXERCISE 5

1. Find the stationary point(s) of the functions below and state if these are local maxima or local minima:

   (a) $y = x^2 - 4x + 5, x \in \mathbb{R}$

   (b) $y = -3x^2 + 18x - 5, x \in \mathbb{R}$

   (c) $y = x^3 - 3x^2 - 9x - 3, x \in \mathbb{R}$

   (d) $y = 11 - 12x + 9x^2 - 2x^3, x \in \mathbb{R}$

   (e) $y = -x^3 - 3x^2 + 7, x \in \mathbb{R}$

2. Find the maximum value of $y = -2x^2 - 8x + 7$, $x \in \mathbb{R}$.

3. Find the stationary point of $y = ax^2 + bx + c$ and show it is a local maximum if $a < 0$ and a local minimum if $a > 0$.

4. The graph of a cubic function $y = f(x)$ in the domain $-2 \leq x \leq 5, x \in \mathbb{R}$, is shown.

   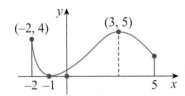

   (a) Write down the co-ordinates of:

      (i) the local minimum

      (ii) the local maximum

   (b) Find:

      (i) the maximum value of y in the domain

      (ii) the minimum value of y in the domain

5. Find the local maximum and local minimum of $y = 4x^3 - 6x^2 - 24x - 14, x \in \mathbb{R}$.

   The graph of $y = 4x^3 - 6x^2 - 24x - 14$, $-2 \leq x \leq 3, x \in \mathbb{R}$, is shown.

   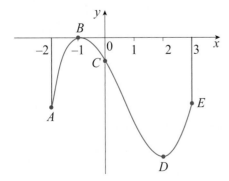

   (a) Find the co-ordinates of A, B, C, D and E.

   (b) What name is given to B?

   (c) What name is given to D?

   (d) Find the range of values of x for which y is decreasing.

   (e) What is the maximum value of y in the domain?

   (f) What is the minimum value of y in the domain?

6. (a) If $f(x) = x^2 + px + 10, x \in \mathbb{R}$, find $f'(x)$. If the minimum value of $f(x)$ is at $x = 3$, find $p \in \mathbb{Z}$.

   (b) If $f(x) = 3 + 8x - 2x^2, x \in \mathbb{R}$, find $f'(x)$.

      (i) Find where the curve crosses the y-axis.

      (ii) Find the maximum value of $f(x)$.

      (iii) For what range of values is $f'(x) > 4$?

   (c) If $f(x) = x^3 - 3x^2 + kx + 2, x \in \mathbb{R}$ has a stationary point at $x = 1$, find k and the co-ordinates of the stationary point.

   (d) The slope of the tangent to the curve $y = x^3 - kx + 7, x \in \mathbb{R}$ at $x = 1$ is -9, find $k \in \mathbb{R}$. Hence, find the co-ordinates of the local maximum and local minimum of this curve.

   (e) $f(x) = (x + k)(x - 2)^2$. If $f(3) = 7$, find $k \in \mathbb{R}$. Hence, find the local maximum and local minimum of $f(x)$.

   (f) $f(x) = ax^3 + bx + c$. Find $a, b, c, \in \mathbb{R}$, if:

      (i) $f(0) = 3$

      (ii) the slope of the tangent at $x = 1$ is -18

      (iii) the curve has a local maximum at $x = 2$

   (g) If $f(x) = x^3 - 3x^2 + kx + 1$ has a stationary point at $x = -1$, find $k \in \mathbb{R}$. Find the local maximum and local minimum of $f(x)$.

7. The level h in centimetres of water varies with time t in hours after 5 a.m. ($t = 0$) according to the equation $h = 16t^2 - 180t + 600$, $0 \leq t \leq 12$. Find the minimum value of the level of the water and when it occurs, to the nearest minute.

8. A cannon fires a shell along the path given by the formula $h = x(40 - x)$, where h is the height of the shell above the ground in metres and x is its horizontal distance in metres from $O(0, 0)$. The shell lands at B.

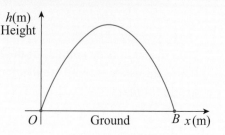

(a) Find:

    (i) how far from O it lands,

    (ii) its maximum height above the ground.

(b) Find the slope of the tangent at
    (i) O and (ii) B.

Curve sketching

The most important points in sketching a curve are the local maxima and minima.

Steps for sketching a curve

1. Find all local maxima and local minima (turning points).

2. Find where the curve crosses:

    (i) the y-axis

    (ii) the x-axis, if possible

3. Find all other points in the domain.

4. Plot a smooth curve on graph paper.

Types of curve

(a) Quadratic curves   (b) Cubic curves   (c) Exponential curves

(a) Quadratic curves: $y = ax^2 + bx + c$

1. Local maxima and minima: $y = ax^2 + bx + c$

    (i) $\dfrac{dy}{dx} = 2ax + b = 0$

        $x = -\dfrac{b}{2a}$

> Quadratic functions always have one and only one stationary point at $x = -\dfrac{b}{2a}$.

    (ii) $\dfrac{d^2y}{dx^2} = 2a$

        If $a > 0$ the slope is increasing $\searrow\!\!\nearrow$ always.

        Therefore, the shape is $\smile$ and $x = -\dfrac{b}{2a}$ gives a local minimum.

        If $a < 0$ the slope is decreasing $\nearrow\!\!\searrow$ always.

        Therefore, the shape is $\frown$ and $x = -\dfrac{b}{2a}$ gives a local maximum.

2. Crossing the axes: $y = ax^2 + bx + c$

   (i) y-axis: $x = 0$: $y = c$ [The curve always crosses the y axis at $(0, c)$.]

   (ii) x-axis: $y = 0$: $ax^2 + bx + c = 0$

No solutions if $b^2 < 4ac$	Two equal solutions if $b^2 = 4ac$	Two different solutions if $b^2 > 4ac$
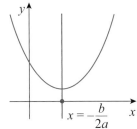		
Does not cross x-axis	Touches the x-axis at the local maximum or local minimum	Cuts the x-axis at two different points

3. The axis of symmetry has the equation $x = -\dfrac{b}{2a}$.

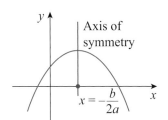

Conclusion

$a > 0$: Shape ⌣	$a < 0$: Shape ⌢
Local minimum at $x = -\dfrac{b}{2a}$	Local maximum at $x = -\dfrac{b}{2a}$
Crosses y-axis at $(0, c)$	Crosses y-axis at $(0, c)$
Axis of symmetry $x = -\dfrac{b}{2a}$	Axis of symmetry $x = -\dfrac{b}{2a}$

EXAMPLE 14

Plot the curve with equation $y = 6 + 2x - x^2$ in the domain $-2 \le x \le 4$, $x \in \mathbb{R}$, by finding the local maximum.

(a) Estimate where the curve crosses the x-axis, correct to one decimal place.

(b) Use the graph to find the range of values of x in the domain for which:

   (i) $f(x) \le 0$ **(ii)** $f'(x) \le 0$

(c) Find the equation of the axis of symmetry of the curve.

Solution

$y = 6 + 2x - x^2$, $-2 \le x \le 4$

1. $\boxed{\dfrac{dy}{dx} = 2 - 2x}$

$\dfrac{dy}{dx} = 0$

$2 - 2x = 0$

$x = 1$ [There is only one stationary point.]

$\dfrac{d^2y}{dx^2} = -2 < 0$

Therefore, there is a local maximum at $x = 1$.

$x = 1$: $y = 6 + 2 - 1 = 7$.

The local maximum is $(1, 7)$.

2. $x = 0$: $y = 6 + 2(0) - (0)^2 = 6$

The curve crosses the y-axis at $(0, 6)$.

$y = 0$: $6 + 2x - x^2 = 0$

$x^2 - 2x - 6 = 0$

Solve this equation using the quadratic formula.

$x = 1 \pm \sqrt{7}$

3.

x	-2	-1	0	1	2	3	4
y	-2	3	6	7	6	3	-2

(a) $E : x = -1 \cdot 6, F : x = 3 \cdot 6$

(b) (i) $f(x) \le 0 \Rightarrow y \le 0$. The y values on the curve on or below the x-axis are:

$$-2 \le x \le -1 \cdot 6, \; 3 \cdot 6 \le x \le 4, \; x \in \mathbb{R}$$

(ii) $f'(x) \le 0$ means that the curve is decreasing or is flat.

$$\therefore \; 1 \le x \le 4, x \in \mathbb{R}$$

(c) Axis of symmetry: $x = 1$

4.

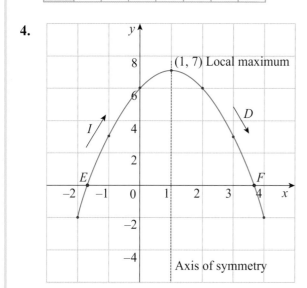

EXAMPLE 15

(a) Plot $y = f(x) = x^2 + 2x - 8$ in the domain $-5 \le x \le 3, x \in \mathbb{R}$, by finding the local maximum and local minimum, if any.

(b) On the same diagram, plot $g(x) = 2x - 6$ in the domain $-2 \le x \le 4, x \in \mathbb{R}$.

(c) Use your graph to find the point at which $f(x) = g(x)$, $x > 0$ and hence estimate $\sqrt{2}$, correct to one decimal place.

Solution

(a) 1. $y = x^2 + 2x - 8$ is a quadratic ($a = 1 > 0$). Therefore, it is shaped as follows: $\smile$

Local minimum is at $x = -\dfrac{b}{2a} = \dfrac{-2}{2} = -1$.

$x = -1$: $y = (-1)^2 + 2(-1) - 8 = -9$

The local minimum is $(-1, -9)$.

2. y-axis: $(0, c) = (0, -8)$

3.

x	-5	-4	-3	-2	-1	0	1	2	3
y	7	0	-5	-8	-9	-8	-5	0	7

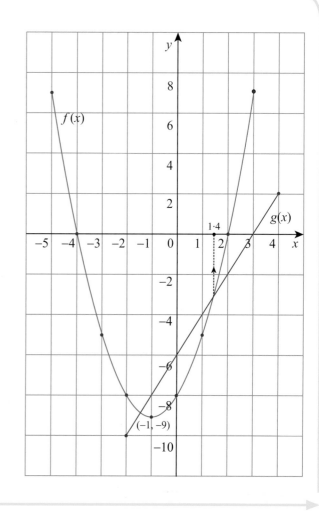

(b) $g(x) = 2x - 6$

This graph is a straight line so you just need to use the extreme points.

x	-2	4
$g(x)$	-10	2

(c) $f(x) = g(x)$

$x^2 + 2x - 8 = 2x - 6$

$x^2 = 2$

$x^2 = \pm\sqrt{2}$

$\therefore \sqrt{2} \approx 1 \cdot 4$

(b) Cubic curves: $y = ax^3 + bx^2 + cx + d$

1. Local maxima and local minima: $y = ax^3 + bx^2 + cx + d$

    $$\frac{dy}{dx} = 3ax^2 + 2bx + c = 0$$

    Solve this quadratic equation to get the stationary points. Test the stationary points in $\frac{d^2y}{dx^2} = 6ax + 2b$ to get the local maximum and local minimum (turning points).

2. Crossing the axes:

    (i) *y*-**axis:** $x = 0$: $y = (0, d)$ always

    (ii) *x*-**axis:** Solve $y = 0$ if you can.

    Shapes:

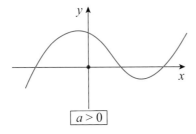

$\boxed{a > 0}$

or

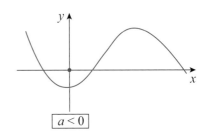

$\boxed{a < 0}$

EXAMPLE 16

(a) Find the co-ordinates of the local maximum and the local minimum of $y = f(x) = 4 - 9x + 6x^2 - x^3$, $x \in \mathbb{R}$.

(b) Plot the curve in the domain $-1 \leq x \leq 5$, $x \in \mathbb{R}$.

(c) Use the graph to find the range of values of x for which: **(i)** $f(x) \geq 0$ **(ii)** $f'(x) < 0$

Solution

$y = 4 - 9x + 6x^2 - x^3$

(a) $\boxed{\dfrac{dy}{dx} = -9 + 12x - 3x^2}$

$-9 + 12x - 3x^2 = 0$

$x^2 - 4x + 3 = 0$

$(x - 1)(x - 3) = 0 \Rightarrow x = 1, 3$

$\dfrac{d^2y}{dx^2} = 12 - 6x$

$x = 1$: $\dfrac{d^2y}{dx^2} = 12 - 6(1) = 6 > 0$

There is a local minimum at $x = 1$.

$x = 1$: $y = 4 - 9(1) + 6(1)^2 - (1)^3 = 0$

$(1, 0)$ is a local minimum.

$x = 3$: $\dfrac{d^2y}{dx^2} = 12 - 6(3) = -6 < 0$

There is a local maximum at $x = 3$.

$x = 3$: $y = 4 - 9(3) + 6(3)^2 - (3)^3 = 4$

$(3, 4)$ is a local maximum.

(b) Crosses y-axis: $x = 0$: $y = 4$

(0, 4) is the point where the curve crosses the y-axis.

x	-1	0	1	2	3	4	5
y	20	4	0	2	4	0	-16

(c) (i) $f(x) = y \geq 0$: Curve is above or on the x-axis from $-1 \leq x \leq 4$, $x \in \mathbb{R}$.

(ii) $f'(x) < 0$: Curve is decreasing from $-1 \leq x < 1, 3 < x \leq 5, x \in \mathbb{R}$.

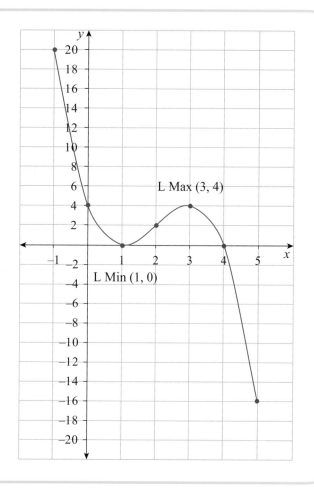

EXAMPLE 17

(a) Find the co-ordinates of the local maximum and the local minimum of the function
$y = f(x) = x^3 - 12x + 2, x \in \mathbb{R}$.

(b) Plot $y = f(x)$ in the domain $-3 \leq x \leq 3, x \in \mathbb{R}$.

(c) Plot $g(x) = -12x + 6$ on the same diagram.

(d) Use your graph to find the point at which $f(x) = g(x)$ hence, estimate $\sqrt[3]{4}$, correct to one decimal place.

Solution

(a) $y = f(x) = x^3 - 12x + 2$

$$\boxed{\frac{dy}{dx} = 3x^2 - 12}$$

$\frac{dy}{dx} = 0$

$3x^2 - 12 = 0$

$x^2 = 4$

$x = \pm\sqrt{4} = \pm 2$ [There are two stationary points.]

$\frac{d^2y}{dx^2} = 6x$

$x = 2$: $\frac{d^2y}{dx^2} = 12 > 0$ ⌣

There is a local minimum at $x = 2$.

$x = 2$: $y = (2)^3 - 12(2) + 2 = -14$

(2, -14) is a local minimum.

$x = -2$: $\frac{d^2y}{dx^2} = -12 < 0$ ⌢

There is a local maximum at $x = -2$.

$x = -2$: $y = (-2)^3 - 12(-2) + 2 = 18$

(-2, 18) is a local maximum.

(b) Crosses y-axis: $x = 0$: $y = 2$

The curve crosses the y-axis at $(0, 2)$.

x	−3	−2	−1	0	1	2	3
y	11	18	13	2	−9	−14	−7

(c) $g(x) = -12x + 6$

This function represents a straight line so you need just two points to draw it.

x	0	1
$g(x)$	6	−6

(d) $f(x) = g(x)$

$$x^3 - 12x + 2 = -12x + 6$$
$$x^3 = 4$$
$$x = \sqrt[3]{4} \approx 1 \cdot 6$$

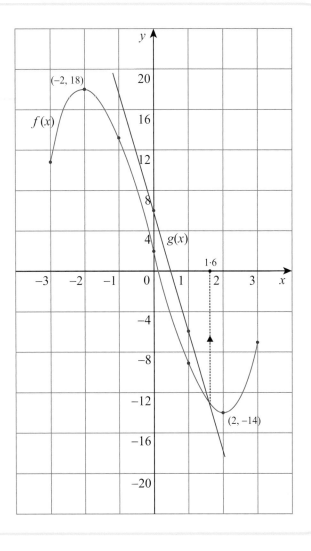

(c) Exponential curves: $y = ka^{bx}$, $k \in \mathbb{N}$, $a > 0$, $a \in \mathbb{R}$

1. These have no local maxima or minima.

2. If $0 < a < 1$, they are always decreasing.
   If $a > 1$, they are always increasing.

3. They never cross the x-axis but **always** cross the y-axis at $(0, k)$ because:
   $x = 0 \Rightarrow y = ka^0 = k$.

4. General shape

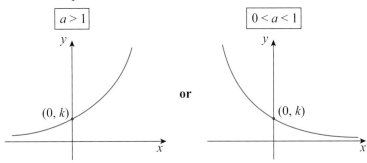

5. To plot these curves, use the x values in the domain to find the y values using your calculator.

6. Remember: $2^{-x} = \dfrac{1}{2^x} = \left(\dfrac{1}{2}\right)^x$

EXAMPLE 18

(a) Plot $f(x) = 3 \times 2^{-x}$ in the domain $-2 \leq x \leq 3$, $x \in \mathbb{R}$.

(b) Plot $g(x) = 5$ on the same diagram.

(c) Use your graphs to estimate the solution of $2^{-x} = \frac{5}{3}$, correct to one decimal place.

Solution

(a) $f(x) = 3 \times 2^{-x} = 3\left(\dfrac{1}{2^x}\right)$

x	-2	-1	0	1	2	3
y	12	6	3	1·5	0·75	0·375

(b) $g(x) = 5$ is the line $y = 5$.

(c) $f(x) = g(x)$

$3 \times 2^{-x} = 5$

$2^{-x} = \dfrac{5}{3}$

$x \approx -0·7$

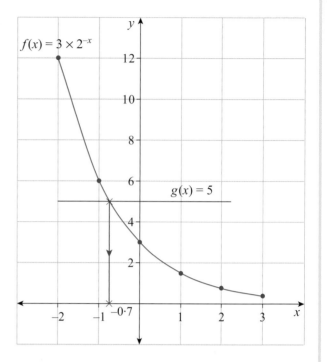

EXERCISE 6

1. Find the co-ordinates of the local minimum of the function $y = f(x) = x^2 - 4x + 2$ and plot it in the domain $0 \leq x \leq 4$, $x \in \mathbb{R}$.

    (a) Use the graph to find:

        (i) the solutions of $x^2 - 4x + 2 = 0$, correct to one decimal place,

        (ii) the range of values of x for which $f(x) < 0$,

        (iii) the range of values of x for which $f'(x) \leq 0$.

    (b) Find the equation of the axis of symmetry of the curve.

    (c) Find the equation of the tangent to the curve parallel to the line $2x - y - 1 = 0$.

2. **(a)** Find the co-ordinates of the local minimum of $y = x^2 - x - 6$ and plot this function in the domain $-3 \leq x \leq 4$, $x \in \mathbb{R}$.

    (b) **(i)** Use the graph to find the range of values of x for which $x^2 - x - 6 \leq 0$.

        (ii) Say why there are no real solutions of the equation $y = -8$.

        (iii) Are there any real solutions to $x^2 - x + 2 = 0$? Why?

3. If $x = 1$ is the axis of symmetry of $y = x^2 + bx + c$, $x \in \mathbb{R}$, find b. Find c if the curve crosses the y-axis at $(0, -3)$.

4. Let $y = f(x) = 3 - 5x - 2x^2, x \in \mathbb{R}$.

   (a) Find $f'(x)$ and hence, the co-ordinates of the local maximum of the curve $y = f(x)$.

   (b) Solve $f(x) = 0$.

   (c) Plot $y = 3 - 5x - 2x^2$ and $2x + y = 0$ on the same diagram.

   (d) Use your graphs to estimate the solutions of $2x^2 + 3x - 3 = 0$, correct to one decimal place.

5. **(a)** Find the co-ordinates of the local maximum and local minimum of $y = x^3 - 6x^2, x \in \mathbb{R}$.

   (b) Find where the curve crosses the axes.

   (c) Plot the curve in the domain $-2 \le x \le 6$, $x \in \mathbb{R}$.

   (d) Find the range of values for which the curve is decreasing.

6. Let $y = f(x) = x^3 - 3x^2, x \in \mathbb{R}$.

   (a) Find $f'(x)$ and hence, find the co-ordinates of the local maximum and local minimum of the curve.

   (b) Plot the graph of $y = f(x)$ in the domain $-1 \le x \le 3, x \in \mathbb{R}$.

   (c) Use your graph to:

   (i) estimate the solutions of $f(x) + 2 = 0$, correct to one decimal place,

   (ii) find the range of values of x for which $f'(x) < 0$.

7. Let $f(x) = x^3 - 3x^2 + 1, x \in \mathbb{R}$.

   (a) Find $f(-1)$ and $f(3)$.

   (b) Find $f'(x)$.

   (c) Find the co-ordinates of the local maximum and local minimum of $y = f(x)$.

   (d) Plot the graph of $y = f(x)$ in the domain $-1 \le x \le 3, x \in \mathbb{R}$.

(e) Use your graph to:

   (i) estimate the range of values of x for which $f(x) < 0, x > 0$, giving your answers correct to one decimal place,

   (ii) find the range of values of x for which $f'(x) < 0$.

8. Let $y = f(x) = 2x^3 - 5x^2 - 4x + 3, x \in \mathbb{R}$.

   (a) Copy and complete the table:

x	-1·5	-1	0	2	3	3·5
y	-9					13·5

   (b) Find $\dfrac{dy}{dx}$.

   (c) Find the co-ordinates of the local maximum and local minimum of $y = f(x)$.

   (d) Plot $y = f(x)$ in the domain $-1·5 \le x \le 3·5$, $x \in \mathbb{R}$.

   (e) On the same diagram, draw the line with the equation $x - y = 0$.

   (f) Use both graphs to estimate the solutions of $2x^3 - 5x^2 - 5x + 3 = 0$, correct to one decimal place.

9. Write $y = 2^{x-1}$ in the form $y = k2^x$, where k is a constant, $0 < k < 1$. Plot the graph of $y = 2^{x-1}$ in the domain $-2 \le x \le 3, x \in \mathbb{R}$. Use your graph to:

   (a) show that there are no solutions of $2^{x-1} = 0$,

   (b) estimate the solution of $2^{x-1} = 3$, correct to one decimal place.

10. **(a)** For $f(x) = x^2$, find the local minimum point and plot the function in the domain $-3 \le x \le 3, x \in \mathbb{R}$.

    (b) On the same diagram as $y = f(x)$, plot $g(x) = 2^x$ in the domain $-3 \le x \le 3, x \in \mathbb{R}$.

    (c) Use your diagram to estimate the solutions of $x^2 = 2^x$, correct to one decimal place.

21.2 Rate of change

We have already learned that: $\dfrac{dy}{dx}$ = rate of change of y with respect to x.

However, when the independent variable is time t, the rate of change of a quantity with respect to **time** (t) is simply called the rate of change of the quantity.

There are many quantities in the real world that vary with time.

Examples: the height of plants, the price of shares, the speed of a car.

▸ A water tank is leaking water at a rate of 20 cm³ per second. This means at a particular instant, the volume V of water in the tank is **decreasing** by 20 cm³ every second.

Mathematically, this is expressed as $\dfrac{dV}{dt} = -20$ cm³/s.

This equation states that if the time changes (increases) by 1 s, the volume changes by -20 cm³ (decreases by 20 cm³).

▸ $\dfrac{dT}{dt} = +5$ °C/h where T is the temperature in °C and t is in hours means that the temperature is increasing at 5 °C per hour.

▸ $\dfrac{dA}{dt} = -10$ m²/minute, where A is area in m², means the area is decreasing at 10 m² every minute.

If the rate of change is greater than zero, the quantity is increasing with time.

If the rate of change is less than zero, the quantity is decreasing with time.

If the the rate of change is equal to zero, the quantity has reached its maximum or minimum value.

EXAMPLE 19

The area A, in metres squared, of an oil slick after t hours is given by $A = -t^3 + 10t^2 + 3t$, $0 \le t < 10$. Find the rate of change of the area when:

(a) $t = 0$ (b) $t = 4$ (c) $t = 8$

Solution

$A = -t^3 + 10t^2 + 3t$

[Always differentiate before you substitute values.]

$\dfrac{dA}{dt} = -3t^2 + 20t + 3$

(a) $t = 0$: $\dfrac{dA}{dt} = 3$ m²/h

(b) $t = 4$: $\dfrac{dA}{dt} = -3(4)^2 + 20(4) + 3 = 35$ m²/h

(c) $t = 8$: $\dfrac{dA}{dt} = -3(8)^2 + 20(8) + 3 = -29$ m²/h

Distance/speed/acceleration

For motion in a straight line:

If s is the distance of a body relative to the origin $O(0, 0)$ at time t, then:

Speed: $v = \dfrac{ds}{dt}$

Acceleration: $a = \dfrac{dv}{dt}$

Units

Distance s: m, cm, km   [s can also be height or depth.]

Time t: seconds, minutes, hours

Speed v: m/s, km/h, cm/s

Acceleration a: m/s^2, km/h^2, cm/s^2

EXAMPLE 20

A car begins to slow down at a marker P in order to stop at traffic lights at Q.

The distance s of the car from P after t seconds is given by $s = 15t - \frac{3}{2}t^2$, where s is in metres.

(a) Find the speed of the car in terms of t.

(b) Find the car's speed at P.

(c) Find the time it takes the car to stop.

(d) Find the car's acceleration.

(e) Interpret the result in **(d)**.

Solution

Start by finding v and a from s.

$$s = 15t - \frac{3}{2}t^2 \quad \bigg| \quad v = \frac{ds}{dt} = 15 - 3t \quad \bigg| \quad a = \frac{dv}{dt} = -3$$

(a) $v = 15 - 3t$

(b) At P: $t = 0$: $v = 15 - 0 = 15$ m/s

(c) The car stops when $v = 0$.

$$15 - 3t = 0$$
$$t = 5 \text{ s}$$

(d) $a = -3$ m/s^2

(e) The minus sign means it is decelerating.

Interpretation of signs for s, v, a, t

1. $s\,(+)$: The body is to the right of the origin.

$s\,(-)$: The body is to the left of the origin.

2. $v\,(+)$: The body is moving to the right.

$v\,(-)$: The body is moving to the left.

3. $a\,(+)$: The body is accelerating.

$a\,(-)$: The body is decelerating.

4. t: $t \geq 0$ always (no negative times).

$t = 0$ is the initial time.

EXAMPLE 21

The distance s in metres of a body from a fixed point A after t seconds is given by $s = 1{\cdot}5t^2 - 48t$

(a) Find how far the body is from the fixed point at:

(i) $t = 0$ (ii) $t = 10$ (iii) $t = 40$

(b) Find the speed of the body at:

(i) $t = 0$ (ii) $t = 10$ (iii) $t = 40$

(c) Find the acceleration of the body.

Solution

$$s = 1{\cdot}5t^2 - 48t \quad \bigg| \quad v = \frac{ds}{dt} = 3t - 48 \quad \bigg| \quad a = \frac{dv}{dt} = 3$$

(a) $s = 1{\cdot}5t^2 - 48t$

(i) $t = 0$: $s = 0$ m   It is at the origin.

(ii) $t = 10$: $s = 1{\cdot}5(100) - 48(10) = -330$

It is 330 m to the left of the fixed point.

(iii) $t = 40$: $s = 1{\cdot}5(40)^2 - 48(40) = 480$

It is 480 m to the right of the fixed point.

(b) $v = 3t - 48$

(i) $t = 0$: $v = -48$

It is moving to the left at 48 m/s.

(ii) $t = 10$: $v = 30 - 48 = -18$

It is moving at 18 m/s to the left.

(iii) $t = 40$: $v = 120 - 48 = 72$

It is moving at 72 m/s to the right.

(c) $a = 3$ m/s^2 It is accelerating.

EXERCISE 7

1. The share price P (€) in a technology company after t years is given by $P = 5 + 14t - t^2$, $0 \le t \le 14$.

   Find the rate of change of the share price when:

   (a) $t = 0$

   (b) $t = 5$

   (c) $t = 12$

2. A population P of eagles, t years after a mating pair was introduced into an area, is given by: $P = 10 + 2t + t^2$.

   Find the rate of change of the population after:

   (a) 0 years

   (b) 3 years

3. The salary s, in thousands of euros, of a professional footballer t years after he started playing for Manchester United is given by $s = 250 + 55t - 9t^2 + t^3$, $0 \le t \le 5$.

   Find the rate of change of his salary after:

   (a) 0 years

   (b) 2 years

   (c) 5 years

4. A jeweller's profits, in hundreds of euros, t days after Christmas is given by $P = -3t^2 + 42t + 50$, $0 \le t \le 7$.

   Find the rate of change in the profit:

   (a) three days after Christmas,

   (b) five days after Christmas.

5. A tank holds 800 litres of oil that takes 70 minutes to drain. The volume V of oil remaining in a tank after t minutes is given by

   $V = 800 \left(1 - \dfrac{t}{70}\right)^2$, $0 \le t \le 70$.

   (a) How much oil is in the tank after 1 hour, correct to two decimal places?

   (b) What is the average rate of change of volume from 0 minutes to 60 minutes, correct to two decimal places?

   (c) How fast is the liquid draining after 30 minutes, correct to two decimal places?

6. A jet is moving along an airport runway. Its distance s in metres from a marker P after t seconds is given by $s = 2t^2 + 3t$.

   (a) Find the jet's speed as it passes the marker.

   (b) Find its acceleration.

   (c) If the jet has to reach a speed of 83 m/s to take off, after how many seconds will it reach this speed? How far from the marker does it take off?

7. A particle moves in a straight line from a fixed point O. Its distance s in metres from O after t seconds is given by $s = 77t + 13t^2 - t^3$.

   Find:

   (a) the speed in terms of t,

   (b) the acceleration in terms of t,

   (c) when the particle comes to rest,

   (d) the particle's speed after 5 seconds,

   (e) the particle's acceleration after 3 seconds.

8. The height h in metres of a missile t seconds after launch is given by $h = t(-5t + 260)$.

   (a) Find the speed of the missile after 10 s.

   (b) Find the acceleration of the missile.

   (c) Find the height of the missile after 10 s.

21.3 Modelling and optimisation

KEY TERMS

Modelling is the process of describing a problem (realistic or otherwise) in mathematical terms. This means writing a quantity in terms of a single variable.

Optimisation is the process of finding the maximum or minimum value of a function.

EXAMPLE 22

The perimeter of the rectangle *BCDE* is 48 cm.

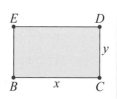

(a) Express y in terms of x.

(b) Express the area A of the rectangle in terms of x.

(c) Find the maximum value of this area.

Solution

(a) $48 = 2x + 2y$

$x + y = 24$

$y = (24 - x)$

(b) Let A be the area of $BCDE$.

$A = xy$

$A = x(24 - x)$

$A = 24x - x^2$

This is the process of modelling. Now for the optimisation.

(c) $A = 24x - x^2$

$\dfrac{dA}{dx} = 24 - 2x$

Maximize the area: $\dfrac{dA}{dx} = 0$

$24 - 2x = 0$

$x = 12$ [There is one stationary point.]

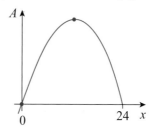

$\dfrac{d^2A}{dx^2} = -2 < 0$

Therefore, there is a local maximum at $x = 12$.

$A_{max} = 24(12) - 12^2 = 144 \text{ m}^2$

This is the process of optimisation.

Steps for modelling and optimising

1. Identify the quantity to be optimised and give it a suitable symbol. For example, A for area.

2. Draw a diagram, if necessary, and put in the variable(s).

3. Write the quantity in terms of this/these variable(s).

4. If there are two variables, eliminate one of these in terms of the other, using some extra information.

5. Hence, write the quantity in terms of a single variable.

6. Differentiate the quantity with respect to the variable. Set it equal to 0 and solve.

7. Put the value of the variable back into the quantity to find the optimum value.

You do not have to do the second derivative in most cases as it is obvious from the context that it is a maximum or a minimum.

Types of optimisation

(a) Geometry   **(c)** Algebraic

(b) Economics   **(d)** Motion

(a) Geometry

EXAMPLE 23

A rectangular sheet of metal 80 cm × 50 cm is used to form an open box (no lid) by removing squares of side x cm from each corner, as shown, and folding up the flaps along the dotted lines.

Show that the volume is given by $V = 4x^3 - 260x^2 + 4000x$. Find the maximum volume of the box.

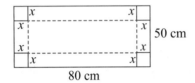

Solution

1. V (volume)

2. Diagram:

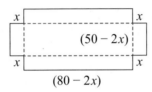

3–5. $V = (80 - 2x)(50 - 2x)(x)$

$x = (4000 - 260x + 4x^2)(x)$

$V = 4x^3 - 260x^2 + 4000x$

6. $\dfrac{dV}{dx} = 12x^2 - 520x + 4000$

$12x^2 - 520x + 4000 = 0$

$3x^2 - 130x + 1000 = 0$

$(3x - 100)(x - 10) = 0$

$x = \dfrac{100}{3}, 10$

There are two stationary points.

Reject $\dfrac{100}{3}$ as it gives $(50 - 2x) < 0$.

7. V_{max} occurs at $x = 10$

$V_{max} = (80 - 20)(50 - 20)10 = 18\,000 \text{ cm}^2$

EXAMPLE 24

A farmer has 800 m of fencing and wishes to make an enclosure consisting of four equal area rectangles, as shown.

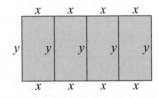

(a) Express y in terms of x.

(b) Express the total area A in terms of x.

(c) Find x, if the total area A is to be a maximum.

Solution

1. A (area)

2. Diagram:

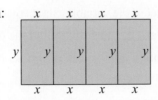

3. $A = 4xy$

4. $800 = 8x + 5y$

$5y = 800 - 8x$

$y = 160 - \dfrac{8}{5}x$

5. $A = 4x(160 - \dfrac{8}{5}x)$

$A = 640x - \dfrac{32}{5}x^2$

6. $\dfrac{dA}{dx} = 640 - \dfrac{64}{5}x$

$640 - \dfrac{64}{5}x = 0$

$x = 50 \text{ m}$

There is only one stationary point. This is a local maximum.

(a) $y = 160 - \dfrac{8}{5}x$

(b) $A = 640x - \dfrac{32}{5}x^2$

(c) $x = 50 \text{ m}$

(b) Economics

Economics insights:

1. Profit (P) = Revenue or income (R) – Costs (C)
2. N objects sold at €x each $\Rightarrow$ Revenue $R = €Nx$

EXAMPLE 25

The fuel economy E (km/l) of an average saloon car is given by $E = -0.00375v^2 + 0.575v - 2$, where v is the speed of the car in km/h.
At what speed, correct to one decimal place, is the fuel economy a maximum?

Solution

1. Fuel economy (E)

3. $E = -0.00375v^2 + 0.575v - 2$

6. $\dfrac{dE}{dv} = -0.0075v + 0.575$

$-0.0075v + 0.575 = 0$

$v = 76.7$ [There is one stationary point.]

Fuel economy is a maximum at a speed of 76.7 km/h.

EXAMPLE 26

A company manufactures and sells shirts. The company's fixed costs are €1500 per week. The production costs are €10 per shirt. For a selling price of €x per shirt, the number N of shirts sold per week is given by $N = -10x + 1200$. If the company sells the shirts at €x each, find:

(a) the weekly revenue in terms of x,

(b) the weekly costs in terms of x,

(c) the weekly profit in terms of x,

(d) the maximum weekly profit.

Solution

(a) For a selling price of €x per shirt, the number sold is N.

Revenue R per week $= Nx = x(-10x + 1200)$
$= 1200x - 10x^2$

(b) Weekly costs:

C = Fixed costs + Cost per shirt × Number of shirts

$C = 1500 + 10(-10x + 1200)$

$C = -100x + 13\,500$

(c) $P = R - C = 1200x - 10x^2 - (13\,500 - 100x)$
$= -10x^2 + 1300x - 13\,500$

Now, for the optimisation of the profit P.

(d) $P = -10x^2 + 1300x - 13\,500$

$\dfrac{dP}{dx} = -20x + 1300$

$\dfrac{dP}{dx} = 0$

$-20x + 1300 = 0$

$x = 65$ [There is only one stationary point.]

Maximum profit:

$P_{max} = -10(65)^2 + 1300(65) - 13\,500 = €28\,750$

(c) Algebraic

EXAMPLE 27

The sum of two numbers is 32. Find the numbers if their product is to have its maximum value.

Solution

1. P (product)
2. Let the numbers be x and y.
3. $P = xy$
4. $x + y = 32$

$y = (32 - x)$

5. $P = x(32 - x) = 32x - x^2$

6. $\dfrac{dP}{dx} = 32 - 2x$

$32 - 2x = 0$

$x = 16$ [There is one stationary point.]

$y = 16$

(d) Motion

EXAMPLE 28

A body moves in a straight line for 10 seconds, its distance s, in metres, from a fixed point ($s = 0$) is given by $s = 25t^2 - \frac{5}{3}t^3$, $0 \le t \le 10$ where t is in seconds.

Find its maximum speed and the distance it is from its starting point ($t = 0$) when its speed is at a maximum.

Solution

1. v (speed)

5. $s = 25t^2 - \frac{5}{3}t^3$

$$v = \frac{ds}{dt} = 50t - 5t^2$$

6. $\frac{dv}{dt} = 50 - 10t$

$50 - 10t = 0$

$t = 5$ [There is only one stationary point.]

7. $v_{max} = 50(5) - 5(25) = 125$ m/s

$s = 25(5)^2 - \frac{5}{3}(5)^3 = 416\frac{2}{3}$ m

EXERCISE 8

1. A 20 m length of cable is bent into a rectangular ring circuit, as shown.

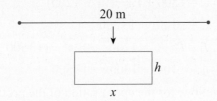

If the length of the rectangle is x:

   (a) express the breadth h of the rectangle in terms of x,

   (b) express the area of the rectangle in terms of x,

   (c) find the area of the rectangle with maximum area that can be constructed in this way.

2. A rectangular sheet of plastic 20 cm by 200 cm is used to make a gutter.

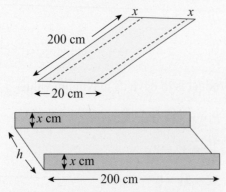

The gutter is made by bending the sheet of plastic along the dotted lines of width x cm.

   (a) Express, in terms of x:

      (i) the width h of the gutter,

      (ii) the volume V of the gutter.

   (b) Find x, to maximize the volume of the gutter.

3. Artwork with a perimeter of 128 cm is mounted inside a rectangular frame. A 1 cm border at the top and the bottom and a border of 2 cm at each side surrounds the artwork, as shown.

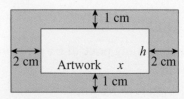

   (a) If x is the length of the artwork, express the width h of the artwork in terms of x.

   (b) Find an expression for the area A of the frame in terms of x.

   (c) Find the maximum possible area of the frame.

4. A box (cuboid) has a square base of side x cm. If the sum of the length of one of the square bases and the height h is 27 cm:

   (a) express h in terms of x,

   (b) express the volume V of the box in terms of x,

   (c) find the maximum possible volume of such a box.

5. An Olympic running track, with perimeter 400 m, has two straights and two semicircular ends, as shown. If the length of each straight is x m and the radius of each semicircular end is h:

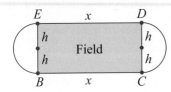

(a) express x in terms of h,

(b) express the area A of the rectangular field $BCDE$ in terms of h,

(c) find x, to maximize the area of the field.

6. The total cost C (€) of producing x units of a computer part per week is given by:

$C = \frac{1}{3}x^3 - 24x^2 + 560x + 1200$. The total

revenue R (€) per week is given by
$R = 400x - 2x^2$.

(a) Express the profit P, per week, in terms of x.

(b) Find $\dfrac{dP}{dx}$ and $\dfrac{d^2P}{dx^2}$.

(c) Find x, to maximize the weekly profit.

7. The value V of shares in euro can be modelled in time t in years by the equation $V = 10 - 2t + 3.5t^2 - t^3$, $0 \le t \le 3$.

Find:

(a) $\dfrac{dV}{dt}$,

(b) $\dfrac{d^2V}{dt^2}$,

(c) the local maximum and local minimum turning points,

(d) the maximum value of the shares.

8. The cost to a travel agency to provide a holiday is €$(150 + 30x)$ per person where x is the number of people that travel. The agency charges each person going on the trip €$(930 - 100x)$ for groups of 8 or less.

If x people travel, find in terms of x:

(a) (i) the total cost C to the agency for a group of x people,

(ii) the total revenue R for a group of x people,

(iii) the total profit P for a group of x people.

(b) Find the value of x that maximizes the profit.

9. Find the minimum product of two numbers that differ by 12.

10. The sum of one number x and twice another y is 35. Find the numbers to maximize their product.

11. A body moves in a straight line from a fixed point O. Its distance s in metres from O after t seconds is given by $s = t^3 - 6t^2 + 9t$, $0 \le t \le 3.5$.

(a) Find:

(i) its speed v in terms of t,

(ii) its acceleration in terms of t.

(b) Plot a graph of s against t using the table below:

t (s)	0	0·5	1	1·5	2	2·5	3	3·5
s (m)								

(c) Find the maximum and minimum distances the body is from the fixed point O.

12. Two rockets were fired straight up in the air at $t = 0$ seconds. The height h in metres that each rocket reached above the ground t seconds after being fired is given by: $h = 84t - 6t^2$. The first rocket exploded after four seconds.

(a) Find:

(i) at what height the first rocket exploded,

(ii) the speed of the first rocket when it exploded.

(b) The second rocket continued to its maximum height. Find its maximum height.

REVISION QUESTIONS

Concepts and skills

1. Let $f(x) = 2x + 1$ and $g(x) = x^2 + 3x + 2$, $x \in \mathbb{R}$.

   (a) Find $h(x) = f(g(x))$.

   (b) Find $f'(x)$, $g'(x)$ and $h'(x)$.

   (c) Solve $h'(x) > 0$.

   (d) Find the equation of the tangent to the curve $h(x)$ at $x = -2$.

   (e) Show that $h''(x)$ is a constant.

2. If $u(x) = 3x^2 + 1$ and $v(x) = x - 2$, find:

   (a) $u'(x)$

   (b) $v'(x)$

   (c) $g(x) = u(x) \times v(x)$

   (d) $g'(x)$

   (e) $u(x) \times v'(x)$

   (f) $v(x) \times u'(x)$

   (g) Show that $g'(x) = u(x) \times v'(x) + v(x) \times u'(x)$.

3. For the curve $y = x^3 - x^2 - 2$, find:

   (a) $\dfrac{dy}{dx}$,

   (b) the equation k of the tangent at $x = 1$,

   (c) the equation l of the tangent at $x = -1$,

   (d) the point of intersection of k and l,

   (e) the points on the curve where the tangents are parallel to the x-axis.

4. The equation of a curve is $y = x^2 - 3x - 4$.

   (a) Show that $P(2, -6)$ is on the curve.

   (b) Find the equation of the tangent k to the curve at $P(2, -6)$.

   (c) Find the equation of the line l through P perpendicular to k.

   (d) Show that l intersects the curve at the point Q, where the curve crosses the y-axis.

   (e) Find $|PQ|$.

5. **(a)** If a company sells x items per week at S cent each, what is its weekly revenue R, in terms of x, if $S = 50x + 20\,000$.

   (b) If the company produces x items per week at a cost of q cents each, find the company's weekly costs C, in terms of x, if $q = 200x$.

   (c) Write down an expression P for the company's weekly profit.

   (d) Find $\dfrac{dP}{dx}$.

   (e) Find the value of x for which $\dfrac{dP}{dx} = 0$, correct to two decimal places.

   (f) Find P when $\dfrac{dP}{dx} = 0$, correct to the nearest euro.

   (g) Show that $\dfrac{d^2P}{dx^2} < 0$.

6. The volume V, in metres cubed of water of height h, in a hemispherical tank of radius 1 m is given by $V = \pi h^2 \left(1 - \dfrac{h}{3}\right)$, where h is the height of the water from its lowest point A in metres.

   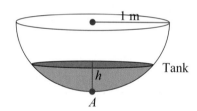

   (a) Find V when $h = 0$.

   (b) Find V when $h = 1$, in terms of π.

   (c) Find $\dfrac{dV}{dh}$ by multiplying out the brackets.

   (d) Find the rate of change of V with respect to h, in terms of π, when:

   (i) $h = 0 \cdot 5$

   (ii) $h = 1$

   (e) Find $\dfrac{d^2V}{dh^2}$.

   (f) At what height is $\dfrac{dV}{dh} = \dfrac{15\pi}{16}$?

7. **(a)** If $y = 2x^3 - 6x^2 + 6x$, find $\dfrac{dy}{dx}$ and show that $\dfrac{dy}{dx} \geq 0$ for all $x \in \mathbb{R}$.

   (b) For $S = 3t^2 + 1$, find:

   (i) the average rate of change of S with respect to t from $t = 3$ to $t = 5$,

   (ii) the instantaneous rate of change of S with respect to t at $t = -3$.

   (c) If $f'(3) = 10$, find $g'(3)$ if $g(x) = 6x^2 - 7f(x)$.

8. **(a)** If $y = 1 - x^2$, find $\dfrac{dy}{dx}$ and show that

$x \times \dfrac{dy}{dx} + 2 = 2y$.

(b) If $y = 3x^2 - 4x + 11$, find x if $\dfrac{dy}{dx} = 0$.

(c) By multiplying out $f(x) = (2x - 1)(x + 2)(2x + 1)$, find:

    (i) $f'(x)$

    (ii) $f''(3)$

Contexts and applications

1. The number of people N, in thousands, entering a shopping centre per hour t hours after it opens is given by $N = 60t - 5t^2$, $0 \le t \le 12$, where $t = 0$ corresponds to 8 a.m.

(a) Copy and complete the table below and use it to plot a graph of N against t.

t (Hours)	0	2	4	6	8	10	12
N							

(b) Find $\dfrac{dN}{dt}$.

(c) Find at what time there is the maximum number of shoppers per hour entering the centre.

(d) Find the maximum number of shoppers per hour entering the centre.

(e) The area between the curve and the t axis is an estimate for the total number of shoppers who entered the centre during opening time. Use the trapezoidal rule to estimate this number.

2. A small manufacturer produces mobile phone covers. It can sell x covers per week at € q each where $q = 125 - \dfrac{5}{3}x$.

(a) Find the manufacturer's total weekly revenue R (€) in terms of x.

(b) The cost C (€) of producing x covers per week is given by $C = 25x + \dfrac{x^2}{3}$. Copy and complete the table below and use it to plot graphs of R and C against x on the same grid.

x	0	15	30	45	60	75
R (€)						
C (€)						

(c) The breakeven point is the point at which the revenue R is equal to the cost C. Mark this point on your graph and find the number of covers per week and the value of R at this point, correct to two significant figures. Find x and R by calculation, correct to two significant figures, and show that you get the same answers as those from the graph.

(d) The profit P is given by $P = R - C$. Show that $P = 100x - 2x^2$.

(e) Find $\dfrac{dP}{dx}$ and hence, find the maximum profit.

3. An aeroplane is flying in an airshow display.

Its height h, in metres, above the ground t seconds after takeoff is given by:

$$h = \begin{cases} t^3 - 18t^2 + 96t + 250, \ 0 \le t \le 9 \\ 385, \ t > 9 \end{cases}$$

(a) Find the plane's height at:

    (i) $t = 0$ **(ii)** $t = 9$

(b) Show that the plane's height is decreasing at $t = 5$.

(c) Find its local minimum height.

(d) Find its local maximum height.

(e) Find the plane's minimum height during the display.

(f) Find its maximum height during the display.

(g) Draw a graph of height h against time t.

4. In an experiment on the motion of a body in a straight line, a student devises an equation for the speed v (m/s) against time t, in seconds, for a computer generated graph of the motion. The formula is $v = t^3 - 20t^2 + 100t$, $4 \le t \le 12$.

(a) Find an expression for the acceleration a at any time t.

(b) Find $\dfrac{d^2v}{dt^2}$.

(c) Find the time at which the body has its minimum speed.

(d) Find the minimum speed.

(e) By copying and completing the table below, plot a graph of v against t.

t (s)	4	6	8	10	12
v (m/s)					

(f) Given that the area between a velocity graph and the t axis is an estimate for the distance travelled by a body in a certain time, use the trapezoidal rule to estimate the distance travelled from $t = 4$ s to $t = 10$ s.

(g) Find the acceleration of the body at:

  (i) $t = 5$ s

  (ii) $t = 10$ s

5. A geographer draws a 2-D model of the coastal terrain in a local area. x is the distance inland from the sea in hundreds of metres measured from sea level and y is the height in hundreds of metres above sea level.

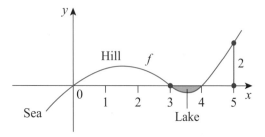

If the equation of the curve f is given by $y = ax(x - 3)(x - 4)$, find:

(a) a,

(b) the x co-ordinate of the stationary points on the curve f in surd form,

(c) $\dfrac{d^2y}{dx^2}$ and find which stationary point is the local maximum and which is the local minimum,

(d) the height of the hill to the nearest metre,

(e) the depth of the lake to the nearest metre.

6. The life expectancy E, in years, of a man who reaches retirement age in 2013 is given by:

$$E = \begin{cases} -\frac{2}{81}t^2 + \frac{36}{81}t + 21, & 0 \le t \le 9 \\ -\frac{23}{21}(t - 30), & t > 9 \end{cases}$$

where t is the number of years after 2013.

(a) Find the value of t that gives the stationary point for $0 \le t \le 9$.

(b) Find $\dfrac{d^2E}{dt^2}$ and state if the stationary point is a local maximum or a local minimum for $0 \le t \le 9$.

(c) Find the value of E at the stationary point for $0 \le t \le 9$.

(d) Plot a graph of E against t using the table. Give each answer correct to one decimal place.

t (years)	0	3	6	9	12	15	18	21
E (years)								

(e) Using the graph, find the year in which the life expectancy is 0 years.

(f) Verify the answer by solving an equation.

7. A box (cuboid) has a square base of side x cm and height h cm. It has no lid.

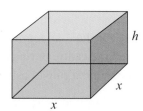

(a) If the surface area is $(24x - 3x^2)$ cm^2, express h in terms of x.

(b) Hence, express the volume V in terms of x.

(c) Find $\dfrac{dV}{dx}$ and hence, find the stationary points of V.

(d) Find $\dfrac{d^2V}{dx^2}$ and use it to find the value of x that maximizes the volume.

(e) Find the maximum volume of the box.

8. A javelin thrower releases the spear from A.

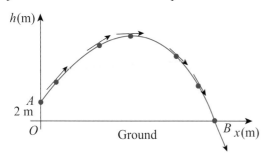

The spear's height h, in metres, above the ground is related to the horizontal distance x, in metres, it has moved from $O(0, 0)$ by the equation

$$h = -\frac{16x^2}{4050} + \frac{16x}{45} + 2.$$

(a) Show that the spear's height is increasing at $x = 30$ m.

(b) Show that its height is decreasing at $x = 70$ m.

(c) Find the spear's maximum height above the ground.

(d) Find $|OB|$, to the nearest metre, where B is the point at which the spear strikes the ground.

(e) Find the slope of the tangent to the curve at B, correct to one decimal place.

9. The graph shows part of a cubic curve with equation $y = f(x) = \dfrac{x^3}{2} + \dfrac{x^2}{4} - 2x - 1$, $x \in \mathbb{R}$.

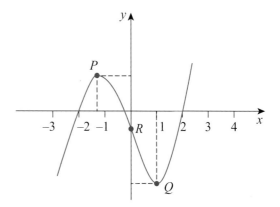

(a) Find the co-ordinates of the local maximum and local minimum, P and Q.

(b) Verify that the curve crosses the x-axis at $(-2, 0)$ and $(2, 0)$.

(c) Find the point R where the curve crosses the y-axis.

(d) For which values of x is $f'(x) < 0$?

(e) Sketch a graph of $f'(x)$ against x.

SUMMARY

1. **Basic rule:**

   $y = f(x) = x^n$

   $\dfrac{dy}{dx} = f'(x) = nx^{n-1}$

2. **Other rules:**

   (a) Multiplication by a constant rule

   $y = \text{constant} \times \text{a function}$

   $\dfrac{dy}{dx} = \text{constant} \times \text{differentiate the function}$

   (b) The constant rule

   $y = \text{constant (on its own)}$

   $\dfrac{dy}{dx} = 0$

   (c) The sum rule

   $y = \text{a sum of functions}$

   $\dfrac{dy}{dx} = \text{differentiate each function individually}$

   Always substitute values after you differentiate.

3. **Curves:**

   (a) $\dfrac{dy}{dx} = $ the slope of tangent to the curve

   $y = f(x)$ at a point (x, y) on the curve

   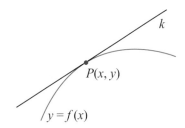

   (b)

	> 0	< 0	= 0
$\dfrac{dy}{dx}$	Increasing I	Decreasing D	Flat / Flat or Flat

(c) Conditions for local maxima and minima

   (i) Local maximum at P

   $\dfrac{dy}{dx} = 0$ at P

   and

   $\dfrac{d^2y}{dx^2} < 0$ at P

   (ii) Local minimum at Q

   $\dfrac{dy}{dx} = 0$ at Q

   $\dfrac{d^2y}{dx^2} > 0$ at Q

   (d) A stationary point is a point at which $\dfrac{dy}{dx} = 0$.

4. **Rate of change:**

   $\dfrac{dA}{dt} = $ rate of change of A

   $\text{Speed} = v = \dfrac{ds}{dt} = \text{Rate of change of distance}$

   $\text{Acceleration } a = \dfrac{dv}{dt} = \text{Rate of change of speed}$

5. **Optimisation:**

   • Model the problem first

   • Differentiate to find local maxima/minima

Answers

Section 1

Chapter 1

Exercise 1

1. (a) 10 (b) 14 (c) 1, 2, 3, 4, 5, 6, 7, 8, 9, 10, 11, 12, 13, 14, 15 (d) 48 (e) 32 (f) 5; 2 is a divisor (g) 2^4; 16 (h) 30; 30; They are equal (i) $2 + 2 + 2 + 2 + 2 = 10$ (j) $2 \times 2 \times 2 \times 2 \times 2 = 32$ **2.** (a) 27 (b) 6 (c) 26 (d) 24 (e) 18 (f) 2 (g) 3 (h) 7 (i) 5 (j) 2
3. (a) $U = \{1, 2, 3, 4, 5, 6, 7, 8, 9, 10, 11, 12\}$, $A = \{3, 5, 7, 9\}$, $B = \{1, 2, 3, 4, 5\}$
(i) $\{1, 2, 3, 4, 5, 7, 9\}$ (ii) $\{3, 5\}$ (iii) $\{7, 9\}$
(iv) $\{1, 2, 4\}$ (v) $\{1, 2, 4, 6, 8, 10, 11, 12\}$
(vi) $\{6, 7, 8, 9, 10, 11, 12\}$ (vii) $\{6, 8, 9, 10, 11, 12\}$
(viii) $\{1, 2, 3, 4, 5, 6, 8, 10, 11, 12\}$ (b) $U = \{5, 6, 7, 8, 9, 10, 11, 12, 13, 14, 15, 16, 17, 18, 19, 20\}$, $C = \{6, 8, 10, 12, 14\}$, $D = \{5, 10, 15, 20\}$
(i) $\{5, 6, 8, 10, 12, 14, 15, 20\}$ (ii) $\{10\}$
(iii) $\{6, 8, 12, 14\}$ (iv) $\{5, 15, 20\}$ (v) $\{5, 7, 9, 11, 13, 15, 16, 17, 18, 19, 20\}$ (vi) $\{6, 7, 8, 9, 11, 12, 13, 14, 16, 17, 18, 19\}$ (vii) $\{7, 9, 11, 13, 16, 17, 18, 19\}$
(viii) $\{6, 7, 8, 9, 10, 11, 12, 13, 14, 16, 17, 18, 19\}$
4. (a) (i) $U = \{6, 9, 12, 15, 18, 21, 24\}$, $A = \{9, 15, 18\}$, $B = \{6, 15, 18, 21\}$ (ii) $12 \notin A$ (iii) The set of natural numbers between 6 and 24 inclusive which are divisible by 3 (iv) $\{6, 9, 15, 18, 21\}$ (v) $\{15, 18\}$ (vi) $\{9\}$ (vii) $\{6, 12, 21, 24\}$ (b) (i) $U = \{1, 3, 4, 5, 6, 8, 9, 10, 11, 12\}$, $C = \{1, 3, 4, 8, 12\}$, $D = \{4, 8, 9, 10, 11\}$ (ii) $\#(C) = 5$, $\#(D) = 5$
(iii) $\{1, 3, 4, 8, 9, 10, 11, 12\}$ (iv) $\{4, 8\}$
(v) $\{1, 3, 12\}$ (vi) $\{5, 6\}$ (vii) $3 \notin D\backslash C$
5. (a) 18 composite; $2 \times 3 \times 3$ (b) 45 composite; $3 \times 3 \times 5$ (c) 11 prime (d) 28 composite; $2 \times 2 \times 7$ (e) 90 composite; $2 \times 3 \times 3 \times 5$ (f) 85 composite; 5×17 (g) 62 composite; 2×31 (h) 79 prime (i) 51 composite; 3×17 **6.** Prime numbers 47, 91   **7.** Not prime; Even number   **8.** Not prime; Divisible by 3
9. (a) 8, 16, 32, 64; Not prime; Even number
(b) 25, 125, 625, 3125; Not prime; Divisible by 5
10. 17 girls, 19 boys   **11.** $3 = 2 + 1$

Exercise 2

1. (a) $A = \{-3, -2, -1, 0, 1, 2, 3, 4\}$
(b)
(c) (i) $0 < 4$ (ii) $-1 > -3$ (iii) $0 > -2$ (iv) $2 > -3$
(v) $-4 < -3$ **2.** (a) -2 (b) -3 (c) -17 (d) -3
(e) -4 (f) 3 (g) -27 (h) -3 (i) 4 (j) 1

3.
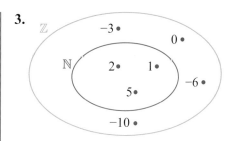

4. (a) $+20$ m (b) -2 m   **5.** (a) -1200 m (b) -1700 m
6. (a) (i) 6168 m (ii) -86 m (b) 6254 m   **7.** 75 °C
8. 503 years   **9.** -1 °C   **10.** €26 000   **11.** 125 °C
12. 180 °F   **13.** €293   **14.** 37 °C   **15.** (a) 2 310 241
(b) $+30$ 094 (c) 2 340 335   **16.** 100   **17.** $-27, -26, -25$
18. $-9, -8, -7$ **19.** (a) -1 (b) -1 (c) 1 (d) 1 (e) 0 (f) -1

Exercise 3

1. (a)
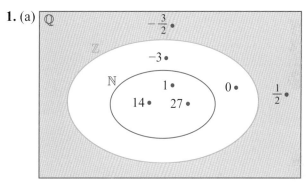

(b) (i) Yes; $\mathbb{Z} \subset \mathbb{Q}$ (All integers are rational numbers) (ii) Yes; $\mathbb{N} \subset \mathbb{Q}$ (All natural numbers are rational numbers) (c) {Rational numbers that are not integers}   **2.** Infinite number; $0 < x < 1$
3.

$$\overset{\frac{1}{6}\ \frac{2}{9}\quad \frac{1}{3}}{\underset{1}{\xleftarrow{\quad}}\ \bullet\ \bullet\quad \bullet\quad\quad\quad \overset{\frac{5}{6}}{\bullet}\quad \underset{0}{\xrightarrow{\quad}}}$$

4. (a) $\frac{4}{5}$ (b) $\frac{3}{7}$ (c) $-\frac{1}{3}$ (d) $\frac{61}{60}$ (e) $\frac{8}{15}$ (f) $\frac{4}{25}$ (g) $\frac{49}{4}$ (h) $\frac{4}{7}$
(i) $\frac{1}{3}$ (j) $\frac{7}{25}$ **5.** (a) $\frac{3}{2}$ (b) 2 (c) $\frac{1}{4}$ (d) $-\frac{2}{9}$ (e) $\frac{35}{18}$ (f) $\frac{3}{2}$
(g) -2 (h) $-\frac{4}{7}$ (i) 2   **6.** (a) 0·6 (b) 0·75 (c) 1·21
(d) 0·78 (e) $-0·2875$ (f) $-3·4$ (g) 0·24 (h) $-5·125$
(i) 7·2 (j) 0·08   **7.** (a) $\frac{5}{8}$ (b) $-\frac{713}{1000}$ (c) $-\frac{107}{50}$ (d) $\frac{141}{25}$
8. €4750   **9.** Treadmill: 36 minutes, Pool: 30 minutes, Weights: 24 minutes, $\frac{4}{15}$ **10.** Son: $\frac{1}{6}$, daughter: $\frac{1}{3}$
11. Mechanical: 315, Chemical: 140, Electrical: 385, $\frac{11}{24}$
12. 287 875   **13.** 75 mph   **14.** $7\frac{11}{12}$ litres   **15.** $2\frac{7}{8}$ cm
16. $13\frac{5}{8}$ km   **17.** $\frac{3}{5}$ **18.** 2   **19.** 18

Exercise 4

1. (a) Irrational (b) Irrational (c) Rational (d) Rational
(e) Irrational (f) Irrational (g) Irrational (h) Irrational
(i) Irrational (j) Rational (k) Irrational (l) Rational
(m) Irrational (n) Rational (o) Rational (p) Irrational

3.

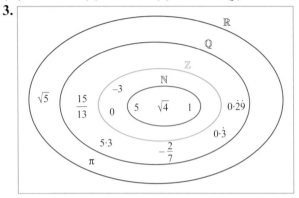

4. $\pi \approx 3\cdot1416$ **5.** (a) 628 m (b) 3·14 **6.** 1·6
7. 18 cm^2

Exercise 5

1. (a) 72 (b) $\frac{69}{4}$ (c) 1·72 (d) $\frac{1}{\sqrt{2}}$ (e) $\frac{3\sqrt{2}}{4}$ (f) 0 (g) π

(h) $\frac{5}{6}$ **2.** (a) 2 (b) 2 (c) $\sqrt{2} - 1$ (d) $\pi - 3$ (e) $\pi - 3$

(f) $\sqrt{3} - \sqrt{2}$ (g) $a - b$ (h) $b - a$

Chapter 2

Exercise 6

1. (a) 50% (b) 25% (c) 60% (d) 48% (e) 160%
(f) 765% (g) 23% (h) 200% (i) 70% (j) 18%

2. (a) 0·2, $\frac{1}{5}$ (b) 0·32, $\frac{8}{25}$ (c) 0·67, $\frac{67}{100}$ (d) 0·18, $\frac{9}{50}$

(e) $0\cdot\dot{6}$, $\frac{2}{3}$ (f) 0·82, $\frac{41}{50}$ (g) 0·04, $\frac{1}{25}$ (h) 0·023, $\frac{23}{1000}$

(i) 0·2475, $\frac{99}{400}$ **3.** (a) 25% (b) $33\frac{1}{3}\% = 33\cdot\dot{3}\%$

(c) $37\frac{1}{2}\% = 37\cdot5\%$ (d) 130% (e) 200% (f) 25%

(g) 400% (h) 80% (i) $66\frac{2}{3}\% = 66\cdot\dot{6}\%$ (j) $10\frac{5}{12}\%$

4. (a) 90% (b) 36% (c) 40% (d) 93·5% (e) 75%
5. (a) 32 (b) 47 (c) €22·80 (d) 9920 (e) €320
6. (a) €2820·95 (b) €413·40 (c) 1 692 561 sq miles
(d) 18 (e) €28·80 **7.** (a) €42 (b) 212
(c) 248·67 million (d) €560 (e) 51

Exercise 7

1. (a) 7×10^{-1} (b) 4×10^{-2} (c) 2×10^{-3} (d) 4×10^{-5}
(e) 3×10^{-6} (f) 5×10^{-10} (g) 1×10^{-4} (h) 8×10^{-13}
(i) 5×10^{-6} (j) 9×10^{-7} **2.** (a) 1×10^5 (b) 1×10^{-1}
(c) 1×10^1 (d) 3×10^5 (e) 1×10^6 (f) 1×10^{-6}
(g) $3\cdot2 \times 10^4$ (h) 1×10^{10} (i) 1×10^0 (j) 1×10^7
3. (a) 1×10^{12} (b) $2\cdot222 \times 10^{-25}$ kg (c) 3×10^8 m/s

(d) $1\cdot4 \times 10^9$ (e) 6×10^{24} kg (f) 1×10^{18} (g) 1×10^{21}
(h) $6\cdot2 \times 10^{-34}$ J s (i) $1\cdot57 \times 10^7$ K (j) $5\cdot6 \times 10^{-15}$ m
4. (a) $2\cdot3 \times 10^{-2}$ (b) 1×10^3 (c) $1\cdot4 \times 10^{-4}$ (d) 2×10^0
(e) $2\cdot43 \times 10^{-5}$ (f) $1\cdot26 \times 10^7$ (g) $1\cdot2 \times 10^{-5}$
(h) $1\cdot4 \times 10^1$ (i) $2\cdot67 \times 10^2$ (j) $5\cdot7 \times 10^{-9}$
5. (a) 0·03 (b) 0·000412 (c) 357 000 (d) 2 000 000
(e) 0·00000056 (f) 0·00006 (g) 0·0001 (h) 100 000
(i) 3·3 (j) 780 000 000 **6.** (a) $2\cdot3 \times 10^0$, 0
(b) $3\cdot5642 \times 10^4$, 4 (c) $1\cdot3 \times 10^{-4}$, -4
(d) $4\cdot765314 \times 10^6$, 6 (e) $5\cdot63 \times 10^{-5}$, -4
(f) $7\cdot3 \times 10^6$, 7 **7.** (a) 15 (b) 100 **8.** (a) -9 (b) 15
(c) 15 **9.** (a) (i) $1000 = 1 \times 10^3$ (ii) 3 (iii) 5
(b) (i) Order of magnitude for km = 3, order of
magnitude for miles = 0, order of magnitude for
Mary's answer = 5, $3 + 0 \neq 5$ (ii) 2701·34; Mary
multiplied by 62 (iii) 2701·34 miles **10.** -6 **11.** 10^7

Exercise 8

1. (a) €13·65 (b) (i) 560 ml (ii) 540 ml (c) $(3\cdot7 \pm 0\cdot2)\ \Omega$
(d) $(4 \pm 0\cdot2)$ mm (e) $(3\cdot8 \pm 0\cdot2)$ cm (f) $(5\cdot85 \pm 1\cdot44)$ cm^2
2. (a) $(13\,600 \pm 544)$ kg/m^3 (b) (i) 80 g (ii) 20%
(c) Error = 7·5%; True mass of wife = 67 kg

Exercise 9

1. (a) 9·87 (b) 0·1 (c) 1·9 (d) 4·785 (e) 0·2639
2. (a) 43·0 cm^2 (b) 50·24 (c) 173·96 (d) 3·012
(e) 459·7 **3.** (a) 479 400 (b) 1·33 (c) 57·32 (d) 6·0
(e) $5\cdot73 \times 10^{-4}$ (f) $5\cdot2 \times 10^{-12}$ (g) $6\cdot00 \times 10^4$
(h) $5\cdot63 \times 10^{-2}$ (i) 7800 (j) 83 000 **4.** (a) 40 (b) 450
(c) 1 (d) 25 000 (e) 10 (f) 500 (g) 540 000 (h) 1
(i) 400 (j) 1 **5.** 12 **6.** 0·37%

Exercise 10

1. 0·69 m/s **2.** -3 °C/h **3.** (a) 6·92 m/s
(b) 12·05 m/s (c) 10·44 m/s **4.** (a) -4000 l/h
(b) -800 l/h (c) -2400 l/h **5.** 10 900 per year

Exercise 11

1. 360 km **2.** $y = 2\cdot5x$ (a) 62·5 (b) 12 **3.** $F = 4a$; 140
4. $I = \frac{1}{3}V$; $\frac{10}{3}$ **5.** (a) $y = \frac{2}{3}x$ (b) $\frac{2}{3}$ (c) 600 **6.** (a) $F \propto x$
(b) $F = kx$ (c) 800 (d) 29·6 N **7.** $k = 5$; $x = 14\cdot4$
8. (a) $w = 18$ (b) $u = 3$, $w = 5$ (c) $w = 45$, $u = 15$, $v = 85$
9. (a) Yes; $\frac{y}{x} = 7\cdot5$ for all values (b) 7·5 (c) $y = 7\cdot5x$
(e) 7·5 **10.** (a) Yes; $\frac{y}{x} = 2 = $ constant
(b) Yes; $\frac{y}{x} = 3 = $ constant (c) No; $(0, 0)$ not on the line
(d) Yes; $\frac{y}{x} = \frac{1}{2} = $ constant (e) No; $y \neq kx$ or $\frac{y}{x} \neq $ constant

Exercise 12

1. $k = 100$ (a) 4 (b) 2·5   **2.** (a) $t = \dfrac{k}{N}$ (b) 300

(c) 25 minutes   **3.** (a) Inversely proportional

(b) $t = \dfrac{k}{v} \rightarrow t = \dfrac{2400}{v}$ (c) 80 km/h

4. (a) As P increases, V decreases (b) $P = \dfrac{k}{V}$

(d) 0·0156 m³   **5.** $x = \dfrac{k}{t}$; $k = 600$; 25 men

6. 16 pumps   **7.** 8·4 days   **8.** 650·24 Hertz

9. (a) 5 (b) $v = \dfrac{5}{m}$; $v = 25$ km/h   **10.** (a) $g = \dfrac{k}{r^2}$

(b) 0·392 m/s²

Revision Questions

1. (a)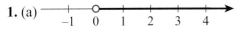

(b)

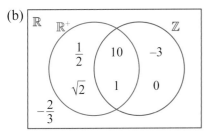

(c) $\mathbb{R}^+ \cap \mathbb{Z} = \mathbb{N}$ (d) The set of negative,
real numbers   **2.** (a) A number divisible by itself
and 1 only (b) (i) $3 \times 3 \times 3 \times 7 \times 13$
(c) $1671 = 3 \times 557$ **3.** (a) 2, 3, 5, 7, 11, 13, 17, 19,
23, 29, 31, 37, 41, 43, 47

(b)

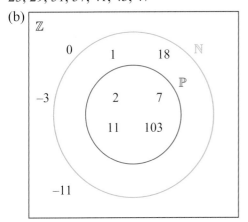

(c) 151, 157, 163   **4.** (a) $3·2 \times 10^3$, $2·157 \times 10^4$,
$2·25 \times 10^4$, $2·5 \times 10^4$ (b) (i) 13 (ii) 15·8
(c) (i) 343·4 cm (ii) 342·6 cm; $A_{max} = 8·726$ m²,

$A_{min} = 8·699$ m²   **5.** (a) $1·6 \times 10^{-6}$ (b) 0·9 N
(c) (i) 8 (ii) 7·4 (iii) 8·1%   **6.** (a) $1·74 \times 10^8$ km
(b) (i) 9 (ii) 7·96 (c) (i) 1005 ml
(ii) 975 ml; 110·55 g of sugar   **7.** (a) $6·2 \times 10^{-2}$
(b) (i) $(1·4 \pm 0·1)$ cm (ii) 1·95 cm²
(c) (i) €43 (ii) €43·15 (iii) 0·35%

8. (a) (i) $2·4 \times 10^{-3}$, 2·4, 10^3, 2200, $2·4 \times 10^3$
(ii) $1·68 \times 10^{12}$ (b) 3·8% (c) (i) 87·5 km
(ii) 156·25 km (d) (i) $I = \dfrac{k}{R}$ (ii) 6·4 Amps

9. (a) (i) The graph is a straight line through the origin
(ii) $\dfrac{2}{5}$ (iii) $y = \dfrac{2}{5}x$ (iv) 81·25 (b) 24 m/s (c) (i) $r = \dfrac{k}{t}$

(ii) 2·65 h   **10.** (a) (i) 23·08% (ii) 25% (iii) 30·77%

(b) 0·0189 (c) (i) −5 (ii) $\dfrac{1}{3}$ mpg/mph (d) 2·5 m

Section 2
Chapter 3

Exercise 1

1. (a) $2x^2$ (b) $3xy^2$ (c) x^2y (d) $-2xy$ (e) $18xy$ (f) $6y^2$
(g) $15xy$ (h) $8x^2y$ (i) $15x$ (j) $7xy$ **2.** (a) $10x + 6$
(b) $-10x + 6$ (c) $2x^2 + 7x$ (d) $2x^2 - 7x$ (e) $15x^2 - 24x$
(f) $-4xy - 2y$ (g) $2xy^2 + 2xy$ (h) $-3x^2y + 3xy$
(i) $x^2y - xy^2 + xy$ (j) $2xy^2 + 4x^2y - 6xy$
(k) $xy + 3x + 2y + 6$ (l) $xy + 7x + 5y + 35$
(m) $xy + 3x - 2y - 6$ (n) $-xy - 8x + 5y + 40$ **3.** (a) $5x$
(b) $-2x$ (c) $-5y$ (d) $3y$ (e) $3x + 8y$ (f) $-19x + 3y$
(g) $7x^2 - y^2 + 9x + 3y$ (h) $9x^2y - 8xy^2 - 2$ (i) $2yz - 8y + z$
(j) $3x^2 + 5xy + 2y^2$ **4.** (a) $-2x - 8$ (b) $7x - 49$
(c) $6x^2 - 24x$ (d) $2x^3 - 2x^2 + 14x$ (e) $-6x - 59$ (f) $4x^2 + x$
(g) $-4x^2 + 13x - 27$ (h) $-x^2 - x + 11$
(i) $-3x^3 + 3x^2 - 10x$ (j) $7x^3 - 3x^2 + 2x$ **5.** (a) $x^2 + 7x + 10$
(b) $6x^2 + 23x + 21$ (c) $y^2 + 13y + 40$ (d) $6x^2 - 13x + 5$
(e) $2x^3 - 2x^2 - 12x$ (f) $2x^3 + 3x^2 + 2x + 1$
(g) $x^3 - 4x^2 + 8x - 15$ (h) $3x^3 + 2x^2 - 12x + 7$
(i) $2x^3 - 7x^2 + 11x - 6$ (j) $2x^3 + x^2 - 5x + 2$ **6.** (a) $x^2 - 4$
(b) $4x^2 - 1$ (c) $16x^2 - 1$ (d) $x^4 - 1$ (e) $9x^2 - 4$ (f) $16x^2 - 9$
(g) $x^4 - 25$ (h) $y^2 - 9$ (i) $9 - x^2$ (j) $x^2 - 4y^2$
7. (a) $x^2 + 2x + 1$ (b) $x^2 + 4x + 4$ (c) $4x^2 + 4x + 1$
(d) $9x^2 + 12x + 4$ (e) $x^2 - 8x + 16$ (f) $4x^2 - 12x + 9$
(g) $25x^2 - 40x + 16$ (h) $x^4 - 22x^2 + 121$
(i) $16x^2 - 40x + 25$ (j) $4x^2 + 12xy + 9y^2$
(k) $a^2x^2 - 2abx + b^2$ (l) $4a$ **8.** (a) $x^3 + x^2 - 4x - 4$
(b) $4x^3 + 12x^2 - x - 3$ (c) $12x^3 - 4x^2 - 27x + 9$
(d) $x^3 + 3x^2 + 3x + 1$ (e) $8x^3 - 12x^2 + 6x - 1$
(f) $2x^3 - 9x^2 + 7x + 6$ **9.** (a) (i) $3x + 2y + 4$
(ii) $-x + 8y - 10$ (iii) $12x - 5y + 29$ (iv) $-13y + 13$
(b) (i) $-x + 8$ (ii) $3x - 2$ (iii) $-2x^2 - x + 15$
(iv) $x^2 - 16x + 64$ (v) $9x^2 - 12x + 4$ (vi) $5x^2 - 14x + 34$
(c) (i) $2x^2 - x - 7$ (ii) $8x^2 - 3x + 9$ (iii) $-13x^2 + 5x - 10$
(iv) $-x - 37$ **10.** (a) 18 (b) 32·5 (c) 22 (d) 45 (e) −45
(f) 225 (g) −3 (h) 68 (i) −37 (j) 36 (k) −79 (l) 56·75

Exercise 2

1. (a) $3(x + 2y)$ (b) $x(x + 3)$ (c) $a(b - c)$ (d) $4x(x - 4y)$
(e) $3(x^2 + 3x - 6)$ (f) $3(x - 3y)$ (g) $8a^2(1 - 2b^2)$
(h) $7x^2y(y - 2)$ (i) $(x - 2y)(3 - 5x)$ (j) $(a + b)(m - 3n)$
2. (a) $(x + 2)(ax + 1)$ (b) $(x + y)(a + b)$
(c) $(a - b)(x + y)$ (d) $(b + 7)(a - 3)$ (e) $(p + 2q)(3n - a)$
(f) $(x + 1)(2x - 3y)$ (g) $(x - 3)(2 - b)$ (h) $(z - 2)(x^2 + y^2)$
(i) $(3x - 2)(1 + 4y)$ (j) $(7 - ax^2)(3 - 2b)$
3. (a) $(x + 7)(x + 5)$ (b) $(x + 9)(x + 3)$ (c) $(x + 9)(x + 2)$
(d) $(x + 18)(x + 2)$ (e) $(x + 18)(x + 3)$ (f) $(x - 5)(x - 10)$
(g) $(x - 11)(x + 10)$ (h) $(x + 11)(x - 10)$
(i) $(x - 10)(x - 11)$ (j) $(x - 15)(x - 3)$ (k) $(2x + 1)(x + 2)$
(l) $(3x + 4)(2x + 5)$ (m) $(4x + 7)(3x + 8)$
(n) $(8x + 3)(2x + 5)$ (o) $(3x - 2)(2x + 3)$
(p) $(4x - 3)(3x + 2)$ (q) $(3x - 8)(2x + 3)$
(r) $(5x - 2)(x + 7)$ (s) $(6x - 11)(2x + 3)$
(t) $(7x - 2)(6x + 1)$ **4.** (a) $(x + 3y)(x + 2y)$
(b) $(x + 7y)(x + 2y)$ (c) $(x - 3y)(x - 2y)$
(d) $(x - 2y)(x + 7y)$ (e) $(5x - 1)(2x + 3)$
(f) $(2x + 5)(x - 3)$ (g) $(7x - y)(x - 3y)$
(h) $(2a + 3b)(a - b)$ (i) $(6x - 1)(5x - 2)$ (j) $(bx + c)^2$
(k) $(2p - 1)^2$ (l) $(9x - 1)(2x + 3)$ **5.** (a) $(2x - 1)(2x + 1)$
(b) $(5x - y)(5x + y)$ (c) $(3x - 4)(3x + 4)$
(d) $(x - ab)(x + ab)$ (e) $(2m - 9n)(2m + 9n)$
(f) $(x + y - z)(x + y + z)$ (g) $(x + 1 - 3z)(x + 1 + 3z)$
(h) (Yoke – Thing)(Yoke + Thing)   **6.** (a) 200
(b) 600 (c) 400 (d) 80 (e) 60 (f) 8000 (g) 240 (h) 28
7. (a) $2(x - 2)(x + 2)$ (b) $2(3a - 2b)(3a + 2b)$
(c) $3(4x + 3y)(3x - y)$ (d) $(y + 2)(x - 1)(x + 1)$
(e) $7(2 - x)(2 + x)$ (f) $4(x - 3y)^2$ (g) $-2(x - y)^2$
(h) $(a - 2)(a + 4)$ (i) $4(2x - 3)(2x - 1)$ (j) $2(a - 17)(a + 17)$

Exercise 3

1. €$(98y - 30x)$ **2.** (a) $P = (2x + 4y + 6)$ m
(b) $A = (xy + 2 + 2y)$ m^2 **3.** $D = xy^2 - x^2y = xy(y - x)$
4. $A = (2000 + 4000y + 2005x)$ c
5. (a) (i) $P = (2x + 2y)$ m (ii) $A = (xy)$ m^2
(b) 100 m; 600 m^2 **6.** (a) $L = (4y + 2x + 6)$ m
(b) $A = (2xy + 4y)$ m^2 **7.** (a) (i) $x + 1$ (ii) $2x + 1$
(b)

Number	Sum
$x = 1$	3
$x = 2$	5
$x = 3$	7
$x = 4$	9
$x = 5$	11
$x = 6$	13
$x = 7$	15

The sum of two consecutive whole numbers is odd.
8. (a) $2\pi r$ (b) $8r$ (c) πr^2 (d) $4r^2$ (e) $4r^2 - \pi r^2$

9. (a) $(2x + 1\cdot5y)$ m (b) $(1\cdot8x + 1\cdot3y + 41)$ m
10. (a) $x(x + 2) = (x^2 + 2x)$ m^2 (b) $(x - 2)x = (x^2 - 2x)$ m^2
(c) $4x$ m^2

Chapter 4

Exercise 4

1. (a) $8x + 9$ (b) $5x - 6$ (c) $21x + 28$ (d) $-3x - 13$
(e) $13x - 23$ (f) $28x - 24$ (g) 12 (h) $2x + 3$
2. (a) $x^2 + 2x$ (b) $3x^2 + 3x$ (c) $-2x^2 + 4x$ (d) $x^2 + 3x + 2$
(e) $2x^2 + 11x + 5$ (f) $15x^2 + 31x + 14$ (g) $x^2 + 3x - 4$
(h) $8x^2 - 2x - 3$ (i) $-25x^2 + 45x - 18$ (j) $36x^2 - 49$
3. (a) $x + 4$ (b) $x - 2$ (c) $x + 3$ (d) $x - 3$ (e) $2x - 1$
(f) $5x - 1$ (g) $2(x + 1)$ (h) $3 - x$ (i) $2x - 1$ (j) $x - 1$
(k) $x + 2$ (l) $-x$

Exercise 5

1. (a) $\frac{3x + 2}{6}$ (b) $\frac{5x - 3}{15}$ (c) $\frac{9x}{14}$ (d) $\frac{7x}{12}$ (e) $\frac{2x}{3}$ (f) $\frac{-5x + 12}{12}$
(g) $\frac{x - 3}{6}$ (h) $\frac{8x + 17}{15}$ (i) $\frac{13x + 5}{12}$ (j) $\frac{-x - 5}{12}$ (k) $\frac{-3x + 4}{4}$
(l) $\frac{2x + 1}{x(x + 1)}$ (m) $\frac{5x + 13}{(x + 2)(x + 3)}$ (n) $\frac{13x + 22}{6(x + 1)(x + 2)}$
(o) $\frac{3x - 19}{(x + 2)(x - 3)}$ (p) $\frac{3(x + 1)}{x(2x - 3)}$ (q) $\frac{x + 14}{5(x - 1)(2x + 3)}$
(r) $\frac{2x^2}{(x + 1)(x - 1)}$ (s) $\frac{8x}{(x - 2)(x + 2)}$ (t) $\frac{-12x}{(3x + 1)(3x - 1)}$
2. (a) $\frac{17x}{10}$ (b) $-\frac{x}{3}$ (c) $\frac{2}{9}$ (d) $\frac{1}{4}$ (e) $-\frac{2}{7}$ (f) $\frac{x^2}{15}$ (g) $\frac{10x^2}{21}$
(h) $\frac{7x^2}{45}$ (i) $\frac{11x^2}{4}$ (j) $\frac{x^2 + x}{15} = \frac{x(x + 1)}{15}$ (k) $\frac{x^2 - 1}{21} = \frac{(x + 1)(x - 1)}{21}$
(l) $\frac{2(2x + 1)}{x - 1} = \frac{4x + 2}{x - 1}$ (m) $\frac{1}{2}$ (n) $\frac{1}{2}$ (o) $\frac{3x}{2}$ (p) $\frac{5}{3}$ (q) -2
(r) $\frac{21}{x + 2}$ (s) $\frac{5}{3}$ (t) $-(x + 2)$

Exercise 6

1. (a) 4 (b) 9 (c) 16 (d) 27 (e) 32 (f) 625
(g) 100 000 000 (h) 1 (i) 1 (j) -1 (k) 16 (l) -243
(m) $\frac{1}{4}$ (n) $\frac{4}{9}$ (o) $\frac{64}{27}$ (p) $-\frac{1}{8}$ (q) $\frac{16}{25}$ (r) $\frac{49}{4}$ (s) $\frac{121}{16}$ (t) $-\frac{125}{8}$
2. (a) $\frac{1}{2}$ (b) $\frac{1}{9}$ (c) $\frac{1}{64}$ (d) $\frac{1}{25}$ (e) $\frac{1}{16}$ (f) $\frac{5}{18}$ (g) $\frac{4}{3}$ (h) $\frac{3}{2}$
(i) $\frac{2}{3}$ (j) 6 (k) $\frac{1}{6}$ (l) 6 (m) $\frac{1}{64}$ (n) $-\frac{1}{27}$ (o) $\frac{8}{27}$ **3.** (a) 27
(b) 5 (c) 125 (d) 16 (e) $\frac{1}{6}$ (f) $\frac{1}{4}$ (g) 1 (h) 8 (i) $\frac{3}{500}$
(j) 28 (k) $\frac{3}{2}$ (l) $\frac{1}{3}$ (m) $10^6 = 1\,000\,000$ (n) -32 (o) $\frac{1}{10}$
(p) $\frac{3}{2}$ (q) $\frac{2}{3}$ (r) $-\frac{2}{3}$ (s) $-\frac{3}{2}$ (t) 1 (u) 3 (v) -3 (w) $\frac{2}{3}$ (x) $\frac{9}{5}$
4. (a) $2^{\frac{7}{2}}$ (b) $3^{\frac{5}{2}}$ (c) $\frac{1}{5^{\frac{5}{2}}}$ (d) $7^{\frac{13}{6}}$ (e) $5^{\frac{3}{2}}$ **5.** (a) a^9 (b) a^{21}
(c) a^4 (d) a^4 (e) $a^{\frac{1}{3}}$ (f) $a^{\frac{3}{2}}$ (g) a^{12} (h) $\frac{1}{a^2}$ (i) $a^{\frac{3}{2}}$ (j) a^5
(k) $a^{\frac{2}{3}}$ (l) $a^{\frac{23}{2}}$ (m) $\frac{1}{a^3}$ (n) $a^{\frac{7}{2}}$ **6.** (a) x^4y (b) $2x^5$ (c) $4x$
(d) $\frac{1}{2x^2}$ (e) 2 (f) $2x^5y$ (g) 2^{2x} (h) $2^{4x}x$ (i) $\frac{2}{x^3}$ (j) $\frac{x^8y^4}{81z^{12}}$
(k) $\frac{5}{2x^2}$ (l) $(a + 3b)^5$ (m) $\frac{b}{xy}$ (n) $\frac{1}{2y^2a^2}$ (o) $2a^2y^2$ (p) $\frac{5}{y}$

Exercise 7

1. (a) $2\sqrt{3}$ (b) $3\sqrt{3}$ (c) $5\sqrt{2}$ (d) $3\sqrt{5}$ (e) $11\sqrt{10}$
(f) $5\sqrt{3}$ (g) $4\sqrt{2}$ (h) $7\sqrt{2}$ (i) $6\sqrt{2}$ (j) $16\sqrt{2}$ (k) $\frac{2\sqrt{2}}{3}$
(l) $\frac{3\sqrt{2}}{5}$ (m) $\sqrt{3}$ (n) $\frac{7\sqrt{3}}{10}$ (o) $\frac{5\sqrt{3}}{6}$ **2.** (a) $3\sqrt{11}$
(b) $-4 + 15\sqrt{3}$ (c) $3x - 7\sqrt{y}$ (d) 0 (e) 0 (f) $5\sqrt{2} + 5\sqrt{3}$
(g) 0 **3.** (a) $2\sqrt{2}$ (b) $\sqrt{6}$ (c) $60\sqrt{3}$ (d) $6\sqrt{3} + 6\sqrt{2} + 6$
(e) $4 + 2\sqrt{3}$ (f) 2 (g) $ab(\sqrt{a} + \sqrt{b})$ (h) $20 + 2\sqrt{91}$
(i) -6 **4.** (a) $\frac{\sqrt{5}}{5}$ (b) $-\frac{\sqrt{2}}{2}$ (c) $\frac{2\sqrt{3}}{3}$ (d) $\frac{2\sqrt{2}}{5}$ (e) $-\frac{\sqrt{3}}{2}$
(f) $\frac{\sqrt{42}}{14}$ (g) $\frac{x\sqrt{y}}{y}$ (h) $\frac{\sqrt{xy}}{y}$ **5.** 11 **6.** (a) $0\cdot 56$ (b) $0\cdot 03$
(c) $0\cdot 53$ (d) $0\cdot 59$

Revision Questions

1. $9x + 7$ **2.** (a) $(8x + 4)$ cm (b) $6(2x + 1)$ cm^2
3. $\frac{2}{3}x$; $\frac{3x}{2}$ **4.** (a) $\frac{6x^2 + 25x + 24}{2x + 3}$ (b) $3x + 8$ (c) $10x + 22$
5. (a) $\frac{1}{x}$ m^{-1} (b) $-\frac{1}{x+2}$ m^{-1} (c) $\frac{2}{x(x+2)}$ m^{-1}
(d) Power $= \frac{8}{5}$ m^{-1}; $f = \frac{5}{8}$ m **6.** (a) $\frac{2}{x-2}$ hours
(b) $\frac{2}{x+2}$ hours (c) The man's speed is greater
(d) $\frac{8}{x^2-4}$ (e) 206 s **7.** (a) $A^{\frac{2}{3}} = \left(\sqrt[3]{A}\right)^2$ (b) 4
(c) $1\cdot 368$ m^2 **8.** (b) 6 g (c) Fraction left after n
half-lives $= \frac{1}{2^n}$ **9.** (a) 192π cm^3 (b) $12\pi x^2$ cm^3
(c) $12\pi(4 - x)(4 + x)$ cm^3 (d) 84π cm^3
10. (a) 3200 (b) 100 (c) $\frac{2^t}{32}$ (i) $\frac{1}{8}$ (ii) 1 (iii) 32
(d) Number in B is less than in A for $t < 5$;
Numbers equal for $t = 5$; Number in B is greater
than in A for $t > 5$

Section 3
Chapter 5

Exercise 1

1. (a) 9 (b) -4 (c) 2 (d) 3 (e) 3 (f) 3 (g) -2 (h) $\frac{3}{2}$ (i) 2
(j) 1 **2.** (a) -2 (b) -7 (c) 1 (d) $-\frac{50}{9}$ (e) $-\frac{1}{2}$ (f) 5
(g) $\frac{14}{3}$ (h) 8 (i) 1 (j) $\frac{9}{4}$ **3.** (a) 2 (b) $-\frac{1}{4}$ (c) 14 (d) 7
(e) 7 (f) 4 (g) 16 (h) 8 (i) 3 (j) 4 **4.** (a) 5 (b) 2 (c) 7
(d) 5 (e) $-\frac{23}{7}$ (f) $-\frac{7}{4}$ **5.** (c) -5 (d) Yes **6.** (a) 23 cm,
69 cm (b) $l = 13\cdot 75$ m, $b = 8\cdot 25$ m, $A = 113\cdot 4375$ m^2
(c) 15 cm, 20 cm, 25 cm (d) 12, 8 (e) 15, 16, 17
(f) Sandra $= 14$ yrs, Anna $= 12$ yrs (g) 15 yrs (h) 16 at
€$1\cdot 50$, 9 at €1 (i) 360 units (j) 7, 8, 9, 10, 11 (k) 80 km
(l) 120 weeks (m) 414 (n) Man $= 40$ yrs; Son $= 20$ yrs

Exercise 2

1. (a) -2, 1 (b) 3, $-\frac{1}{2}$ (c) $\frac{7}{2}$, $\frac{7}{2}$ (d) 0, 3 (e) 0, $\frac{7}{3}$ (f) 0, 2
(g) 0, 3 (h) 0, $\frac{1}{9}$ (i) 3, -3 (j) 0, $\frac{1}{4}$ **2.** (a) 5, -5 (b) 2, -2
(c) -3, 5 (d) -11, 3 (e) -1, $-\frac{1}{2}$ (f) $\frac{5}{4}$, $\frac{2}{3}$ (g) -6, $\frac{2}{3}$
(h) $-\frac{8}{7}$, 1 (i) 2, 3 **3.** (a) -25, 1 (b) -4, 3 (c) -1, 2
(d) -1, $\frac{4}{7}$ (e) $-\frac{1}{3}$, 3 **4.** (a) $-\frac{3}{2}$ (c) Yes, it is a solution
5. (a) $1 \pm \sqrt{31}$; $6\cdot 57$, $-4\cdot 57$ (b) $1 \pm \sqrt{10}$;
$4\cdot 16$, $-2\cdot 16$ (c) $\frac{19 \pm \sqrt{345}}{8}$; $4\cdot 70$, $0\cdot 05$ (d) $\frac{1}{2}$, $-\frac{2}{3}$
(e) $\frac{5 \pm \sqrt{73}}{4}$; $3\cdot 39$, $-0\cdot 89$ (f) $\frac{4 \pm \sqrt{22}}{3}$; $2\cdot 90$, $-0\cdot 23$
(g) $\frac{-4 \pm \sqrt{30}}{7}$; $0\cdot 21$, $-1\cdot 35$ (h) $\frac{-4 \pm \sqrt{22}}{2}$; $0\cdot 35$, $-4\cdot 35$
(i) $\pm\sqrt{3}$; $1\cdot 73$, $-1\cdot 73$ (j) $\pm\sqrt{8} = \pm 2\sqrt{2}$; $2\cdot 83$, $-2\cdot 83$
6. (a) 2 equal real roots; 2, 2 (b) 2 real roots; 0, 3
(c) 2 real roots; -1, 5 **7.** -3 **8.** (a) $x^2 - 3x + 2 = 0$
(b) $x^2 - 6x + 9 = 0$ (c) $x^2 + 3x + 2 = 0$ (d) $x^2 + x - 30 = 0$
(e) $4x^2 - 8x + 3 = 0$ **9.** (a) $-\frac{1}{3}$, $\frac{5}{2}$ (b) -1, 3 (c) 2, 3
(d) 2, 6 (e) $0\cdot 3$, $-3\cdot 3$ **10.** (a) $x = 2$, 5; $y = 4$, 7
(b) $x = -\frac{2}{3}$, $\frac{5}{2}$; $t = \frac{1}{3}$, $\frac{7}{2}$ (c) $x = 1$, $\frac{4}{3}$; $y = 6$, 7
(d) $x = 3$, 7; $x = -3$, 6, -2, 9 (e) $x = \frac{3}{5}$, 4; $y = \frac{13}{5}$, 6
11. (a) 12 (b) 4 (c) 50, 190 (d) $3\ \Omega$ (e) 2 s, 14 s
(f) $l = 24\cdot 05$ m, $b = 11\cdot 10$ m (g) $l = 10\cdot 8$ m,
$w = 7\cdot 8$ m (h) 2 (i) $|PQ| = 5$ cm, $|PR| = 12$ cm,
$|QR| = 13$ cm

Chapter 6

Exercise 3

1. (a) 16 (b) $\frac{1}{4}$ (c) $10\,000$ (d) a (e) e^2 (f) 2 (g) $4^{\frac{2}{3}} = \sqrt[3]{16}$
(h) $(a - 1)^2 = a^2 - 2a + 1$ (i) $\frac{4}{9}$ (j) $1\cdot 44$ **2.** (a) 5 (b) 11
(c) 7 (d) 5 (e) 24 (f) 12 (g) -3 (h) 13 (i) 2, 4 (j) 5 (k) $\frac{3}{2}$

Exercise 4

1. (a) $y - 4$ (b) $\frac{y}{3}$ (c) $\frac{y-4}{3}$ (d) $\frac{100I}{PR}$ (e) $\frac{2\pi lp}{w}$ (f) $\frac{v^2 - u^2}{2S}$
(g) $\frac{S - 2\pi r^2}{2\pi r}$ (h) $\frac{mV}{a - V}$ (i) $\pm\sqrt{\frac{A}{\pi h}}$ (j) $\pm\sqrt{\frac{3V}{\pi h}}$ (k) $\frac{v^2}{5g}$ (l) $\frac{4\pi^2 k}{HT^2}$
(m) $\frac{2D^2}{3}$ (n) $\pm\sqrt{\frac{2H}{g}}$ (o) $\pm\sqrt{\frac{2A}{x}}$ (p) $\pm\sqrt{\frac{r - a}{b}}$
(q) $3P + b$ (r) $\frac{5Q + 3l}{9}$ (s) $\frac{6}{L - 9}$ (t) $dt + s$ (u) $\pm\sqrt{Q - 3f}$
(v) $\pm\sqrt{\frac{M + 1}{z}}$ (w) $\frac{b^2 - A^2}{4c}$ (x) $\pm\sqrt{\frac{2E}{C}}$ (y) $\pm\sqrt{v^2 - 2as}$
2. $s = \frac{(q - p)^2}{4}$; $1\cdot 69$ **3.** $r = \sqrt{\frac{V}{\pi h}}$; 2 cm
4. $\frac{500D^2}{h}$; $6366\cdot 8$ km **5.** $A = \frac{17C}{t + 1}$; $A = 68$ mg;
$t = 16$ yrs

Exercise 5

1. (a) 2^2 (b) 2^4 (c) 2^7 (d) 2^{12} (e) 2^1 (f) 2^4 (g) 2^{-4} (h) 2^4
(i) $2^{-\frac{7}{2}}$ (j) $2^{-\frac{1}{2}}$ (k) 2^4 (l) 2^0 **2.** (a) 3^2 (b) 3^{-1} (c) 3^{-2}
(d) 3^4 (e) 3^{-3} (f) 3^3 (g) 3^6 (h) $3^{\frac{3}{2}}$ (i) 3^{-4} (j) 3^2 (k) 3^4
(l) 3^2 **3.** (a) 2^{2x} (b) 2^{-x} (c) $2^{\frac{x}{2}}$ (d) 2^{3x} (e) 2^{4-x} (f) 2^{1+3x}
(g) 2^{5x-1} (h) 2^{4x} (i) 2^{8x-1} (j) 2^{-3x} (k) 2^{x+2} **4.** (a) 3^{2x}
(b) 3^{-2x} (c) 3^{-2x} (d) 3^{2x} (e) 3^{2x+4} (f) 3^{-x} (g) 3^{2x+1}
(h) 3^{2x+1} (i) 3^{2x-4} **5.** (a) 2 (b) -2 (c) 3 (d) -2 (e) $\frac{4}{3}$
(f) $-\frac{3}{2}$ (g) $\frac{3}{2}$ (h) $-\frac{3}{2}$ (i) 3 (j) -8 (k) $\frac{3}{2}$ (l) 4 (m) -6
(n) $\frac{7}{4}$ (o) $-\frac{5}{4}$ (p) 4 (q) $-\frac{4}{3}$ (r) $\frac{1}{2}$ (s) $\frac{6}{5}$ **6.** (a) $2^{-\frac{7}{2}}$; $-\frac{15}{2}$
(b) $3^{\frac{13}{3}}$; $-\frac{1}{6}$ (c) $2^{\frac{7}{2}}$; $\frac{5}{8}$ (d) $5^{\frac{11}{2}}$; 4 **7.** (a) 17
(b) $1\frac{1}{2}$ months **8.** (a) 51 (b) 2 months **9.** 1 month
10. (a) €4000 (b) €64 000 (c) 30 yrs

Chapter 7

Exercise 6A

1. $(2, 3)$ **2.** $(2, 1)$ **3.** $(2, 4)$ **4.** $(2, 3)$ **5.** $(1, -2)$
6. $(1, 1)$ **7.** $(2, 3)$ **8.** $(4, 3)$ **9.** $\left(-\frac{27}{2}, -7\right)$
10. $\left(\frac{17}{8}, -\frac{1}{2}\right)$ **11.** $(4, 1)$ **12.** $(8, -4)$ **13.** $(6, -4)$
14. $(4, 10)$ **15.** $(-5, -3)$ **16.** $\left(2, \frac{1}{2}\right)$ **17.** $(2, 1)$

18. $a = 8, b = 0·5$ **19.** $a = 14, b = -6$ **20.** $a = \frac{18}{5}$,
$b = -\frac{3}{5}, V = 3·6 \text{ m}^3$

Exercise 6B

1. 71, 64 **2.** 7, 4 **3.** 3, -5 **4.** 17, 12 **5.** 72, 24
6. 6, 6 **7.** $l = 32$ m, $b = 25$ m, $A = 800$ m^2
8. (a) $x = 5, y = 1$ (b) $P = 24$ cm, $A = 35$ cm^2
9. (a) $x = 12, y = 8$ (b) $P = 60$ cm, $A = 100\sqrt{3}$ cm^2
10. 7 cm, 7 cm, 3 cm **11.** €15 000 at 2%, €5000 at 3%
12. Bankwin shares cost €4·80, Academic Enterprise
shares cost €6·20 **13.** 37 of 5c coins, 4 of 10c coins
14. 8 of 5-mark questions, 5 of 12-mark questions
15. 108 car spaces; 54 truck spaces **16.** 10 litres of
each **17.** 37·17 g of 90% alloy, 15·93 g of 80% alloy

Exercise 7A

1. $(4, 3) (3, 4)$ **2.** $(-6, -7) (7, 6)$ **3.** $(1, 2) (2, 1)$
4. $(-2, -3) (3, 2)$ **5.** $(2, 6) (6, 2)$ **6.** $(4, 2)$; The line
is tangent to the curve **7.** $\left(\frac{27}{11}, \frac{29}{11}\right) (3, 1)$ **8.** $(-2, 3)$
$\left(\frac{3}{2}, -4\right)$ **9.** $(0, -5) \left(\frac{5}{2}, 0\right)$ **10.** $(-1, 3) (3, -5)$

Exercise 7B

1. 11, 8 *or* $-8, -11$ **2.** 23, 19 **3.** 15, 8
4. $\left(\frac{3+\sqrt{5}}{2}, \frac{3-\sqrt{5}}{2}\right), \left(\frac{3-\sqrt{5}}{2}, \frac{3+\sqrt{5}}{2}\right)$ **5.** 45 m, 80 m
6. $(-3, -5) \left(\frac{11}{5}, \frac{27}{5}\right)$ **7.** $x = 4, y = 3; l = 9$ cm, $b = 4$ cm,
$A = 36$ cm^2 **8.** $x = 0·8$ m, $y = 0·6$ m, $V = 0·24$ m^3
9. *Ulysses* 40 km/h, *Jonathan Swift* 74 km/h
10. $\left(\frac{12}{5}, -\frac{3}{5}\right) (3, 0)$

Chapter 8

Exercise 8

1. (a) $x > 9, x \in \mathbb{R}$ (b) $x < 9, x \in \mathbb{N}$ (c) $x \leq -1, x \in \mathbb{R}$
(d) $x \geq 12, x \in \mathbb{R}$ (e) $x > 15, x \in \mathbb{R}$ (f) $x \leq -9, x \in \mathbb{R}$
(g) $x \geq -4, x \in \mathbb{R}$ (h) $x \geq -2, x \in \mathbb{R}$ (i) $x < -1, x \in \mathbb{R}$
(j) $x > -5, x \in \mathbb{R}$ (k) $x > \frac{7}{4}, x \in \mathbb{R}$ (l) $x \geq -\frac{7}{2}, x \in \mathbb{R}$
(m) $x \leq 15, x \in \mathbb{Z}$ (n) $x \leq -\frac{1}{18}, x \in \mathbb{R}$ (o) $x \leq \frac{4}{3}, x \in \mathbb{R}$
(p) $x < -\frac{34}{13}, x \in \mathbb{R}$ (q) $x < \frac{1}{8}, x \in \mathbb{R}$ (r) $x < -\frac{1}{9}, x \in \mathbb{R}$
(s) $x \geq -\frac{1}{8}, x \in \mathbb{R}$ (t) $x \leq \frac{3}{10}, x \in \mathbb{R}$ **2.** (b) $x < 9, x \in \mathbb{N}$

(i) $x < -1, x \in \mathbb{R}$

(l) $x \geq -\frac{7}{2}, x \in \mathbb{R}$

(t) $x \leq \frac{3}{10}, x \in \mathbb{R}$

3. (a) $\{1, 2, 3\}$ (b) $\{-2, -1, 0, 1, 2, ...\}$
(c) $\{-4, -3, -2, -1, 0, 1, ...\}$ (d) $A = 1, 2, ..., 10, 11\}$;
$B = \{7, 8, 9, 10, 11, 12, ...\}$; $A \cap B = \{7, 8, 9, 10, 11\}$
(e) $A = \{1, 2, 3, 4\}$; $B = \{1, 2, ..., 8\}$;
$B / A = \{5, 6, 7, 8\}$ (f) $P = \{-4, -3, -2, ...\}$,
$Q = \{-3, -2, -1, ...\}, P / Q = \{-4\}$

Revision Questions

1. (a) $\frac{-1 \pm \sqrt{5}}{2}$ (b) (i) 6 (ii) 64 (iii) $\pm\sqrt{8} = \pm 2\sqrt{2}$
(c) 4 mins **2.** (a) $(8, 3)$
(b) (i) $A = \{... -1, 0, 1, 2, 3, 4\}$
(ii) $B = \{-3, -2, -1, 0, 1, ...\}$

(iii) $A \cap B = \{-3, -2, -1, 0, 1, 2, 3, 4\}$
(c) $a = -1, b = 1, c = 2$ **3.** (a) $N = -8000x + 32\,000$
(b) $P = Nx - 10\,000$ (c) $P = -8000x^2 + 32\,000x - 10\,000$
(d) €14 000 (e) €2 **4.** (a) $k = 3 \cdot 2, H = \dfrac{256\,L^2}{25\,r^2}$
(b) The room costs €72 per night. The breakfast
costs €12 (c) $\left(\dfrac{11}{5}, \dfrac{2}{5}\right)$ (2, 1) **5.** (a) $-2 \pm \sqrt{5}$ (b) 3 years
(c) $x = 4, y = 1$ **6.** (a) $-\dfrac{1}{2}$ (b) $k = \dfrac{17}{2}$
(c) (i) $x^2 - 4x - 5 = 0$ (ii) $12x^2 - 11x + 2 = 0$
(d) Speed = 3 m/s, time upstream = 20 mins,
time downstream = 4 mins **7.** (a) (6, 10)
(b) (i) 5050 (ii) 1, 2, 3, 4, 5, 6, 7, 8, 9, 10, 11
(c) (ii) $C = -750x + 49\,000$ (iii) $R = -50x^2 + 3100x$
(iv) $P = -50x^2 + 3850x - 49\,000$ (v) €54 **8.** (a) 6
(b) White tiles cost €5·50, red tiles cost €8 (c) −7, 4
9. (a) $\dfrac{E - IR}{I}$ (c) $U(-2 \cdot 15, 0)$ $V(0 \cdot 15, 0)$ $W(0, -1)$
10. (a) 85° (b) 24, 26 (c) (i) 104·9 m (ii) 5 s

(iii) 3 s, 7 s

Section 4
Chapter 9

Exercise 1

1. (a) −8 (b) 5 (c) First term is −8, add 5 each time
to get successive terms (d) 22, 27, 32, 37
(f) $-8 + (n - 1) \times 5 = 5n - 13$ (g) 157 (h) Infinite
sequence **2.** (a) 3 (c) $3n + 8$ (d) (i) 119 (ii) 308
(iii) 311 **3.** (b) n^3 (c) 10648 **4.** (a) 3
(c) $T_n = 2 \times 3^n$ (d) 3 **5.** (a) (i) 1 (ii) 4 (iii) 19
(iv) 31 (b) T_{32} or 32nd term **6.** (a) 3, 8, 15, 24, 35
(b) T_{10} or 10th term **7.** (a) (i) −23 (ii) −28 (iii) −253
(iv) −258 **8.** (a) 2, 1, $\dfrac{1}{2}$, $\dfrac{1}{4}$, $\dfrac{1}{8}$ (b) T_9 or 9th term

9. (a)

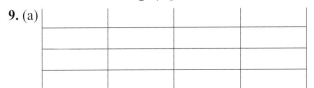

(b) 5, 9, 13, 17

(c)

n	T_n
1	$5 = 5 + 4 \times 0$
2	$9 = 5 + 4 \times 1$
3	$13 = 5 + 4 \times 2$
4	$17 = 5 + 4 \times 3$

(d) $4n + 1$ (e) 41 (f) 15th stage

10. (a) (i) and (ii)

No. of sides N	Sum of interior angles, T_n
3	$180° = 180° \times (3 - 2)$
4	$360° = 180° \times (4 - 2)$
5	$540° = 180° \times (5 - 2)$
6	$720° = 180° \times (6 - 2)$

(iii) $180°(n - 2)$ (b) 1440° (c) 23 sides
11. (a) (i) 23 (ii) $6n - 1$ (b) (i) 16 (ii) 31 (iii) $3n + 1$

Chapter 10

Exercise 2

1. Arithmetic   **2.** Geometric   **3.** Neither
4. Geometric   **5.** Geometric   **6.** Arithmetic
7. Geometric   **8.** Geometric   **9.** Geometric
10. Arithmetic   **11.** Neither   **12.** Arithmetic
13. Geometric   **14.** Neither   **15.** Geometric
16. Arithmetic   **17.** Arithmetic   **18.** Geometric
19. Geometric   **20.** Arithmetic

Exercise 3

1. (a) (i) 3 (ii) 19 (iii) 8 (iv) 8 (b) $T_5 = 35$, $T_6 = 43$
2. (a) (i) 5 (ii) 3 (iii) 1 (iv) −2 (v) −2 (b) −1, −3, −5
3. (a) (i) 4 (ii) 7 (c) 291   **4.** (a) (i) −3 (ii) −4 (c) −83
5. (a) (i) $\dfrac{1}{2}$ (ii) $\dfrac{1}{3}$ (c) $\dfrac{35}{6}$

Exercise 4

1. (a) 4, 19, 14, 24, 54, 609 (b) 4, 2, 0, −104, −204
(c) 5, 8, 9, $\dfrac{59}{2} = 29\dfrac{1}{2}$, 41 (d) 15, 24, 66 (e) 180 kg
(f) 9·15 km (g) 108 (h) (i) 24 000, 27 000, 30 000,
33 000, 36 000 (ii) Yes (iii) $a = 24\,000$, $d = 3000$
(iv) €141 000   **2.** (a) 2, 2, $2n$ (b) 1, 2, $2n - 1$
(c) 7, −2, $9 - 2n$ (d) 3, 0·5, $\dfrac{n + 5}{2}$ (e) −1, −3, $2 - 3n$
(f) −6, 4, $4n - 10$ (g) x, −1, $x + 1 - n$
(h) $b, c, cn + b - c$ (i) $\dfrac{1}{2}, \dfrac{1}{2}, \dfrac{1}{2}n$ (j) 4, 4·1, 4·2, ...; 4,
0·1, 4·7 km   **3.** (a) $a = 2$, $d = 1$; 2, 3, 4, 5, 6 (b) $a = 2$,
$d = 2$; 2, 4, 6, 8, 10 (c) $a = 5$, $d = 2$; 5, 7, 9, 11, 13
(d) $a = 1$, $d = 3$; 1, 4, 7, 10, 13 (e) $a = -2$,
$d = 5$; −2, 3, 8, 13, 18 (f) $a = \dfrac{2}{3}$, $d = \dfrac{1}{3}$; $\dfrac{2}{3}$, 1, $\dfrac{4}{3}$, $\dfrac{5}{3}$, 2
4. (a) $2n$, 14 (b) $9 - 2n$, −25 (c) $3n - 4$, 59
(d) $-2n - 1$, −85 (e) $\dfrac{3 - n}{2}$, −16 (f) $\dfrac{n + 2}{2}$, 30
(g) $\dfrac{15 - 5n}{2}$, −85 (h) $a + n - 1$, $a + 11$ (i) $a + (n - 1)d$,
$a + 44d$ (j) $\dfrac{4n - 1}{6}$, $\dfrac{191}{6} = 31\dfrac{5}{6}$ **5.** (a) T_{13}
(b) T_{62} (c) T_7 (d) T_{10} (e) April 16th (f) (i) 24
(ii) 66 (iii) 20 (iv) 50

Exercise 5

1. (a) $n(n + 7)$, 638 (b) $n(2n + 10)$, 2368

(c) $n(10n - 27)$, 8190 (d) $\dfrac{n(13 - n)}{4}$, −270

(e) $\dfrac{n(3n - 19)}{2}$, 3861 (f) $\dfrac{n(2n + 1)}{12}$, 388

(g) $n(12 - n)$, −925 (h) $\dfrac{n(2x + 3n - 3)}{2}$, $12x + 198$

(i) $\dfrac{n(n + 1)}{8}$, 657 (j) $\dfrac{n(3n - 9)}{2}$, 825 **2.** (a) 2550

(b) 2500 (c) 500 500 (d) 3575 (e) 201 000

3. (a) 5, 2 (b) 10, 14, 18, 22 (c) −35 (d) −105

4. (a) €2250 (b) €1 904 000; €63 200 (c) €377 500

(d) 63; 1020 (e) 14, 1225 (f) 4092 **5.** (a) (i) 2

(ii) 7 (iii) 2 (iv) 5 (v) $\dfrac{n(5n - 1)}{2}$ (vi) 3404 (b) (i) −5

(ii) −5 (iii) −5 (iv) 6 (v) 79 (vi) $6n - 11$ (vii) 2816

(viii) $n(3n - 8)$ (ix) 29 200 (c) (i) 3 (ii) 8 (iii) 2600

(iv) 3 (v) 5 (vi) 2 (vii) 69

Exercise 6

1. (a) First differences: 2, 3, 4, 5, ….; second differences: 1, 1, 1, … (b) First differences: 5, 7, 9, 11, ….; second differences: 2, 2, 2, … (c) First differences: 2, 4, 6, 8, ….; second differences: 2, 2, 2, … (d) First differences: 8, 14, 20, 26, ….; second differences: 6, 6, 6, … (e) First differences: −3, −5, −7, −9, ….; second differences: −2, −2, −2, … (f) First differences: −6, −10, −14, −18, ….; second differences: −4, −4, −4, … (g) First differences: −4, −6, −8, −10, ….; second differences: −2, −2, −2, … (h) First differences: 2, 3, 4, 5, ….; second differences: 1, 1, 1, … (i) First differences: 5, 8, 11, 14, ….; second differences: 3, 3, 3, … (j) First differences: $3t + 1, 5t + 1, 7t + 1, 9t + 1$, ...; second differences: $2t, 2t, 2t$, … **2.** (a) 43, 65 (b) 70, 90 (c) 115, 167 (d) 65, 98 (e) −27, −23 **3.** (a) 2, 5, 10, 17 (b) 2, 8, 18, 32 (c) −1, −1, 1, 5 (d) 2, −1, −6, −13 (e) 0, 1, 6, 15 **4.** (b) 1, 3, 6, 10, 15, 21 (c) (i) First differences: 2, 3, 4, 5, 6 (ii) Second differences: 1, 1, 1, 1; The sequence is a quadratic sequence.

Revision Questions

1. (c) $N = 3n + 2$ (d) 32 (e) 22 **2.** (a) $7 - 2n$ (b) 3, 1, −1, −3 (d) Slope = −2 (e) $\dfrac{3}{2}$ (i) $\dfrac{11}{2}$ (ii) $\dfrac{3}{2}$ **3.** (b) 7, 9, 3, 1, 7, 9, 3, 1 (c) 3 (d) 0, 4, 4, 0, 0, 4, 4, 0; 4 **4.** (b) Any term − previous term = constant = −5 (c) (i) 1000 (ii) −5 (d) 945 litres

(e) 101st day **5.** (c) $2n$ (d) $n + 2$ (e) $3n + 2$ (f) 98 hours **6.** (a) 2000, 2350, 2700, 3050 (b) Any term − previous term = constant = 350 (c) $a = 2000$, $d = 350$ (d) $350n + 1650$ (e) 5150 m (f) 7th day (g) 47 100 m (h) 7 **7.** (c) $N = 6l + 2$ (d) $n = 14l - 1$ (e) $n = \dfrac{7N - 17}{3}$ or $N = \dfrac{3n + 17}{7}$ (f) 314 (g) 80 (h) 137 **8.** (a) −11, −20 (b) −11, −9 (c) −11, 2 (d) $2n - 13$ (e) 1, 11 **9.** (a) (i) −7 (ii) 3 (iii) 42 (iv) 42 (v) 2289 (b) 736 **10.** (a) (ii) $22 - 2n$ (iii) −14°C (b) (i) 25 (ii) 13 (iii) 25 (iv) 325 **11.** (a) (i) −5 (ii) 7 (b) −5, 2, 9, 16 (c) 2895 **12.** (a) 4, 7, 10 (b) 61 (c) 650

Section 5
Chapter 11

Exercise 1

1. (a) 62·8 km/h (b) €5·40; 90c per can (c) No (d) 160-page refill pad (e) 870 ml bottle (f) 416 m² (g) 36·25% (h) $\dfrac{2}{3}$ **2.** (a) 5×10^{-2} m (b) $2·7 \times 10^{-3}$ km (c) $5·4 \times 10^{6}$ m² (d) $2·6 \times 10^{-4}$ m² (e) $6·8 \times 10^{-4}$ m³ (f) 5×10^{3} kg (g) $5·6 \times 10^{-6}$ m³ (h) 5×10^{3} cm³ (i) 5×10^{-3} m³ **3.** (a) 20 m/s (b) 30 m/s (c) $27\dfrac{7}{9}$ m/s = 27·8 m/s (d) 12·5 m/s (e) 36 km/h (f) 56·16 km/h (g) 10·8 km/h (h) 90 km/h (i) $20\dfrac{5}{6}$ m/s = 20·8 m/s (j) 32·4 km/h **4.** 13 gallons **5.** 6697·6 km **6.** 8847·6 m **7.** 4·16 **8.** 2·44 m; 1·62 feet **9.** (a) 52 500 m² (b) $5·25 \times 10^{-2}$ km² (c) 5·25 hectares (d) 13 acres **10.** 120 yards **11.** (a) $1·08 \times 10^{9}$ km/h (b) $6·7 \times 10^{8}$ mph

Exercise 2

1. (a) £659·36 (b) $1091·20 (c) CAD$1216·80 (d) R12 248 **2.** (a) €366·57 (b) €788·64 (c) €1457·42 (d) $5406·13 (e) £120·85 (f) 1783·70 rupees **3.** (a) $1620·43 (b) €513·75 **4.** (a) (i) €66·73 (ii) 707·30 HKD (b) 2248 THB (c) 2544·91 THB **5.** (a) €645·21 (b) €678·43 (c) €33·22 **6.** (a) $\dfrac{5}{4}$ (b) $y = \dfrac{5}{4}x$ (c) €250 (d) £240 (e) €1 = £0·80; Exchange rate from £ to € is constant over this period

Exercise 3

1. €270·60 **2.** £346·80 **3.** €219·56 **4.** €357 **5.** €378·51 **6.** €62·39 **7.** €60·86 **8.** (a) €38 610 in Luxembourg (b) €40 920 in Finland **9.** €35 593·22; €42 711·86 **10.** €21 049

11. €6000; €2700 **12.** (a) €37 (b) €13·91 (c) €20
(d) €70·91 (e) €429·09 **13.** (a) €2240 (b) €2373·06
(c) €12 270 (d) €39 116·94 yearly; €3259·75 monthly
14. €48 000; €1933·06 **15.** €57 490
16. (a) €68 644 (b) €2745·76 (c) €45 432·16

Chapter 12

Exercise 4

1. (a)

CP (€)	SP (€)	Profit (€)	% Profit	Profit margin
100	150	50	50	$33\frac{1}{3}$%
180	300	120	$66\frac{2}{3}$	40%
250	312·50	62·50	25	20%
50·40	72	21·60	42·86	30%
72	160	88	122·2	55%

(b)

CP (€)	SP (€)	Loss	% Loss
100	75	25	25
172	87	85	49·4
170	100	70	41·2

2. (a) 20% (b) €1073·52 **3.** 14·3% **4.** €446·25
5. (a) €6210 (b) 76·2% (c) 43·2% **6.** 20%
7. (a) €30 000 (b) €19 755·09

Exercise 5

1. (a) €2131·25 (b) €206·72 (c) 4·2% (d) 9·3%
(e) €277·28 **2.** (a) €420 (b) €3780 (c) €1209·60
(d) €4989·60 (e) €103·95 **3.** (a) €1350 (b) €13 425·84
(c) €14 775·84 (d) €1275·84 (e) 9·45% **4.** (a) €4650
(b) €1046·25 (c) €158·23 (d) €7196·25 **5.** €405
6. (a) (i) €10 300 (ii) €10 609 (iii) €10 927·27
(b) (i) €25 625 (ii) €26 265·63 (iii) €26 922·27
7. (a) €10 302·25 (b) €23 622·32 **8.** (a) €20 665·13
(b) €14 111·17 **9.** (a) 1·57% (b) 2·4% **10.** €10 250
11. €16 120 **12.** 4% **13.** €28 295·79 **14.** 1·32%
15. 41·4% **16.** €26 520; €2·50 **17.** €20 000
18. 5%, €2500 **19.** (a) €11 411·66 (b) €10 710; Option 1
20. 5% **21.** €2125 **22.** €45 999 **23.** 20%
24. (a) €13 500 (b) €12 150 **25.** 43·75%

Revision Questions

1. (a) (i) €16·20 (ii) 23·5% (iii) 28% (b) (i) 20 days
(ii) 15 days **2.** (a) €10 506 (b) 2·5% **3.** (a) €1560
(b) 192% (c) €38 768·06 (d) €51 660 (e) 25%
4. (a) (i) 4 hrs (ii) €475·20 (iii) €21·30 (b) €852
(c) €210·80 (d) €147·80 (e) €34·08 (f) €33·37
(g) €636·85 **5.** (a) €336 866·63 (b) (i) 266 (ii) €26 600
(iii) 38·7% (iv) €7140 **6.** (a) 34·6 (b) 28·74 (c) 17%
(d) Mass = 183·12 pounds, height = 66·93 inches
7. (a) €1 = £0·8394 (b) €655·23 (c) €1 = £0·7983
(d) £534·86 **8.** (a) €571·34 (b) 6·5% (c) €2432
9. (a) (i) €50 000 (ii) €20 000 (b) −7500 euro/year
(c) $V = 50 000 - 7500t$ (d) 1 August 2016 (e) 20·5%
10. (a) 8·208 m^2 (b) 377 tiles (c) 3·2% (d) 10 boxes
(e) 23 (f) €1045·50

Section 6
Chapter 13

Exercise 1

1. (a) 4 Re (b) −7 Re (c) −3$\sqrt{2}$ Re (d) 4i Im (e) 7i Im
(f) 9i Im (g) −5i Im (h) $\sqrt{3}i$ Im (i) $\sqrt{2}i$ Im (j) $\frac{1}{\sqrt{7}}i$ Im
(k) $\frac{\sqrt{3}}{4}i$ Im (l) $\frac{3}{4}i$ Im **2.** (a) 7 Re (b) −9 Re (c) 7i Im
(d) −9i Im (e) 16$\sqrt{2}$ Re (f) −9 Re (g) 18i Im
3. (a) −i (b) 1 (c) i (d) −1 (e) 3 (f) 2i (g) 3i (h) 4i
(i) −1 (j) −11i (k) 18i (l) i (m) 2i (n) 32i

Exercise 2

1. (a) 2 + 3i, 2, 3 (b) 5 − 7i, 5, −7 (c) −6 + 5i, −6, 5
(d) −7 − 4i, −7, −4 (e) 0 − 3i, 0, −3 (f) $\frac{7}{3}$ + 0i, $\frac{7}{3}$, 0
(g) $\frac{1}{2}$ + $\frac{3}{2}i$, $\frac{1}{2}$, $\frac{3}{2}$ (h) −8 + $\frac{3}{4}i$, −8, $\frac{3}{4}$ (i) $\sqrt{2}$ − $\sqrt{3}i$, $\sqrt{2}$, −$\sqrt{3}$
(j) $-\frac{1}{\sqrt{2}}$ + $\frac{3}{2}i$, $-\frac{1}{\sqrt{2}}$, $\frac{3}{2}$ **2.** (a) 3 + 4i, 3, 4 (b) 4 + 7i, 4, 7
(c) 7 + 11i, 7, 11 (d) 3 + 7i, 3, 7 (e) 5 + 13i, 5, 13
(f) −3 + 11i, −3, 11 (g) 0 − 5i, 0, −5 (h) −6 + 9i, −6, 9
(i) 7 − 2i, 7, −2 (j) 11 − 5i, 11, −5 (k) −3 − 6i, −3, −6,
(l) −7 − 9i, −7, −9 (m) −15 − 22i, −15, −22
(n) −3 + 0i, −3, 0 (o) −3 + 11i, −3, 11 (p) 5 − 22i, 5, −22
(q) $\sqrt{2}$ + 3i, $\sqrt{2}$, 3 (r) 3 + 2$\sqrt{3}i$, 3, 2$\sqrt{3}$ (s) $-\frac{1}{2}$ − i, $-\frac{1}{2}$, −1
(t) $\sqrt{7}$ − $\frac{3}{2}i$, $\sqrt{7}$, − $\frac{3}{2}$ (u) (3 + y) − xi, 3 + y, − x
(v) x + (y − 3)i, x, y − 3 **3.** (a) (x + 2) − 3i, x + 2, −3
(b) (x + 7) − 2i, x + 7, −2 (c) 7 + (x − 2)i, 7, x − 2
(d) y + (5 − x)i, y, 5 − x

Exercise 3

1. (a) (2, 7) (b) (3, 18) (c) (17, 52) (d) (11, –5)

(e) (–3, 7) (f) (–7, –6) (g) $\left(\frac{1}{2}, \frac{3}{2}\right)$ (h) $\left(\sqrt{2}, -\frac{7}{2}\right)$

(i) (6, –5) (j) (–8, 11) (k) (x + 1, –2) (l) (–2, y + 3)

2. (a) 1 + 0i (b) –3 + 0i (c) 0 + 5i (d) –5 + 6i (e) –7 – 2i

(f) $\frac{1}{2} + \sqrt{2}i$ (g) $-\frac{2}{3} + i$ (h) $5 - \frac{11}{3}i$ (i) $4 + \frac{3}{\sqrt{2}}i$

(j) $\frac{1}{\sqrt{2}} + \frac{1}{\sqrt{2}}i$ (k) (y – 1) + 2i (l) –3 + (a – 2)i

4. (a) (3, 4) (b) $\frac{4}{3}$ (c) 5 **5.** P (3, 3) (a) 3 + 3i

(b) 1 (c) 1 (d) $\sqrt{18} = 3\sqrt{2}$

Chapter 14

Exercise 4

1. (a) 9 + 9i (b) 14 + 12i (c) 14 + 8i (d) 13 + 20i
(e) 3 + 12i (f) 8 + 18i (g) 19 + 17i (h) 13 + 3i
(i) 2 + 14i (j) (x + y) + 5i **2.** (a) 10 – i (b) 2 – 6i
(c) 19 + 4i (d) –12 – i (e) –10 + 2i (f) –9 + 8i (g) 10 – i
(h) 5 + 5i **3.** (a) 9 + 8i (b) 4 + 5i (c) 7 – 8i (d) 23 + 6i
(e) $\frac{1}{2} + 7i$ (f) $2\sqrt{3} + 4i$ (g) 2x – 2i (h) 9 + 4xi
4. (a) 10 + 7i (b) 11 – i (c) $-\frac{21}{2} - 6i$ (d) 12 – 2i
(e) y + 5i **5.** (a) –5 – i (b) –3 + 2i (c) –2 + 7i
(d) 0 + 8i (e) –8 + 9i (f) 14 – 11i (g) 1 – 2i
(h) $-\sqrt{3} - 3i$ (i) (x – y) – 6i (j) (x – y) + (x + y)i
6. (a) 13 + 4i (b) (0, 0) → (–2, 8); –2 + 8i
(c) (0, 0) → (7, –13); –7 + 13i (d) –9 – 4i

Exercise 5

1. (a) 12 + 8i (b) 55 + 50i (c) 42 + 14i (d) –22 – 33i
(e) 24 – 6i (f) 55 – 5i (g) 20 + 10i (h) 24 + 12i
(i) –1 – 4i (j) –2 + 3i (k) 5a + 5bi (l) k + 2ki
(m) ka + kbi (n) 10 + 10i (o) 1 – 10i (p) –4 – 5i
(q) 3 – 7i (r) –11 – 8i (s) –32 – 50i **2.** (a) –6 + 0i
(b) 13 + 15i (c) 2 + 12i (d) 1 – 3i (e) –28 – 24i
(f) 17 + 12i (g) $-\frac{9}{2} - \frac{9}{2}i$ (h) 17 + 21i (i) 1 + 6i
(j) 3 + 3i **3.** P(–5, 12), 13 (a) –10 + 24i; 26
(b) 20 – 48i; 52 (c) $\frac{5}{2} - 6i$; $\frac{13}{2}$ **4.** (b) P(–4, –2);
Q(4, 2); R(–8, –4); S(–2, –1) (c) Slope of OP = $\frac{1}{2}$,
$|OP| = 2\sqrt{5}$; Slope of OQ = $\frac{1}{2}$, $|OQ| = 2\sqrt{5}$;
Slope of OR = $\frac{1}{2}$, $|OR| = \sqrt{80} = 4\sqrt{5}$; Slope of
OS = $\frac{1}{2}$, $|OS| = \sqrt{5}$ **6.** (a) 6 – 9i (b) –6 + 2i (c) 0 – 7i

Exercise 6

1. (a) 5 (b) $\sqrt{5}$ (c) $\sqrt{41}$ (d) $\sqrt{29}$ (e) $\sqrt{40} = 2\sqrt{10}$

(f) $\sqrt{2}$ (g) 25 (h) $\sqrt{13}$ (i) 2 (j) $\frac{\sqrt{5}}{3}$ (k) 1 (l) $\frac{\sqrt{5}}{4}$

2. |z| = 5, |w| = 13 (a) $8\sqrt{2}$; 18 (b) $2\sqrt{65}$; –8
(c) 10; 10 (d) $2\sqrt{13}$; 8 (e) $\sqrt{146}$; 14 (f) $\sqrt{401}$; –3
(g) 1; 1 (h) 1; 1 **3.** (b) |z| = 5, |w| = 5 (c) $5\sqrt{2}$; $\frac{25}{2}$
4. (a) $\sqrt{(7 + y)^2 + (3 - x)^2}$ (b) $\sqrt{(x + 3)^2 + (y - 2)^2}$
(c) $x^2 + y^2 = 25$, Centre (0, 0)
(d) $(x + 7)^2 + (y + 5)^2 = 6$, Centre (–7, –5)
5. (a) ±24 (b) ±3 (c) ±3 (d) $\pm\frac{5}{3}$

Exercise 7

1. (a) 2 – 5i (b) 7 – 11i (c) 3 – 7i (d) $\sqrt{3} - i$
(e) a – ci (f) 3 + 2i (g) –5 + 2i (h) 4 – 6i (i) 3 + 0i
(j) –2 + 0i (k) 0 – 5i (l) 0 + 7i (m) –2 – 3i (n) –1 – 5i
(o) $\sqrt{3} + 6i$ (p) 8 + 3i (q) (x – 7) – 2i (r) (x – 2) – (y + 3)i
(s) (x + 3) + yi (t) (4x + y – 2) + 3i **2.** (a) 6i (b) 6i
(c) 6 + 22i (d) 6 + 22i (e) 4i (f) 4i (g) 6 + 14i (h) –3 – i
(i) –3 – i (j) 6 + 16i (k) 6 + 16i (l) 3 – 11i (m) –3 + 5i
3. (a) 15 – 21i (b) –8 + 32i (c) 7 + 11i (d) 12 – 22i
(e) 4 – 3i (f) 8 – 22i (g) 3 – 15i (h) 17 + 29i (i) 26 + 0i
(j) 13 + 29i **5.** (a) –15 – 8i (b) $\sqrt{3} - i$

Exercise 8

1. (a) –4 + 6i (b) 5 + 5i (c) 6 + 17i (d) –13 + 13i
(e) –5 + 0i (f) 19 – 9i (g) 2 + 8i **2.** (a) 26 – 2i
(b) 0 – 34i (c) –14 – 22i (d) 26 + 2i (e) 26 + 2i
(f) 0 + 34i (g) –22 –14i (h) $\sqrt{34}$ (i) $\sqrt{20} = 2\sqrt{5}$
(j) $\sqrt{680} = 2\sqrt{170}$ (k) $\sqrt{680} = 2\sqrt{170}$ **3.** (a) –3 + 12i
(b) –3 + 5i (c) –4 + 2i (d) –3 + 2i (e) 9 + 11i (f) 4 – 3i
(g) –5 – i (h) 11 – 2i **4.** (a) 2 (b) 13 (c) 29 (d) 45
(e) 5 **5.** (a) –11 + 60i (b) –2 – 2i (c) –4 + 0i (d) 0 + 8i
6. (a) –4 + 3i (c) 10; 5 (d) Halved modulus, no rotation
7. (a) –6 – 8i (c) 10; 10 (d) Anticlockwise rotation
by 90°, modulus unchanged **8.** (b) 4 – 2i
(d) $\sqrt{20}$; $\sqrt{20}$ (e) Anticlockwise rotation by 270°,
modulus unchanged **11.** (b) 9 + 12i **12.** (b) 4 – 6i

Exercise 9

1. (a) 0 – 3i (b) 0 + 7i (c) 0 + 5i (d) $0 - \frac{2}{3}i$ (e) $\frac{6}{5} + \frac{3}{5}i$
(f) $\frac{14}{29} - \frac{6}{29}i$ (g) $-\frac{10}{13} - \frac{15}{13}i$ (h) $\frac{3}{5} + \frac{1}{5}i$ (i) $\frac{3}{5} - \frac{1}{5}i$
(j) $\frac{7}{13} - \frac{4}{13}i$ (k) $\frac{11}{5} - \frac{2}{5}i$ (l) $-\frac{3}{25} + \frac{29}{25}i$ **2.** (a) 1 + 2i
(b) $\frac{1}{5} - \frac{2}{5}i$ (c) $\frac{4}{25} - \frac{3}{25}i$ (d) $\frac{7}{25} + \frac{24}{25}i$ (e) $\frac{3}{5} - \frac{4}{5}i$
(f) $\frac{11}{5} + \frac{2}{5}i$ (g) $\frac{11}{25} + \frac{2}{25}i$ (h) 1 – 2i (i) $\frac{1}{5} + \frac{2}{5}i$ (j) $\frac{11}{5} - \frac{2}{5}i$
(k) $\sqrt{5}$ (l) $\sqrt{5}$ (m) $\sqrt{5}$ (n) $\sqrt{5}$ (o) $\frac{1}{5}$

Exercise 10

1. x = 2, y = 3 **2.** x = –3, y = 3 **3.** x = –4, y = 3
4. x = 1, y = –6 **5.** x = 2, y = 1 **6.** x = 4, y = –2

Revision Questions

1. (a) $30 - 5i$ (b) (ii) 5 (c) (i) $7 + 2i$ (ii) 90

2. (a) $3 - 4i$; 5 (b) (ii) $7 - 2i$ (c) $-i$ **3.** (a) (i) $\sqrt{34}$
(ii) $\sqrt{136} = 2\sqrt{34}$ (iii) $\sqrt{136} = 2\sqrt{34}$ (iv) $\sqrt{136} = 2\sqrt{34}$
(b) (i) $0°$ (ii) $90°$ **4.** (a) $-12 + 5i$ (b) (i) $2 + 8i$
(ii) $0 - 6i$ (iii) $\sqrt{68} = 2\sqrt{17}$ (iv) 6 (c) (i) $6 + 2i$
(ii) $c = 2, d = 3$ **5.** (a) $3 - 3i$ (b) $x = 0, y = 3$
(c) $3 + 4i, 5 + 12i$ (i) 126 (ii) $18 > 8\sqrt{5}$ **6.** (b) (i) $1 - 2i$
(ii) No (c) (i) $1 + 3i$ (ii) $k = -3, t = -5$ **7.** (a) $-13 - i$
(b) (i) $5 + 5i$ (ii) $-2 + 5i$ (iii) $5 - 5i$ (c) 50 (d) (i) $x = -4$,
$y = -\frac{1}{2}$ (ii) $s = \frac{8}{25}, t = -\frac{6}{25}$ **8.** (b) (i) $5 + i$ (ii) $\frac{1}{13} + \frac{5}{13}i$
(c) (i) $P(1, 1)$; Slope of $OP = 1$ (ii) $\frac{1}{2} - \frac{1}{2}i$; $Q\left(\frac{1}{2}, -\frac{1}{2}\right)$;
Slope of $OQ = -1$ (iii) 2 **9.** (a) $k = \pm 8$ (b) (i) $-1 + 3i$
(ii) $\sqrt{10}$ (c) (i) $P(-9, 6)$; Slope of $OP = -\frac{2}{3}$
(ii) $-2 - 3i$, $Q(-2, -3)$; Slope of $OQ = \frac{3}{2}$
10. (b) (ii) 5 (iii) $\frac{4}{25} - \frac{3}{25}i$ (c) 4225

Section 7
Chapter 15

Exercise 1

1. (i) (a) $S = \{(2, 1), (4, 5), (6, 7), (8, 3)\}$
(b) $D = \{2, 4, 6, 8\}, I = \{1, 3, 5, 7\}$
(c) It is a function (ii) (a) $S = \{(3, a), (3, b), (2, c)\}$
(b) $D = \{2, 3\}, I = \{a, b, c\}$ (c) It is not a function
(iii) (a) $S = \{(1, 5), (2, 5)\}$ (b) $D = \{1, 2\}, I = \{5\}$
(c) It is a function (iv) (a) $S = \{(1, a), (1, b)\}$
(b) $D = \{1\}, I = \{a, b\}$ (c) It is not a function
(v) (a) $S = \{(a, d), (b, e), (c, f)\}$ (b) $D = \{a, b, c\}$,
$I = \{d, e, f\}$ (c) It is a function
2. (a) It is a function; $D = \{a, b, c\}, I = \{1\}$
(b) It is not a function; $D = \{1, 2\}, I = \{a, b\}$
(c) It is a function; $D = \{1, 2, 3, 4\}, I = \{1, 4, 9, 16\}$
(d) It is not a function; $D = \{1, 4\}, I = \{-2, -1, 1, 2\}$
(e) It is a function; $D = \{1, 2, 3, 4\}, I = \{0\}$
3. (a) (i) -1 (ii) -9 (iii) -6 (b) (i) 4 (ii) 9 (iii) 0·25
(c) (i) -10 (ii) -20 (iii) 50 (d) (i) -10 (ii) -14
(iii) -7 (e) (i) 8 (ii) -8 (iii) $\frac{125}{8}$ **4.** (a) 17 (b) -4 (c) $\frac{3}{2}$
(d) 3 (e) $\frac{11}{2}$ (f) -3 (g) 2·5 (h) 1 **5.** (a) 5, 9, -4
(b) $1, \frac{1}{2}, 2, -3$ (c) $8, \frac{1}{2}, \frac{17}{8}$ (d) (i) 44 (ii) 9
(e) 0, 0, 4 (f) $\frac{1}{54}, -4$ (g) 5, 5, 5, 5 (h) 1, 3
6. (a) $11, 2x + 9, 13 - 4x$ (b) $0, 4 - 4t^2$ (c) $1, \frac{3}{x + 4}$ (d)
$13, s + 4, s^2 - 2s + 5$ (e) $\frac{3}{4}, 12p^2 - 8p + 2$
(f) $12, 3 \times 2^{3x-1}$ **7.** (a) 1 (b) 15 (c) 1, 6 (d) 4 (e) 4

(f) 4 (g) -4, 2 (h) -2, 0, 1 **8.** (a) -20 (b) -3 (c) 4
(d) -3, 1 (e) $a = -1, k = -2$ (f) $a = 5, b = 2$

Exercise 2

1. (a) 15 (b) -7 (c) -1 (d) 2 **2.** (a) $-4x^2 - 12x - 8$,
5   $2x^2$ (b) $4\sqrt{2x + 4}, 2\sqrt{2x + 1}$ (c) $\frac{1}{2x + 5}, \frac{2}{x} + 5$
(d) $3^{\sqrt{x}}, 3^{\frac{x}{2}}$ (e) $\frac{x^2 - 1}{3}, \frac{x^2 - 2x + 1}{9}$ (f) $\frac{1}{x^3}, \frac{1}{x^3}$
(g) x, x **3.** (a) $\frac{11}{3}$ (b) $k = 2, b = 3$

Exercise 3

1. 9 **2.** -2 **3.** 37 **4.** 0 **5.** 6 **6.** 2 **7.** 0
8. 2 **9.** $\frac{2}{3}$ **10.** 3

Chapter 16

Exercise 4

2. (a) $y = -x + \frac{7}{3}$ (b) $y = \frac{4}{3}x - 3$ (c) $y = 7x - 0·5$
(d) $y = 0x + 5$ (e) $y = -x + 8$
3. (a) Linear $f(x) = y = -\frac{2}{3}x - \frac{1}{3}$
(b) Linear $h(x) = y = \frac{3}{5}x + 4$
(c) Linear $C(r) = y = 2\pi r + 0$ (d) Non-linear
(e) Linear $F(p) = y = -\frac{1}{64}p + 13$ **4.** (a) $y = 3x - 2$
(b) $y = -2x + 10$ (c) $y = -\frac{2}{5}x + \frac{19}{5}$ (d) $y = -\frac{1}{3}x + \frac{7}{3}$
(e) $y = -7x + 11$ **5.** (a) $V = -180t + 500$
(b) $\theta = \frac{9}{5}T + 32$ (c) $y = -\frac{3}{2}x + 6$ (d) $P = \frac{3}{2}t + 5$
6. (a) $\frac{3}{2}$ (b) $\frac{1}{2}$ (c) 2 (d) -3

Exercise 5

1. (a) $V = -4000t + 50\,000$ (b) $7\frac{1}{2}$ years
(c) $12\frac{1}{2}$ years **2.** $s = -300t + 6000$; 20 mins
3. Linear, $y = \frac{1}{8}x + 1$ **4.** (a) B (b) (i) $P = 0·24t + 7·6$
(ii) 24·4 million (c) 0·334 million/yr = 334 000/yr
5. (a) Membership fee = €250; Cost per round = €30
(b) $C = 30n + 250$ (c) €1750 (d) 25 **6.** (b) 500;
$n = -5t + 200$; 40 days

Chapter 17

Exercise 6

2. (a) x: $(-1, 0), (1, 0)$; y: $(0, -1)$
(b) x: Does not cross; y: $(0, 1)$ (c) x: $(2, 0), (3, 0)$;
y: $(0, 6)$ (d) x: $(1, 0), (2, 0)$; y: $(0, -2)$ (e) x: $\left(\frac{1}{2}, 0\right)$;
y: $(0, 2)$ (f) x: $\left(\frac{2}{3}, 0\right), (2, 0)$; y: $(0, -4)$ (g) x: $(-1, 0)$,

(3, 0); y: (0, 3) (h) x: $\left(\frac{1}{2}, 0\right), \left(\frac{7}{2}, 0\right)$; y: (0, 7)

(i) x: Does not cross; y: (0, 7) (j) x: $\left(\frac{-7-\sqrt{137}}{4}, 0\right)$, $\left(\frac{-7+\sqrt{137}}{4}, 0\right)$; y: (0, –11) **3.** (a) (0, –1) min;

$x = 0$ (b) (0, 1) min; $x = 0$ (c) $\left(\frac{5}{2}, -\frac{1}{4}\right)$ min; $x = \frac{5}{2}$

(d) $\left(\frac{3}{2}, \frac{1}{4}\right)$ max; $x = \frac{3}{2}$ (e) $\left(\frac{1}{2}, 0\right)$ min; $x = \frac{1}{2}$

(f) $\left(\frac{4}{3}, \frac{4}{3}\right)$ max; $x = \frac{4}{3}$ (g) (1, 4) max; $x = 1$

(h) (2, –9) min; $x = 2$ (i) $\left(\frac{5}{2}, \frac{3}{4}\right)$ min; $x = \frac{5}{2}$

(j) $\left(-\frac{7}{4}, -\frac{137}{8}\right)$ min; $x = -\frac{7}{4}$ **4.** (a) 20 > 0, 2 points

(b) 1 > 0, 2 points (c) 676 > 0, 2 points (d) 0, 1 point
(e) 16 > 0, 2 points (f) 65 > 0, 2 points
(g) 169 > 0, 2 points (h) 0, 1 point

Exercise 7

1. (a) –2·4, 0·9 (b) –1·6, 3·6 (c) 0·3, –3·3
(d) –0·6, 2·3 (e) –1·5 (f) –1, 1·5 **2.** (a) (i) (0, –3)

(ii) (–3, 0), $\left(\frac{1}{2}, 0\right)$ (iii) $\left(-\frac{5}{4}, -\frac{49}{8}\right)$ **3.** (b) (i) –1·8 °C

(ii) 9 °C (iii) 1·8 hours (iv) 1·6 hours, 4·4 hours
(c) $a = 1$, $b = -6$, $c = 7$ **4.** (b) (i) 375 cm (ii) 1 cm,
39 cm (iii) 400 cm **5.** (b) (i) 24 m (ii) 0·9 s, 3·9 s
(iii) 30 m (c) 29·8 m (d) 0·7 % **6.** (b) (i) 600 m
(ii) 150 m **7.** (a) 2, 10 (b) $2 < x < 10, x \in \mathbb{R}$
8. (a) $x < 25, x \in \mathbb{R}$ (c) (i) €780 (ii) €12·50
(iii) €6, €19 (iv) 25, 100 (d) €781·25 **9.** (a) $B(3, 0)$
(b) $C(0, 6)$ (c) $A(-1, 0)$ (d) $p = -3$, $q = 6$, $r = 9$ (e)
$D(0, 9)$ (f) $P\left(-\frac{1}{3}, \frac{20}{3}\right)$

Chapter 18

Exercise 8

1. (a) $x = -1.9, -0.3, 2.1$; y: (0, –1)
(b) $x = -4.3, -1.7, 1.1$; y: (0, 8) (c) $x = -1, 2$;
y: (0, –2) (d) $x = -3, 1$; y: (0, –3) (e) $x = 2.7$; y: (0, –2)
2. (a) 1 root (b) 3 roots, 2 equal (c) 3 roots (d) 1 root
3. (a) x: (–2, 0), (1, 0), (2, 0) y: (0, 4) (b) x: (–2, 0),
(0, 0), $\left(\frac{1}{2}, 0\right)$; y: (0, 0) (c) x: (0, 0), (1, 0); y: (0, 0)

(d) x: (0, 0); y: (0, 0) (e) x: $\left(\frac{3-\sqrt{13}}{2}, 0\right)$, (2, 0),
$\left(\frac{3+\sqrt{13}}{2}, 0\right)$; y: (0, 4) (f) x: (2, 0), (3, 0), (4, 0);

y: (0, 24) (g) x: (–1, 0), $\left(-\sqrt{\frac{2}{3}}, 0\right), \left(\sqrt{\frac{2}{3}}, 0\right)$; y: (0, –2)

(h) x: (0, 0), $\left(\frac{2}{3}, 0\right)$; y: (0, 0) (i) x: (–1, 0), $\left(\frac{2}{5}, 0\right)$,

$\left(\frac{3}{4}, 0\right)$; y: (0, 6) (j) x: (–5, 0); y: (0, –10) **4.** (a) 800

(c) (i) 700 tonnes (ii) 2004 (iii) 2007
5. (a) –2·2, –1, 0·7 (b) 3·6 (c) –1·2, 0, 3·2
(d) –0·9, 0·5, 4·4 (e) –2·6, –0·4, 2 (f) 0·8
(g) –2·6, 0·3, 2·3 **6.** (c) 1·5, 3, 4·5
7. (b) –0·6, 1, 1·6 **8.** (b) –1·3, 0·9 (c) 3

Exercise 9

2. (a) $y = (x + 2)^2$ (b) $y = f(x - 4)$ (c) $y = f(x - 6)$
(d) $y = f(x) + 5$

Chapter 19

Exercise 10

1. (b) 1·6 (c) 1·4 **2.** $k = 0.5$, $a = 3$ **3.** (a) 20 000
(b) (i) 80 900 (ii) 327 000 (d) 13 days **4.** (a) 60
(b) 68 (d) 11·6 hrs **5.** (a) 1280 (b) €40 (c) 8 yrs

Exercise 11

1. (b) (1·4, 2·6) **2.** (b) –0·9, 1·2
3. (b) 0·3 days, 5·3 days **4.** (b) (0, 1)
(c) (i) 1·4 (ii) –1·7 **5.** (a) $A(0, 4)$, $a = 8$
(b) $c = 2$ (c) $B(2, 8)$

Revision Questions

1. (c) 0·4 s, 3·1 s (d) 17 m (e) 0·2 s, 4 s, 5·8 s
2. (c) (i) 96 cm³/h (ii) 72 cm³/h (iii) 11 hrs, 22 hrs
(iv) 9 cm³/h **3.** (a) $A(-1, 0)$, $B(6, 0)$ (b) $D(1, 10)$
(c) $E\left(\frac{5}{2}, \frac{49}{4}\right)$ (d) $F\left(\frac{5}{2}, 7\right)$ (e) $|EF| = 5.25$

4. (a) 5 A (d) (i) 1·4 A (ii) 4·5 s (e) 4 s
5. (a) $0.06x - 400$ (b) €2300 (c) €25 000
6. (a) 0·2 (b) 1200 (e) (i) 2300 (ii) 6·5 days
(f) $P = 1000(1.2)^t$ **7.** (b) (i) 2^{19} (ii) 2^{63} (c) $N = 2^{R-1}$
(d) 9.2×10^{15} m (e) 1.5×10^{11} m (f) 61 333

Section 8
Chapter 20

Exercise 1

1. (a) 5 m/s (b) 5 m/s (c) Straight line – Constant
slope **2.** (a) 27 (b) 30 **3.** (a) (i) –2, (ii) –1
(b) –2·5; V is decreasing (c) –2·5 **4.** (a) $\frac{2}{3}$ (b) 1

(c) 1 (d) 1 **5.** (a) 200 mA/V (b) 333·$\dot{3}$ mA/V; $\frac{dI}{dV}$

Exercise 2

1. (a) $2x$ (b) $6x^2$ (c) 4 (d) $12x$ (e) $-3x^2$ (f) $-15x^2$

(g) $\frac{2x}{5}$ (h) x^2 (i) $\frac{4x}{5}$ (j) $-\frac{9x^2}{4}$ **2.** (a) 2 (b) a (c) $6x - 5$

(d) $2ax + b$ (e) $12x^2 - 10x + 6$ (f) $3ax^2 + 2bx + c$

(g) $x^2 - 10x + 2$ (h) $\dfrac{8x}{3} - \dfrac{2}{5}$ (i) $15x^2 - \dfrac{6x}{5} + \dfrac{4}{3}$

(j) $3x^2 - 2x + \dfrac{1}{3}$ **3.** (a) $-x$ (b) $4 + \dfrac{2x}{3} - 3x^2$

(c) $-3x^2 + \dfrac{4x}{5} - 1$ (d) $-4(1 + 3x^2)$ (e) $\dfrac{1 - 2x}{5}$

4. (a) $2x + 1$ (b) $16x - 2 = 2(8x - 1)$ (c) $6x^2 - 2x - 1$
(d) $3t^2 - 1$ (e) $18v - 12 = 6(3v - 2)$ (f) 1
5. (a) 1 (b) 19 (c) 2 (d) $3x^2 - 8x + 5$; $6x - 8$ (e) 51; –38
(f) 60; –46 **6.** (a) –2 (b) $m = -1$; $x + y + 3 = 0$
(c) $m = 10$; $10x - y + 2 = 0$ **7.** $\dfrac{3}{5}$ N/m per sec =
0·6 N/m per sec **8.** (a) 1 (b) $\pm$ 2 (c) –1, 2
9. (a) 9·2 °C (b) 28·1 °C (c) Midnight (d) –1·67°/hr
(e) Midday (Noon) **10.** 36π m³/m **11.** (a) –20
(b) –10 (c) $a = -9$, $c = 14$

Chapter 21

Exercise 3

1. (a) 3 (b) 1 (c) 10 (d) 6 (e) $-\dfrac{1}{4}$ **2.** (a) $x + y - 4 = 0$
(b) $15x - y + 4 = 0$ (c) $5x - y - 10 = 0$
(d) $77x - y + 86 = 0$ (e) $12x - y + 20 = 0$
3. (a) (–1, 1) (b) (2, –4) (c) (3, 1) (d) (1, –6)
4. (a) (1, –1) (b) (–1, –6) (c) (–1, 0), (2, –9)
(d) (–2, –3), (1, 0) **5.** (a) (2, 13) (b) (–3, 13),
(2, –82) (c) $(-2, -9)$, $\left(-\dfrac{2}{3}, -\dfrac{239}{27}\right)$ (d) (3, –15)

(e) $(x_1, y_1) = (0, 12)$, $(x_2, y_2) = (4, -20)$

Exercise 4

4. $x < 0$, $x \in \mathbb{R}$ **5.** $x > 4$, $x \in \mathbb{R}$ **6.** (a) Increasing
(b) Increasing (c) Decreasing; accelerating at $t = 1, 2$
and decelerating at $t = 3$ **7.** (a) Increasing
(b) Increasing (c) Decreasing (d) Decreasing
8. (a) Increasing (b) Increasing (c) Decreasing

Exercise 5

1. (a) (2, 1) L Min (b) (3, 22) L Max (c) (–1, 2) L Max;
(3, –30) L Min (d) (1, 6) L Min; (2, 7) L Max
(e) (–2, 3) L Min; (0, 7) L Max **2.** 15

3. $\left(-\dfrac{b}{2a}, \dfrac{4ac - b^2}{4a}\right)$ **4.** (a) (i) (–1, 0) (ii) (3, 5)

(b) (i) 5 (ii) 0 **5.** (–1, 0) L Max; (2, –54) L Min
(a) $A(-2, -22)$; $B(-1, 0)$; $C(0, -14)$; $D(2, -54)$;
$E(3, -32)$ (b) L Max (c) L Min (d) $-1 < x < 2$, $x \in \mathbb{R}$
(e) 0 (f) –54 **6.** (a) $2x + p$, –6 (b) $8 - 4x$ (i) (0, 3)
(ii) 11 (iii) $x < 1$, $x \in \mathbb{R}$ (c) $k = 3$; (1, 3) (d) $k = 12$;
(–2, 23) L Max; (2, –9) L Min (e) $k = 4$; (–2, 32)
L Max; (2, 0) L Min (f) $a = 2$, $b = -24$, $c = 3$ (g) $k = -9$;
(–1, 6) L Max; (3, –26) L Min **7.** 93·75 cm; 10·38 a.m.
8. (a) (i) 40 m (ii) 400 m (b) (i) 40 (ii) –40

Exercise 6

1. (a) L Min (2, –2) (i) 0·6, 3·4 (ii) $0·6 < x < 3·4$,
$x \in \mathbb{R}$ (iii) $0 \le x \le 2$, $x \in \mathbb{R}$ (b) $x = 2$ (c) $2x - y - 7 = 0$
2. (a) L Min $\left(\dfrac{1}{2}, -\dfrac{25}{4}\right)$ (b) (i) $-2 \le x \le 3$, $x \in \mathbb{R}$
(ii) No points of intersection of $y = -8$ and the curve
(iii) No, based on answer to (ii) **3.** $b = -2$, $c = -3$
4. (a) $f'(x) = -5 - 4x$; L Max $\left(-\dfrac{5}{4}, \dfrac{49}{8}\right)$ (b) –3, $\dfrac{1}{2}$
(d) –2·2, 0·7 **5.** (a) (0, 0) L Max; (4, –32) L Min
(b) (0, 0) (6, 0) (d) $0 < x < 4$, $x \in \mathbb{R}$ **6.** (a) $3x^2 - 6x$;
(0, 0) L Max; (2, –4) L Min (c) (i) $x = -0·7, 1, 2·7$
(ii) $0 < x < 2$, $x \in \mathbb{R}$ **7.** (a) $f(-1) = -3$; $f(3) = 1$
(b) $3x^2 - 6x$ (c) (0, 1) L Max; (2, –3) L Min
(e) (i) $0·7 < x < 2·9$, $x \in \mathbb{R}$ (ii) $0 < x < 2$, $x \in \mathbb{R}$

8. (a)

x	–1·5	–1	0	2	3	3·5
y	–9	0	3	–9	0	13·5

(b) $6x^2 - 10x - 4$ (c) $\left(-\dfrac{1}{3}, \dfrac{100}{27}\right)$ L Max; (2, –9) L Min

(f) $x = -1·1, 0·4, 3·1$ **9.** $\dfrac{1}{2} \times 2^x$ (a) Curve does not

cross the x-axis (b) 2·6 **10.** (a) (0, 0) L Min (c) –0·8, 2

Exercise 7

1. (a) Increasing at €14 per year (b) Increasing at
€4 per year (c) Decreasing at €10 per year
2. (a) Increasing at 2 eagles per year (b) Increasing
at 8 eagles per year **3.** (a) Increasing at
€55 000 per year (b) Increasing at €31 000 per year
(c) Increasing at €40 000 per year **4.** (a) Increasing
at €2400 per day (b) Increasing at €1200 per day
5. (a) 16·33 l (b) –13·06 l/min (c) –13·06 l/min
6. (a) 3 m/s (b) 4 m/s² (c) 20 s, 860 m
7. (a) $77 + 26t - 3t^2$ (b) $26 - 6t$ (c) 11 s (d) 132 m/s
(e) 8 m/s² **8.** (a) 160 m/s (b) –10 m/s² (c) 2100 m

Exercise 8

1. (a) $10 - x$ (b) $10x - x^2$ (c) 25 m² **2.** (a) (i) $20 - 2x$
(ii) $4000x - 400x^2$ (b) 5 cm **3.** (a) $64 - x$
(b) $264 + 62x - x^2$ (c) 1225 cm² **4.** (a) $27 - x$
(b) $27x^2 - x^3$ (c) 2916 cm³ **5.** (a) $200 - \pi h$
(b) $400h - 2\pi h^2$ (c) 100 m

6. (a) $-\dfrac{1}{3}x^3 + 22x^2 - 160x - 1200$

(b) $\dfrac{dP}{dx} = -x^2 + 44x - 160$, $\dfrac{d^2P}{dx^2} = -2x + 44$ (c) 40

7. (a) $-2 + 7t - 3t^2$ (b) $7 - 6t$ (c) $\left(\dfrac{1}{3}, \dfrac{523}{54}\right)$ L Min;

(2, 12) L Max (d) €12 **8.** (a) (i) €$(150x + 30x^2)$
(ii) €$(930x - 100x^2)$ (iii) €$(780x - 130x^2)$ (b) 3
9. –36 **10.** 8·75, 17·5 **11.** (a) (i) $3t^2 - 12t + 9$

(ii) $6t - 12$ (c) Maximum distance = 4 m, minimum distance = 0 m   **12.** (a) (i) 240 m (ii) 36 m/s (b) 294 m

Revision Questions

Concepts and skills

1. (a) $2x^2 + 6x + 5$ (b) $f'(x) = 2$; $g'(x) = 2x + 3$; $h'(x) = 4x + 6$ (c) $x > -\frac{3}{2}$, $x \in \mathbb{R}$ (d) $2x + y + 3 = 0$
2. (a) $6x$ (b) 1 (c) $3x^3 - 6x^2 + x - 2$ (d) $9x^2 - 12x + 1$
(e) $3x^2 + 1$ (f) $6x^2 - 12x$ **3.** (a) $3x^2 - 2x$
(b) $x - y - 3 = 0$ (c) $5x - y + 1 = 0$ (d) $(-1, -4)$

(e) $(0, -2)$; $\left(\frac{2}{3}, -\frac{58}{27}\right)$ **4.** (b) $x - y - 8 = 0$

(c) $x + y + 4 = 0$ (e) $\sqrt{8} = 2\sqrt{2}$ **5.** (a) $50x^2 + 20\,000x$
(b) $200x^2$ (c) $20\,000x - 150x^2$ (d) $20\,000 - 300x$

(e) 66·67 (f) €6667   **6.** (a) 0 m^3 (b) $\frac{2\pi}{3}$ m^3

(c) $2\pi h - \pi h^2$ (d) (i) $\frac{3}{4}\pi$ (ii) π (e) $2\pi - 2\pi h$ (f) $\frac{3}{4}$ m

7. (a) $6x^2 - 12x + 6 = 6(x^2 - 2x + 1) = 6(x - 1)^2$ for all $x \in \mathbb{R}$ (b) (i) 24 (ii) –18 (c) –34   **8.** (a) $-2x$ (b) $\frac{2}{3}$
(c) (i) $12x^2 + 16x - 1$ (ii) 88

Contexts and applications

1. (a)

t (Hours)	0	2	4	6	8	10	12
N	0	100	160	180	160	100	0

(b) $60 - 10t$ (c) 14:00 or 2 p.m. (d) 180 (e) 1400

2. (a) $125x - \dfrac{5x^2}{3}$

(b)

x	0	15	30	45	60	75
R (€)	0	1500	2250	2250	1500	0
C (€)	0	450	1050	1800	2700	3750

(c) 50 covers/week; €2100 (e) $100 - 4x$; €1250
3. (a) (i) 250 m (ii) 385 m (c) 378 m (d) 410 m
(e) 250 m (f) 410 m   **4.** (a) $3t^2 - 40t + 100$
(b) $6t - 40$ (c) 10 s (d) 0 m/s

(e)

t (s)	4	6	8	10	12
v (m/s)	144	96	32	0	48

(f) 400 m (g) (i) –25 m/s^2 (ii) 0 m/s^2

5. (a) $\frac{1}{5}$ (b) $\dfrac{7 \pm \sqrt{13}}{3}$ (c) $\dfrac{d^2y}{dx^2} = \dfrac{6x - 14}{5}$; L Max at $x = \dfrac{7 - \sqrt{13}}{3}$, L Min at $x = \dfrac{7 + \sqrt{13}}{3}$ (d) 121 m

(e) 18 m   **6.** (a) 9 (b) $-\frac{4}{81}$; L Max (c) 23 years

(d)

t (years)	0	3	6	9	12	15	18	21
E (years)	21·0	22·1	22·8	23·0	19·7	16·4	13·1	9·9

(e) 30 years   **7.** (a) $6 - x$ (b) $6x^2 - x^3$ (c) $12x - 3x^2$; $(0, 0)$; $(4, 32)$ (d) $12 - 6x$; V_{max} at $x = 4$ (e) 32 cm^3

8. (c) 10 m (d) 95 m (e) –0·40   **9.** (a) $\left(-\frac{4}{3}, \frac{25}{27}\right)$ L Max; $\left(1, -\frac{9}{4}\right)$ L Min (c) $(0, -1)$ (d) $-\frac{4}{3} < x < 1$, $x \in \mathbb{R}$